D1175158

PARLIAMENT, POLITICS
AND ELECTIONS
1604–1648

PARLIAMENT, POLITICS AND ELECTIONS
1604–1648

edited by

CHRIS R. KYLE

CAMDEN FIFTH SERIES
Volume 17

CAMBRIDGE
UNIVERSITY PRESS

FOR THE ROYAL HISTORICAL SOCIETY
University College London, Queen Street, London WC1 6BT
2001

Published by the Press Syndicate of the University of Cambridge
The Edinburgh Building, Cambridge CB2 2RU, United Kingdom
40 West 20th Street, New York, NY 10011–4211, USA
10 Stamford Road, Oakleigh, Melbourne 3166, Australia

First published 2001

A catalogue record for this book is available from the British Library

Library of Congress Cataloging-in-Publication Data

Parliament, politics and elections, 1604–1648 / edited by Chris R. Kyle.
p. cm. — (Camden fifth series; v. 17)
Includes bibliographical references and index
ISBN 0-521-80214-8
1. Great Britain. Parliament—History—17th century—Sources. 2. Great Britain—
Politics and government—1603–1649—Sources. I. Kyle, Chris R. II. Series.

DA20.C15 vol. 17
[JN534]
941 s—dc21
[328.41'09'032]

00-045550

ISBN 0 521 80214 8 hardback

SUBSCRIPTIONS. The serial publications of the Royal Historical Society, *Royal Historical Society Transactions* (ISSN 0080–4401) and Camden Fifth Series (ISSN 0960–1163) volumes may be purchased together on annual subscription. The 2001 subscription price (which includes postage but not VAT) is £60 (US$99 in the USA, Canada and Mexico) and includes Camden Fifth Series, volumes 17 and 18 (published in July and December) and Transactions Sixth Series, volume 11 (published in December). Japanese prices are available from Kinokuniya Company Ltd, P.O. Box 55, Chitose, Tokyo 156, Japan. EU subscribers (outside the UK) who are not registered for VAT should add VAT at their country's rate. VAT registered subscribers should provide their VAT registration number. Prices include delivery by air.

Subscription orders, which must be accompanied by payment, may be sent to a bookseller, subscription agent or direct to the publisher: Cambridge University Press, The Edinburgh Building, Shaftesbury Road, Cambridge CB2 2RU, UK; or in the USA, Canada and Mexico: Cambridge University Press, Journals Fulfillment Department, 110, Midland Avenue, Port Chester, NY 10573–4930, USA.

SINGLE VOLUMES AND BACK VOLUMES. A list of Royal Historical Society volumes available from Cambridge University Press may be obtained from the Humanities Marketing Department at the address above.

Printed and bound in the United Kingdom by Butler & Tanner Ltd, Frome and London

CONTENTS

ACKNOWLEDGEMENTS

This volume is the result of many discussions with colleagues working in the field of parliamentary history. All have, at one time or another, pointed out the reliance of historians on certain types of parliamentary documents to the exclusion of other important material. All have lamented how difficult it is to find anything in print which was not the diary of an MP, and why we should do more to highlight the wide range of parliamentary sources available to early modern historians. Therefore, this edition is designed to go some way towards addressing these lacunae. I wish to acknowledge not only the invaluable comments raised by my fellow contributors, but also the support and friendship of many who have worked in this field. In particular, Michael Graves who, as an exemplary Ph.D. supervisor, first encouraged me to look beyond traditional parliamentary sources, and did much to mould my attitude towards Parliament. Both David Dean and Pauline Croft have provided tremendous assistance over the years and have been more than generous in sharing their knowledge of early modern Parliaments. A hard-working but very pleasant summer of 1999 was spent in the company of Norman Jones at the Henry E. Huntington Library and his ideas on how to interrogate parliamentary sources have done much to shape my own opinions. Others whom I must mention are Tom Cogswell, Richard Cust, Stuart Handley, David Hayton, Paul Hunneyball, Sean Kelsey, Henry Lancaster, Patrick Little, Giles Margetts, John Morrill, David Smith, Andrew Thrush, and Marcy Norton for her help in translating from the Spanish. On a final note, this volume would not have made to the press by the deadline without the tremendous support and enthusiasm of the series editor, Andrew Pettegree, who from the outset wholeheartedly encouraged its production and contents. The completion of the manuscript would not have been possible without the unwavering support of Dympna Callaghan through many trans-Atlantic crossings and even more phone calls. Her intellectual gift is unparalleled and her brilliance, humour and warmth have immeasurably enhanced my life.

The editor and contributors would like to acknowledge warmly the following libraries and individuals for permission to publish the documents: the Bodleian Library, Oxford, British Library, Hampshire Record Office, His Grace the Duke of Buccleuch, His Grace the Duke of Rutland, House of Lords Record Office, Hull City Council, Public Record Office and Weymouth Museum.

Chris R. Kyle
June 2000

NOTES ON CONTRIBUTORS

Simon Healy has written extensively on Yorkshire, the East Midlands and North Wales for the 1604–29 section of the History of Parliament, London. Forthcoming publications include essays on the young Oliver Cromwell, the Welsh cattle trade and parliamentary elections in early Stuart England, while in the longer term he plans to publish a critical edition of parliamentary debates on the Union project in 1604–7 and a study of relations between central and local government in early Stuart Yorkshire.

Chris R. Kyle is Visiting Assistant Professor at Syracuse University. Formerly a Senior Research Fellow at the History of Parliament, London, he is the author of a number of articles on early Stuart Parliaments and is co-editing, with Jason Peacey, *Parliament at Work: Parliamentary Committees, Access and Lobbying Under the Tudors and Stuarts* (forthcoming). He is currently writing a monograph entitled 'Politics and Society: The Toponomology of the Palace of Westminster in Sixteenth and Seventeenth Century England'.

Jason Peacey is a Research Fellow at the History of Parliament, London, and is the author of a number of articles on politics, patronage and print culture in the seventeenth century. He is currently editing a collection of essays on the trial of Charles I, and is preparing monographs on 'Politicians, Pamphleteers and Propaganda in the English Civil Wars', and on 'The Political Life of a Pamphleteer: William Prynne'.

Brennan Pursell received his Ph.D. at Harvard University in March 2000. He has published articles in *The Sixteenth Century Journal* and *History* and is currently working on his first book, 'The Winter King', a study of Elector Palatine Friedrich V.

David Scott is a Senior Research Fellow in the History of Parliament Trust, London. He has written several articles and essays on British politics in the 1640s and co-edited for the Royal Historical Society Camden Series *The Journal of Thomas Juxon, 1644–1647*.

ABBREVIATIONS

BIHR	*Bulletin of the Institute of Historical Research*
BL	British Library, London
Bodl.	Bodleian Library, Oxford
Bowyer	David Harris Willson, ed., *The Parliamentary of Robert Bowyer 1606–1607* (Minneapolis, 1931)
CJ	Commons Journal
CKS	Centre for Kentish Studies
CSPD	*Calendar of State Papers, Domestic Series*
GL	Guildhall Library
Hasler	P. W. Hasler, ed., *The History of Parliament: The House of Commons 1558–1603* (3 vols, London, 1981)
HCA	Hull City Archives
HJ	*Historical Journal*
HLQ	*Huntington Library Quarterly*
HLRO	House of Lords Record Office
HMC	Historical Manuscripts Commission
HR	*Historical Research*
JBS	*Journal of British Studies*
LJ	*Lords Journal*
OA	Original Act
P&P	*Past and Present*
PER	*Parliaments, Estates and Representation*
PH	*Parliamentary History*
PRO	Public Record Office, Kew, London
RO	Record Office
SR	A Luders et al., eds, *Statutes of the Realm* (11 vols, London, 1810–28)
STC	A. W. Pollard and G. R. Redgrave, *A Short Title Catalogue of Books Printed in England, Scotland and Ireland and of English Books Printed Abroad, 1475–1640*, second edition revised by W. A. Jackson, F. S. Ferguson and K. F. Pantzer (3 vols, 1976–91)
TRHS	*Transactions of the Royal Historical Society*
VCH	*Victoria County History*

INTRODUCTION

Chris R. Kyle

Early modern English Parliaments were institutional events: institutional
because they occupied a significant role in the governance of the
realm, and after the Reformation Parliament statute law became
omnicompetent.[1] Furthermore, they established and followed (more or
less) fixed procedures and had a permanent clerical staff. However,
they were also events, summoned and dissolved at irregular intervals
by the monarch, at least until the passage of the Triennial Act in
February 1641.[2] The very nature of the assembly and its power, influence
and role in English society and politics has been hotly debated by
historians for many years and continues today to fill the pages of
scholarly journals and the catalogues of publishers. No less controversial
than the nature and role of the assembly is the impact and validity of
its sources, official and unofficial. It is the aim of this introduction and
the ensuing editorials and documents to discuss and deconstruct the
nature of parliamentary sources and how they can be utilised in the
study of parliamentary history.

In recent years the publication of documents relating to Parliament
has concentrated on the diaries of MPs. These works, of immense
value to all early modern historians, are important sources but they
should not be viewed as the only material of relevance to the study
of parliamentary history. The documentary output relating to early
seventeenth-century Parliaments is vast and covers aspects of procedure,
lobbying, elections, legislation, debate, foreign policy, high politics and
local affairs. In line with this, the aim of the present collection of essays
is to highlight the importance of a wide range of parliamentary material.
In doing so it furthers not only our knowledge of the institution
but also provides insights into the importance of the centre–locality
relationship, local politicking amongst members of the gentry, the day-
to-day working of Parliaments and high politics. The volume covers
five different but overlapping aspects of parliamentary history. Designed
to stand alone but also to form a coherent whole, the documents
examine parliamentary debates, ambassadorial letters, the procedural

---

[1] G. R. Elton, *The Parliament of England, 1559–1581* (Cambridge, 1986), pp. 32–9; David
L. Smith, *The Stuart Parliaments, 1603–1689* (London, 1999), p. 205 n. 99.

[2] 16 Charles I cap. 1. But see the contemporary discussion on the frequency and calling
of Parliaments discussed in Pauline Croft, 'Annual Parliaments and the Long Parliament',
HR lix (1986), pp. 155–71; *idem*, 'The Debate on Annual Parliaments in the Early
Seventeenth Century', *PER* xvi (1996), pp. 163–74.

operation of Parliament, elections, politicking and correspondence between MPs and their constituencies. The pieces reproduced here cannot hope to encompass all the different types of source material for Parliament but they cover a wider diversity of sources than is normally found in such a collection. It is hoped that in presenting this information, scholars will not only find the individual articles useful, but also recognize the importance of looking at what the institutional, local and foreign sources can tell us as well as moving parliamentary history beyond the normal concentration on journals and diaries.

One of the important lessons from 'post-revisionist' history is that we have started to expand the range of sources that are used in the study of Parliament and to look at questions which cannot be answered by reference to the Journals. Work by Pauline Croft,[3] Richard Cust,[4] Tom Cogswell,[5] Norman Jones[6] and Sean Kelsey,[7] in particular, has provided a picture of Stuart Parliaments viewed from outside the gates of Westminster. The work has encompassed the print culture of Parliament, the iconography of the institution, the circulation of the speeches of MPs, political libels and the impact of legislation on the wider community. But in-depth research of this fresh approach to Parliament remains in its infancy and subjects such as the daily functioning of the institution, propaganda, political accountability and the socio-economic impact of Parliament on Westminster remain little understood.[8]

Furthermore, in order to understand Parliament and the wider world, some conception of its institutional character is necessary. Contrary to the strict revisionist position adopted by Sir Geoffrey Elton, early Stuart historians have broadened their focus from examining the 'official' sources of Parliament and have concentrated on the speeches and

---

[3] Pauline Croft, 'Libels, Popular Literacy and Public Opinion in Early Modern England', *HR* lxviii (1995), pp. 266–85; *idem*, 'The Reputation of Robert Cecil: Libels, Political Opinion and Popular Awareness in the Early Seventeenth Century', *TRHS* 6ᵗʰ ser. i (1991), pp. 43–69.

[4] Richard Cust, 'News and Politics in Early Seventeenth Century England', *P&P* cxii (1986), pp. 60–90; *idem*, 'Politics and the Electorate in the 1620s', *Conflict in Early Stuart England*, ed. Richard Cust and Ann Hughes (London, 1989), pp. 134–67; Richard Cust and Peter Lake, 'Sir Richard Grosvenor and the Rhetoric of Magistracy', *BIHR* liv (1981), pp. 40–53.

[5] Thomas Cogswell, *The Blessed Revolution: English Politics and the Coming of War, 1621–1624* (Cambridge, 1989); *idem*, 'Thomas Middleton and the Court, 1624: A Game at Chess in Context', *HLQ* xlviii (1984), pp. 273–88.

[6] Norman L. Jones, *God and the Moneylenders: Usury and Law in Early Modern England* (Oxford, 1989).

[7] Sean Kelsey, *Inventing a Republic: The Political Culture of the English Commonwealth* (Manchester, 1997).

[8] The volume *Parliament at Work: Parliamentary Committees, Access and Lobbying under the Tudors and Stuarts* (Boydell and Brewer, forthcoming) edited by myself and Jason Peacey, adds further to our knowledge of how Parliament operated on a day-to-day basis.

debates of Members, particularly those scribbled down by the bur-
geoning number of parliamentary diarists in the 1620s and 1640s. That
it has been possible to do so, owes much to the publications of the Yale
Centre for Parliamentary History – 'a heroic project' in the words of
John Morrill.[9] For the 1620s, only 1624 remains completely unpublished
and work is well advanced on the production of the diaries of the Long
Parliament.[10] These volumes have highlighted the importance of diaries
for an understanding of Stuart Parliaments as well as saving the valuable
research budgets of historians previously forced to trek the length and
breadth of England and to travel to Ireland and the United States.
The Yale Centre has also included many other types of documents
relating to Parliament, including accounts of elections, some texts of
bills, newsletters and separates. But before drawing these into the orbit
of this discussion it is worth highlighting the nature of the 'official'
sources in the early seventeenth century.

The surviving Commons Journals for the early Stuart period are a
far cry from their Tudor antecedents and 1640s counterparts.[11] Through
the vagaries of fire and survival, many of the Journals are the rough
notes of the Underclerk written on the floor of the House rather than
the fair copy shorn of references to speakers and what they said.[12] Thus
what has come down to us are Journals, especially for the 1620s, which
do record speeches and debate in detail and are not simply a record
of the formal business of the House. Clearly, in the 1620s the Commons
attempted to impose tighter restrictions on the Journal,[13] but it remains
a valuable record of debate until the Short Parliament and the order
of the Commons to the Clerk assistant, John Rushworth, not to take
notes of anything other than formal proceedings.[14] In addition, debates
in *both* Houses and the proceedings of the Parliament can be recon-
structed from the material in the House of Lords Record Office.
Although most of the Commons' archive was destroyed by fire in 1834,
the Main Papers of the Lords do contain much of value to those
interested in the Commons. A wealth of documents deals with committees in the Lower House, including the notes of their proceedings,

---

[9] John Morrill, 'Reconstructing the History of Early Stuart Parliaments', *Archives* xxi
91 (1994), 67.
[10] See below n. 45.
[11] *CJ*, i. 139–1057.
[12] It is tempting to attribute the loss of the fair-copy Journals not to fire, but to the
light fingers of Sir Simonds D'Ewes. His 'borrowing' of the Elizabethan Journals is well
known and his parliamentary diary for 1624 (BL, Harl. 159) is based partly on the
Underclerk's Journal. On D'Ewes and the Elizabethan Journals see David Dean, *Law-
making and Society in Late Elizabethan England* (Cambridge, 1996), p. 3.
[13] See *Proceedings 1628*, p. 2; Sheila Lambert, 'The Clerks and Records of the House of
Commons, 1600–1640', *BIHR* xliii (1970), pp. 215–31.
[14] *CJ*, ii. 12. I am grateful to Jason Peacey for this reference.

whilst many petitions and papers concerning grievances and the activities of MPs (political and procedural) can also be found there. The Main Papers should be regarded not only as a source for the history of the Lords but for the Commons as well.

Given the recent debates on the nature of parliamentary sources, and private diaries in particular, it is increasingly important to emphasise the problematic nature of many of the parliamentary diaries. Did the author have a particular bias? Was he present at the day's proceedings or did he write down an account relayed from another witness? How can we be sure that the diarist captured both the exact words and the tone of the speaker(s)? When we have ten versions of a particular speech, which one should we believe? I do not wish to dwell long on this matter as the question of the reliability of these diaries as accurate accounts of the proceedings of the Commons was answered some time ago by J. H. Hexter, and much of the subsequent debate has added little to our knowledge. But John Morrill has offered the radical solution that we should not quote directly from the Journals and diaries, but paraphrase them after reading and collating all the available accounts.[15] Furthermore, Morrill has provided a timely reminder of the importance of comparing the various diaries and not simply relying on one account, for example the dependence of Conrad Russell on the synopses of John Pym, and Robert Ruigh, whose work on the 1624 Parliament relied mainly on the diaries of Pym and Sir William Spring.[16] However, it is easy to exaggerate the problem. One point that Morrill, Jansson and David Smith all note is that it is necessary to employ good historical working practices – a point that surely no one will argue with.[17] In examining the proceedings of the Commons we should follow the ten guidelines that Morrill has suggested,[18] and also note that his analysis of the diaries illustrates the fact that 'time and time again the *similarity* of the accounts to one another (if rarely the precise replication of words and sentences) allows us to be confident that we are getting the gist of what is spoken'.[19] Perhaps this is also true of Morrill's own experiment in lecture notes in which he reviewed the notes of his students after

[15] J. H. Hexter, 'Parliament under the Lens', *British Studies Monitor* iii (1972–3), pp. 4–15; *idem*, 'Quoting the Commons, 1604–1642', *Tudor Rule and Revolution*, ed. DeLloyd J. Guth and John W. McKenna (Cambridge, 1982), pp. 369–91; Morrill, 'Reconstructing the History', pp. 67–72; *idem*, 'Paying One's D'Ewes', *PH* xiv (1995), pp. 179–86; *idem*, 'Getting Over D'Ewes', *PH* xv (1996), pp. 221–30; Maija Jansson, 'Dues Paid', *PH* xv (1996), pp. 215–20.

[16] Conrad Russell, *Parliaments and English Politics, 1621–1629* (Oxford, 1979), p. xix; Robert E. Ruigh, *The Parliament of 1624: Politics and Foreign Policy* (Camb. MA, 1971).

[17] Smith, *Stuart Parliaments*, pp. 13–14; Morrill, 'Reconstructing the History', p. 71; Jansson, 'Dues Paid', p. 220.

[18] See Morrill, 'Reconstructing the History', p. 71.

[19] *Ibid.* p. 70.

lecturing for five minutes on parliamentary diaries. He found that

one had tried hard to summarize all that I said; one had only noted points she did not already know; and the third had written down not so much what I had said as his reflections and commentary on what I had said. Two had drawn closely on my actual words (but one more closely than the other), one had used his own (and wittier) language. In 50 years time how easily would such surviving notes allow a reconstruction of my lecture or my personal bearing as I lectured?[20]

But here it is important not to burn the lecture notes of the recent graduate in a celebratory pyre, but, to apply the guidelines of Hexter and Morrill to *read* the lecture notes, *compare and contrast* them and reach an *informed* opinion. The unanswered question is, do the *collected* notes of Morrill's students accurately reflect what he said? In entering into the debate on this subject, I must confess (before someone else points it out) that I am equally guilty of directly quoting what MPs said in Parliament. But after spending the last fifteen years working with the parliamentary diaries of the 1620s, I see little need to paraphrase and no need to refrain from quoting the Journals and diaries. Not least because if we do not trust historians to read all the diaries and select the most accurate account, then why should we trust their own paraphrases?

Thus I believe that the problem of the usage of diaries has been exaggerated. Problems of conflicting evidence, misdating and value tend to sort themselves out. Following Hexter, it is true that 'the axes along which it turns out to be worth grading the narratives of the early Stuart Parliaments are completeness, competence and coherence. Bias and point of view enter the picture occasionally but rarely. Any problems that may arise on those scores, as in the case of Eliot's *Negotium Posterorum*, are best dealt with "ad hoc." '[21]

Moving beyond the eye-catching nature of the diaries there remains a vast amount of parliamentary information. Parliamentary separates have been used by Wallace Notestein, Tom Cogswell and Richard Cust to illustrate the widespread circulation of news about parliamentary debates, especially the speeches of Commons grandees such as Sir

[20] Morrill, 'Paying One's D'Ewes', pp. 185–6.
[21] Hexter, 'Quoting the Commons', p. 391.

Edward Coke, Sir Edwin Sandys and John Eliot.[22] In addition, MPs frequently reported parliamentary news to their constituencies and friends;[23] MPs and peers ordered copies of bills, speeches and royal addresses;[24] boroughs sent delegations to Westminster to assist their MPs;[25] petitions flooded into Parliament;[26] committee lists were hung in the lobby of the Commons which was open to the public;[27] and on occasion, petitions and grievances were posted around London and Westminster.[28] This wealth of parliamentary material has also high-lighted the theoretical construct of parliamentary secrecy. It seems clear that there was widespread knowledge, at least among the élite, of parliamentary debates and individual speeches. We may argue over the degree of the 'trickle-down' effect,[29] but the overall conception of Parliament as a *public* institution agrees with Jason Peacey's comment when discussing the 1640s 'that secrecy was not enforced, while the determination of publishers ensured that it could not be enforced'.[30] The logical development from this point is to look at the impact of print in the parliamentary arena. In conceptualising Parliament from the standpoint of print it is clear that much more source material exists than just the official proclamations and statutes. This has been recognised by historians working on the 1640s but much less so by their early Stuart colleagues.[31] Throughout the 1620s and the 1640s, MPs

[22] Wallace Notestein and Frances Relf, eds, *Commons Debates 1629* (Minnesota, 1921), *CD 1629*, pp. xx–xli; Cust, 'News and Politics', pp. 60–90; idem, *The Forced Loan and English Politics 1626–1628* (Oxford, 1987), pp. 155, 158, 168; Thomas Cogswell, 'Politics and Propaganda: Charles I and the People in the 1620s', *JBS* xxix (1990), pp. 187–215; idem, 'Underground Verse and the Transformation of Early Stuart Political Culture', *Political Culture and Cultural Politics in Early Modern England*, ed. S. D. Amussen and Mark A. Kishlansky (Manchester, 1995), pp. 277–300.

[23] See, for example, the correspondence of John Lister with the Hull corporation in Hull RO, L. 166–70, and the numerous letters reproduced in the Yale *Proceedings in Parliament* volumes. I am grateful to Simon Healy for the Hull references.

[24] Vernon Snow, ed., *Parliament in Elizabethan England: John Hooker's Order and Usage*, (New Haven, 1977), p. 172. For a specific incidence see HLRO, Main Papers, 13 March 1624, order for Lord Danvers to have a copy of the Goathland manor bill.

[25] Chris R. Kyle and Jason Peacey, ' "Under cover of so much coming and going": Public Access to Parliament and the Political Process in Early Modern England' in *idem*. eds, *Parliament at Work* (forthcoming).

[26] See for example the Guildhall collection noted below, p. 7. Scribal petitions can be found in vast quantities in HLRO, Main Papers.

[27] *Proceedings 1614*, p.99; *CD 1621*, ii. 32.

[28] PRO, STAC 8/128/11, pt. 2; GL, Broadside 23.105. I am grateful to Andrew Thrush for the PRO reference.

[29] Derek Hirst, *The Representative of the People?* (Cambridge, 1975), p. 181.

[30] Jason Peacey, 'Making Parliament Public: Privacy, Print and Political Accountability during the Civil Wars and Interregnum'. I am grateful to Dr Peacey for showing me a copy of his paper in advance of publication.

[31] See, for example, Alan Cromartie 'The Printing of Parliamentary Speeches, November 1640–July 1642', *HJ* xxxiii (1990), pp. 23–44; Sheila Lambert, ed., *Printing for Parliament,*

and peers were subjected to a barrage of petitions and lobbying documents, some of which were printed in many copies and distributed to all Members of both Houses. The extent of this degree of lobbying is clear, not least from a collection in the Guildhall Library, London, in which one MP, probably a member of the grievances committee, amassed at least 60 individual printed petitions during the 1621 Parliament.[32] At least 120 different printed petitions survive from the 1620s alone, some of which were printed in many 'hundreds' of copies.[33] This deliberate mass lobbying of MPs, which continued despite a Lords order on 5 April 1624 to stop petitions to Parliament being printed,[34] illustrates how widespread the notion had become of Parliament as an effective forum for the grievances of individuals, companies and the commonweal.[35]

Print was also the favoured medium for the sermons preached to Parliament;[36] woodcuts circulated depicting such newsworthy events as the fall in 1621 of the notorious patentee, Sir Giles Mompesson;[37] Ben Jonson,[38] John Dee[39] and John Taylor the Water Poet immortalized

1641–1700 (List and Index Society, xx, 1984); *idem*, 'The Beginning of Printing for the House of Commons, 1640–1642', *The Library*, 6th ser. iii (1981), pp. 43–61.

[32] GL, Broadsides. These are scattered throughout the Guildhall collection. They are undated, but are identifiable by cross-referencing against the 1621 Journals and debates and by annotations in the same hand.

[33] S. R. Gardiner, ed., *Reports of Cases in the Courts of Star Chamber and High Commission* (Camden Society, new ser., xxxix, 1886), 37–40; PRO, STAC 8/128/11, pt. 2. In 1641 Robert Jager, attending at Westminster to help with business for Sandwich, informed the corporation that with their case to be freed from the subsidy, 'I have put it forth to print that every men of the House may have one'. CKS, Sa/C4, unbound letters, Robert Jager to Sandwich, 10 March 1641. I owe this reference to Jason Peacey.

[34] William A. Jackson, ed., *Records of the Court of the Stationers' Company, 1602–1640* (London, 1957), p. 166.

[35] I am currently engaged in research on these petitions. My preliminary findings were given in a paper entitled 'Parliament, Print and Petitions in Early Seventeenth Century England' at the North American Conference on British Studies (Cambridge MA, 1999).

[36] *Prayers for the Parliament* (?1604); *Prayers for the Parliament* (?1605–6); *A Prayer for the Speaker of the Commons House of Parliament* (London, ?1606); Society of Antiquaries, Broadside no. 176, *Prayers for the Parliament* (1621); John F. Wilson, *Pulpit in Parliament* (Oxford, 1970); H. R. Trevor-Roper, 'The Fast Sermons of the Long Parliament', *Essays in British History Presented to Sir Keith Feiling*, ed. Trevor-Roper, (London, 1964), pp. 85–138.

[37] Society of Antiquaries, Broadside no. 182.

[38] C. H. Herford, Percy and Evelyn Simpson, eds, *Ben Jonson* (11 vols, Oxford, 1925–52), viii in *Epigrammes* (1612), no. 24. See also Jonson's description of the King's procession to Parliament in 1604, *B. Jon[son]; His Part of King James his Royall and Magnificent Entertainement . . .* (London, 1604).

[39] John Dee, *To the Honorable Assemblie of the Commons in the present Parlament* (1604), Corpus Christi College, Oxford, F.A.1.10 (38, 39); Henry E. Huntington Library, San Marino, California, RB 41808, 41809; Bodleian, 4°.S.2 (7a, b) JUR; Ashmole MS 133 (3, 4); Lincoln College, Oxford, O.3.15; BL, RB C.21.b.25 (2).

Parliament in verse;[40] printed breviates of bills were available to MPs in the chamber and at committee meetings;[41] while those interested in lobbying or knowing who sat in Parliament could purchase lists of MPs and peers, some engraved not only with names but also with representations of peers seated in the Lords and MPs sitting in St Stephens.[42]

It is partly through this reflection upon the wide range of extant parliamentary material that certain conclusions can be drawn about Parliament in the 1620s and its relationship with the Short and Long Parliaments. Analysing Parliament through an examination of the myriad sources pertaining to it allows us to see a picture far removed from the Russellian event of the 1620s. It challenges the revisionist position that Parliament in the 1620s increasingly became a body of no use to the Crown and little to the Commonweal. Indeed, it illustrates that Parliament was increasingly viewed as the 'body of the whole realm' to which, in the face of royal policy, the gentry and wider populace turned in order to remedy grievances and to act as a national sounding-board. Furthermore, collating the parliamentary material shows just how prevalent this view was and that Parliament played a more significant and newsworthy role than has been generally accepted hitherto. The extent and nature of the parliamentary material emphasises Cust's notion of a more politicised institution than that discussed by Conrad Russell and Mark Kishlansky.[43] And this politicisation of Parliament was a development which happened both within the chambers and in the community at large. It is viewed in this light that the documents reproduced here interact with one another and emphasise the public and private awareness of Parliament.

Simon Healy's chapter, 'Debates in the House of Commons, 1604–1607', reproduces the unpublished notes and diaries of the first Jacobean Parliament of 1604–10 and in doing so continues the publication of the proceedings of the early modern English Parliament. Leicester Uni-

---

[40] John Taylor, *The Subjects Joy for the Parliament* (1621), Society of Antiquaries, Broadside no. 177.

[41] See for example BL, Harl. 7608, fols 382v–87; GL, Broadside 23.120. Alford took notes on the dorse of his copy of this petition whilst sitting in the House that morning. For other examples see GL, Broadside 24.31; Society of Antiquaries, Broadside no. 216; Hampshire Record Office, Jervoise Papers, Scrapbook TD/540; BL, Harl. 7607, fols 393–404; The Queen's College, Oxford, Sel.b.229, no. 2; GL, Broadsides 23.122, 123.

[42] Society of Antiquaries, Broadside nos 281, 282. See also no. 221 for a rare engraving of Convocation with a list of the Members present in 1624. See, for example, *The Names of the Knights for Parliament 1625* (1625). Numerous other lists are noted in the *STC*, 2nd edn, i. 351–2.

[43] Russell, *Parliaments and English Politics*; Mark A. Kishlansky, *Parliamentary Selection: Social and Political Choice in Early Modern England* (Cambridge, 1986); Cust, 'Politics and the Electorate', esp. pp. 136, 158–62.

versity Press has published the private diaries of the proceedings of the House of Commons for 1559–1601,[44] while the Yale Centre for Parliamentary History and various individuals have undertaken the editing of the debates of the sessions covering the period from 1610 to 1641.[45] However, the sessions of 1604–7 have been covered less adequately. A comprehensive edition of the fullest diary, kept by Robert Bowyer during the sessions of 1605–6 and 1606–7, was published by D. H. Willson, who interpolated many of the notes made by Sir John Holles and Sir Thomas Wilson into his footnotes.[46] However, this still leaves a number of other sources for the first three sessions of James's first Parliament either unpublished or edited in abbreviated form. These are reproduced here in full, with appropriate cross-referencing to Bowyer and other published sources:

1. the diaries and notes kept in all three sessions by Sir Edward Mountagu, which are partially calendared in *HMC Buccleuch*.
2. the notes of Sir Robert Cotton in British Library, Titus F.IV.
3. Sir George Manners' account of the opening weeks of the 1604 session in Belvoir Castle MS 14.

[44] T. E. Hartley, ed., *Proceedings in the Parliaments of Elizabeth I* (3 vols, Leicester, 1981–95).

[45] Elizabeth Read Foster, ed., *Proceedings in Parliament 1610* (2 vols, New Haven, 1966); Maija Jansson, ed., *Proceedings in Parliament 1614 (House of Commons)* (Philadelphia, 1988); Wallace Notestein, Frances Helen Relf and Hartley Simpson, eds, *Commons Debates 1621* (7 vols, New Haven, 1935); Maija Jansson and William B. Bidwell, eds, *Proceedings in Parliament 1625* (New Haven, 1987); William B. Bidwell and Maija Jansson, eds, *Proceedings in Parliament 1626* (4 vols, New Haven, 1991–6); Mary Freer Keeler, Maija Jansson Cole, and William B. Bidwell, *Proceedings in Parliament 1628* (6 vols, New Haven, 1977–83); Wallace Notestein and Frances Helen Relf, eds, *Commons Debates for 1629* (Minneapolis, 1921); Wallace Notestein, ed., *The Journal of Sir Simonds D'Ewes from the Beginning of the Long Parliament to the Opening of the Trial of the Earl of Strafford* (New Haven, 1923); Willson H. Coates, ed., *The Journal of Sir Simonds D'Ewes from the Final Recess of the Long Parliament to the Withdrawl of King Charles from London* (New Haven, 1942); Maija Jansson, ed., *Proceedings in the Opening Session of the Long Parliament* (3 Nov. 1640–20 Mar. 1641, 2 vols, London, 2000); idem, ed., *Two Diaries of the Long Parliament* (Gloucester and New York, 1984); Willson H. Coates, A. S. Young and Vernon F. Snow, eds, *The Private Journals of the Long Parliament* (3 vols, New Haven, 1982–92). See also the parliamentary volumes in the Camden series: Samuel Rawson Gardiner, ed., *Parliamentary Debates in 1610* (Camden Soc., OS, xxxi, 1862); Lady de Villiers, ed., 'The Hastings Journal of the Parliament of 1621', in *Camden Miscellany* (Camden Soc., 3rd ser., xxxiii, 1953); Samuel Rawson Gardiner, ed., *Notes of the Debates in the House of Lords 1621* (Camden Soc., OS, ciii, 1870); Frances Helen Relf, *Notes of the Debates in the House of Lords, 1621–1628* (Camden Soc., 3rd ser., xlii, 1929); Samuel Rawson Gardiner, ed., *Notes of the Debates in the House of Lords, 1624 and 1626* (Camden Soc., 2nd ser., xxiv, 1879); idem, ed., *Debates in the House of Commons in 1625* (Camden Soc., 2nd ser., vi, 1873).

[46] David Harris Willson, ed., *The Parliamentary Diary of Robert Bowyer, 1606–1607* (Minneapolis, 1977).

Publication of these sources fills one of the few remaining gaps in the parliamentary diary sources for the early seventeenth century.

Brennan Pursell, in 'War or Peace? Jacobean Politics and the Parliament of 1621', has translated and edited two letters from the Spanish Ambassador to England, Count Gondomar, to the Infanta Isabella. These letters offer a fascinating insight into James's attitude to Parliament and his reasons for adjourning it in December 1621. Furthermore, they illustrate the close relationship between James and Gondomar and how the Spaniard was made privy to the most intimate secrets of state. Gondomar gained his knowledge not only from the King but also in private conversations with Prince Charles, George Villiers, Marquis of Buckingham, and Sir John Digby. In relaying this information to the Infanta, Gondomar offered a unique perspective on Jacobean high politics and revealed himself to be very well informed on the debates in the House of Commons. The letters add substantially to our knowledge of the November–December sitting of the 1621 Parliament as well as providing further evidence on the King's relationship with the Lower House. Gondomar emerges as an astute and witty reporter although, as Pursell notes, one who was overly prone to 'rambling syntax.'

In my own chapter, ' "It will be a Scandal to show what we have done with such a number": House of Commons Committee Attendance Lists, 1606–1628', I have transcribed a series of House of Commons committee lists from 1606 to 1628 which are annotated with the attendance of MPs. The subject-matter of the legislation and select committees ranges widely through public and private matters, such as the bill for better attendance in the Commons (1610), purveyance (1624) and the naturalization of a physician, Samuel Bave (1626). This material illustrates a wealth of issues of importance not only to parliamentary historians but also to all those who study the early modern period. The documents themselves reveal an astonishing apathy in attendance amongst those named to committees, as well as shedding further light on the workings of the Lower House, both by MPs and the nascent bureaucracy. The publication of the lists greatly increases our knowledge of how parliamentary committees operated in the early seventeenth century as well as providing valuable biographical information on important Members, such as Sir Edward Coke.

Jason Peacey's chapter, 'Tactical Organization in a Contested Election: Sir Edward Dering and the Spring Election at Kent, 1640', concerns a notebook of Dering pertaining to the Kent county election for the Short Parliament of 1640. The notebook offers an important insight into the degree of planning and preparation which went into some contested parliamentary elections. While other early seventeenth-century elections reveal evidence of concerted organisation, and even of the creation of poll books, documentary evidence about such activities is extremely rare. The circumstances surrounding the Kent election are well known, and have been explored thoroughly by scholars like Professor Mark Kishlansky. What this document provides, however, is new evidence regarding the mechanics of an election campaign. Dering, evidently aware of the popularity of his rival, Sir Roger Twysden, and of the organisation with which the latter sought to secure support prior to the poll, recognised the need to organise his own campaign. The result was the list of more than 600 freeholders in the county, and Dering's notes thereon. In the weeks before the election, Dering identified those who planned to vote for himself and Twysden in a way which indicates a concerted effort to undertake an 'opinion poll' across the entire county, and one which must have required the assistance of a number of friends. Furthermore, on the day of the election and in the weeks which followed, Dering endeavoured to record the way in which the freeholders voted, perhaps recognising – on the basis of past experience at Kent county elections – the possibility of electoral malpractice by the sheriff. By keeping a record of events at the election, therefore, Dering may have felt prepared for any dispute and any parliamentary investigation as well as for future elections. Examination of Dering's list also offers important evidence about the areas within the county where he was most influential, and illustrates the patterns of voting by both parish and county region.

David Scott in ' "Particular Businesses" in the Long Parliament: The Hull Letters, 1644–1648', has transcribed and edited 117 letters sent to Hull corporation by its MPs and friends at Westminster between 1644 and 1648. This correspondence reveals an unrivalled source for analysing the interaction between centre and locality during the civil war period, as well as providing unique evidence concerning the workings of the Long Parliament and its committees, the exercise of patronage and influence at Westminster, and the lobbying and management tactics employed by wealthy boroughs such as Hull to manipulate parliamentary proceedings to their own advantage. The letters reveal hitherto unknown interest groups and factional alignments at Westminster, and chart changing opinion in the Houses towards the King, the Scots and the settlement of peace. Most importantly, the letters shed light on the activities of MPs as parliamentary men-of-business – a very rare phenomenon for the seventeenth century. Through the letters we are afforded a view of political life at Westminster behind the scenes, and the picture of parliamentary politics that emerges bears little resemblance to the one depicted by most historians, in which lofty national issues predominate. Hull MPs spent much of their time in an altogether different environment, in which bribery and committee-packing were rife. Yet at the same time the wealth of detail in the letters about national events and constitutional issues also indicates the existence of a politically aware and engaged audience in the localities. The 117 letters in question form a nearly unbroken series over the civil war years, and can be regarded as a discrete collection in themselves. Scott has included detailed notes on the correspondence, plus biographical studies of the MPs involved and an analysis of the wider political context in which they operated.

As this volume illustrates, it is necessary to take the search for Parliament in the wider world beyond the boundaries of parliamentary diaries and the official Journals, and yet the publication of primary sources which are not Journals or diaries has lagged behind the historiography. Notwithstanding the fact that the Yale Centre has published many documents concerning elections and politicking, these have received little historical attention. In highlighting these documents, as well as in presenting unpublished proceedings of the first Jacobean Parliament, it is hoped also that Parliament may be seen through the eyes of its contemporary audience and participants as an institutional event which needs to be viewed not only from an institutional per-spective but from outside the gates of the Palace. Healy's chapter further demonstrates that parliamentary notetaking and reporting became increasingly commonplace, whilst Pursell reveals the avid interest shown in Parliament by ambassadors. My chapter shows that we need to expand our range of sources when examining Parliament and avoid over-reliance on the journals and diaries for the activities of MPs. Peacey's development of the Kent electoral politics through the use of local sources again highlights the importance of looking beyond the chambers to understand parliamentary behaviour – a point also germane to Scott's edition of the Hull letters. It is thus one of the aims of this volume to show that Parliament generated a far greater body of documentation than has previously been acknowledged to have been part of its *œuvre*.

DEBATES IN THE HOUSE OF COMMONS, 1604–1607

Simon Healy

Introduction

Although the authors of the journals and speeches reproduced below all came from the East Midlands and were loosely related to each other, they offer three widely differing viewpoints of the proceedings of the House of Commons during the parliamentary sessions of 1604 and 1606–7. The Rutland manuscript concentrates on the privilege dispute over election returns which dominated the opening weeks of the 1604 session, while Sir Robert Cotton was chiefly concerned to record procedural precedents for use in subsequent Parliaments, and Sir Edward Mountagu focussed on the House's legislative activity.[1]

For the most part, these diaries are not as comprehensive as the official Journals, nor do they give as full an account of key speeches as is provided by the diaries of the MPs Robert Bowyer and Sir Robert Harley, which are already in print.[2] However, they add a considerable number of details, and offer the historian a view of the Commons as seen through the eyes of three members who were less interested in the cut and thrust of daily debate than Bowyer and Harley, and thus perhaps more accurately reflect the interests of many ordinary members.

One key factor which emerges clearly from all of the accounts printed below is the active role played in the politics of these sessions by the King, a constant influence on the daily proceedings of the House, and whose resolution of the Buckinghamshire election dispute is amply detailed by Manners and Cotton. Mountagu also had a keen appreciation of the King's role, giving the royal speeches, messages and exhortations rather more prominence in his diary than the debates within the chamber. Such an interest is hardly surprising, for two reasons: first, the authors of the accounts were keen to know the mind of their sovereign, still new on the throne and still a relatively unknown quantity to all but his closest advisers; secondly, James arrived on the

---

[1] For further discussion of the priorities each author brought to his account, see the introductions to the relevant manuscripts below.

[2] D. H. Willson, ed., *The Parliamentary Diary of Robert Bowyer 1606–1607* (Minneapolis, 1931), which reprints Harley's account in its footnotes.

throne with a positive agenda, that of union and a moderate church settlement, the enactment of which necessarily entailed the management of Parliament on a weekly, or even a daily, basis.[3] All of this is a far cry from the ageing regal cynic whose extended sojourn at Royston in the autumn of 1621 played a significant part in the collapse of that Parliament, or the King who spent a good deal of the 1624 session trying to escape from the firm commitment to war with Spain which his son Prince Charles, his favourite the Duke of Buckingham and a significant proportion of MPs proposed to force upon him.[4]

The one significant revelation within the journals printed below is the light Mountagu's papers shed upon the agenda contained in his keynote speech of 23 March 1604, which raised what he described as 'greeffes injoyned me by the country to make knowen'. The most important was a complaint about the threatened deprivation of ministers for failure to subscribe to the 1604 Canons. Such protests were inevitable from a county which had been a centre of the Presbyterian movement in the 1580s, and was to see fifteen non-conforming clergy removed from office over the coming year. Mountagu himself took on an important role in the controversy in February 1605, when he presented a petition to the Privy Council on behalf of the suspended ministers.[5] The other major concern his speech addressed, about enclosure and depopulation, was proved to be well founded by the riots provoked across the Midlands by this grievance in the late spring of 1607.

The positive action on religious policy which Mountagu recommended to his listeners was concealed within his deceptively innocuous complaint about 'the Intollerable burdene vexation travayle & charge of the commissaries courtes'. A draft of this speech, printed below, lists no less than sixteen separate complaints against the ecclesiastical courts. In proposing a solution, he quickly dismissed any expectation of reform from a Convocation packed with episcopal placemen, recommending instead the revival of the legislation which had underpinned Thomas Cranmer's earlier attempt to codify canon law and church discipline: 3&4 Edward VI, cap. 11, 'An Act that the King's Majesty may nominate thirty-two persons to peruse and make ecclesiastical laws'. This long-defunct statute allowed the King to appoint sixteen clergy and sixteen laymen to examine and redraft the entire canon of ecclesiastical law on their own authority, subject only to royal assent. Mountagu added

[3] For which see R. C. Munden, 'King, Commons and Reform, 1603–4' in *Faction and Parliament* (Oxford, 1978), ed. K. Sharpe, pp. 43–72.

[4] C. Russell, *Parliaments and English Politics 1621–9* (Oxford, 1979), pp. 121–203; T. Cogswell, *Blessed Revolution* (Cambridge, 1989).

[5] W. J. Sheils, *Puritans in the Diocese of Peterborough* (Northamptonshire Record Society publications xxx; Northampton 1979), pp. 79–86, 110–12; *HMC Buccleuch*, i. 237–8; *HMC Montagu of Beaulieu*, pp. 45–8.

his own recommendation that the review be completed

> during this parliament (for I do not like to refer it to commissioners hereafter) that there wer a convenient number chosen oute of both howses, & they to view, search & examine ... And then to bring them in articles into the house ... And then to present them to his majestie for his Royall assent/

This proposal served the godly agenda admirably well, removing control of ecclesiastical legislation from Convocation to Parliament at a stroke, while paying little more than lip-service to the royal prerogative.[6] As such, it stood no chance whatsoever of passing into law, and in the event even the King's suggestion of a conference with the clergy to discuss the issue engendered a protracted quarrel about whether the Commons could be ordered to meet with Convocation.[7]

The Diaries

None of the accounts printed below appears to be original notes taken on the floor of St Stephen's chapel, although all were probably written up while the relevant sessions were still fresh in the authors' minds. As far as they go – and two only cover the first few weeks of the 1604 session – all given a broadly chronological account of the sessions, although to a variable extent they address thematic concerns: this is most true of Cotton's account of the session of 1606–7, which was clearly compiled as a record of precedents for the procedures and standing orders of the House to be consulted by future Parliaments.

(1) Belvoir Castle, Rutland MS 14, fols 201–8
Journal of parliamentary proceedings from 19 March to 6 April 1604, tentatively ascribed to Sir George Manners.

Presumably compiled either by or at the behest of Sir George Manners, the only member of the Earl of Rutland's family then sitting in the Commons, the original text of this diary is unavailable for consultation, and this transcript has been taken from a photocopy held by the History of Parliament Trust.

The Rutland diary begins as a general account, but becomes increasingly focussed upon the Goodwin v. Fortescue election debate which

---

[6] Northants. RO, Montagu MS 29/7, below, p. 95; *SR*, iv. III–12; D. MacCulloch, *Thomas Cranmer* (New Haven, 1996), pp. 500–3, 533–4.

[7] *CJ*, i. 172–3, 175–6, 178, 235, 988–9; Mountagu Diary, below p. 69.

came to dominate the first two weeks of business. Its account of the debate of 23 March, at which the Buckinghamshire election controversy was first raised, is by far the fullest of any known source, recording the detailed arguments and legal precedents.[8] It makes equally careful note of Speaker Phelips' report of 29 March upon the conference of the previous day at which the Commons justified their proceedings to the Lords and judges,[9] while its record of the debate of 30 March includes several speeches unnoticed in any of the other surviving narratives.[10] The last major speech recorded in the journal, Griffith Payne's outburst of 3 April at the second reading of the purveyance bill, focusses on the same issue from a different angle, taxing the House with insulting the King, Council and judges with its claim to jurisdiction over elections. This is followed by a further recapitulation of the Commons' justification for their actions. Curiously, the diarist gives only a brief summary of the King's final adjudication of this dispute on 5 April.

Other major events of the first two weeks of the session are generally recorded in less detail. The King's speech at the opening of the session receives only a few lines, while the lengthy agenda for business laid before the House by Sir Robert Wroth and Sir Edward Mountagu on 23 March are merely listed and noted to have been committed. The other significant privilege dispute at the start of the session, the arrest of Sir Thomas Sherley for debt during the King's entry into London four days before the start of the session, is covered in much less detail than the Buckinghamshire election, except for the debate of 27 March which followed Sherley's examination at the bar of the House.[11]

(2) BL, Cotton MSS, Titus F.IV, fols 3–10.
Sir Robert Cotton's journal of parliamentary proceedings 19 March–4 April 1604.

In later life, Cotton himself referred to a diary kept during the parliamentary sessions of 1604–10, and there is strong circumstantial evidence to identify Titus F.IV as this manuscript. Probably compiled shortly after the dissolution, in 1611 or early 1612, the account is in the hand of Cotton's associate Ralph Starkey.[12]

---

[8] Other accounts may be found in *CJ*, i. 151–2, 934–5; Cotton Diary; Mountagu Diary.
[9] *CJ*, i. 158, 938 are the only other accounts to match Manners for detail.
[10] *Ibid.* i. 159–60 gives a fuller text but does not name the speakers, and *ibid.* i. 939–40 is almost as comprehensive, but the Rutland account is the only one to include speeches by Sir John Mallory, Richard Martin, Edward Hext and William Wiseman.
[11] For other accounts of this debate, see *CJ*, i. 155, 936–7; Cotton Diary.
[12] The attribution is discussed at length in Elizabeth Read Foster, ed., *Proceedings in Parliament 1610* (New Haven, 1966), i. pp. xliii–xlvii; K. Sharpe, *Sir Robert Cotton, 1586–1631* (Oxford, 1979), pp. 251–2.

Cotton, or the source he used for the first day of the session, was one of the many members who failed to gain admittance to the King's opening speech in the Court of Requests on 19 March, which perhaps explains the care with which he noted the insult offered to Sir Herbert Croft when the latter was excluded by one of the guards on the door. He made detailed notes of the King's speech when it was repeated on 22 March for the benefit of those denied access on the earlier occasion.

The journal gives details of Sir William Maurice's enthusiastic speech of 29 March in favour of the union; like the good antiquarian he was, Cotton copied down the Welsh proverb which Maurice insisted foretold James's role in uniting the kingdoms.[13] His antiquarian interests inclined him to be more interested in precedent than politics, and thus it is perhaps not surprising that he garbled the seven-point agenda put forward by Sir Robert Wroth on 23 March. By contrast, the privilege disputes over the Buckinghamshire election and the arrest of Sir Thomas Sherley were exactly the sort of material he wished to retain for future reference, and it is not surprising that he collected detailed notes on both.[14] With an eye for the telling detail, he was the only diarist to note the important information that Bishop Mathew of Durham had vouched for Sherley's parliamentary privilege at the time of his arrest.

One minor incident which offers some suggestion as to the way in which Cotton compiled his diary was his description of the first reading of the apparel bill on 24 March: he noted the provisions of the bill and its rejection, which, he observed, 'did seem a litle odd'. Mountagu's journal makes it clear that the House disliked the clause allowing the Privy Council to make law by proclamation, but the Clerk's Journal, upon which Cotton probably based his account, does not go into the details of the debate, which would explain the author's perplexity.[15] However, Cotton clearly had access to other sources in the compilation of his diary: his report of Henry Yelverton's speech of 30 March on the Buckinghamshire election case is so disproportionately detailed that it seems likely he had access to the original; while his account of the proceedings against Griffith Payne on 3 April, which noted that 'the matter sleepeth', implies that he had access to at least one set of notes written during the session.

Cotton's account ceases abruptly in the middle of a page with a mention of the reading of the bill against the export of iron ordnance

[13] *CJ*, i. 158, 938. For another example of Cotton's interest in Welsh history, see BL, Cotton MSS, Julius F.VI, fol. 303.

[14] He was particularly well placed to do so in the case of the Buckinghamshire election, as he was named to the committee to justify the Commons' decision to the Lords on 27 March, and that to confer with the judges about the same issue on 5 April. *CJ*, i. 156, 166.

[15] *Ibid.* i. 152; Mountagu Diary.

on 4 April; unlike the Rutland account, it does not even record the final resolution of the Buckinghamshire election dispute on the following day, which would have made a more logical endpoint to the journal. One can only speculate upon the reasons for this sudden break: Cotton may simply have run out of time or felt that the effort of compiling a comprehensive journal was unlikely to serve his chief purpose, namely, to provide a catalogue of precedents for use in future Parliaments.

The editor gratefully acknowledges the generous assistance of Christopher Thompson, whose earlier transcript of this diary has been an invaluable aid in the preparation of this edition.

(3) Northamptonshire Record Office, Montagu MSS 29, 30.
Sir Edward Mountagu's journal of parliamentary proceedings and associated notes for speeches, 19 March–7 July 1604

Mountagu's account is the only surviving journal known to have been kept throughout the session. It is supported by two separate accounts of debates from 21 April to 15 May, and drafts of two of Mountagu's own speeches: one against the abuses of commissaries' courts which he probably used to commend the agenda he laid before the House on 23 March, the other on the annexations' bill, which was presumably intended for the debate of 4 July 1604, although Mountagu notes that it was never delivered. The speeches were clearly drafted in preparation for the relevant debates, while the diary was probably compiled either during or shortly after the end of the session from notes taken on the floor of the House.

The journal shows relatively little interest in the privilege disputes with which the session began, contrasting sharply with the detailed coverage these incidents received from both Cotton and Manners. On 23 March Mountagu made a half-hearted attempt to follow the details of the Buckinghamshire election dispute, but quickly lost interest, and concluded 'this matter was long debated with diver arguments pro & con especially by the lawyers'. He made more detailed notes on the debate of 29 March, and recorded the King's final settlement of the dispute on 5 April in some detail, underlining the key decision 'that the writt shoulde be graunted to go oute of the lower house'.[16]

Mountagu demonstrated a consistently low interest in political issues, recording only a handful of individual speeches after the opening week of the session, and summarising lengthy debates in a single sentence. As might be expected, religious affairs were occasionally favoured with slightly fuller coverage, and he presumably believed that the debates

---

[16] Mountagu Diary, pp. 64–5. The separate for the debate of 29 March has not been found.

on the union, concerning the change of name and the nomination of the Union Commission, were of significance, as he covered these in two separate papers.[17]

Mountagu's chief purpose in keeping a journal lay in its record of the passage of bills, particularly those likely to be of use to him a county magistrate. To this end he made a painstaking record of most items of legislation which came before the House, noting the title of each bill (and occasionally its sponsor) and making marginal notes about committal, engrossing, third readings and rejections. In the opening weeks of the 1604 session he even numbered each bill, which suggests that he was initially planning to compile a systematic record of bills submitted during the session.

(4) BL, Cotton MSS, Titus F.IV, fols 93–106.
Sir Robert Cotton's account of precedents during the session 18 November 1606–5 July 1607.

This digest of proceedings follows an entirely different format from the one Cotton had used for the 1604 session, being a detailed list of precedents, generally in chronological order, rather than a journal of debates. The change of format may owe something to the fact that Cotton had been added to the committee for privileges at the start of the second session on 5 November 1605.[18] Most of the incidents recorded can be traced in the Commons Journal, which Cotton clearly relied upon heavily in the preparation of this account. However, a few came from other sources, and in one case, a procedural ruling of 21 February 1607, Cotton's account clarifies an ambiguous note in the Commons Journal.[19]

(5) Northants. RO, Montagu MS 30.
Sir Edward Mountagu's diary of the session 18 November 1606–20 May 1607 (with a handful of notes on debates thereafter).

Mountagu's account follows the same format as in 1604. He may have felt somewhat out of his depth in a session dominated by the legal technicalities of the proposed union with Scotland, as his notes on the key debates rarely attempt to unravel the complex issues being discussed, and become increasingly perfunctory. The only speech for which he kept separate notes was that by Sir Edwin Sandys on 28 April 1607, an important intervention which moved the debate away from technical

---

[17] Northants. RO, Montagu 29/71, 73.
[18] CJ, i. 256.
[19] Cotton Diary, p. 107.

questions on to the wider consideration of the desirability of the full
legal and commercial union proposed by the King.[20] James responded
by sending the House a bill for repeal of hostile laws, the first positive
step towards a legal union, which the Commons did their best to ignore
by provoking a privilege dispute over their freedom of speech on the
union question. Mountagu recorded this flurry of activity in unusual
detail, but before the House returned to the issue Mountagu was sent
down to Northamptonshire to assist in the suppression of the enclosure
riots in the Midlands. He resumed his seat in the Commons on 26
June, only a week before the prorogation, but did not resume his diary,
which concludes with a brief summary of the passage of the hostile
laws bill.

Editorial Conventions

Transcriptions of the diaries have largely retained their original spelling,
punctuation and capitalization, except that the letters I and J, U and
V have been altered to conform to modern usage, and 'ff' has been
replaced by a single letter, capitalized or otherwise as seems best in the
circumstances. Words crossed out in the text appear ~~thus~~, and while
items in [square brackets] are editorial interpolations, those in (rounded
brackets) are original; it should be borne in mind that the authors were
not always consistent in closing brackets they had opened. The handful
of words which have defied the editor's paleographical efforts are
?preceded by a question mark. Finally, it should be noted that standard
seventeenth-century abbreviations have been silently expanded, with
the exception of Sir Edward Mountagu's abbreviations for the remark
'committed', which have been left unaltered; he eventually settled on
the term 'cottd'. Names of those recorded in the debates who were
MPs at the time have been printed in **boldface type** for easier visual
reference, with the exception of Mr. Speaker (Sir Edward Phelips),
whose title occurs too often for this to be of any use.

---

[20] Briefly calendared in *HMC Montagu of Beaulieu*, p. 50. For other reports of this
speech, see *CJ*, i. 364, 1035–6; *Bowyer*, pp. 255–61.

Diary of Sir George Manners, March–April 1604
(Belvoir Castle, Rutland MS, fols 201–8)

[f.201]

19 Marcij 1603: his majesties speache in his oration grounded upon thes[e] three specyally

Fyrst his majesties comminge to the crowne by his right & dyscent with soe genera[ll] [ap]plause to all his subjects of this kingdome, that whylest he lyved he would never be unmyndfull of theire acknowledgments & kyndeness.

Secondly the peace that came by his majesty both outward & inward at home, whereby all merchants had free traffique, and all warrs which were in her late majesties tyme were ?omyeted

Thyrdly touchinge the trewe relygyon & servyce of Almighty god which he devyded into three sorts, fyrst the professors of the religyonat home which ys establyshed which he allowed of & never purposeth to change, the second Catholicks which he called papysts, who seeke to have wars forreyn or outward, thyrdly Sectaries who sought for reformacion at home & soe troubled th'estate.

After this speache by **Mr. doctor Herbert** in the lower house delivered, **Sir Edward Phillipps** was commended from the king by hym to be a fitt man for the speaker & so elected by the lower house, & by them to be presented Thursday followinge videlicet 22 marcij 1603.

[Thursday 22 March]

At which day Mr. Speaker was presented to the king betwene one & two of the clock in the afternone, and all being ended in the upper house he came in to the lower house, and after he had taken his chere, & sylence commanded, then was a speeche made by **Sir William Fletewood** one of the knights in Buckingham shyre in the behalf of **Sir Franncs Goodwyn** the other knight elected & retorned by Mr. Shereffe, & yet stayd & not fyled by the clerk of the crowne one Sir [blank] Coppyn,[21] and therefore the matter was commytted to certeyne commyttees to examyne the cause but not censure yt, but to relate yt to the house, & the house to determyne of yt, & this to be done the next day in the morninge at nyne of the clock by the commyttees, then to be opened to the house & censured by the house.

Also yt was then opened to the house that **Sir Thomas Sherley** beinge elected A burges for the parlyament was after his eleccion arrested in London and for hym it was determyned that a *habeas corpus*

---

[21] Sir George Coppin.

should be awarded to the shereffs of London to bringe hym in the next day, And a serjeant at armes sent for that serjeant who arrested hym & the party that caused hym to be arrested.

Also yt was moved, that one Danyell Tasse[22] one of the gard at the dore of the upper house, kept out certeyne burgesses dysgracefully, to the indignytie of the lower house, wherein are knights gentlemen & others of good sort & reckoninge burgesses, assembled by the kings commandement for the servyce of hym & of the realme, And therefore yt was ordered by the house that a serjeant at armes should bringe hym in the next dey, thoughe some of the pryvy counsell moved to have yt commytted.

Then was redd a byll for the falsyfyinge of recoveries ageynst enfants commynge in, eyther as tenants or vouchees, & then the court arose.

Fryday the xxiÿth of marche
there was propounded to the house a speache by **Sir Robert Wrothe** knight, to these severall effects, fyrst that the book of commen prayer might be establyshed & confirmed, Secondly that there might be some course taken for wards & theire lands by a peyment & not by wey of wardshipp, Thyrdly ageynst Purveyors whome he termed the hell hounds of England, [**f.201v**] fourthly ageynst Monopolies fyftly transportacion of ordynance, Sixtly concerninge the offycers of th'exchequer, Sevently dispensacion of penall statuts, for which causes there was a commyttment made to several commyttees gentlemen of good sorte to consyder of these things, & to bring them to some heads that bylls might be drawen to releive the inconveyniencs thereof.[23]

Next to this was moved to the house by **Sir Edward Mountague** that certeyne abuses might be reformed, & that the house would have consyderacion thereof for the good of the subjects, which were these, the intollerable burden upon the subjects in ecclesyasticall & commissarie Courts.[24]

Then secondly the suspencion of mynisters learned & grave beinge good pastors & preachers. Thyrdly the generall yll growinge to the subjects by convertinge of tyllage into pasture. These things also thus moved were commytted to a grave commyttment to be consydered of, howe to be reduced to a good head, & a good provysion for the generall good of the kingdome.[25]

Thyrdly yt was moved by one **Mr. Wentworth** a lawyer that yt

---

[22] *CJ*, i. 152 refers to him as Brian Tash.

[23] *CJ*, i. 150–1. For the context of this speech, see N. R. N. Tyacke, 'Wroth, Cecil and the Parliamentary Session of 1604', *BIHR* l (1977), pp. 120–5.

[24] For a draft of which speech, see below.

[25] For which also see Mountagu's own account and *CJ*, i. 151.

might be examyned by the house, whether there were any in the house,
that were there as members not warraunted.

This being done then the clerk of the crowne for the cause betwene
the right honorable **Sir John Fortescue** knight Chancellor of the
duchie & one of the pryvy counsell, & **Sir Franncs Goodwyn** knight
was sent for, and by the house examyned what retornes he had from
the shereffe of Buckinghamshire, touchinge the knights of the shyre,
who brought in two wrytts & ij indentures with two severall retornes,
By the fyrst wrytt yt appeared yt bare *Teste xxxjo Januarij Anno primo
Jacobi Regis Anglie* & c. and upon that wrytt was retorned an eleccion
made 22 Februarij as appeared by the indenture, of **Sir Franncs
Goodwyn** & **Sir William Fletewood** knights, and upon the retorne
of the wrytt yt appeared that **Sir Franncs Goodwyn** was outlawed,
soe that therefore yt should be enferred, that the eleccion was not good,
and the wrytt of the parlyament was retornable 19 Marcij, Before xix°
marcij the kinge awarded another wrytt for an newe eleccion recytinge
the fyrst wrytt, & the outlawry, And that therefore they should proceede
to a new eleccion which was done, & the second wrytt dated before
the xixth day of marche, & by that second wrytt, **Sir John Fortescue**
was elected & retorned, And which of these twoe knights should be
accepted to be the member of the house was the questyon. That **Sir
Franncs Goodwyn** should be the member of the house, yt was spoken
by **Sir William Fletewood**, that the eleccion of Sir Franncs was
good by lawe fyrst for that the eleccion commanded by the wrytt was
performed, for thoughe he were outlawed yet he was (*idonens*) able to
gyve good counsell & to advyse, And by the retorne, the statute of
7H4[26] was performed, which was that the eleccion should by the shereffe
in pleno Com' by indenture, And that retorne by indenture should be
good, soe that then there was a concludinge posytyve lawe.

Then he alledged that the retorne of the shereffe was voyd as to the
outlawry, & but a negacion & surplus, for by the wrytt he was but to
make his eleccion in the full County, which done & retorned the
commandement of the kinge was performed, & further the shereffe had
not to doe.

Yt was also by the seyd **Sir William Fletewood** alleged, that the
retorne of the fyrst wrytt was not retornable until the xix th of marche,
then to award a second wrytt for eleccion was voyde, for until the fyrst
wrytt was retornable, the second could take noe effect. [**f.202**] And
the fyrst was not dyscharged by the awardinge of the second, nether
could be dyscharged but by a supersedeas And soe inferred that the
fyrst elecc[ion] was good & ought not to be rejected.

And in fortyfyinge of this posycion many lawyers spake & muche to

---

[26] Elections statute, 7 Hen. IV, cap. 15. *SR*, ii. 156.

the same effect, & they vouched a case in the parlyament 35 Eliz. Reginae of Fitzherbert outlawed & was admytted.[27]

To encounter this yt was alledged by some other lawyers, that the fyrst eleccion was voyde, & by the words of the wrytt, relyinge cheiffly upon the word (*idonens*) for that a person outlawed could not in lawe be sayd, *idonens*, for that he was out of the law, & therefore not fytt to be a law maker, Also yt was sayd that he could not use an accion in his name & for his owne use, nether could he in law be a sufficyent wyttnes, nether a Juror for a tryall nor to serve as an indytor, Also the words of Bracton were cited *de utlagatis qd gerit capud lupium* & soe fytter to consume then to preserve, & therefore not fytt to be a member of that house, and these insertyons were secopnded & followed but not with soe many for **Sir John Fortescue** as for **Sir Franncs Goodwyn**. Then the questyon was whether of them were the member of the house, and the questyon was this, as many as would say that **Sir Franncs Goodwyn** should be the member of the house, say, yea, & those that were of that mynde that **Sir John Fortescue** was to be the member of the house to say, noe, and the voyce of the yea carryed yt to **Sir Franncs Goodwyn**, who was sworne & came into the house & tooke his place, and the clerke of the crowne commanded to syle the wrytt, whereby he was retorned knight of the shire.

Then the cause concerninge Danyell Tasse of the gard was brought in questyon, aboute his insolent & prowde speche in callinge some of the burgesses (good man burges)[28] he was brought in by the serieant at armes, to the barre, & uppon his knees acknowledged his fault desyred pardon of the house & yt was graunted of the grace of the house, upon a speeche used by the Kinge in his behalfe, & not for any good lykinge the house had of Danyell Tasse who was a very tall proper man.

Then yt was moved in the behalfe of one **Chubbe**[29] who was a burges & a collector for this subsydie, a treasorer for the meamed soldyers, & some thinge infyrme in his body, that his apparance might be excused, and a wrytt awarded for a newe eleccion in his place.[30] And lykewyse that suche as were retorned for ij placs, notyce should be taken for what place they served & newe wrytts for newe eleccion to the other place.

Afterwards yt was agreed that a *habeas corpus* should be awarded to the shereffs of London to bringe the body of Sir Thomas Sherley uppon

[27] Thomas Fitzherbert was arrested upon outlawry for debts owing to the Crown and others on the day of his election for Newcastle-under-Lyme. He was adjudged to have been properly elected, but denied parliamentary privilege. Hasler, ii. 125–6.

[28] Thus implying that the burgesses were not gentlemen.

[29] Matthew Chubbe, MP for Dorchester.

[30] The House disapproved of this request, but followed due process by referring the request to the privileges' committee. *CJ*, i. 152.

mundey next, & the serieant at armes to bring in the serieant who arrested hym & the party who caused hym to be arrested, that the cause might be censured by the court.

Setterdey 24 marcij
was moved an acte concerninge apparrell, that all former acts touchinge apparell might be revocated, & order set downe by the kings pro-clamacion what apparell ought to be used by euery sort of people, and this byll was presently reiected by the house, as unfytt to be reteyned. Then was moved that the act of 32 H8 Ca:[31] for lymytacion of prescripcion might be explaned with some addycion thereunto con-cerninge ?rent chargs & other [**f.202v**] things out of the statute. Then was moved to have commytees f[or] abrogatinge lawes unnecessary & retayninge of lawes necessary for the comenwelthe & comen good for ordynary Justyce.

Then was moved the statuts ageynst fugytyves to have yt revyved, and lykewyse the statute of primo Eliz. for the saffety of her mats. person,[32] that the lyke might be for the kinge, these were moved by **Mr. serieant dodrige** & thought fyt to come in by wey of byll.

There was then moved that the statuts in primo Marie concerninge ryotts, routs & unlawfull assemblies might be revyved, for that by primo Eliz. yt was revyved but duringe her mats. lyffe & to th'end of the next parlyament after,[33] & for noe longer tyme.[34]

Next was compleynt made to the house of the abvse commytted by certen pags upon a boy of one of the burgesses, for drawing or haylinge ?by the taverne, for wyne & Cakes taken at the house of one Will'm C[arter] of Westmr., & for layinge the boyes cloake to pawne for ijs. vjd. for the wyne & cakes, the vyntener & one Bryan Ashton his man were ?brought to the barre, & the cause examyned; ;the vyntner sayd he was not at home and his man delyuered to the custody of the serieant untill mundey, then to be ordered as the commyttees should seeme good, and soe the court in regard the Sermon was begune & Satterdey beinge the xxiij[th] of marche was the day his majesty began his raigne, & in the afternoone ?dyvers of the noblemen knights & gentlemen shewed themselves to the kinge & ran at tylte in the tylte yard at Whytehall.

---

[31] 32 Hen. VIII, cap. 2. *SR*, iii. 747–8.
[32] 1 Eliz. I cap. 3 Recognition of the Queen's title. *SR*, iv. 358–9.
[33] 1 Mary (April) cap. 12; 1 Eliz. I cap. 16. *SR*, iv. 211–14, 377.
[34] None of these motions for revival of statutes is mentioned in *CJ*, i. 152, 935.

Mundey 26 marcij.

A report of the commyttees touchinge the wards was made by **Mr. Bacon**, who spake of sundry dysputes touchinge wards & that court both pro & contra, fyrst yt was moved by hym ~~what~~ how the kinge ~~could no~~ might be answered to his contentment to that which was to be propounded vnto hym, videlt. an yerely rent or somme whatsoeuer or in what manner soeuer in respect of the wardshippe when yt should happen, fyrst yf the kinge should accept ageynst the thinge propounded, that the lyke was neuer offred to kinge in his state and gouerment as kinge of England, begynninge at the ereccion of tenures & contynuynge to this dey.

Then yt was sayd that his majesty might be very well answered, that thes cause of Scutage was onely invented to defend the kinge & this realme ageynst the Scotts, & nowe the realmes being conioyned in dyscent & bloud to his majesty & his heyres, the cause of the wards dyd cease, & soe ought the effect, which ys the wardshippe lyvery & prymer seasen.

yt was sayd by **Sir Thomas Heskett** Attorney of the courts of wards & lyueries, that certeyne tenures were of the kinge by his graunt to keepe the castell of Dover & dyuers other castells, which were not gyven as the former, which were knights servyce, & demaunded what should become of those, Answere was made by the house that provysyon might be made aswell for the one as the other.

Then was moved the manner howe to proceede in this accion, for that yf yt were a matter of commen Justyce, that ought to be by byll, but ?yt beinge a matter of grace, yt ought to be proceeded in, to the kinge by wey of petycion, & that was the opynyon of the lower house, And ?the most honorable wey of porceedinge herein, the lower house sent to the lords yelded vnto, [**f.203**] And from them were sent downe in message to the lower house the lord cheiffe Justyce of England, namely Sir John Popham, Mr. Justyce Yeluerton & Doctor Swayle, who reported to the house that the lords were well content to admytt a conferrence, & delyuered the nomber of the lords to be thyrtie, an[d] the lower house appoynted theyre nomber threescore to mete theire lordshipps the next morninge at nyne of the clock in the withdrawynge house nere to the higher house. Then lykewyse in that conferrence the lords willed by theire messengers that in that commyttment speche might be had concerninge purveyors for theire abuses to the subiects, And also the payment of respect of homage, which was a generall charge to the subiects, which was yelded vnto by the lower house. And the lords lykewyse offered to have conference at any tyme touchinge of any thinge concerninge the generall good of the kyngdome.

After this yt was moved a relieffe of certeyne captaynes & offycers to be had for their servyce in Ireland being englyshemen, there maymed & there hurt, which was commytted to dyvers commyttees.

Also yt was moved that a declaracion might be had generally what things are treason.

Lykewyse for graunts made to the kinge & by the kinge, what should & ought to be good & what not, & that reasonable construccion might be had thereof.

Then yt was moved that Justycs of peace uppon bylls of indytement might upon an *ignoramus* found dyscharge the prysoner as Justycs of oyer & determyner & to convey them to the place where they dwell yf they have dwellings, els to the place where they were borne, as rouges accordinge to the statute of 39 Eliz.[35]

Further yt was moved pro & contra touchinge a retorne made by the bayliffs & commen counsell of shrewsbury, concerninge theire burgesses, Mr. shereffe would not accept yt, & the [sic they] certyfyed yt under the towne seale, & for theire eleccion by the bayliffs & commen counsell the vouched a partyculer act of parlyament in 23 H.8.

Moreover there was moved a partyculer acte concerninge clothyers in the County of Surrey, but that receyved at this time int'upcyion by the comminge in of the lord cheiffe Justyce & others.

Lastly was moved this dey the cause of **Sir Thomas Sherley** who was attended by the shereffs of London & by them brought to the parlyament, deferred to the next day then to be brought in upon a new *habeas corpus*.

27 marcij Tuysdey

was moved by **Sir George More** an act for the relieffe of clothyers in Gylford, & that wooll might be stayed & not soe generally transported, but that conveynyent might be kept in the realme to sett the subiects on work, And to that was added an other act to be made, that noe cloth should be carryed beyond the seas, unbarbed, unrowed, nor unshorne.

Next to this was **Sir Thomas Sherley** brought to the barre upon *a habeas corpus* by the shereffs of London, beinge arrested in London, videlt. 15 marcij last, where he was elected a burges in Sussex the xiiij[th] of February before, and vpon the *habeas corpus* was retorned *execucio patet in quondam scedula*, and by the scedule yt appeared that he was arested upon a pleynt in London at the sute of one Sympson of 3000*li.*, then upon an execucion of 3000*li*, thyrdly an other pleynt of 3000*li.*, Another pleynt of 2000*li.* & fyftly & lastly a pleynt of 300*li.*, which **Sir Thomas Sherley** desyred the pryvyledge of the house, and whether he should have the pryvyledge or not was the fyrst questyon, The second questyon

[35] 39 Eliz. I cap. 4. *SR*, iv. 899–902.

was admyttinge he should have his pryvyledge then whether Sympson dyd lose his execucion & dett for euer.

One **Mr. Wynche** a lawyer sayd, that yt were good to advyse whether he ought to have the pryvyledge or not, for that yf he had the pryvyledge yt might be matter in doubt whether the execucion were gone & the party without remedy, And to th'end he might have the pryvyledge, he took a diversytie, where he was dyscharged by the act of the party. And where he was sett at liberty by the act of lawe, for beinge dyscharged by the act of the party, the execucion was also dyscharged, but being pryvyledged by the act in the lawe, he was pryvyledged of th'arrest, & so the execucion was but suspended & not merely determyned. And by him yt was sayd that this wrytt from the house was but a *supersedeas* for the tyme of the parlyament.

Serieant Hubberd sayd that Sir Thomas ought to have priviledge *veniendo* & *redendo* and that the execucion was suspended & not determyned nor dyscharged for euer.

Mr. Recorder of London[36] moved two poynts, fyrst whether the priviledge were to be graunted upon th'execucion. Secondly, yf the pryviledge were graunted, then whether the seyd Sir Thomas was discharged and lykewyse the Shereffs of London.

Serieant doddryge wished that conference myght be had with the iudges whether that by the priviledge graunted th'execucion were not discharged, for he seemed in opynyon to bend to that syde; that the execucion was discharged, and then Sympson lost his dett.

Serieant Tanfeild moved to know whether Sympson had notyce or intellygence that the sayd Sir Thomas was elected a burgesse, whiche yf he had and then arrested hym he sayd, that then Sir Thomas ought to have his privilege & the dett dyscharged.

Bacon doubted whether if he had priviledge, whether the dett was gone or not and therefore wyshed the house to suspend their iudgement in regard of th'execucion, and to procede to censure the iudgement agaynst Sympson & Beecher the credytors who procured ytt and ageynst Watkyn the Serieant who arrested hym.

Dyatt sayd that the verball informacion of Sir Thomas as to sey that he was a burgesse was nott suffycyent to surcesse the arrest but the retorne of recorde, and that the arrest *sedente cur.* was the contempt. And further sayd that the execucion was but suspended by aucthorytie of lawe, and yet yf that aucthorytie dyd erre th'execucion was gone.

Serieant Snygge prayed that the court would be advysed, and he cyted this case, that yf one were indetted to dyvers and afterwards procured hym selffe to be indyted of felony & had his booke that he is not dyscharged of the dett. Lykewyse he sayd, that yf Sir Thomas

---

[36] Sir Henry Mountagu.

procured hym selffe extraordynarylie to be a burgesse he ought not to have his priviledge.

Yelverton junior sayd that the punyshment was not yett rype for the parties, for that yt was yett questyonable whether Sir Thomas was a member of the house or not.

The Kyngs Solycytor[37] sayd that there was not any booke to warraunte his enlargement and therefore good to advyse before any act done.

Heskett th'attorney of the Courte of wardes moved that xij lawyers of the house & xij gentlemen of the house myght consider of this cause by a commytment and here [**f.204**] the counsell on both sydes whiche was yelded, and the day Fryday next the Inner Temple hall in the afternone, and the counsell on both syds to ~~here the~~ attend the commyttees.

Next after was delyuered to the house by **Mr. Bacon** what had passed betwene the lords of the higher house and the commyttees of the lower house touchynge a conferrence concernynge wardes, and the proposicions whiche the lower house propounded for their grieffs were these.

The lyvynges taken & seased in present, the marryags of wardes ageynst their lykings or els myghty sommes of money for the same hardely euer after to be recouered.

These former grieffs to be reduced into an yerely payment or yerely revenue.

The Kyngs officer to be considered.

An offer of them selves in tyme of servyce.

The maner to atteyne by wey of peticion.

Thus this delyuered yt seemed by the reporter, that the lords dyd enterteyne yt as with a willyngnes to ioyne with the lower house, so that yt myght be done in modesty playnes & order.

But afterwards the lords sent a message to the lower house by Sir Edward Coke his majesties attorney accompanyed with three others, wishing of the lower house that there myght be a conferrence betwene the lords of the higher house & the nether house, that the nether house might shewe cause why they had admytted **Sir Franncs Goodwyn** into the house as a member thereof & refused **Sir John Fortescue**, the seyd **Sir Franncs Goodwyn** beinge a man outlawed at the tyme of the eleccion. And soe by a second wrytt ~~certyfyed~~ dyrected to the shereffe commaundinge hym to proceede to a newe eleccion, which the shereffy dyd, & choyce was made of newe, & **Sir John Fortescue**

---

[37] Solicitor-general Sir Thomas Fleming, MP for Southampton.

elected by the second wrytt, & retorned yet not admytted but reiected.

This message delyuered, Mr. Attorney & they who accompanyed hym went out of the lower house to the wtidrawinge house, untyll the house had consydered of an answere, & consyderacion had, the house sayd that the lyke had neuer byn before hard or seene, that the should delyver a reason unto the lords why they dyd yt, but yt was sayd by the house that they were iudges in the parlyament, thoughe not iudges of the lawe, and theire iudgment beinge past yt ought not to be called into questyon, so that then they were not mynded to yeld to the lords any reason what moved them to doe yt, yet in all humblenes, they would attend the kinge at his appoyntment, & yeld hym theire reasons why they dyd ytt, and then Mr. Attorney & the others with hym were brought in ageyne to the house, and receyved an answere by the mouth of Mr. speaker to the effect aforeseyd & soe departed, and at Mr. Attorneys comynge in, the house dyd not knowe that yt was the kings pleasure that the lords should move the lower house to the effect aforeseyd, but afterwards they dyd understand, that yt was the kings pleasure. And therefore the house send **Sir John Stanhopp** & **Sir John Harbert** to the kinge about the seyd cause, who returned not to the house. And after three of the clock in the afternoone the house rose, & met **Sir John Stanhopp** & **Sir John Harbert** who returned andwere that yt was his mats. pleasure to have Mr. Speaker with threescore of the house to be before his majesty at Whytehall on Wennesday the next dey followinge by eight of the clock in the morninge. Yet before the house dyd ryse the seyd 27th dey of marche there was red a byll touchinge the preservacion of mannors & copy-houlds lands, [**f.204v**] also an other byll for costs in physicions.

An other touchinge brewers in London & the suburbes & within ij myles of the same to be within the survey of the brewers of London, & that noe farrener should be permytted unles he was free; this byll was throwen out at the fyrst readinge as not fytt to be reteyned.

28 marcij Wennesdey

Mr. Speaker & the lower house assembled earely, & yt was determyned by the house which threescore of the house should accompany Mr. Speaker to the kinge, to delyver to his majesty the causes & reasons that moved the house to accept of **Sir Franncs Goodwyn** to be theire member, & then to meete the next morninge at the lower house ageyne.

29 marcij Thursdey

A byll was redd that the liberties gyven to the commons of this kingdome by the auncyent charter of magna Carta might be confyrmed.

Then was moved by Mr. Speaker that there had byn delyuered to hym an informacion by one Bryon Brydger, a mynister, which Mr. Speaker termed rather to be a lybell, the effect whereof consysted of three poynts[38]

1. First that all Bysshopps of this kingdome that urged men to subscrybe to ceremonies of relygyon were Antychrists.
2. Secondly that all Bysshopps that take upon them to rule as Justycs in temporall causes are Imytators of Antichriste.
3. Thyrdly that the last yere the kingdome was infected with suche lyke bushopps.

The seyd Bryan was brought to the barre, thouge, before that he came in, yt was alledged he was not sound memory, vpon his comynge in, he was examyned by Mr. Speaker who wrytt that informacion; he answered, hym selffe, he was asked who was of counsell with hym and what were theire names, he sayd he might not tell that for that yf he dyd, he thought murther might ensue, he answered euery questyon too hym propounded very substancyally, that noe imperfeccion could be thought to be in hym, but that the informacion was upon mature beliberacion by the helpe & assystance of others, he sayd he wrytt yt in a Scryvners house in Westm[inste]r, & was prysoner in the whyte lyon in Southwork, the scryvener & keper of the lyon were sent for to be examyned before the commyttees. The course with hym was that sixe of the house commyttees for that purpose should examyne hym, & that he should be sent to the tower by warrant from the house.

After this & next unto yt Mr. Speaker began to make relacion to the house of his message delyuered by hym from the house to the kinge & of the answere of the kinge & of the iudges.[39] Fyrst he alledged the

Motyves of the house
Secondly presydents
Thyrdly iudgements

Motyves. That there was eyther one member to many or els one member wantinge.

The causes that moved them was the kings wrytt, & the eleccion by indenture & soe vertyfyed & therefore the eleccion good by the statute of 7 of H.4 [**f.205**]

That the outlawries ageynst hym were, one of them in 31 Eliz. Rne. for 60*li.* at the sute of one Johnson. The dett before the outlag, dyscharged by Johnson as appeared, by his acquittans. The second

[38] Text in *CJ*, i. 157.
[39] Concerning the Goodwin v. Fortescue election dispute.

outlawry was 39 Eliz. Rne. as pdct. Hacker for xvj*li.* whiche was also satysffied as appeared by Hackers acquyttance.

Then he served in 39 Eliz. and in 43 Eliz. and admytted a member and that now at his eleccion no outlawry was spoken of and the outlawry was layd in London.

For presydents

That this was not done of the house as merely of them selves without regard but by presedents one in 39 H.6 the lyke in Anno primo Eliz. Reginae,[40] another in 23 Eliz. Reginae then one Fludds case[41] & had his priviledge, In 35 Eliz. Reginae 3 presydents, one of them Fitzherberts[42] case, the second one Kylligreys[43] case case ageynst whom there were 52 outlawryes the thrydd Sir Water Hawcourts case ageynst whom there was xviij outlawries.[44]

Judgements

Fyrst the statute of 7 H.4 fully performed by the eleccion & retorne
Then that the Sheriffs retorne as to the outlawry was ?negacion & surplus
Then that the second wrytt was without warrant, the fyrst not dyscharged by super'ser. [*sic superioribus?*]
Then the Statute of 31 Eliz. Reginae that yf there were no wrytt of proclamacion into the shire where the party dwelt, the utlagary should be voyd.
Then the two generall pardons th'one in 39 Eliz. Reginae th'other 43 Eliz. Reginae.[45] Then that the utlagary in 31 Eliz. Reginae was Francis Godwyn armigerum, in 39 Eliz. Reginae Francis Godwyn generosum/ whether this in lawe should be intented the same man.

The answere of his majestye was delyuered by Mr. Speaker to be full of grace & favour, wytt & wysedome, that he could not so amply delyuer ytt as his majestye had done and desyred pardon therein, yett to the best of his remembrance he would so nere as he could make report of ytt.

[40] This was John Smith, MP for Camelford in 1559, allowed to retain his seat after a close run division. Hasler, iii. 397–8.

[41] *CJ*, i. 158, names this man as 'one Vaughan outlawed'. i.e. Walter Vaughan, returned for Carmarthenshire in 1576 but outlawed before the next session began in 1581. Hasler, iii. 552–3.

[42] Thomas Fitzherbert.

[43] Presumably John Killigrew of Arwennack, MP for Penryn in 1584, 1586 and 1597, although no privilege case is mentioned in Hasler, ii. 396–7.

[44] Sir Walter Harcourt was arrested on the day after the end of the 1593 session at the behest of Sir John Fortescue. Hasler, ii. 250.

[45] 39 Eliz. I cap. 28; 43 Eliz. I cap. 19. *SR*, iv. 952–7, 1010–14.

Fyrst his majestye beganne, saying that he should be very lothe to alter his former tune of love in so highe a degree to any of his subiects, by bryngyng yt nowe into any contestacion fyndynge in them no myslyke of loyaltie but only for mystakynge the lawe, saying further, nay he must say ad [*sic* as] god sayd, thoughe he punyshed the Israelyts yet he loved them. Alledgyng that that he dyd was by his counsels & judges and that the house had done rashely without calling his counsell thereunto or the judges.

For by the eleccion his majesty sayd that an auncyent counsellor of estate not of his bryngyng in, but such as he found had bene a counsellor long before and by hym approved & allowed was disgraced, and yet indifferent to his majestye whiche of them had served, regard having bene had that non should have been iniured. And whether were capable of that place his matter [*sic* majesty] desyred for matter of lawe the advyse of his counsell and of the iudges, and thereupon there opynyons were that he was not capable and so his majestye awarded the new wrytt.

To that, that the seyd Sir Francis had served twyce synce.

To that his majestyes answere was that his offence was the greater, for that he was not outlawed for the dett, but for his contempt ageynst the lawe, Also his majestye sayd, that Sir Frauncs was out of the proteccion of the lawe whiche was dyshonorable and then no reason why suche a honorable house should have a dishonorable member.

And as to the priviledges that came to the house, his majestye sayd that they came from the crowne and so admytted to the house, wherein, the tyme they came in was to be respected, as whether in the tyme of an infant, or of a tyrant or usurper. [**f.205v**]

Then the last poynt consystynge of lawe his majestie willed myght be delyvered by the judgs and for that cause the judges made eleccion of the lord chieffe Justyce of England to be the mouthe of them all.

Whiche lord chieffe Justyce was charged by the kynge upon his loyaltie to hym & the [*sic* oath] of a judge to deluyer the lawe for his opynyon & the others.

Whose answer was that he would doe ytt willyngly and accordynge to the lawe.

Then fyrst he beganne with the wrytt that was fyrst awarded, and the retorne thereof, alledgynge that the house had not to medle with the retorne for the retorne was made to his majesty into his court of chauncery, then no man had to doe with the retorne but the kynge to whom to whom [*sic*] yt was retorned.

Next he sayd that the opynyon delyuered by the seyd lord chieffe Justyce & for hym & the other judges was, that the retorne of the

Shereffe was suffycyent to reject Sir Francis. Also the seyd lord chieff Justyce cyted a case in 35 H.6 that one outlawed was refused to be a member of the parlyament.

Also he cyted the booke of 1 H.7 where divers of the parlyament in the tyme of R.3 who were withdrawen from the house untyll a byll was made to restore them and they were restored, and then come in and so was the record.

Further that the resolucion of the judgs in 35 Eliz. Reginae among them was that a person outlawed was not *idonens*.

And touchynge the two generall pardons in 39 & 43 Eliz. Reginae that by lawe he styll stood a person outlawed ageynst all men untyll he had sued his *scire facias* ageynst the party in the accions.

And by the statute of 7 H.4 he graunted the statute to be so, and that yet by an other Statute he should have forfeyted one hundreth pounds, yf he knewe hym to be outlawed and dyd not retorne hym outlawed.

Then the kinge demaunded how yt should be knowen Sir Frauncis to be the man outlawed.

Yt was answered by the retorne of the shereffe to be (eandem franciscum).

The kinge also asked whether yt were not voyd for want of a proclamacion

Yt was answered that that must be by judgement of the court declaratory & not otherwyse voyde.

Then yt was wayd by the kinge that he hard say that some other judge or judges were of that opynyon that the outlawry was voyde by the two generall pardons, & yt was Mr. Justyce Willyams.

Who answered & sayd that he dyd hould that opynion formerly but havinge better deliberated upon the matter upon the view of his books & consyderacion of the seyd pardons was of the mynde of my lord chiefe Justyce & the other judges.

And upon this hearinge & deliberacion the kinge requyred foure things to be consydered, some course, A resolucion, A conference, & upon the conferrence to delyver theire opynyons to the lords of his counsell & soe at that tyme noe more of that.

Then afterwards there came a message from the higher house to the lower house, by the lord cheiffe Justycs, Mr. Barron Clerk, Mr. Justyce Fenner, Sir John Crook & Mr. Attorney General which was

A most joyful byll of recognycion of the successyon of the crowne to be in the kings majesty by right & dyscent of enherytance [**f.206**] which byll was thryce red that day.[46]

Afterwards an other message from the upper house to the lower house by Mr. Doctor Carewe & Mr. Doctor Stanhoppe.

A byll of restytucion in bloud of Erle of Southampton.
An other for iij of the children of the Erle of Essex
An other for the restoringe in bloud of the Erle of Arrundale.

Frydey xxx° marcij

One **Mr. Johnson** made a mocion Alehouse keepers to be depryved upon dysorder by them to be commytted & afterwards never to be admytted.

Next to this **Sir Robert Wyngfeyld** entred into dyscourse of the reasons of the house delyvered to the kinge, why the reteyned **Sir Francis Goodwyn** & dysallowed of of **Sir John Fortescue**, And delyvered his mynde, that the house had fyrst consydered of the retorne, then advysed, & after resolved, & so judgment gyven which he thought might not, nor ought not to be altered, & the matter thus havinge byn handled, noe reason nowe to impugne yt, And thoughe that the judges were judges of the lawe, yet they were judges of the parlyament, further he sayd that yt was chyldyshe to conclude one dey & revoke the same an other dey, And howe farre this trenched & wrought into the pryvyledge of the house, he wyshed every good member thereof to have some consyderacion of the future tyme as well as of the present, And alledged further that yt should be dyshonorable, that lawe books should prynted & delyvered out one wey & the role to be an other wey, and that yt was as dangerous that men might not be assured of the lawe as yt is delyvered out in books in prynte, but that the construccion thereof should merely depend or rest in the harte of the judge, And as thoughe yt should be as yt should please hym to expound & therefore was not of that opynion to have any conference with the judges, but to resolve what answere to make to the pryvie counsell to satysffie the kinge.

Sir George More seyd that he thought a conference fytt to be had, yt could not doe any hurte, but good might ensue, & used in his speache that yt was more saffe to goe after, then afore to breake the yce, & as the former thought not fytt he was of that mynde.

Sir Frauncis Bacon he thought yt fytt A conference upon two poynts, one for the satisfaccion of the kinge, the other for the pryvyledges

---

[46] Enacted as 1 Jac. I, cap. 1. *SR*, iv. 1017–18.

of the house, whereby eyther might be well performed & the kinge fully satisfyed.

Sir John Mallery ageynst any conference respectinge yt was a thinge done alredy, not to be reversed, respectinge the auncyent pryvyledges of the house & the advysed course & resolucion of the house had formerly taken. [**f.206v**]

Mr. Frauncis More Respect cheiffly to be had howe farre we were drawen into, & therefore substance of the matter cheiffly to be consydered of, the other noe grett matters, the substance by hym seemed to be the retorne of the fyrst wrytt, the other the outlawry, for the retorne yt was not untyll the fyrst dey of the parlyament, secondly the outlawry, And the lyke be presydent had byn allowed, A conference with the judges he thought fytt.

Mr. Martyn That A comyttment might be, whether this house mey take notyce of the retorne before the house be fully sett.

Then whether the person outlawed mey be receyved & thereupon cyted the booke that he might be an executor for the good of an other, & soe a good member by that reason. Thyrdly the teste of the second wrytt, before the fyrst wrytt retornable.

Mr. Yelverton Thought fytt, nether to have commyttment nor conference, for yf there were yt shewed both, levytie, crueltie, & cowardnes.

Levytie too muche this dey A member to morrowe non.
Cruelty to take awey any perfett member, as the hand to beare the fleshe were cruelty.
Cowardnes in leavinge to persevere in any such good acte, which yelded unto were the wey to have *A quo warranto* brought for the rest. Further he sayd that the retorne ought not to bee before the dey for then all the knights & burgesses were in the petty bagge, untyll that dey, And then upon suggestyons newe wrytts, & then when will the court come to perfettnes, many other insertyons he used nether to have commyttment nor conference.

Mr. Thomas Crewe Thought fytt that the judgment ought not to be reversed, nether could yt beinge done, And fyrst he alledged the matter was performed, which was the kings comaundement by the wrytt, the other matter was the person outlawed for the contempt, whyche contempt was pardoned as to the kinge, for the contempt was to the kinge for his non apparance, he incyted much upon the awardinge of the second wrytt before the dey of the retorne of the fyrst, and soe was ageynst any conference with the judges, but wyshed A consyderacion had of the matter to be delivered to the lords of the counsell for the satysfaccion of the kinge.

Mr. Dyott Fyrst a full resolucion of this Court, yf not then A conference of this house for resolucion, & then to delyver the resolucion to the lords of the pryvy counsell.

Sir Frauncis Hastings sayd that he should be sory to have yt termed to be any dyfference betwene the kinge & this house, yet held yt fytt to speake with the judges.

Mr. Headley,[47] **a lawyer** he sayd that the questyon was merely upon the retorne, & who should conferre & judge of the retorne.[f.207]

[Sir] Robert Rath[48] Sayd that he was sory that any such bone should be throwen into the house, & was of that opynyon that noe speache should be had with the judges.

[Mr.] Hext that yt was fytt that speech might be had with the judges.

[Sir] Edward Hobby Repeated his majesties words to conferre what to resolve, and yf we did resolve, then not to goe to the judges, but to acquynte his majesties counsell with yt.

[Si]r Frauncis Barrington to have the house to resolve & then to determyne of some answere to be made to his majesties counsell.

[Mr.] Wyseman when we be resolved then to gyve the resolucion to the lords of the counsell.

[Mr.] Lawrence Hyde Noe conference with the judges, but to determyne of a resolucion & to gyve the same to the lords of the counsell in wrytinge.

[Mr.] Fuller Fytt to be A conference with the judges.

[Mr.] Recorder [of] London[49] Noe conference with the judges, but to determyne & resolve and therewith to acquynte the lords of his majesty's counsell.

And afterwards the questyon was propounded to the house, And the house dyd determyne & resolve, that the judgment gyven could not be altered, & appoynted A commyttment whereof the gentlemen that before had spoken were commyttees, & ten more added unto them, to consult of the resolucion for the answere to the lords of the counsell, this dey in the afternoon to meete in the Chequer chamber & the next morning to relate yt to the house, that the house mey gyve theire consents.

31 marcij Setterdey
Was red a byll concerninge the restytucion of the Erle of Southampton, nex A byll for the restytucion of Robert sonne of the late Erle of Essex & of Frances & Dorothee daughters of the late Erle theire father.

---

[47] Thomas Hetley, MP for Huntingdon.
[48] i.e. Wroth.
[49] Sir Henry Mountagu.

Also an act for the restytucion of Thomas Howard th'only child of Phillip late Erle of Arundale his father to the erledome of Arundale & Surrey. Also an acte for the exchange of certeyne lands reiected at the fyrst readinge. An acte to dysable from henceforth any person from being a member of the house beinge outlawed or in execucion the fyrst dey of the parlyament. An act ageynst transportinge wooll & cloathes unrought beyond the seas, thereby to sett poore men on work.

iij severall bylls concerninge Alehouses.
An acte ageynst Purveyors & Carttakers.
An act for the naturalizinge of Margarett Countesse of Nottingham & of her children & to her to have dower.
An act for the trewe makinge of hatts.
An act for the takinge awey of Clergy from them that stabb others.
[**f.207v**]
An act ageynst Purveyors.
An act for the restrayninge of fryvolous accions.
An act concerninge extorcion.
An act for the better execucion of penall lawes.
An act ageynst pluralyties of benefyces.
An act to take awey clergy from steylers of cattell & sheepe.
An act for the releiffe of prysoners.
An act for the countynuance of the makinge of capps.
An act concerninge laborers.
An act concerninge tanninge of leather.

Tercio Aprilis

An act concerninge proces & pleadings in th'exchequer.
A proviso to the byll of the naturalizinge of the countesse of Nottingham.
An act agenst depopulacion & restreyninge of enclosures & convertinge of tyllage into pasture.
An act for the preservacion of records of leets & of Court barrons, Cast out of the cou[rt?]

Gryffyn Payne a burges of the burrowe of Wallingford in Berkshire, who was maior of the towne, in the act ageynst Purveyors used a speche for theire defence, for that he was A Purveyor, and in the end of his speche he taxed the whole house in dealinge very hardly.

1. Fyrst in dyshonoringe of the kinge.
2. Secondly in dysgrace ageynst the counsell.
3. Thyrdly in dysgrace of the judges.

4. Lastly that the house went about to hange some of his servants.

And therefore he was brought to the barre, to answere his mys-demeanors ageynst the house.

1. To the fyrst poynte, in that the kinge by a second wrytt had commaunded a newe eleccion, & by the second eleccion Sir John Fortescue was rejected & Sir Frauncis Goodwyn receyved, soe the kinge thereby dyshonored.

2. Secondly he sayd that in regard Sir John Fortescue had not the place therefore he beinge of the honorable pryvie counsell was dysgraced.

3. Thyrdly for that the judges had delyvered theire opynyons that the lawe was that one outlawed was not capable of the place, & that the house had gyven hym admyttance, therefore he thought the judges dysgraced.

4. Fourthly he confessed his rashenes in sayinge that the house went about to hange some of his servants, in that he dyd see the vehemency of the house ageynst Purveyors.

After his answere gyven, he was taken from the barre by the serjeant at armes, beinge withdrawen, the house consulted, And dyd determyne that yf he stoode upon his defence, then to censure hym in the dyscreacion of our Speaker, which we would ratyfie, And yf he confessed his faults then the house would shewe mercy, beinge brought in ageyne to the barre by the serjeant, he acknowledged his faults in all the proposycions ageynst hym & had mercy, And yet because the princypall offycer of the towne he was censured to be sequestred from the house, And yet [**f.208**] his allegacion to the contrary was that the foote might as well chose the head as the head the foote, but he styll standeth sequestred, And the opynyon of the gretest sort in the house was, that he might not be retorned, yet regardinge yt might concerne dyvers other members in the house, there ys noe judgement sett downe but a sequestracion of hym.[50]

After this, then was entred into speche the grett matter concerninge the house & the members thereof, nowe brought into questyon in the cause betwene **Sir John Fortescue** & **Sir Frauncis Goodwyn** wherein were dyvers gentlemen, that spake bouldly & confydently, wherein were touched, whether accordinge to the kings speche, the house had power to examyne the retorne of knyght & burgesses. Then his majesty's speech, that the house had had done yt by too muche precypytacion, Then in [?mak]inge of outlawes, Fourthly the retorne

[50] Payne's sequestration was reversed on 6 March 1610. *CJ*, i. 406.

of the shereffe ?yt [Good]wyn *fuit utlagat* &c. every of these poynts were dysput[ed in th]e house, & the house resolved of theire determynacion to the answere of the kinge, which for that yf yt were by verball delyverie, there might be mysprysyon, And therefore upon many consults in the end to the grett hynderance of other grett busynes, yt was sett downe in wrytinge, & his thyrd day of Apryll delyvered to the lords of the counsell, as the resolucion of the lower house, & all the cyrcymstancs that induced them to admytt of **Sir Frauncis Goodwyn**, & to refuse **Sir John Fortescue**, And the messenger from the house was **Sir Frauncis Bacon** with fourescore knights & gentlemen, the matter of wrytinge ys entered of record, And ys extant to be had for money.

Next to this was red a byll of restytucion in bloud of Sir Thomas Lucas knight, for murtheringe & kyllinge of Sir William Brookes.

Then an Act for the restytucion of William Pagett esquyer the onely sonne of Thomas late Lord Pagett.

Quarto Aprilis

An act ageynst transportacion of any ordynance, & gun mettall, & shott, Iron ordynance, Iron myne & Iron oare.

Then an act ageynst transporting of clothes unrought.

An act for apparrell, ageynst wearinge of clothe of sylver & of gould, & gold lace, & of lace mixt with gold & sylver.

Then an act concerninge recusancy, & the dett thereby growinge to the kinge upon the statuts of 23 & 39 Eliz.[51] [**f.208v**]

5 Aprilis

Mr. Speaker came to the house after nyne of the clock and ther was a second tyme redd a byll concernynge extorcion which done

Mr. Speaker propounded 2 thyngs, one his absence so longe which was by reason of his majesties commandment to attend, The other a message from the kynge. The message was to my remembrance, that his majestye sayd he had receyved a partchment by the lords of his honourable counsell, sent as a ?bond ?horse, whether as a resolucion of the house, or as reasons or motyves for A conference with the judges he could not tell. And Mr. Speaker further delyvered as I tooke ytt, that the kynge dyd not protest, onely as by the worde of A kynge but of his fayth to god that he ment not any abrydgement of any priviledge, and so lykewyse would not that the house should detract any thynge from hym, and therefore willed that a conferreinge might be had betweene the judges & the lower house in the afternoone at Whytehall before the lords of the Counsell at three of the clock. And for that

[51] 23 Eliz. I cap. 1; 39 Eliz. I cap. 7. *SR*, iv. 657–8, 904–9.

occasyon the house appoynted xxx^tie lawyers & gentlemen to meete there.

6 Aprilis[52]
And this day I hard his majestye was at the caryinge of the case and hath ended ytt & entered that a newe eleccion shalbe and nether of them to have the place.

Sir Robert Cotton's Diary of the 1604 Session
[BL, Cotton MS Titus F.IV, ff.3–10:]

[**f.3**]
Observatyones of the proceedinges in the parlemente held at Westeminster *Anno primoe et Secundo Jacobi Regis* &c.

The said parleamente begane one Monday the xix^th of March 1603

Upon the said firste daye the Lordstuard for that tyme, beinge the Earle of Nottingham Came in to the Chamber caled the white halle, wher the Courte of Requeste is usually held every terme and ther firste Called all the knights and burgeses then returned for the Lower house, and after they were Called, appointed **Sir Robarte Wroth, Sir John Lusone**[53] and some foure more[54] to give the oath of Supremasye and allegeance to all the knights and Burgeses before they entered to sitt in the parleamente house, which done they entred the house and tooke every one ther place: Then **Mr. Secretary Herbarte** Comended from the kynge **Sir Edward Phillippes** Serjante at Lawe to be their speakere, who with litle opposityone was elected and agreed uppon although himselfe made refusall by shewing his imperfectyones for so great a burden, but at lenght brought to the Cheare; by **Sir John Herbarte** and **Sir John Stanhope** privie Counselores and some fewe otheres;[55] wher sittynge after a litle pawse he stood upe and moved the house to graunte him two requests the one to release him againe the other that they would take no offence yf he Could procure the king to accepte and comend some other: Then sittynge downe againe rose and asked the house whether a bill should be redd, accordinge to the Custome, which was desired, the bill was that recoveryes suffered by an Infante should bynd no more then a fine. Befoore the oath was

---

[52] This is a report of the decision reached on the previous day, after which the house adjourned for Easter. *CJ*, i. 167.

[53] Sir John Leveson, MP for Shropshire.

[54] The names of the twelve men commissioned to take the oaths of the rest of the House are recorded in *CJ*, i. 140.

[55] *Ibid.* i. 141 states that Phelips was seated by Herbert and Sir Edward Stafford.

minestred the same day the kinge in the highere house was to make an oratyone aswell to the Lower house as upper house and desired that they might be all presente but the prese in the upper house beinge greate and the dores [**f.3v**] moste straightly kepte they Could nott get in, **Sir Herbert Croftes** one of the house pressynge earnestly at the doores was thruste backe by one Brian Tase one of the guarde and Called him goodman Burgesse whereof he Complayned to the house,[56] which the house tooke as a greate wronge and indignetyes to them, & soe Comaunded the serjante that attended the house to cause him to appeare before them one fridaye following and then adjurned the Courte tyll Thursdaye when they entended to present the speaker to the kinge.

Thursdaye the 22ᵗʰ of March
On Thursdaye after prayeres sayd by the Clerke of the house and the speaker, Comyttyes was Nomynatede to examyne Matteres and to make them ripe for to be broughte into billes or otherwise to be ordered by the house[57] About xj of the Clocke the same daye,[58] word was brought to the house that the kynge and lords were sett in the higher house, whether the Speaker with the knights and burgeses repaired: There the kynge by waye of Repetycione delivered againe the effecte of his orratyone made one Mondaye before which contayned these pointes.[59]

1 Firste a thankes givinge to the state that had so peacably and with a Joyfull consent of hearts receavede him into that kyngdom, protestynge his great desire to answere so good an acceptance by beinge Carefull for the kingdomes good.

2 Then shewed his greate desire to have the kingdom of England and scotland and as by Nature they were but but one intyre Iland Not seperated by Mountaynes, woods, seas, or greate Rivere, but as it weare an imagenary partycion that in Manye places the very bordereres knewe not Certenly wher the true devysione was, soe he beinge now one heade of bothe he should not be a head of a devided bodie. [**f.4**]

3 Then he tould them that he had broughte peace with him peace abroade and peace at home, peace abroade for that never since he was a kinge had he any warre with any kynge Christyan, Nor any kynge Christyan with him, and prayed that ther never might be, which he would ever endevoure by all good meanes to bringe to passe, peace at

---

[56] *Ibid.* i. 142.

[57] This is not recorded in the Journal, although a committee of privileges was named on this day, *ibid.* i. 149–50.

[58] *Ibid.* i. 142 puts this at two o'clock in the afternoon.

[59] Having gone to so much trouble to obtain a hearing of this speech, the Commons had it entered in the Journal, *ibid.* i. 142–6.

home because in him all auntyente Controversies were styll at an end, as that of Lancaster and yorke, and for a securety to come, he had brought with him Issue.

4 Then he shewed howe he found here two Religeons and one greate secte Not worthie the Name of a religeon: the firste a religeone estableshed and maintayned by the state which he proffessed to be of perswading him selfe that yt was accordinge to the exprese word of God the other the Catholicke or popishe Religeone, whose Churche he saith he thought in his Contyence was the Mother Church, but that of late yeares diveres errores and superstytiouse opiniones were crepte into yt which he desired that all Christyane princes would endevore to cutt of and that he would use the best Care and paines in that behalfe and meete them halfe waye to accomplish so good a worke; that all princes of Christendome beinge at unitie they Mighte the better resiste the common enemye. of the Papiste he said ther were two soarts, the Clerks and the Laycks and that the Clerks such as are caled semenaryes preestes & Jesuits were insufferable in this state for that they perswade disobedience and allineate the subjectes Mindes from their prince, and that they held that the pope not onely as a generall bishoppe tooke upon him the ruling of all ecclesiastycall Matteres thorowgh Christendom but as an Emperore of the world Claimed a powere to depose kynges and Emperores and to dispose at his pleasure kyngdomes & monarchies; And that the Layke were of two soartes old [**f.4v**] and yonge, the yonge he hoped might by good perswasiones be reduced from their false opiniones, and the ould becuase he did beleeve that many or moste of them were good and lovinge subjects he would have them used with noe extreme severitye: the secte whom he Caled puritanes he said were dangerouse and of a violente sperite, and willed the Bishopes to have a care for the suppressynge of them.

5 Lastely he exhorted the whole house of parleament to be carefull in makynge houlsom Lawes for the good of the kingdom, to repeale Lawes that were superfluouse & Idle, and to looke that they made not over manye Lawes, for by such the future ages might be much trubled &c.

Fridaye the 23ᵗʰ of March.
The Commones beinge come to gether about 8 of the Clocke in the Morninge after prayeres said[60] **Sir Robert Wroth** made the first motyone wherin he sett downe diveres matteres to be considered of and ordered in that parleamente, firste a Confirmatyone of the Commone booke[61] 2. the ease of the servitud of wards 3. Monopollyes

---

[60] For the form of which, see *ibid.* i. 150.
[61] i.e. The Book of Common Prayer. *Ibid.* i. 151.

4. Transportacion of ordinance 5. reformatyone of Purvayores and Cartetakeres;[62] the same daye **Sir Edward Montague** Moved for a Reformatione of certen greevances in his Country which he said were three viz: 1. that diveres preachers were suspended for refusyinge to use certayne ceremonyes prescribed them, and for preaching againste the pope and popishe doctryne 2. that the abuses in the Comyssaryes Courte were greate and over burdenouse 3. that diveres Contrary to the Lawe and comon welth of the Country, converted a great quantitie of arable land in to pasture;[63] Theise Matteres and the formore Moved by **Sir Robarte Wroath** Comyttes wer Nomynated to examyne.[64]

The same daye Bryane Tayse of the guarde [**f.5**] that had abused the House by ill termes was brought in to the house and kneelinge upon his knees at the Barre Confessed his fault, and was pardoned in Marcy not in Justyce the kynge being partly meanes for his favore.

That day also the Contentyon between **Sir John fortescue** and **Sir Francys Goodwine** aboute knighte of the sheere was decided; The Controversy was, that wher **Sir francys Goodwine** was returned by the sherife havinge the More voyces, **Sir John Fortescugh** procured a Newe writte to the sherife to make a Newe ellectyone for that Sir Francis stood outlawed, which cause was expressed in the writte upon this Sir John was secondly Chosen, The Mattere was firste debated in the House before any of them admitted; Some held that outlary was a suffityente cause to keepe a Man from beinge a Membere of that house; some held otherwise and made their Argumente upon the words of the writte which were to returne *Idoneos et sufitientes homines* and not *Legales*:[65] But, **Mr. Francys More** the lawiere held that although in his opinione a man outlawed was Not fit to Make Lawes, yet because the outlray of Sir Francys was pardoned by acte of parleamente as to all the world excepte againste him that sued him, he was inabled to be of the house; And so with a generall concente of the house Sir Francys was admitted and Sir John rejected.[66]

Sattordaye the 24th of March 1603
The fourth daye some billes were Redd one about apparrill; theffecte wherof was that because the statutes in force were too traight[67] to be

---

[62] Wroth included two other grievances, dispensation from penal statutes and abuses of writs and Exchequer procedure. *CJ*, i. 151; Mountagu Diary, p. 55; Manners Diary, p. 22.

[63] *CJ*, i. 151; Mountagu Diary, p. 55; Manners Diary, p. 22.

[64] For which see *CJ*, i. 151.

[65] The wording of the writ for return of knights of the shire as recorded in *CJ*, i. 140 specifies *duos Milites, Gladiis cinctos, magis idoneos et discretos*.

[66] The Manners Diary has the fullest account of this debate, see above p. 23–24.

[67] [*Sic*] straight.

obeyed, and the penaltyes unpossyble to be answered, that Statute for apparrell shalbe repealed and both the appointe of the kynd of apparrille and the [**f.5v**] penalty to be referred to the kynge and Counsell provided that the penaltye exceed Not the value of the apparrell used againste the said proclamatyone, This receaved noe second readinge by the more number of voyces which did seem a litle odd.[68]

Another bill was redd aboute the Explanacion of a Statute Made 32 Hen.8. concerning limetacion of prescriptyon.[69]

Att tenne of the Clocke the Court brake upp by reasone of a sermon made at westminster by the deane beinge the daye of the kinges enterance in to the kyngdome yearly solempnized.

Mondaye the 26ᵗʰ of Marche 1604
one Mondaye the Matter of the wards moved amonge other thinges by **Sir Robarte Wroth**, and comitted to diveres to examine on Tuesday[70] before **Sir Francys Bakone** made reporte of upon which reporte a questyone was made whether it should be proceeded in by bill or petycione, and the house agreed by petycione,[71] and withall the Lords of the higher house was requested to conferre with the Comittyes aboute that matter who consented Most willingly and desired withall that the Matter of respecte of Homage might be Coupled with the Matter of the Wardes, and that they might with those comittyes treate of the Matter of purvayores, and especially Cartetakers all which the house consented unto;[72] the Mesuage [*sic*] from the lords was brought to the house by the Lord Chiefe Justyce and Mr. Justyce yelvertone; upon their conferrences viz. the Committyes with the lords, the Matter of **Sir Francis Goodwine** about his ellectyone and admittance in to the house for a knight of Barkeshire[73] was caled in questyone by the lords, who intymated that the kinge Conceaved some displeasure of the house proceeding therin therfor it was agreed that **Sir John Stanhope** [**f.6**] And **Sir John Herberte** privie Counselleres & Memberes of the house should move the kynge that hee would be pleased to admitt to his presence our speakere to deliver to his Majestie

---

[68] See the Mountagu Diary for the reasons, p. 56. The bill was rejected by 125–75, *CJ*, i. 152.

[69] 32 Hen. VIII, cap. 2. *SR* iii. 747–8.

[70] The committee for Wroth's motions met on the afternoon of Friday 23 March. *CJ*, i. 151.

[71] The heads of Bacon's report are printed in *CJ*, i. 153; the fullest summary of the wardship debate is in the Manners Diary, p. 26.

[72] See *CJ*, i. 154; Mountagu Diary, p. 57.

[73] [*Sic*] Buckinghamshire.

that that which was don was accordinge to the priveliges of the house, and No waye did or could prejudice his honor.[74]

Tusdaye the 27ᵗʰ of March 1604
On Tusdaye Morninge after some fewe billes redd the Serjant at Armes broughte into the house to the Barre **Sir Thomas Sherley**, the ij Sherifes of Londone, one Simpsone who sued out an executyone against **Sir Thomas Shereley** and watkynes the Serjante who arested Sir Thomas on tusdaye the xvᵗʰ of March, 1603. beinge the daye that the king wente in state thorough Londone: Simpson and watkynes beinge delinquentes kneeled at the Barre Sir Thomas and the Sherifes standinge, a Counselor at lawe was admitted to speake for simpsone and watkynes; It was objected againste them that they had broken the privelidge of the house in arestynge Sir Thomas beinge Chosen a Burgese of the house; their Answer by their Counsell was that they were sorye that they had offended and desired that yf they Might not be pardoned yet that their punishmente might be the Lesse for that they protested that they knewe Not that Sir Thomas was a burgis of the house, the reason that moved them so to think was that in the kinges proclematyone before the parleamente, thellectores of the knights and Buirgeses should not chose Men outlawed, and they understandinge that Sir Thomas was outlawed presumed that he was No member of the house, also that theire shuite was entered longe before the electyone, & therfore before he was invested in the house and so prayed the favorable constructyon of the [**f.6v**] house; Sir Thomas to the outlarye replyed that as soone as he found he was outlawed did reverse the utlarye by a *supersedias*, the Coppy wherof he had in his hande to shewe under the offyceres hande, and touchinge their knowlyge of him to be a Burgese he said he tould them that they might kise the Towere for arrestynge him a Burges And that the Bishope of durhame[75] cominge by the same Instante to the officeres said also so muche, but they regarded Not this havinge once laide the Executyone upon him. This matter was spoken to by diveres, the points were theis firste whether it were a breach of the privelidge to areste one returned but Not invested a burgis yt was Answered by **Serjante Hubbarte**,[76] that he thought it was by reason that a burgis aftere that he was elected Muste be allowed a Conveniente tyme to come the Citty towards the parleamente which he expressed in iiij latten words viz: *eundo, sedendo, morando, et*

---

[74] The debate on the Goodwin v. Fortescue case took place on the morning of 27 March, when the objections Lord Cecil raised at the conference on the afternoon of 26 March were reported to the House. See *CJ*, i. 155–6; Manners Diary, pp. 29–30; Mountagu Diary, pp. 58–59.

[75] Tobie Mathew, Bishop of Durham, 1595–1606.

[76] Serjeant Sir Henry Hobart, MP for Norwich.

redeundo, another point and the greateste of all was, whether yf **Sir Thomas Sherley** should be receaved out of Executyone to be a membere of the house the executyone could be No more lye againste him & so the Creditore lose absolutly all his Monye **Serjante Tanfeeld** was of that oppinione and some otheres; but **Sir Frances Bacone** thought otherwise and that he was out of executyone but duringe the tyme of the Parleamente, No otherwise then yf one be in prisone and the prisone be fired and the party escape he shall not be out of executyone because it was act *de deie* he Compared it also to a case, that yf a sherife should take one in executyone & die and the prisoner therby escape before an other be chosen &c: but this Matter beinge doubtefull, and the Lords havinge sent from them Mr. Atturney generall and some ij Masteres of the Chauncery to the house who stayed without [**f.7**] yt was ordered that **Sir Thomas Sherley** and Simpson with the Sergeante should returne from whence they came and attend againe on Fryday followinge Then Mr. Atturney generall Sir Edward Cooke delivered to the house that the Lords desired that before they should joyne with the House to confer upon the Matter of the Wardes proposed by the House and the Mattere of the Homage and purvayores proposed by the Lordes, that the house would be pleased to conferr also of the proceedinges ~~of~~ aboute the ellectyone of **Sir Francys Goowine** [*sic*]; They beinge departed out of the house and attendinge their answere without the Courte was demaunded their oppinione herin diveres spake[77] to that poynte and all concluded to answere, that it stood Not with the dignetye or privelidge of the house to bringe in questyone or to conferre with the upper house of Matteres alredye adjudged by the house and so the Messengeres beinge againe admytted into the house to receave their answere the Speaker tould them that it was Not the pleasure of the house to conferre with the Lords of that matter, After some more motyones of that matter and some fewe billes redd, Mr. Atturney accompanied with three Masteres of the Chancery viz. doctor Carye, doctor Home and Mr. Tyndall came againe from the Lords,[78] and shewed the house that the Lords againe required conferrence of that matter of **Sir Francys Goodwine** and that the kynge had Comannded them so to doe herupon after good and long delyberatyone, yt was concluded that the house intended by their speaker to satysfye the kynge in that pointe and to delivere to his Majestie the Cause of their refusall of suche Conferrence of matteres fully adjudged: so the Courte brake upe at iij of the Clock in the afternoone beginninge before viij the same Morninge.[79]

[77] For further coverage of the debate, see *CJ*, i. 155; Manners Diary, pp. 29–30.
[78] *CJ*, i. 156 mentions only Sir Edward Coke and Dr Hone.
[79] The time of the adjournment is confirmed by Manners Diary, p. 30.

wensday the 28. of march 1604 [**f.7v**]

upon wensdaye mornynge by sixe of the Clock the house beinge for the moste parte come to gether[80] **Sir John Herberte** made reporte of the mesuage [*sic*] that he and **Sir John Stanhope** made to the kynge accordinge to the directyone of the House, He said the kyng was by informatyone Much moved against the procedinge of the house about **Sir Francys Goodwine** whose priviledges he Mente by all waies and meanes as much to maintayne and Confirme as ever any his predecessores had done, but desired that xij Lawyeres and threescore knights and Burgeses[81] with the speaker might come to him to the Courte at White hall to satysfye him in that pointe which was done, but what they should delyvere to the kynge after much debate, was that wee did as of our selves come unto his Majestie Not to give the reasone of our Judgmente in that case, but to satysfye him of the erevocablenes of our Judgments in so high a Courte beinge Never before demanded an accompte of our proceedings there and so the Courte brake upe at viij of the clocke and the Lawieres with 60. gentlemen wente to the Court.

Thursdaye the 29th of March. 1604

The Lord Cheefe Justyce of England[82] Lord cheife Justyce of the Comone please[83] Lord cheife Barrone[84] Justyce Clerke, Justyce Crooke and the kynges atturneye[85] came as Messengeres frome the upper house and delivered to the Nether House a byll ingrossed whose tytle was a moste Joyfull and Juste recognitione of his Majesties moste immediat Lawfull & true righte to the Crowne of Englande[86] which after their departure, was ordered by the House with greate willingenes and Joye to be redeliverede then was it moved to be Redd againe the second tyme and so the third that as the upper house had bene forwarde in passynge it, the Lower house might [**f.8**] not shewe them selves but as forward in giving it passage and correspondente goodwill in Confirminge it there **Mr. George More**[87] spake to the Byll with great likynge and approbatyone, but desired that beinge a Matter of Importance it myght be committed that yf any tittle were omitted by errore of the Clerke or other wise it

---

[80] *CJ*, i. 156 states that the House was not held to be full enough, and three bills were read before Herbert made his report.

[81] *CJ*, i. 157. The lawyers are among the first named to this delegation.

[82] Sir John Popham.

[83] Sir Edmund Anderson.

[84] Sir William Peryam. Not noted to have been sent in *CJ*, i. 158.

[85] Sir Edward Coke.

[86] Enacted as 1 Jac. I, cap. 1. *SR*, iv. 1016–17.

[87] i.e. Sir George More, MP for Guildford.

myghte be added, but the fervente zeale of the House was such that they would suffer Noe delayes but redd it all three tymes in one houres space; On **Sir Williame Morris** a Welch Man as he said spake unto that Bill and desired ther Mighte be Added to that bill the Tytle of Emperore of greate Brittanye for that he did observe that an old provesee among the Welchmen was in the kinge in parte performed by that he had seene, and an other parte performed as he had Credibly heard and wished that yt might be fully fulfylled herafter the prophesee as he pronounced it was; A kinge of Brittyshe Bloud in Cradle Crowned with lyones Marke shall Joyne all brittyshe ground, restore the Crose and male this Ile Renowned.[88]

This day after that the speaker had made relatione of the kynges Answer to the 12 Lawieres and 60 knights and Burgesses the Consideratyon of the Answer was putt of tyll the Nexte daye being Fridaye.[89] This daye also was brought to the House from the Lords by Mr. doctor Carewe and doctor Stanhope,[90] three billes for the Restoringe of the Bloud of Henry Earle of Southampton, Thomas Earle of Arundell; and Earle of Essexe[91] and his two sisteres, None of them Redde for the shortenes of the tyme.

Friday the 30th of March 1604
On Fridaye Mornynge **Sir Robart Wingfeeld [f.8v]** verrye bouldly spake in defence of the judgemente givene by the House for receaving as a Member **Sir Francis Goodwine** and rejectynge **Sire John Fortescugh** deliveringe his opinione that the kynge was misinformed by those Neare him, and that the sheriffe, in the return of the Writte with the indorsemente, that it appeared by record that **Sire Francys Goodwine** stood outlawed and so Not Meete nor ssuffityente to be a Member of the House, was Not privie to that indorcemente but cogged in by some other againste which abuse hee spake without all feare and lyke a faithfull member of the House and Concluded a Refusal of Conferring with the Lords or Judges of that Judgment alredy paste. Nexte him spake **Mr. Yelverton** of Grayes Inne with great applawese for gravitye, bouldnes and Judgemente shewinge that yf alteration of the former Judegmente should be Made it would shewe Levitye Cruelty and Cowardlynes, Levitye in varying from former proceedinges, which he sayd Could not be allthoughe the Judgment had been erronyouse being once paste, for sayth hee, in the kynges bench or Comon please, inferryore Courtes to that Judgemente Cannot be altered that terme,

---

[88] For an alternative translation of this prophecy, see Mountagu Diary for 31 March.
[89] *CJ*, i. 158; Manners Diary, p. 34.
[90] Sir Matthew Carew and Sir Edward Stanhope, *CJ*, i. 158.
[91] Robert, 3rd Earl of Essex.

and therfor because every partyculer daye of the Parleament was a Terme, it Could receave Noe Alteracion besides that he proved it a Moste true and substanshiall Judgemente, the Matter having bene firste Moved to the house then agreed one both sides with good delyberacion and therupon Judgment givene; he tooke awaye the objectyons againste it; first that the kinge had Not to doe in the Alteracione of the Electyone by a Newe Writte, but that yf the knight had died before the Returne, or by attainture of Treasone or become Lunatyke (all which was objected) yet the Sherife was Not to make his returne Not before his daye beinge the firste daye of the parleamente and then the parleamente beinge in force was to send out their warrant [**f.9**] For a Newe Writte and Not the kinge by his Lord Chauncelore for by that meanes the Lord Chauncelore and his under officeres might make the Knightes and the Burgeses for the parleamente. Crueltye he thought the Courte Might be Charged with yf it should teare a ~~sundere~~ sound Member from the bodye, for although a surgeane Mighte well Cutt of a Corupte and putrefyed member from the bodye, yet to pull vyolently from the body a sound Member were an intollorable Crueltye. To Avoyd the thirde Imputacion of Crueltye he wished them to consider howe fare the overthrowe of the authoritie of that Courte would extend to the undoing of all their estats, which ruled and governed all and Not to feare the greatnes of **Sir John Fortescugh** whom he also for Many respects had Juste Cause to honore Nor to thinke that the kynge would otherwise then the establishinge of all the priveleges of that house; for said hee the kynge most Royallye willed the Comyttyes to goe againe to gether and to Consydere of their Resolutyone wishing they Mighte Justefye their formore proceedinges and yf they could Not amonge them selves resolve, then to conferre with the Judges and so resolve, and their resolutyon to signefye to the Lords of the privie Counselle Not as parleament men, but as such as might beste informe the kynge at his returne & Wheras it was objected that the Judges had given their oppiniones What was the Lawe in that Case beinge to demaunded of the kynge that the outlarye Made Sir Francys uncapable beinge Not reversed by a *scire facias*; he sayd the Judges sayd true for the Lawe, but that was Nothinge to the decre of the Courte of parleamente for the Courte of parleamente had powere to decree and Judge by discretyone and Not by the positive Lawes, that it was objected No presidente Could be shewed for the Lyke Judgemente, he Answered that ther [**f.9v**] was Nevere the lyke case and so concluded that he would have no Conferrence with the Judges or the Lords but that the Kynge should be informed that their Judgmente they Could not altere and the Reasones that bothe Moved theire Judgementes and the resolutyone to stand to it, to be writtene and delivered to the kynge for his satysfactyone.

Mr. More a Counselor at Lawe[92] shewed that where as it was objected that it touched the Kynges honnore Not to harken to the second Writtes, yt could Not be so, for that writtes wente out Comonly by Clarkes the kynge Nevere privie to them.[93] **Mr. Crewe,**[94] **Sir Francis Hastynges, Mr. Hide,**[95] **Mr dyott**[96] **Sir Edward Hobye** and otheres[97] all spake to stand to the Judgmente but to certefye the kynge, Soe the Courte agreed that this daye all the Lawieres that spake and Serjants and some knights and gentlemen should be Comyttyes to penne the reasons of the Courtes proseedinges for Judgement and for the Establishinge thereof to be delyvered to the kynge for his satys-factyone Upon the deliverye of those Reasones to the kynge the kynge appoynted the Comyttyes for that Cause and Judges and the Lords of the parleamente to meete before him at Whit hall there the kynge propounded the Reasones and presidents to the Judges who agreede unto them, but my Lord Cheife Justyce was aboute to disprove by an other Reasone that **Sir Francis Goodwine** was Not duly Chosen, herupon the kinge desirouse to Comprimitt the Matter made offere to the Lower House to be contented that Sir Francis should Not be also and that a Newe Writte should be sente out to ellecte an other Knight in his place which upon the suite of Sir Francis the House agreed upon and so a warrant was Made from the House for the Newe Writte, and Not from my lord Chauncelore which the Chauncelore offered to doe but [**f.10**] was stoutely impugned by the House, for therin Might have bene the greateste breache of their privelige: And so that Controversie fineshed with the kynges good approbatyone of the Judgmente & Courage of them of the Lower House.

Mondaye the 2 of Aprill 1604
diveres Billes Redd amongeste the Reste the ladye Nottynghames Bylle for her Naturallizinge being a Scotte the Bill was mended by the Comittyes because it did not stretch to the Naturalizinge of any Children she should have any where and by what persone soever.[98]

Tusdaye the 3 of Aprill 1604
diveres Billes Redd one **Griphin Paine** Burges for Wallingford inveyed against the byll for punishing of ?Mene purveores sayenge that the house resisted the kynges pleasure withstood the privie counsel; Croste

[92] i.e. Francis Moore, MP for Reading.
[93] These speeches are reported anonymously in *CJ*, i. 159.
[94] Thomas Crew, MP for Lichfield.
[95] Lawrence Hyde, MP for Marlborough. See Manners Diary, p. 37.
[96] Anthony Dyott, MP for Lichfield.
[97] For the fullest details of which see Manners Diary, pp. 36–37.
[98] Second reading and committal. Cotton was not named to the committee. *CJ*, i. 162.

the Judges and Nowe went aboute in that bill to hange the kynges servantes because fellonye is sett downe of purveyores offendinge the Lawe; He was Called to the Barre, and there did confesse his faulte and asked forgivenes of the House but because he was Maiore of Wallingford he was Comaunded to departe the house till the house had Considered of that pointe, and as yet is Not returned and the matter sleepeth.[99]

Wenesdaye the 4ᵗʰ of Aprill 1604
A Bill againste Transportacion of ordinance of Irone or Bullets or Irone ore or Iron Myne. Another againste transportynge of Cloth undressed.

Sir Edward Mountagu's Diary of the 1604 Session
[Northants. RO, Montagu MS 30:]

A note of the things that wer donne the first parliament of King James 19 march 1603.

The first day being *Monday the 19 of March*
After the King was gonne to the Chirch/ The Lord High steward which was the Erle of Nottingham, cam into the usuall place in Westminster & after he had called all the knights citesens & Burgesses & sworne some to the supremacy The rest went into the courts next the parliament house & there wer sworne by certayne of the house appoynted commissioners for the Lord Steward: And there ~~remayned~~ most of them remaynd expecting to be sent for into the higher house.

The Kings majestie after he was satt & all the Lords placed & the King demaunding once or twice whether [the] lower house was come & answer being made they wer, though in deed the tenth wer not there: His majestie putting off his cap & crowne & putting yt on agayne made a most excellent speach shewing the cause of the calling the parliament to be three: first to shew his thanckfull for ther generall acceptacion of him secondly the benefitts receyved therby which was individuall to his person: & these to be fower/ 1 union of the two kingdomes 2 outeward peace & traffique with all princes: 3 Inward peace at hom & Successeon in his children 4 Religion/ Thirdly the making & execution of laws the making to be allwas at a parliament, the execution allwaes after to stand uppon sincerity & constant courage.

He amplified all these continuing is speach almost an houre concluding the eloquence of a King to stand one playnes & sincerity:-

---

[99] *CJ*, i. 162; See Manners Diary, pp. 38–39; Mountagu Diary, p. 63. Payne's suspension was reversed on 6 March 1610. *CJ*, i. 406.

After this the Lord Chauncelor made a speach not much differeng from the course in former parliaments & willed the lower house to chuse a speaker & to present him to his majestie one Thursday next:

This donne All those that wer in the higher house whereof my selfe was one, returning into the lower which was almost full, & staying till **Mr. Vicechamb.**[100] & **Sir Jhon Herbert** the only privy counsellors then retorned of the house wer come: An Auncient parliament man made complaynt unto them of the wrong that they wer not sent for into the higher house.

Sir Jhon Herbert stood up & shewd how sorry he was for yt & how his majestie was told they wer come/ repeated shortly the heads of his majesties ~~head~~ speach/ & when he had donne that according to the custome he propounded a speaker, thincking **Sir Edward Phelips** to be a fitt man. There was a greate pause after this, the house not naming any at last he being named agayne some few cried a Philips: some cryd no: no: but then an ancient parliament man directing the house sayd yt was not sufficient to say no: but they must propound some other, so som cry Phelips agayne: some one or two cry **Sir Edw Hobby**: some one some an other: but yt being putt to the question as many as will have a Phelips sa I: most cryed I: & the rest no some few crid no/ & so Phelips ~~was sett~~ stood up & made an eloquent speach in disabling himselfe which donne they cried a Phelips & then he was placed in the chayre where he [made] two peticions to the house: the first that though they would not accept of his excuse that yet he might make was to the king for his discharge: thother that they would protect him as they had commanded him/

And so we departed for that time.

Thursday 22 March

One Thursday 22 Mr. Speaker was assented, The King most graciously to satisfie the greffe of the house repeated his speach unto them: And then as many as could possibly stand wer lett in & the doores sett open: nay [*sic*] when the King was ready he sent a Serjeant at armes to call up the lower house that so they might com in: this did notably please the house.

The Speaker returned & sett in his place: & going aboute according to the custome to reade a bill/ **Sir William Fleetewood** knight returned for one of the Knights of Buckingham shire made knowe a grevance of **Sir Frauncis Goodwin**, who though he wer elected by the voyce of the county & as he thought returned, yet was not called and admitted & going to the clerke of the crowne to ~~see~~ know the reason he refused to show him the returne as the ?felow whereuppon desyred that the clerke myght be sent for to know the cause/ which

[100] Sir John Stanhope, MP for Newtown, Isle of Wight and vice-chamberlain of the household.

being put to the house command was geven that he should be sent for.

After stept up **Serjeant Sherley** who declared that in February last **Sir Thomas Sherley** was elected burgesse from Steining in Sussex & the indenture sealed & deliverd And that the 15 of March when the king went through London the sayd Sir Thomas riding to attend his majestie was arrested & layd in the counter. It was orderd that *habeas corpus* should be awarded to fetch the prisonner & that the sergeant should fetch the delinquents, both the partie that arrested him as also he at whose sute he was arrested:

Then motion was made for committees to be nominated for the examining of the privileges of the house, some stick there was at yt at the first but put to the question It was agreed there should be a committee which accordingly was named:

Then **Sir Herbert Croft** made complaynt of Brian Tash ~~who keepe~~ one of the guard for that the first day of the parliament som the burgesses pressing to go into the higher house he thrust them oute & sayd nay goodman burgesse you must stay a while:[101] Some debate there was about this but at last ordered that he should be sent for by the sergeant:

Then the Speaker moved because that Saterday was a day of triump & that some seates wer to be made because all the house could not sitt/ for in deed yt wer so full that the stood half way into the middle of the house/ whether they would be pleased to rejorne the courte till Monday: divers wer of opinion that yt was not in our power to rejorne but only in the king/ but **Sir Edw: Hobby** sayd that there was presedents to the contrary yet the Question being put to the house they determined to sitt & not to rejorne yt: And appoynted 8 of the [clock] in the morning for the usuall hower of sitting

Then was red this Bill:

1 Bill	An act touching common recov-
read agayne ~~28~~ 27 March	eries agaynst Infants.
committed 13 Ap: engrossd	
17 Aprill: passed:	

& so we parted for that day/ that bill read.

Friday 23 [March]

After prayers read: **Sir Robert Wroth** stept up & made this motion first for confirmation of the booke of common prayer lately sett oute by his majesties auctoryt. And that consideracion might be had of these grevances following, first for wardship that the king might have a composition & the subjecte freed [from] that tenure: Secondly agaynst

---

[101] The exclusion of an MP from the King's speech seems to have been compounded by Tash's implicit assumption that burgesses were not gentlemen.

purveyors: 3 agaynst monopolies 4 agaynst licences of Alienation, 5 agaynst transporting of Iron ordinance, 6 agaynst abuses of theschq.[102] & 7 agaynst dispensation of statutes.[103]

This motion was well liked of & committed to have bills drawen & to be sett on that after noone.

My selfe next to him delivered further greefes injoyned me by the country to make knowen ~~there greeffes~~ to the hou[se] first the Intollerable burdene vexation trayvale & charge of the commissaries courtes as now they are used 2 the suspention of grave learned & soberminded ministers for not observing certayne ceremonies long time by many disused/ 3 the depopulation & dayly excessive conversion of tillage into pasture.[104]

This motion yt pleased the house to committ likewise as the former & to be sett on on Monday.

One **Mr. Wentworth** a lawyer he moved ij poynts to the house one for the Infirmities of yt in lacking some of the members, an other for the deformitie having more than yt ought to have, vid. certayne burgesses newly appoynted for the universites.

After some debate aboute the former matter especially concerning **Sir Frauncis Goodwines** case the clerke of the crowne was sent for in ~~to being~~ who brought two returnes & deliverd them into the house.

The former writt bore *teste 30 Jan*, the election was 22 Feb & Sir Frauncis Goodwin & Sir William Fleetewood wer returned but one the returne the sheriff had certefied that Sir Frauncis stood outelawed & therefor not fitt: whereupon an other writt was sent unto ~~uppo~~ them *teste 16 Marcij* & the election 21 of March & Sir Jhon Fortesc[ue returned]

This matter was long debated with diver arguments pro & con especially by the lawyers & at lenght determined by the house that the first returne was good & that the sheriffe administered more then he ought to do, & so Sir Frauncis was sworne & admitted into the house.

Then was called in Brian Tash the yeoman of Guard who confessed that he called one goodman Burgesse and confessed his fault because of his majesties former grace to us the day before was pardoned & relasted without fees.

In the After noone the committees mett ~~for the~~ to consider of those things propounded by **Sir Robert Wroth**.

For the confirmation of the booke of common prayer lately sett forth yt was orderd that some few of the committee should looke into the old & this new & reporte the alteracions & explanations & what else

---

[102] i.e. The Exchequer.
[103] *CJ*, i. 150–1.
[104] See also *CJ*, i. 151.

was thought fitt in ~~these~~ the booke to receyve examination & to ~~reporte there~~ bring in yt uppon wedensday to the committees to receyve further debate.

For the matter of wardship yt was ordered to be moved to the house that a conference might be had with the Lords to see if they would joyne with us in making a peticion to the king to geve us leave to treate of those matters & to offer him a project:

For purveyors yt was ordered that some few lawyers should draw a bill & bring yt in uppon wedensday to be further considered of.

The rest of the matters the day being short wer referred to Tuesday nest & this is theffect of this days worke:

Saterd. 24 [March]
Saterday complaynt was made agaynst pages & other for abusing of the servaunts of some of the house carying them to tavernes by force & there leaving the cloakes and other things in pawn. some wer appoynted to examine the abuses & to punish thoffenders:[105]

2 bill 28: 2 read committed March 24 Ap: brought in & dashed	A bill read the like: An act to take away writts of errors in certayne cases.
3 bill comitted 18 Aprell Ingrossed passed	A bill: the like: An act concerning apparell ~~but for the~~ theffect was to repeale all the old lawes & that the king with thadvise of his counsell & proclamation should from time to time limitt what apparell & Jewells every degree should weare: but for this latter clause yt was rejected.[106]
4 bill 11 Aprill 2 read committed 1 May dashed	The like: An act of explanation for limitacion of prescription made 32 H.8[107]

There was a committee chosen for repeale of statutes/
Att ten of the clock Mr. Speaker rose & went to a sermond in

[105] See also *CJ*, i. 152 and the Manners Diary, p. 25.
[106] The House was always reluctant to pass legislation which gave statutory authority to the royal prerogative.
[107] 32 Hen. VIII, cap. 2. *SR*, iii. 747–8.

West[minster] being the first day of the kings entrance.

Monday 26 March 1604

5 bill	An act to confirme to the subjects
2 Ap: 2 read and committed but	of England ther ancient lib-
not thought a good bill but a	erties & priveleges.
new to be made:	
6 bill	An act of explanation of the
28 2 reading & committed	statute for forcible entries made
13 Ap: ingrossd 17 Ap: passed	8 H.6.[108]
7 bill	An act for mending certayne
31 Mar 2 read: committed	imperfection of a statute 8 El:[109]
11 May dashed	for making Hatts

Mr. Hext being some days before hissed at in a speech which he made he this day made a motion for more reverence to be used in that place, which was generally likd of.

Sir Oliver Sct. Jhon made an excellent speach & his motion was for releffe of Captaynes & Captaynes fellows now without meanes to live:

A greate committee of all Knights of shirs & divers others was chosen to sitt of yt on Friday next in the parliament house: but yt was to extend only to English men that had served in Ireland:

~~Mr. Bac~~ **Sir Frauncis Bacon** related what had passed at the committee for **Sir Robt. Wrothes** motion, especially the agreement for wards: whereuppon 24 wer selected to go to the Lords to pray a conference. the Lords gave answer that they liked well of the motion & that they would send unto us an answer for that & aboute certayne other things & therefore desired the lower house would sitt a while/

they sent the Lord Chefe Justice of England with some others unto us declaring ther allowance to confer with us concerning that matter & also propounded to us two other grevances: *vid.* respit of Homage: & matter of purveyors & cart takers desiring a conference with us aboute them also/ And likewise if ther wer any other greevances they would willingly joyne with us to confer them/ The time the desired to be that after noone the place in the outeward chamber & there number to be xxx: we assented unto yt & chose as the fashion & manner ~~is 6o~~ dubble there nomber which was 6o.

In the after noone we mett but the chamber was filled with as many

---

[108] 8 Hen. VI, cap. 9. *SR*, ii. 244–6.
[109] 8 Eliz. I cap. 11. *SR*, iv. 494–59.

more of the lower house as was nominate but the Lords misliked of yt & so most wer putt oute & they only called by bill that wer nominated:

Sir Frauncis Bacon in a very good speach delivered unto them the manner of our proceading & desired ther Lordships to joyne with us in the peticion to his majestie to geve us leave to treate of the matter concerning the wards/ the Lords answered that they would move yt to the house & we should have answer:

Then they propounded to us the matters of Respite of Homage & purveyors, **Sir Francis Bacon** shewed how yt should be delivered to the house to know there pleasures.

Then the Lords Rose & went into the higher house desiring us to stay a while: when they came oute agayne the Lord Cecill delivered a very fine speach, but in thend propounded unto us the matter of **Sir Francis Goodwins** concerning his election & that if we had any auctority He would shew us there reasons of there dislike but answer was made we had no auctority to treate of that matter: & so wee Brake of.

Tuesday 27 [March]:

8 Bill 12 April 2 read cottd	An act aboute Ingrossing & transporting of wooll & ~~yarne~~.[110]
9 Bill 2 read 4 Aprill cottd	An act what cloth may be carried beyond seas unbarbed, unrowed & unshorne:
10 Bill	An act for preservation of mannors & coppyhold lands
11 Bill 31 May dashed	An act for costs in prohibition.
12 Bill rejected & first reading	An act that the Brewers within five miles of London should be subject to company of brewers.
Wedensday 28 [March] 13 Bill 12 April 2 read cott:	An act for reedifying all the decayd sea coste townes & for the increase of mariners:

This day we went to the King who Mr. Speaker delivered the reasons of the commons there ~~choosing~~ taking in **Sir Frauncis Goodwin** to

---

[110] Neither *CJ*, i. 155 or 936 mention any such measure on this day; it was probably the bill given a first reading on 11 April. *CJ*, i. 167.

the house/ the matter Require a speciall reporte what was donne at that time:

Thursday 29 March:
This day on brian Bridger a minister delivered a peticion to Mr. Speaker as he was comming to the house whom the Speaker caused to be stayed by the serjeant, & shewed the peticion to the house which was chifely agaynst the bishops terming there goverment Antichristian & them selves antichrists. The man was knowed by diverse of the house to be lunatike & so affirmed: but at this tyme he answered soberly & as yt should seeme with advisement so that the house thought fitt to send him to the tower:[111]

Mr. Speaker related to the house what was donne before the King & what message he was to retorne from his majestie which in effect was this:

First that he should reporte the course that was taken & the resolucion of the Judges:–2 that we should proceede to some resolucion amongst our selves: 3 If we wer not resolved then to resorte to the Judges: & lastly if we did resolve that we should make repayre to his counsell by whom we should know his majesties pleasure:

Our proceedings herein is to referred to a discourse by yt self.[112]

This donne there wer sent from the Lords The two Lord cheffe Justices, Baron Clerke,[113] Justice Fenner,[114] Serjeant Crooke & Mr. Atturney:[115] with this act:

1 Bill from the Lords: first red that day & passed with grete choutes:[116]	A most joyfull & Just recognition of the Immediate, lawfull & undoubte[d] succession discent & right of the Crowne.

After this the Lords sent us three other billes.

2 bill from the Lords read 31 March: 2 read 2 Ap: comtt 11 Aprill passed	One for the restoring therle of Southampton

3 bill from the Lords read 31 March: 2 red 2 Apr	Thother for restoring the Sonne & two daughters of therle

---

[111] See *CJ*, i. 157–8 and the Manners Diary, pp. 30–31.
[112] This paper has not been found.
[113] Robert Clarke, Exchequer Baron.
[114] Edward Fenner, Justice of King's Bench.
[115] Sir Edward Coke.
[116] i.e. Shouts. The bill passed without committal. See *CJ*, i. 158; Cotton Diary, p. 48–49.

committed 11 Aprill passed   of Essex

4 bill from the lords   The third for restoring the Erle
read 31 March: 2 read 2 Aprell   of Arundell
committed: 11 Aprill passed

Friday 30 March
?More what was donne more then the debating of **goodwin** cause[117]

Saterday 31 March
Sir William Morrice made a long speach aboute the union delivering
the Kings petegree & to have him called Emperor this was advysed
on/ or rather put of.
    Som few days before[118] he had used a speach to such like effect &
utterd this old proverbe of welsh translated by Sir Jhon Harington.[119]

    A King of Brittish blood in cradle crowne
    With lion marke shall joyne all british growne
    Restore the crosse & make the Ile renoune

Mr. Frauncis Tate translated the welsh proverb thus

    The crowned child
    having the lion in his skin
    And gayned the crosse
    Shall have Brutes Island withoute devision
    And from thence forth shall better & better

14 Bill   An act for exchang of lands.[120]
read & rejected

15 bill   An act to disable outelawed
twise read: committed   persons & persons in execution
13 brought & ingrossed: to be of the parliament house
18 Aprill dashed:

A message from the lords

[117] For which see *CJ*, i. 159–60, Cotton Diary, pp. 49–51.
[118] 29 March, Cotton Diary, p. 49.
[119] Mountagu presumably meant the courtier and poet Sir John Harington of Kelston,
Somerset rather than John, 1st Baron Harington or his brother Sir James Harington,
knight of the shire for Rutland.
[120] The details of this bill are not recorded in *CJ*, i. 160, Manners or Cotton.

5 bill from the Lords

read: 2 read 2 Aprill commt.
12 Aprell passed

An act for naturallising the Lady Margarett Countesse of Notingham.

16 bill
2 read 4 Aprill comitted

An act agaynst transporting of woolen cloths undressed & setting the poore on worke.

17 bill

An act to explane the act of Ed 6 concerning alehowses

18 bill
[1]1 Aprill 2 read: dashed

A bill touching wines Innes ale-howses & tavernes.[121]

19 bill
21 Ap comttd.[122]

An act for repressing alehowses agaynst the lawes

20 bill
2 read 3 Ap: com'tt

An act for the better execution of the statutes touching pur-veyors & carte takers

21 bill
this bill not thought fitt

An act agaynst stabbing & taking away clergy in some cases, this bil was deliverd in by **Mr. Bond**, but misliked yet not rejected: because yt might beget a good bill.

22 bill
2 red: committed: *quere*
when yt was first read 17 Ap:
Ingrossed: 17 Ap: passed

An act auctorising Justices of peace to deliver certayne pri-sonners oute of the goale & for setling poore prisonners after delivery

Monday 2 Aprill 1604
23 bill
21 Aprill comtd

An act agaynst puritanes //this was brought in on Saterday by **Sir Frauncis Hastings**//

---

[121] *CJ*, i. 940; not recorded in *CJ*, i. 160.
[122] Mountagu seems to have confused this measure with two other bills concerning alehouses which were first read on 18 April. *CJ*, i. 176.

24 bill
23 Ap: comtt'

An act for the restrayning frivo-
lous actions.

25 bill
2 read 5 Aprill com'tt
18 Ingrossd 20 passed

A bill concerning extorcion/ at
the committ: yt was intituled An
act for better executeon of Justice

26 bill

An act for better execution of
penall statutes

27 bill

An act agaynst plurality of benefices.

28 bill
28 A: Ingrossed 7 May
passed

An act to take away clergy from
cattle & sheepe stealers

29 bill
committed ~~13 Aprill ingrossed~~[123]
28 Ap: ingrossed 7 May dashed

An act for releffe of prisoners

30 bill
28 dashed

An act for the continuing of
making Caps.

31 bill
28 Ap comttd 8 May
passed:

An act for explanation of 5 Ell
concerning laborers.[124]

32 bill
28 Ap: comttd

An act concerning tanning of
leather

A message from the Lords who brought these bills

6 bill from Lord
1 read 2 Apr: 12 Ap: cotted
17 Ap: passed

A bill for the restoring the Lord
Pagett

7 bill from Lords
1 read 2 Aprill 12 Aprill cott
17 Aprill passed

A bill for restoring Tho Lucas in
blood:

---

[123] Mountagu presumably confused this bill with that for forcible entries, engrossed on
13 April. *CJ*, i. 170.
[124] The Statute of Artificers, 5 Eliz. I cap. 4. *SR*, iv. 414–22.

Tuesday 3 Aprill:

33 bill	An act concerning processe &
2 read 4 Aprill comtt	pleadings in the courte of thes-
24 Ap: passed	chequer this bill brought in by
	Sir Edw: Hobby:

34 bill	An act agaynst depopulation &
14 Ap: 2 read dashed	therein to prevent such Inclosure

35 bill	An act for the more autenticall
rejected at the first reading:	ingrossing & reserving courte
	rolls of leete & courte barons.

At the second reading of the bill agaynst purveyors: on **Griffin Payne**, maior & burgesse for Walingford spake agaynst the bill & used these words that this parliament, we had dishonored the King, disgraced the counsell, discredited the opinion of the Judges, & now we sought to hang his majesties servants.

For these words he was brought to the bar ~~but~~ he denied that he sayd we had dishonored the king: but that the kings pleasure was somwhat touched, the rest of the speache he confessed. The house because he was his majesties servaunt wer more Inclined to mercy than severity & so uppon his submission & confessing his fault was pardoned: but because yt stood doubtefull whether he might serve there or no because he was maior: therefore he was sequestred till the houses pleasure further knowen.[125]

After was brought in the writing for his majesties satisfaction which was sent to Ingrossing And because yt was to be deliverd in that after noone, we appoynted to sitt agayne in the house.

After noone	
36 bill	An act for a courte of marchants
39 2 read dashed	in London concerning only
	marchants.

This long bill read, & the writing brought in ingrossed we sent yt to the Lords of the counsell, having no further commission but to deliver yt: & to intreate there Lords for his majesties further satisfaction/

This to be referred to the discourse at large.

[125] Payne was allowed to take his place in the House again on 6 March 1610. *CJ*, i. 406.

Wedensday 4 Aprill

37	An act agaynst transportation of
13 Apr: cott	Iron ordinance gun mettall Iron
17 Aprill passed	ore, Iron mettall, & Iron shott:
	This was returned from the
	Lords with ?such amendments &
	proviso as yt was dashed

38	An act for apparell restrayning
11 Aprill 2 read committ	the excessive wearing of cloth
18 Ingrossed: 21 App	of gold, cloth of tissue, cloth of
passed	silver & gold & silver lace/

39	An act for thexplanation of a
17 Aprill 2 read: dashed	proviso 29 Ell for the discharge
	of arerages by recusancy after
	death or submission:[126]

Thursday 5 Aprill

Mr. Speaker cam not till ten a clock:

After Mr. Speaker had geven the bill of extorcion a second reading & yt was committed: he told us that he was to shew unto us two things the first the cause of his absence, the second a message from his exce[llent majes]tie/ the cause of his absence was a commanndement from the king to geve his attendance betwene 7 & 8 a clock.

The message consisted of divers partes, first to make knowen that uppon Wedensday he had receyved from us a parchment, contayning many particular reasons, but whether our resolute answer, or else reasons to satisfie him, & not to tie. Secondly a princely protestacion not only by that love which he bore to all his subjects which was infinite nor by the word of king but by his fayth to God, to geve us all privileges without detraction of the lease, So we would not seeke to detract that from him that in Justice did belong unto him: he had seene what we had done but not as yet judged: And did desire as a good king, and commaund as a King to prepare that there may be a conference betwene us & the Judges, before his counsell that so he may Judge & lay the fault where yt is, And because he would not long dwell in the contrariety that we should come ~~that we should come~~ with some competent number of the gravest this after noone/

Hereuppon there were some xl selected my selfe being one & we went presently to confer for the strengtthening the reasons.

One thing is to be remembered that yt was moved that we should

---

[126] 29 Eliz. I cap. 6 (cl. 6). *SR*, iv, 772.

be sutors to his majestie to be present him selfe at the conference and not to have yt related to him by the counsell, this caused some dispute by reason of the difference of opinion, but being put to the question the house overruled yt & so the privy counsell of the house wer sent to move his majestie who most gratiously gave us audience in the counsell chamber which was then the place where his majestie useth to heare the sermons and there uppon some debate of both sides & this poynt urged to the judges that was never before, that the first writt was not well returned & that in truth nether **Sir Frauncis Goodwin**, nor **Sir Jhon Fortescue** could be by these writts, his majestie ordered that nether the one nor other should be & that a new writt should go to choose an other: <u>& that the writt shoulde be graunted to go oute of the lower house/ & this we all assented to:</u> his majestie used many mo loving & gracious speaches unto us and at last not only pardoned them that had spoken <u>most & stoutest in this cause but thought the best of them/</u>[127]

In the forenoone when the committees ~~sate the~~ went to the conference the house sate ~~but no~~ So that I know not what was donne after, but I heard that ther was a bill sent from the Lords & the courte rejorned till Wedensday in Easter weeke.[128]

Wedensday 11 Aprill

40 bill	An act agaynst transporting
13 Aprill cotted	brogging & ingrossing of woll & wollen yarne
41 bill	An act of explanation of the
16 Ap: 2 read: cott:	common law in certayne cases of letters patents

Sir Fran Bacon declared that he had obeyed the houses command in attending his majestie but had no authority to make reporte because the committees had not mett, whereuppon yt was moved that the committees should go & confer together & so geve reporte to the house, which accordingly was donne & then **Sir Fr. Bacon** related: after whose speach on **Mr. Brooke** an outeward Barrister[129] charged the committees for exceeding there auctority & would have had them cald oute by the ?7 or x^ty & to have answered yt at Barr, but yt was answered by divers & the house satisfied and all ?relent to the [?for]mer motion &

---

[127] These phrases are underlined in the text.
[128] *CJ*, i. 167. The bill assured lands to the Dean and Chapter of Windsor.
[129] Christopher Brooke, MP for York.

order taken to give his majestie thanks by [?Mr. Speaker].[130]

Thursday 12 Aprill
This day wer read no new bills but only bills of the second reading:

After dinner we went with our Speaker to geve his majestie thancks & had audience in the privy gallery & there his majestie made a notable speach to us agayne.

Friday 13 Apr.

42 bill	An act concerning Vernon &
30th hard the counsel	Power.[131]
4 May dashed	
43 bill	An act to explane an act the
30 June passed	43 of Ell for the Nevills sale of
	land.[132]

This day Mr. Speaker related to us his majesties speach.

After was handled **Sir Tho: Sherley** his cause & Simpson & the serjant sent to the tower:[133]

Saterday 14 [April]

44	An act for ~~make~~ sale of Edward
2 May comitt	Downes his land for payment of
16 June passed	his debtes.

A message from the Lords by Justice Gawdy Baron Savile Serjeant Crooke & Mr. Atturney to have a conference aboute the greatest & wayghtiest matter to be handled this parliament touching the union & to meete this afternoone in the wonted place at two of the clock: the nomber of the lords to 40/we assented to yt & appoynted 100.

In the afternoone The Lord Chancelor/ declaring that we had allraedy acknowleged his majesties Just & lawfull title to the crowne, both the kingdomes being now united in his person as head, both bound in allegeanc to him & both united in religion, this was the Act of God for which we wer bound to geve thancks, and allready donne & therefore not to be talked of.

---

[130] For this debate, see *CJ*, i. 168. Mountagu's account is difficult to read as it is crammed on to the bottom of a page.

[131] Dispute between Sir Robert Vernon and **Sir William Herbert** over conveyance of lands in Montgomeryshire.

[132] Enacted as 1 Jac. I cap. 36.

[133] Sherley had been arrested shortly before the start of the session, while under parliamentary privilege.

The care of the King to have these established hath thought of some things fitt to be propounded, not to the lords alone nor to the commons alone but joyntly to both as one body. This being the first parliament All the princes of the world had an eyewhat would be donne at this time whefore thes things wer fitt further to be thought of.

First the diversity of the names of this one Iland England & Scotland, which very division of name hath bene the cuase of spenting much blood & because this was no new thing yt was shewed that in H8: time when a match was talked of betwene Ed the 6 & this kings mother that was in proposition to bring them to one name, to witt Brittayne & therefore now to be propounded for the uniting of the union.

Secondly there different lawes & different customes, nether of the parliament of England & Scotland can do this of a sodayne, & therefore that by the auctority of both ther may be appoynted of the nobility Clergy & commons selected commissioners to see what lawes are to be taken away what to be new made what to be else donne for the perfecting of the union.

If this should be liked of (not meaning that the acts of the commissioners should binde) but to relate the proceedings in full parliament & there to have them ratified.

His majesties pleasure was that we should fall to publike busines of those to such as wer most publick especially this: & that all other busnes should be layd aside till something wer effected in this.

We had no commission but to hear ther Lordships propositions & ~~the~~ relating them to the house they should ~~withoute have~~ have answer, they desired yt might be with all speed convenient/ & still remembred us that in this we wer not devided but staid as one body.

While we wer in the conference the house sate & red

45 bill	A very long bill betwene the
passed 25 Aprill	colleg of Windsore & therle of Hartford.[134]

We came to the relating of yt which being donn Mr. Speaker rose/[135]

Monday 16 Aprill

46 Bill	An act for the true receyving of
comttd	Homage & fealty by the greate chamberlane of England for &

[134] Enacted as 1 Jac. I cap. 32.
[135] The text breaks off abruptly at the bottom of the page; this was presumably the motion for Recorder Mountagu to report the proceedings of the conference to the House on 16 April.

on the behalfe of the Kings majestie.

Sir Frauncis Hastings motion for the establishing of religion & for the increasing, settling, continuing & mayntayning a learned ministry: this was cottd to be considered of.

Mr. Speaker delivered unto us that he had receyved a message from the kyngs Majestie that he understood where wer devers greeffs complayned of touching commissaries courtes & that we dealt in matters of discipline & therefore wished that there might be a conference betwene the Bishops & us, which was consented to:[136]

47 bill	An act aboute brede well.[137]
27 Aprill comitted	
28 June dashed	

The reporte was made of the Lords conference concerning the union: & day geven till Wedensday morning & then to have yt debated in the house & after the Lords to be sent to what time we would confer agayne.

Sir Thomas Sherleys cause & the presidents read: & after debate in the house this concluded

That he was to have privelege: but because the creditor might not loose his debte, nor the Warden of the Fleete be in danger for an escape, ordered that he should not be delivered till peticion made according to former presidents for the saveing of them:

Tuesday 17 [April]
The house was sett before I came but I hard there had bene red ij bills.

48	A bill aboute Mrs. Lucas to
May 10 dashed	reverse the act made the last 24 Aprill committed parliament.[138]
49	A bill aboute defeating a trust by one Freake.[139]

[136] This was one of the three points Mountagu himself had moved on 23 March.
[137] Bill to confirm the charter of the Bridewell Hospital. *CJ*, i. 173.
[138] The 1601 act made the estate of the late Edward Lucas liable to legacies in the will of John Flowerdew. *CJ*, i. 175.
[139] Unidentified but, in the context, presumably the Le Grys v. Cotterell estate bill. *CJ*, i. 175.

~~Sir Rob~~

One **Ty** had written a letter to Mr. Speaker which he made knowen to the house wherein he had somwhat taxed the speaker/ & so confessed his error/[140]

50	An act for a subsedie of
5 Jun comttd	Tonnage & Pondage
14 Jun passed	

Mr. Speaker renewed his motion aboute conference with the bishopps as he was directed by message from his majestie & delivered certayne reasons which he read because he would not ?mistay yt, the message was delivered by the Bishop of London to him & then yt was propounded that our conference should be with the convocation house but we utterly refused yt:

51	**Sir Tho Sherleys** peticion
comtt: ingrossed 20	twise read & committed.[141]
Aprill: passed 27 Aprill	

Wedensday 18 Aprill
the house sat before I came.[142]

52	An act to avoyde the number of
21: committed	alehouses ~~A new byll for suppressing of number of Alehowses & disorders in the/ brought in by~~ **Mr. Hext** & ~~read~~ & disorders in tipling houses// brought in by **Mr. Hext** & read.
53 bill:	An act for all merchants to have
passed	free liberty to trade in all countreys.

Mr Speaker deliverd unto us that his majesties Intention by commanding a conference with the convocation was not to bring in new precedents or to abridge our former liberties & therefore liked well we should

[140] John Tey, MP for Arundel. *CJ*, i. 175.

[141] Sherley attempted to resolve his privilege case by undertaking to settle the debt for which he had been arrested and exonerate the Warden of the Fleet from any liability for his release under parliamentary privilege.

[142] The only bill Mountagu missed was another relating to alehouses. *CJ*, i. 176.

confer with the Lords Bishopps or Lords of Parliament./

And willed us to fall into the matter of union so that day was spent on that.

Adhuc Wedesday 18 Aprill[143]

This day we receyved a message from the lords being a bill aboute diminucion of Archbishopps etc.

And the BB[144] desired time to geve answer for the conference.

Thursday 19 Aprill

the reasons for mayntayning of the bill of purveyors were committed back agayne to the committees.

A message from the Lords who brought three privat bills[145] ~~all private~~
~~An acte~~
~~Mr. Speaker~~

An other message from the Lords wherein they did approve of our care for the bill of Iron ordinance, but for the stay of them that wer ready to be shipped because they had yt but by relation from us & therefore we best knew the certaynty of yt therefore that we should move yt our selves to the Speaker & they would be [sic] geve us there best assistance.

For the Conference with the BB, the Lords yelded to have one with us uppon Saterday in the greate chamber & there nomber to be 30: we appoynted 60:

Bill 14   Mr. Speaker sat that after
                                           noone & red 14 private bills./

Friday 20 Aprill
The house was sett before I came.[146]

bill   A private Bill for Sir Tho: Jermy.
11 Jn dashed

bill   A bill for the well ordering of
25 Aprell dashed   Spinners & weavers & agaynst

---

[143] This note is at the top of a new page in the manuscript.

[144] i.e. Bishops.

[145] Two private bills were brought from the Lords on 19 April, one for naturalization of Sir George Home, the other for confirmation of letters patents to Home. *LJ*, ii. 782.

[146] Mountagu must only have missed prayers, as Jermy's bill is the first item of business recorded in *CJ*, i. 179.

transporting woll & wollen cloths.

bill

25 Aprill comtt

19 May dashed:

An act to take away the benefitt of clergy from some kinde of manslaughter:

bill

27 Ingrossed

An act for releffe of playntiffs where the party in execution have bene set at liberty by the parliament.[147]

Satterday 21 [April]

2 read comtt

7 May passed

A bill aboute Alehouses brong in by **Mr. Hext**

No new bills this day but we herd the reporte of the Kings speach reported by **Mr. Bacon**/[148] see all things in a paper by them selves/[149] conference for religion put of & conference for union or[150]

adhuc Saterday

these bills sent from the lords

1 An act for naturalising Sir George Hume knight Lord Treasor of Scotland his wiffe & children/ passed
2 An act for naturalising Lodovick Steward duck of Lennox & James the Lord daubeney[151] passed
3 An act for confirmation of letters patents to Sir George Hume/ passed
4 An act against diminution of Archb: & BB & for avoyding dilapidations/ passed

Monday 23 [April]

bill

26 comttd 28 Ingrosd

7 May passed:

An act for the quiet setling of the lands of Sir George Rodney deceased.[152]

bill

An act for explanation of the

---

[147] i.e. The bill to provide a remedy for the dilemma posed by Sherley's privilege case.
[148] i.e. Sir Francis Bacon.
[149] Northants. RO, Mountagu MS 29/71, for which see pp. 96–99.
[150] Text ends abruptly at the bottom of a page.
[151] Esme, Lord D'Aubigny.
[152] Enacted as 1 Jac. I, cap. 31.

30 May dashed   statute 27 H 8 cap 18 aboute
                                        Cole.[153]

Sir Francis Bacon related our procedings with the Lords one Saterday
aboute the union, see in the paper by yt selfe.

Tuesday 24 [April]
bill   An act for the true making of
                                        all kinde of wollen cloths & for
                                        alnaging selling and transporting
                                        the same.

bill   An act that no recusant con-
                                        victed, or any attaynted of
                                        forgery or perjury or any
26: commtt.   outelawed person or contemner
                                        of the law to be of the par-
                                        liament.

bill   An act for inlargement of trade
2 read comttd   of his majesties subjects in for-
                                        rayne countrys

bill   An act how many Coopers,
2 read comtt: Brewers & vinegar men may
                                        keepe

Wedensday 25 Aprill
bill   An act to put in execution the
25 Ap: comttd   statutes agaynst shooting in
19 May dashed   guns & preserving feasants &
                                        partriges & agaynst killing of
                                        hares.

26 cotted: 2 May   An act to restrayne all persons
Ingrossed: 8 May passed   from marriage till there former
                                        ~~husbandes &~~ wives & husbands
                                        be dead.[154]

---

[153] The 1536 Act concerned the taking of ballast from the Thames. *SR*, iii. 550.
[154] Enacted as 1 Jac. I, cap. 11.

Thursday 26 [April]

bill	An act for establishing divers land of Edward late duke of Sommersett:

Friday 27 Aprill

bill	An act for Caltrop to make his wiffe a joynture.[155]
2 red comitt	
1 May Ingrossed 14 May passed	
bill	An act for erecting a church of Melcome Regis & making yt the parish church of Radipole:
2 read commtt:	
a new bill brought	
bill	An act to restryne weares, stangs etc. uppon greate rivers.
comttd	
bill	An act to establish divers orders concerning clothers spinners weavers & sheeremen:
bill	An act agaynst new buildings & agaynst inmates in & neer London etc.
2 read comtt	

Saterday 28 Ap
The house sate before I cam.[156]

~~2 read comttd~~	~~An act concerning tanning of leather~~
bill	An act to prevent overcharging the country by stewards of courte leets & courte barons.
7 May comtt: 19	
passed:	
bill	An act to declare the mariages of the ministers of the Gospels of Christe to be lawfull.
11 May comttd	
bill	An act to retayne his majesties subjects in there due obedience. this had an other title: ?laid for
The former parte of this bill	
passed:	

[155] Enacted as 1 Jac. I, cap. 34.
[156] Three bills had been read and two reported from committee before the point at which Mountagu's notes begin.

execution of the statutes agaynst
recusants.

I went into the courte of wards having ther a matter of hearing/ so
that I know not what was donne in my absence[157] but after my ~~coming~~
returning these matters

bill	} sleepe	An act agaynst grub-
2 read committ		bing up of coppice
		woods
	} & new	
	} bill to	
bill	} be put	An act for pre-
2 read committd		servation of wood &
		timber
	} in	

bill   An act for reformation of abuses
6 May committ   in theschequer[158] agaynst Sheriffs
                              collectors of subsidie & other
                              accomptants.

bill   An act for the true measuring of
22 May comttd   oates.
16 June passed

This day we had or conference agayne with the Lords aboute the
union/ see the matters handled in that discourse.[159]

Monday 30 Aprill
bill   An act agaynst the false making
10 comttd   of mildernex & poledavies
21 June passed   whereof the sale cloth for ship-
                              ping is made.

bill   An act to ~~make~~ inable Sir Hugh
3 May dashed   Losse to sell land for payment of
                              his debts.

bill   An act concerning taking
2 read comt   Apprentices

---

[157] During Mountagu's absence the house received complaints about purveyance, sent
two messages to the Lords and read two bills.
[158] i.e. The Exchequer.
[159] Northants. RO, Montagu MS 29/73, printed below.

6 May Ingrossed
8 May passed

21 May passed: An act touching tanners cur-
                                            riers & shomakers

A message from the Lords who sent a bill for naturalising Kin losse.[160]
Vernon & Power cause debated by counsell at Bar.[161]
The ~~aftern~~ Lords sent to us to have a conference this afternoone aboute
the union/

Tuesday 1 May
bill   An act for Butlers land.[162]
2 read comttd

bill   An act for continuance & explan-
5 May comtt   ation of the statute of Rouges
19 May passed   made 39 Ell.[163]

This morning we receyved a letter from the King which see in his
place.
   This afternoone we conferred with Lords for the poynts of the
commission in the union.[164]

xij bills red this after noone   The house sate that after
                                            noone & red xij private bills.[165]

Wedensday 2 May
bill   An act for reformation of abuses
3 May comitt   in alehouses lately converted into
                                            Inns.

Thursday 3 May
bill   An act about children of stran-
Quere the title of the bill   gers demised.[166]

---

[160] Sir Edward Bruce, Lord Kinloss.
   [161] *CJ*, i. 193 states that the suit was between Sir Robert Vernon and **Sir William Herbert**.
   [162] To confirm an entail made by Henry Butler upon the marriage of his son William. *CJ*, i. 193.
   [163] The 1597 Vagrancy Act, 39 Eliz. I cap. 4. *SR*, iv. 899–902.
   [164] Northants. RO, Montagu MS 29/73.
   [165] For which see *CJ*, i. 194.
   [166] A bill to give children born in England to alien parents the status of denizens. *CJ*, i. 197.

22 May dashed

bill 3 May comttd: 25 May passed:	An act for assartes

Friday 4 [May]

bill 11 May comttd/	An act for the erecting of a parish church of the burrow of blinley
bill 14 June 2 rea: dashd	An act for the true Imployment of the releefe for the poore/
bill 4 May comtt 17 May passed:	The Lord of Kin losse his bill.

Saterday 5 [May]

bill	An act agaynst letters patents for transporting of sheepskin.[167]
bill comtt: 25 May dashed	An act for registring Judgement etc.[168]
comtted bi'	An act to take away abuses of customers.[169]
bill first Read: dashed	An act having a long title, but theffect was to have the names of aliens to be registred.[170]

This day the house concluded of the poynts to be conferred on with the Lords for matters of Religion:

A message from the Lords to confer aboute the purveyors appoynting yt to be to morrow in the afternoone. But the house disliked to sitt on & the sabboth day & refused that but sent to the Lords to appoynt an other day who did appoynt Tuesday morning/

---

[167] The bill must simply have been tabled at this point, as no reading is recorded in *CJ*, i. 199.

[168] A bill to register legal judgements which might affect land titles. *CJ*, i. 199.

[169] i.e. Customs officials.

[170] 'For the better safety of the realm, that his Majesty may take notice where aliens and strangers are inhabiting.' *CJ*, i. 199.

Monday 7 May

bill	An act for the better explanation
14 May comtt	of the statute of bankrupts.
13 Jun passed:	

Tuesday 8 [May]

bill	An act aboute drayning the
12 May comttd	fenns:

comtt	An act betwene Le Grice &
21 May Ingrossd	Cottrell
2 July passd	

An act aboute explanation of the statute for releffe of the poore.

A message from the Lords who sent these bills 3 bill

26 comtt: L.	An act agaynst withcraft
passed: 7 June	

11 May comtt/ Lo:	An act for the restoring of Lord
passed:	Will Howard etc.

22 May passed: L	An act for naturalising Sir Jhon Ramsey

And that they would conferr on Monday for the matters of Religion/

Wedensday 9 [May]

bill	An act for due proffe of ped-
dashed	egrees & discents

bill	An act for explanation 5 Ell. for
2 read dashed	Tanners[171]

bill	An act concerning wherry men &
2 read comtt/	water men.
22 May passed	

bill	An act for costs in a prohibition.
2 read comtt/ dashed	

[171] 5 Eliz. cap. 8. *SR*, iv. 429–36.

bill	An act to take away all excuse for comming to the church.[172]

Thursday 10 [May]

bill 25 May Ingrossd. dashd:	An act for the continuance of lawes & mayntenance of the navy & setting mariners on worke.
bill dashed when it came to Ingrossing	An act for preventing false dice
bill 2 read comttd	An act for the explanation & more due execution of a decree for tythes in London

Friday 11 [May]

dashed: bill	An act agaynst bringing in for-rayne woolls.

Sateday 12 [May]

bill 2 read dashed	An act concerning vagrants & wandring shomakers that go aboute with naughty ware.
first read comtt 29 May passed/	An act for naturalising Sir Roger Astons lady.

Monday 14 [May]

bill 31 May passed:	An act for recovery of small debts in London.

Tuesday 15 [May]

bill 2 read comtt	A bill of Henry Le Grice.

A message from the Lords who sent these bills[173]

---

[172] Not mentioned in *CJ*, i. 204, 967–8.

[173] Two other bills, for Exchequer procedure and the Trinity College-Mounson land exchange, were also sent down at this time. *CJ*, i. 210.

bill LL 22 Jun dashed.	An act agaynst killing of deer & conies.
LL bill passed: passed	An act: An act for naturalising diver of English borne beyond sea:[174]

This day one Jhones a printer delivered a bill to Mr. Speaker which charged the B: of London with high treason the Speaker red but only the title but would not reade the bill, the party was reteyned with the serjeant till further examination had of him by Mr. Speaker.[175]

[Blank page in MS][176]

Saterday 19 May bill 22 comttd 12 Jun passed:	An act that Jhon Tiball may make his wiffe a joyncture & sell land.[177]
bill 23 May comttd: 25 Ingrossed 11 Jun passed:	An act for building a church in Melcombe Regis, this is a new bill the old was changed.
bill L	A message from the Lords who sent ij bills
bill LL: 31 May comttd 22 Jun passed	An act for the assignement of certayne soms of money for the defraying of the charge of his majesties honorable household.
bill L: 22 June comttd: passed	An act for Apparrell./
~~bill~~	~~An act concerning whery men &~~

[174] Thomas Glover, Margaret Mordant, Francis Collymore, Alexander Daniell, Nicholas Gilpine and Mary Copcote. The bill was enacted as 1 Jac. I, cap. 29.

[175] See *CJ*, i. 210.

[176] On Monday 14 May Mountagu was granted leave of absence to attend a lawsuit he had pending the following day at the Guildhall [*CJ*, i. 209]; there are no entries for 16–18 May, but he left a blank page at this point in his parliamentary diary.

[177] Enacted as 1 Jac. I, cap. 37.

~~2 May passed:~~   ~~watermen.~~[178]

Monday 21 [May]
A message from the Lords aboute answer to their desire for conference in the matter of wards they appoynted Friday/ & ther nomber 30.
   They sent two bills

bill Lo.	A bill for the Lady Kildares
26 May comttd	Joyncture.[179]
13 Jun passed	

bill Lo.	An other bill to enable Tho
26 May comttd.	Throgmorton to sell land to pay
15 Jun passed:	his debts.[180]

Tuesday 22: [May]
bills passed: A bill for Berwick.

Wedensday 23 [May]

bill:	An act for the sale of Sir Tho:
4 Jun passed:	Rowse his land for payment of
	his debtes.[181]

bill	divers bills aboute Alehouses.[182]
committed.	

   We sate this afternoone.
   A message from the Lords who sent a bill.

26 May passed: An act for confirming the queens
                                                        Joyncture presently read.[183]

23 comtt: 7 Jun	A new bill of Hatts.
passed:	

[178] The third reading of this bill was deferred until Monday 21 May; it eventually passed on 22 May. *CJ*, i. 215, 222.
[179] Enacted as 1 Jac. I, cap. 18.
[180] Enacted as 1 Jac. I, cap. 28.
[181] Enacted as 1 Jac. I, cap. 30.
[182] Three of the various bills for regulation of alehouses were all consigned to the same committee. *CJ*, i. 222.
[183] *CJ*, i. 224 states that this bill received first and second readings the following morning, but *ibid.* 978 concurs with Mountagu.

Thursday 24 May

bill comttd LL 19 Jun passd	An act for naturalising therle of Mar.
bill 9 Jun comttd.	An act: agaynst usury.
bill 2 read dashed.	An act agaynst Inconveniences of barges going by the river of Lee.[184]
passed	Sir Tho: Erskins bill for naturalising.[185]

A message from the Lords who sent ij bill

bill Lo 15 June passed	one for naturalising Sir J Drommond.[186]
bill Lo. 15 Jun passed:	Thother for Sir James Hay.[187]

Friday 25 [May]

bill 16 Jun comttd 30 June passed	An act agaynst brokers.
bill dashed.	Gill Warrens bill for confirming a decree.[188]
bill 1 Ju: comttd:	An act for reformation of abuses in Informers in penall statutes.
bill uppon committment	An act for ~~explanation~~ the beter execution of the statutes 39

---

[184] i.e. the Lea river to the north-east of London. This reading is not recorded in *CJ*, i. 224–5, 978–9.

[185] Enacted as 1 Jac. I, cap. 17.

[186] Enacted as 1 Jac. I, cap. 24.

[187] Enacted as 1 Jac. I, cap. 21.

[188] *CJ*, i. 225 merely cites this as a bill 'for confirmation of a decree in Chancery made for payment of money and re-assurance of a lease'. It was presumably the bill committed on 2 June [*ibid*. 231], but there is no record of its being dashed, as Mountagu states.

left till next Session.	Elisabeth concerning Tillage.
bill	An act for releffee of poore burrows & townes corporate:
Saterday 26 [May] bill 6 Jun comttd passed:	An act aboute setling those that are infected with the plauge.[189]
bill	An act to avoyde all decests in clothing diing & dressing the same.
bill 30 May comttd: 11 Jun passed:	An act that those that shall be restored in blood shall take the oath of supremacy.
bill Lo. 2 read comttd 7 June passed:	An act for change of lands betweene Trinity college in Cambrige & Sir Tho: Mounson.
bill 30 May cott: 8 June passed:	An act for the better exevutions of former statutes agaynst shoting in guns killing phesants partriges Hares etc.

Mr. Tay[190] made a motion agaynst the bishop of Bristows booke for answering the objections made at the conference aboute the union.[191]

The house found them selves much aggreeved at the booke & thereuppon sent to the Lords to confer for some order to be taken in yt.

A message from the Lords.

The booke was new to them & therefore they would consider of yt at our next ~~meeting~~ sitting we should heere from them, they wer determined to sitt on Monday but we did adjourne our sitting till Wedensday.[192]

[189] i.e. Plague.

[190] i.e. John Tey, MP for Arundel.

[191] John Thornborough, *A Discourse plainely proving the evident Utilitie and urgent necessitie of the desired happie Union of the two famous Kingdomes of England and Scotland* (London, 1604), repr. in *Harleian Miscellany*, ix. 95–105. This outcry occasioned the book's suppression, see *HMC Hastings*, iv. 2.

[192] Because of the feast of Whit Sunday on 27 May.

bill Lo: They sente us withall a bill
15 Jun comttd.   Agaynst abuses in paynting.
21 June passed:

Whitsontide.

Wedensday 30 May
   A message from the Lords who sent

bill LL   The bill of union; presently read.
1 Jun ingrossed: 2 passed

bil   An act for confirmation of letters
4 Jun comttd./   patents.[193]
Ingrossed.

An other message from the Lords who sent 3 bills.

bill LL   An   act   agaynst   deditious
1 Jun reade 6 J comttd: popish & lascivious bookes.
5 July dashed

bill LL   An act for H Jerningham to sell
7 Jun comttd.   lands to pay his debts.[194]
passed:

bill LL   An act for naturalising of the
9 Jun read   Vincents.[195]
15 Jun passed.

Mr. Speaker delivered us his majesties pleasure to attend him that
afternoone: which accordingly with the Speaker we did in the greate
banquetting rom ther we attend and conceyvd some greeffe at his
majesties speach.
   The Lords sent us word to have a conference aboute the bishop of
Bristows booke, there number 24 & ours was 50.

---

[193] To Sir George Home, *CJ*, i. 228.
[194] Henry Jernegan of Norfolk. Enacted as 1 Jac. I, cap. 33.
[195] Enacted as 1 Jac. I, cap. 38.

Thursday 31 May
~~bill LL~~   ~~Jernaghan~~[196]

bill   An act to make the contracts of
4 Jun comttd   Infants voyd withoute consent of
                                      parents & gardeans

A message from the LLs to put of the conference of Religion till
Monday: next.

Friday 1 June
The house sate before I came.

bills   A [*sic*] for the false packing of
1 Jn Ingrossed: Hopps.[197]
11 Jn passed:

Saterday 2 Jun
bill   An act to incourage the seamen
20 Jun comttd   of England to take fish.
30 Jun passed.

A message from the Lords who sent the bill for laborers & the bill for
Berwick with amendments.

Monday 4 [June]
bill   An act for a learned ministry.
4 Jun comttd
7 Jun passed

bill   An act agaynst pluralitie of bene-
4 Jun comttd   fices with cure.[198]
11 Jn passed

   This afternoone we mett with the Lords aboute matters of religion
who refused to joyne with us in a peticion. And the bishop of London
read a writing from the convocation, inhibiting the bishopps to confer
with us, for that the layity hadd not to meddle in these matters now

---

[196] Mountagu crossed this out because he had already made a note of the bill when it
arrived from the Lords the previous day.
[197] i.e. The bill was reported on this day. *CJ*, i. 230.
[198] These bills were assigned to the committee appointed to consider Mountagu's
motion of 23 March.

the King had graunted them Letters patents prosesting [*sic*: protesting] that if they did proceed they would appeale to the King.

Tuesday 5 June
bill   An act for Garbling of Spices.
Ingrossed & 11
passed[199]

bill   The continuance of Statutes.
[5] June comttd:
[22] June passed[200]

bill   An act to avoyde haunting in
5 Jun passed.   Alehouses Taverns & Inns.

Mr. Speaker delivered us a message, from his majestie, ~~which was~~ from him selfe gracious to us comfortable consisting of these partes

1 The motive of some conceyte of unkindenes
2 The cause of his relation & sending for us
3 his princely satisfaction

For the first when he looked into the greate gravity of the house the like whereof had not been, And the continuance of the parliament & litle donne & so much time spent in privelege whereof he had as greate regard as our ~~selfes~~ selves, & some delayes of other matters, and not that haste in some matters which he looked for: This moved a jelousy: for never Prince esteemed better of a people then he did of us and oute of this love of his, rather as a parent by way of admonition moved him the last time to speake as he did unto us & not to taske us of ~~of~~ ingratitude.

Then he doth absolutely resolve him selfe we have not proceeded in any thing agaynst him noting our dutifull & tender regard in taking these things he sayd unto us so tenderly and our desire to geve him satisfaction.

He noted how since that time we have proceeded with speede in those things which he did desier.

And gave us thancks And that we should not troble our selves to geve him satisfaction he being fully satisfied:

[199] The date of this third reading is not noted in *CJ*, i. 236–7, 989–90.
[200] The dates are lost by a tear in the page. *CJ*, i. 232, 244.

Wedensd. [6 June]
Matter of second readings & ~~re~~[201]

Thursd 7 June
7 Jun comttd   A bill for Archery.[202]
13 Jun 2 read dashed.[203]

A message from the Lords to geve us meeting for the Bishop of Bristows booke on Saterday.

bi LL   An act for naturalising Jhon
15 Jun passed: Guerdon the deane of Sarum.[204]

LL   An act for restitution of Litleton
21 June passed: in blood:[205]

Friday 8 [June]
bill   An act for frustrating a release
                                           of Edm Penny & others.[206]

Sir Frauncis Hastings related what had passed at the conference for religion & shewd the partes of the prohibition which the B of London read/
     The house tooke yt in ill parte/ chose a committee to consider of that: & to draw a peticion for ~~ cerem~~ tolleration of ceremonies.

Saterday 9 Jun
bill   ~~An act for naturalising of the Vincents.~~

bill   An act for releeffe of those that
comttd: use the trade of Skinners.
13 Jun 2 read: dashed

comttd bill   A new bill/ to take away clergy
Ingrossd 21 Jun passed   in some cases of manslaughter.

---

[201] Presumably 'reports'; five bills were reported to the House on 6 June. *CJ*, i. 233.
[202] The printed *CJ* [i. 233, 237] misread the title of this bill as being 'for the maintenance of artillery'.
[203] The bill was committed at its second reading on 7 June, but reported as being unfit to continue on 13 June.
[204] John Gordon, Dean of Salisbury. Enacted as 1 Jac. I, cap. 22.
[205] Enacted as 1 Jac. I, cap. 26.
[206] Edmond Penning. *CJ*, i. 234.

bill comtt: 11 June passed:	An act about fishing in Devon Sommersett & cornewale
bill 1 read rejected	An act of repeale of som parte of the statute 21 H 8: for persons to take farmes.[207]
Monday [11 June] bill 11th ~~Jun passed~~	~~Teballs bill:~~
Tuesday 12 [June] bill 22 Jun comttd	An act agaynst atturneys & clarkes in the courtes of common pleas & kings bench.
bill read rejected:	An act for reforming thoffice of Garbler in to the Kings hand:
bill 2 read: rejected	An act for suppressing innov- ation in the church of England/ theffect was to take an oath ~~for~~ to the goverment & ceremonies.
Wedensday 13 [June] bill 2 Jun ~~comttd~~ dashed	An act for explanation of the statutes in prohibitions & consultacions/[208]
bill 14 Jun comttd passed	An act for the better observation of orders in theschequer[209] by vertue of the Queenes privy seale:
bill 13 June comttd: 22 June passed	An act for avoyding multiplicity of leasses by Archb. & BB:/

This morning the peticion was presented to the house for the tolleration

---

[207] i.e. Leases of church lands. *CJ*, i. 235. 21 Hen. VIII, cap. 13. *SR*, iii. 292–6.

[208] 'in spiritual causes' *CJ*, i. 237.

[209] i.e. Exchequer.

of ceremonies: twise read & ordered to be sent to his majestie/[210]

Thursday 14 Jun
bill
2 read cotted
20: Ingrossed
21 Jun passed

An act agaynst masters of colleges etc. to be maried and agaynst keeping there wives in the college.

bill

A new bill for tithes in London.[211]

Friday 15 Jun
   passing of bills

Saterday 16 Jun:
bill
20 Jun comtted/
28 Jun passed

An act ~~agaynst~~ for reforming of abuses in taking pilchards in Devon & Cornewall:

bill
18 Jun comttd
28 Jun passed

An act for the better discovery of Simony.

A message from the Lords who sent the bill of Rouges[212] with good amendements/ And Calthrops bill.

LL
19 Jun passed.

And for naturalising Sir Jhon Kennidy:[213]

Monday 18 June
bill
2 read comttd

An act for releeffe of parsons & vicars of cure of soules.

bill
twise read: comttd
27 Jun passed

An act for disburdening of clergymen of such offices as hinder them in there divine callinges & cure[s]

bill
2 read comttd.

An act for the true making & serching of wollen clothes.

[210] The petition is printed in *CJ*, i. 238. No order for presentation to the King is recorded for that day.
[211] The bill was given a first reading on the recommendation of the committee for the earlier bill. *CJ*, i. 238–9.
[212] i.e. Rogues.
[213] Enacted as 1 Jac. I, cap. 23.

A message from the Lords to desire a conference aboute the bill of Tonnage & Pondage, there number 30 to morrow in the depict chamber[214] we appoynted 60/

Tuesday 19 Jun
bill   An act for naturalising Sir Will
22 Jun passed: Brownes children.[215]

bill   An act to compell deputy lieu-
2 read dashed: tenants   &   Treasorers   to
                                      accounte:

Wedensday 20 [June]
bill   An act for reviving the statute
dashed   for hempe.

bill   An act for abuses in making
cottd: starch.

bill   An   act   aboute   wharffs   in
comttd   London/

Thursday 21 June
bill   An act for better releffe of min-
dashed   isters in corporate townes.

Friday 22 June
bill rejected:[216]   An act for the payment of per-
                                      sonall tithes vid: the xxty parte
                                      of every ones gaynes.

bill rejected   An act for assigning oute of every
                                      impropriation   a   convenient
                                      portion for the cure.

bill passed   An act agaynst Scandalous min-
                                      isters.

bill twise read comttd/   An act for reviving certayne stat-
                                      utes expired by the death of the
                                      Queene.

---

[214] *Camera Picta* or Painted Chamber.
[215] Enacted as 1 Jac. I, cap. 27.
[216] The rejection is recorded in *CJ*, i. 996a but not *ibid*. 244.

[Saturday] 23 June
[I] was at the common place, the case for serjeante ?James [?then]
being argued:

| [bill] | A bill to avoyd overlength of clothes.[217] |

[Mo]nday 25 June:

bi[ll]	An act agaynst unlawful hunting & killing of deere.
bill	An act to avoyd all decepts in clothing diinge & dressing of clothes.
2 read dashed	

Tuesday 26: [June]

bill	A bill aboute Tanners shomakers Curriers etc: the former bill sent to the Lords was dashed & was repealed 5 El: wheruppon this new bill was brought in.
18 Jun comttd: 2 July	
passed	

This day **Mr. Vicechamberline**[218] shewd us that he had recyved a
letter from his majestie which was read & now is printed: aboute matter
of subsidy.[219]

A message from the Lords who sent ij bills/

presently read &	1 An act for the execution of the statute agaynst Jesuits prests recusants.
27 Jun comttd	
1 July passed	
	2 a proviso for Tiball bill:/

Wedensday 27: [June]
The motion being made aboute collection for the poore according to
auncient order vid. every knight of shire x^s & a burgess v^s/ they misliked
to be tied by a presedent but to have yt arbitrary which being put to
the question uppon the old order: the house was divided the No: 126
the I: 119.[220]

---

[217] Second reading; rejected. *CJ*, i. 245.

[218] Sir John Stanhope, MP for Newtown, Isle of Wight.

[219] The King declined any offer of subsidy the Commons might vote.

[220] Mountagu has confused the motion which was to double the traditional contribution
of 5*s.* per knight and 2*s.* 6*d.* per burgess. This motion was rejected.

A day or two after they yelded a voluntary contriute [*sic*] which comm: to:

Thursday 28: [June]
The house having understanding of a blow his majestie had with a horsse they sent **Mr. Vicechamberline** presently to see his majestie who tooke the kindenes of the house in good parte.[221]

bill dashed:	An act for Increase of livings of vicars with Cure of souls.

A message from the LL: ij bill/

bill LL 29 June read 2 Jul cottd 4 July passed	1 An act for the releffe of Tho: Lo.[222]
bill LL passed.	2 For naturalising of Newton sholemaster.[223]

The message to desire a conference ab[out] the continuance of statutes, there number 30 at the greate chamber on Saterday And for the matter of the convocation, & the bishop of bristows booke the same committees to have auctoryty to confer of those.

We assented to yt & desired at that time a conference aboute the bill of recusants Jesuits etc. which they had sent unto us:

Friday 29 June	
bill 2 read rejected:	An act for cancelling defacing & avoyding of the deedes of Corbetts case to avoyd the deede of Sir Walter Mildemays
bill 2 read comttd	An act for Sir Christopher Hatton to sell land for payment of debtes.
bill	An act for the better releffe of the

---

[221] Motion of Sir Edward Hoby. *CJ*, i. 247–8.
[222] Thomas Lovell.
[223] Adam Newton, tutor to Prince Henry.

2 read ~~rejected~~   preachers of Norwich & Gloster.
   comttd/[224]

Saterday 30 June
bill   An act agaynst swearing & taking
ingrossed   the name of God in vayne.
3 July passed

A message from the Lords ij bills

bill LL: 1 An Act for confirmation of
2 July read 5 July   letters patents
cottd but disliked

LL: 2 the bill of the plauge with
                         amendement.

bill   An act agaynst Inmates
2 July comttd

Tuesday 3 July
A message from the Lords ij[225]

1 the garbling of Spices with amendments.
2 the bill for the haunting of alehouses with amendments.

A desire of a conference this afternoone at the presence in white hall
aboute the continuance of statutes by the same comttees/

Wedensday 4 July
A message from the Lords who returned ij bills with amendments

1 Nevells bill[226]   } by & by passed.
2 agaynst brokers   }

An other message from the Lords ij bills

                         1 the   amendement   of   con-
                         tinuance of statutes.

[224] Although technically committed, no committee was named and the bill was ordered
to sleep until the next session.
[225] i.e. Bringing down the following two bills.
[226] Estate bill for Sir Henry Neville of Byrling, Kent, enacted as 1 Jac. I cap. 36.

twise read & comtt:

2 An act proceeding from the Kings most princely wisdome & care of his Royall progenny for the perpetuall & indissolubly annexing of lands to the crowne etc.[227]

Thursday 5 July
We sent to have a conference aboute the kings bill[228] which was yesterday twise read & committed, the Lords returned us answer to have yt present to the nomber of 20 in the greate chamber & withall they desired a conference aboute the bill of free trade we assented & appoynted 40/

Friday 6 July
The conference was reported aboute the former bill & the kings bill was thought fitt to sleepe till the next Session.

Saterday 7ᵗʰ [July]
The Session ended & prorouged till the 7 of Feb: next.

Notes and Drafts of Speeches made by Sir Edward Mountagu during the 1604 Session

Northants. RO, Montagu MS 29.
Mountagu 29/7 Notes on abuses of commissaries' courts, 1604
[Endorsed] Some notes of the generall abuses of the commissaries courtes

First the multitudes of the courtes as the Bishops courte the chancelors courte & the Archdeacons courte they having one manner of proceeding, being of the same king & having in them for the most parte the same & no other officers:

Secondaly the commones of those courtes as ij every fortenight whereby some are constrayned to go every fortenight x or xij miles & some more: both winter & sommer besides the delay of causes for 2 or 3 yeares: drawing thereby greate charge to the subject: for the proctor is to have for every time iij*s*. iiij*d*. for his fee & for the acte every day iiij*d*.

---

[227] Mountagu drafted a speech on this subject, Northants. RO MS 29/44, for which see below, pp. 102–3.
[228] i.e. the annexation's bill.

Thirdly besides the usuall days wherein they keepe courtes there are oftentimes private courtes purchased agaynst men to there greate molestacion/

Fourthly beside the oftennes of the courtes they make men to come at other times when they list: to the offic & ther they wayght ij or iij days to be examined of what articles they list to propound/ & then they must come agayne before the next courte to putt in there answer, And the next courte they must be there to have there answers admitted: And thus under color of dispatch & riddance the weary oute men:

[Margin] these may be reduced to one

Fiftly that those who are no ecclesiasticall persons do exercise ecclesiasticall censures.

Sixtly: the chancelor & Archd: are Justices of peace whereby when they can not prevayle by the church censure to vex a man, they will committ him to prison by ther other auctority/

Seaventhly the officers in these courtes have place also in the courtes above so that uppon appeales there is much wrong nay many times caveats put in that there can be no inhibitions graunted.

Eyghtly there unreasonable fees & intollerable exactions.

Ninthly there oathe ex officion urging men to accuse them selves which if they refuse to do streyght they excomunicate/ And if they answer then they will take advantage uppon some unnessary circumstances & many other trikes they have in this course to gett money.

Tently the proctors swearing for there clients whereoute riseth many offences: & wrongs sometimes to others.

Eleventhly there excommunications for triffles & for the fees ther quicke absolucions/ both donne in one & the self same courte: in one day:

Twelthly the sending oute of Apparitors to spie faults & then if the churchwardens do not present they are punished, only with there pursse/

Thirtenth no fault to grosse & filthy but yt shuffled up for money.

Fourt'hly there easy admitting of compurgators.

Fiftenthly ther proctors oaths uppon bills of expenses.

Sixteently the Apparitours sommoning withoute warrant & there processe of *quorum nomina.*

Whereas we should conceyve hope of redresse of these things by the convocation house: the Clerkes ar not chosen by free voyce but by the Bishops letters & ~~sending~~ gathering of hands by the Apparitor, so that commonly the Chanc: & Archdea: are the clerkes or else those whom they will nominate/

I thinck yt hard to meete with or to make any one law to informe these & such like abuses, & therefore in my poore opinion I thinck the

Statute 25 He: 8: cap 19:[229] confirmed by 1 Ell: 1:[230] to be the best president we can worke by: Se likewise 3 Ed 6: cap 11.

That statute[231] gave auctority to the King to nominate 32 persons wherof 16 to be of the clergy, & xvj of the temporalty of the upper & nether house of parliament/ To view, Search & Examine the constitutions ordinances & Cannons provinciall & Sinodall, and such as should be thought by the more parte of them worthy to be abrogated and admitted should be abolished, And such other as should be approved to stand with the lawes of God & consonant to the lawes of this Realme should stand in strenght (The Kings most Royall assent first had & obteyned to the same.

Now ther is a proviso in that law that such ordinances etc. already made which be not repugnant to the lawes & customes of this realme nor to the hurte of the Kings prerogative shall be used as they wer before, untill such time as they be viewed searched or otherwise ordered or determined by the sayd 32 persons or the more part of them:

3 Ed 6. ca 11 the King during three years might appoynt 16 Spirituall men & 16 Temporall men to examine & compile ecclesiasticall laws: & devers articles concerning those matters, but tooke no effect.

So would I now during this parliament (for I do not like to refer it to commissioners hereafter) that there wer a convenient number chosen oute of both howses, & they to view, search & examine, what constitutions & cannons are fitt to stand & what to be left oute, And then to bring them in articles into the house, & they to allow of those which in there wisedomes they shall thinck fitt to stand And then to present them to his majestie for his Royall assent/ And those constitutions with this grave deliberation only to stand & be in force & the rest to be adnulled & abrogated: And then a booke to be published of them that all men may know them as they do the other statutes of the Realme, And this to continue for a triall till thend of the next parliament:

If this motion like the lower house then some to be sent to the Lords of the higher house to acquaynt them with yt, & to know there pleasures/

---

[229] 25 Hen. VIII, cap. 19, 'Act for the submission of the clergy to the King's Majesty'. *SR*, iii. 460–1.

[230] 1 Eliz. I cap. 1, Act of Supremacy. *SR*, iv. 350–5.

[231] 3&4 Edw. VI cap. 11, 'An act that the King's Majesty may nominate 32 persons to peruse and make ecclesiastical laws'. *SR*, iv. 111–12.

Notes on Union Debates of 21–27 April 1604
[Montagu MS 29/71]

Sir Francis Bacons relation of the Kings speach the 21 of Aprill 1604 made the day before

The King diswarned all that wer not ~~of the~~ parliament ~~house~~ men being a matter not for gasers.

He devided the speach into iiij parts/ 1 an Introduction.

2 a confutacion or solucion of doubtes we had used

3 an exxplanation & declaration of his true meaning

4 by way of example a kind of project of modell or frame of his intencion to passe from him.

The introduction consisted of 3 poynts 1 a delivering of the cause for which he had required our accesse 2 some note of our proceeding, 3 with what minde we should come to heare.

The cause drawing now neare to a conference to declare his meaning & to show his cristall brest:

For the notice of our proceeding/ our courses to be far from his expectacion in our debate & thought yt should have bene passed ~~with~~ as the recognition was/ & found fault with the common & ordinary talke of yt abroade.

The adomonition he deserved attention first in regard of his person 2 for the matter being the greatest & wayghtiest cause.

The solucion of doubte which wer/ 1 matter of Honor, 2 matter of law, 3 foresight of perill, 4 an Informality or misplacing to geve a name before the Kings

For Honor allowed that the nation had bene famous victorious & triumphant this honor was not to be divided for him & he had most interest in this And yf the halfe have be so honored the whole would be more.

For law yt was no meaning to alter them but in those weherein necessity required.

The name to be but a signe.

For the perill: Scotland should make an accession to England for the name before the thing he ~~thought~~ allowed him not a subject that thought yt was not allready donne:

The haste he required, because he was interessed in yt in Honnor & yt was already geven by forayne princes secondly for profite This was in his owne power desiring but our advise & corroboration.

That Scotland should begin before us, this was honor to us & Scotland should agree & would make them.

For the 3 poynte/ he did require 3 things & three things he did disclame.

He did require first that there should be a union 2 that with our assents he might take uppon him the name of King or monarch of Brittayne, 3 that there might be a commission for

He did disclame first that he ment not to suppresse the name or take away the name of England he preserves that & takes but his owne, 2 he had no meaning to alter the fundamentall lawes, liberties or priveleges of the kingdome that was the parte of Tirant, but in some where a necessity required yt 3 that he had no Intention that offices of england should bestowed on the Scottish & referred us in that poynct to his booke/ he had tasted allready of our obedience.

For the 4th poynct he dev read a writing dictated by his majestie which was a forme how we should set downe our assent to the proposition.

This direction geven

That the writing should be communicated to the house but with no intention to prejudicate the conference nor to try us to this forme but to shew his meaning/

Here should come in the Kings project

This after noone we conferred with the Lords.

[Monday 23 April]

On Monday **Sir Francis Bacon** made relation what had passed at the conference[232] which he devedede into 3 partes The entrance Substance & Issue:

The entrance what God had performed in this union & thother what the King had propounded/ to both which we wer to apply [sic ?apply] our conference/ The Lords according to the direction of the house began to us.

The Substance of 3 parts/ first the word Incorporated wherein was doubted somwhat was involved/ 2 the manner of naming commissioners: 3 the name yt selfe whether presently to be geven/ After some debate yt was desired that we should geve our reasons/ And if we did thinck there wer inconveniencs in those things they might be explaned & cautions geven.

The Issue because of the Inversion of there propositions & our Instruction we wer forced to leave of & to know the pleasure of the house.

Uppon this Sir Francis gave his Advise to the house first that there mandates might be more free 2 Whatsoever any man sayd at the meeting yt might be taken by way of objection not resolucion 3 that we might confer amongst our selves before we went to the Lords.

---

[232] Briefly related in *CJ*, i. 182.

That afternoone was appoynted by the comittees to meete in the parliament house which they did & so likewise on Tuesday the afternoone at both times the house was full:

Short heads of the objections[233]

first every change must be eyther by urgent necessity or evident utility:
2. *a ?conjugatis.* The King & Kingdome are relatives, that the King should change his name & not the people change theres in name & laws Impossible.
3. Honor: It can not worke an Immediate change.
4. A change of formes & writts etc:
5. we should now loose the preferment of presciency[234] which we have:
6. If we make a King of new name we must alter our lawes:
7. by the name there is a present ?commonplace of the people
8. dangerous in succession bringing in the title of Malcome.[235]
9. It could not stand with our oath of supreamacy

[Tuesday 24 April]
Uppon Tuesday morning Mr. Speaker delivered unto us a message he had receyvd from his majestie consisting of 3 partes.[236]

first a gracious allowance of freedome of speach in the matter & to all persons.

Secondly a gracious request that we would so prepare our selves that at the conference franckly & freely to discover our selves/ for his meaning was not to Impeach us in any thing & that the Judges should attend to resolve any differencs.

Thirdly ~~that we~~ a gracious admonition that we would not resolve before hand but as we should be induced by reasons.

Ob.[237] The King is aunciently descended of the King of Brittayne so that yf we make him King of Brittayne he is in the remitter & so an overthrow of ther lawes and present goverment/ exampled by the Ile of Man.

Sir Roger Ashton[238] brought us the Kings minde not to loose the name of England but to have the king of Brittayne added to his stile to forrayne princes & England to hold her rights by yt selfe & Scotland her:

The stile to be King of Brittayne and Fraunce with the Iles adjaccent:

---

[233] *CJ*, i. 184 contains the slightly different list of objections reported by Bacon on 25 April.
[234] i.e. Diplomatic precedence.
[235] Bacon chose to ignore this anti-Scots remark in his report of the debate.
[236] *CJ*, i. 183–4.
[237] i.e. Objection.
[238] Sir Roger Aston, MP for Cheshire.

26 [April]

Som heads of **Sir Edwin Sands** his speach.[239]

Uniting of kingdomes are in three sortes, first by mariage, 2 by children, 3 by conquest. In all these no precident for change of name, exampled by the Low Countrys Belgia:// Norway Denmarke & Swethen though they wer once in one man yet changed not there name, Italy, Spayne, meaner Dukedomes, The Duke of Hetruria cam by conquest to Sienna Pisa: etc. by conquest yet never changed his name he would have ben titled King which was refused by the Pope who answered that yf he gave him the name he must geve him the kingdom:

Reason sheweth yf that A title of King can not be geven but a title of the kingdome must follow:

The new title can not be brought in till the old be taken away.

We crosse our selves in this parliament in the recognition we have made.

The ground that one King hath reference to an other is the reference they have to ther subjects so that yt may not be one forrayne & an other at home:

A kingdome is indivisible & therefore we can nott allow the name of Brittayne which compriseth the whole & thenad England & Scotland:

Friday [27 April]

there was retorned to the house the course the comittees had taken for ordering the ~~conference~~ objection when they should come to the conference, which was allowed by the house & they appoynted divers to every parte.[240]

Notes on union debates 27 April–15 May 1604
[Montagu MS 29/73]

[Endorsed] Matters of the union & how yt was proceeded in.

[Saturday 28 April]

~~Uppon Saterday the 28 of Aprill the Lords sent unto us to have a conference with us agayne~~

~~Uppon Saterday~~ we had a conference with the Lords & these matters debated as may appeare in the note: which the Lords allowed well of & gave greate commendacion to the speakers promising to relate to his majestie the truth of things.

[239] See also *CJ*, i. 186–7.
[240] Reported by Bacon. For the names of those chosen to speak at the conference, see *CJ*, i. 188–9.

[Monday 30 April]

The next day [*sic*] we had a conference agayne & that was about the matter of the union & the commission: when we mett there Lordships told us that uppon our debate the Judges *rebus stantibus* wer opinion that as yet the name could not be proceeded in & therefore that was to stay & now we wer to proceede to the poynte of the commission, w made answer our auctoryty was but to heare what there Lordships would propound so that w wer only but to heare & to say nothing at that time whereuppon we brake of.

[Tuesday 1 May]

Uppon May day we had some what a sharpe letter from his majestie,[241] & that afternoone we agreed to confer with the Lords.

And these poynts wer propounded
first that there might be a commission
2 Each house to chuse there commissioners
3 That tere should be a competent nomber of commissioners nether to few nor to many
4 The commission to be returned to the next Session of this parliament.

The time to sitt of yt to be the first of October
The place to be at London.
And these poyncts to be drawen into act & for that to appoyncy ~~to~~ subcommittees to frame yt & then to refer yt to the house/
After the comttees had selected subcommittees for framing such an act:
Sir Frauncis Bacon related there proceedings to the house, & shewed us a writing which was read by him selfe, but nothing spoke to by the house.

[Thursday 10 May]

On Thursday the 12 May[242] the Lords sent to us That commissioners must be named before the act could be proceeded in because there names must be inserted & therefore desired that we would ~~fall to the~~ elect them. The Lords had chosen 14 desiring a proportion accordingly, They desired agayne a conference of the greate committee the time & place they left to our selves, And as they will come prepared with there commissioners named so we likewise would do the same, & they desired presently to know our nomber: which sent word should be 30:

---

[241] *CJ*, i. 193–4.
[242] This message was received on Thursday 10 May, see *CJ*, i. 206.

[Tuesday 15 May]
On Tuesday 15 the Lords & the great ~~cott~~ committee mett, but nothing done but reciproque geving in the names which ~~are~~ wer these

The Lord Treasurer   }
The Lord Admirall   }
Therle of Southampton   }
Therle of Pembroke   }
Therle of Northampton   }
The bishop of London }
The bishop of Duresme   }
The bishop of Sct Davis   }
The Lord Carie   }
The Lord Cecill   }
The Lord Zouch   }
The Lord Mounteagle }
The Lord Sheffeld   }
The Lord Evers   }

For the commons
Sir Frauncis Bacon   }
Sir Tho: Heskett   } common lawyers
Sir Law: Tanfeld   }
Sir Henry Hubber[243]   }

Sir Jhon Bennett   } civilians
Sir Daniell Dun   }

Sir Jhon Stanhop   } privi consellor
Sir Jhon Herbert   }

Sir Henry Belingsly[244]   }
Mr. Askwith[245]   } merchants
Mr. Tho: James[246]   }
Mr. Hen Chapman[247]   }

Sir Edw Stafford   } Imbassadors
Sir Henry Nevell   }

[243] Sir Henry Hobart.
[244] Sir Thomas Billingsley, MP for London.
[245] Robert Askwith, MP for York.
[246] MP for Bristol.
[247] MP for Newcastle-upon-Tyne.

The lord Buckhurst[248]
Sir George Carew vic[250]
Sir Tho: Rigway[251]
Sir Jhon Savile
Sir Rob: Mansell
Sir Hen: Wittrington[253]
Sir Tho: Strickland
Sir Ralf Gray
Sir Tho Lake
Sir Tho Holcroft

The Lo: Clinton[249]
Sir Edw: Hobby
Sir Fran: Hastings
Sir Rob: Wroth
Sir Rich Buckley[252]
Sir Tho: Chalenor

Draft speech on the annexations bill, July 1604
[Montagu 29/44]

A speach sett downe in writing that yt may not be mistaken for the
stay of reading the bill of annexation: from reading but yt was not
spoken because etc.[254] 1 Ja:

Mr. Speaker, considering how this bill came came recommended I
desire rather to speake for the stay if reading yt a while then to speake
agaynst yt when it is read.

Yf I were worthy or had place of accesse to his majestie I had rather
deliver what I have to say to him selfe than heere: but fayling of that &
now being one of his common counsell I will discharge my consciance
in delivering my poore advise.

And if any heere which have accesse to his majestie will truly deliver
what I shall say I will thanck them for yt & to that end I speake.

Yf this lawe passe from us as yt hath donne from the lords then yt
must be presented to his majestie either to geve liffe to yt or to dash
yt.

If he dash yt yt may breed wonde & suspition.
If he geve liffe to yt then yt becoms a law.
Yf yt become a law then yt is eyther of force or no force.
Yf of no force then we have taken care in vayne.

---

248 Robert, Lord Buckhurst, MP for Sussex.
249 Thomas, Lord Clinton, MP for Lincolnshire.
250 Vice-Chamberlain to the Queen. *CJ*, i. 208.
251 Sir Thomas Ridgeway, MP for Devon.
252 Sir Richard Bulkeley, MP for Anglesey.
253 Sir Henry Widdrington, MP for Northumberland.
254 The bill was given two readings in the Commons on 4 July 1604, but ran out of
time and was allowed to sleep until the next session on 6 July. *CJ*, i. 252–3.

If of force then these Inconveniencies arise.

First as greate to touch to his majesties prerogative honor & reputacion as any thing that ever I saw tendred

Secondly yt can not but breed discontent in the Succession to be bound by a perpetuity & never a man heere but would be angry to be bound so & we see how every parliament we are trobled with cutting them of.

Besides these I fayle in my judgement If there may not arise two mischeffe to the crowne.

First to Include land that will hardly hold oute the rent they are now letten for:

Secondly to exclude certayne land which common reputacion are thought already not to be disseevered from the crowne.

These reasons may seeme weake to your Judgements but to me they avayle much

Therefore not to hold you long: God hath geven this kingdome to his majestie which I pray God he may in his owne person long Injoy my advise to him is that he should possess his owne with as great free[dom] as ever any of his ancestors have done: And that the bill may stay [at] his pleasure for the Readeing:

Sir Robert Cotton's Diary of the 1607 Session
[BL, Cotton MS Titus F.IV, fols 93–106:]

[f.93]

3ª Sessio 1 Parliamenti Jacobi Regis que incipit 18 Novembris Aº 4ᵗᵒ 1606 continuat usque 5ᵗᵒ Julij 1607

The Commons according to a messuage [*sic*!] delivered to them by the Speaker from the King, doe attend his Majestie in the upper house the afternoone of the first day of this Session, where first a speach is made unto them by the Lord Chancelor (which is not a usuall course and then by the King.[255]

His Majesties answere to a peticion of greevances exhibited the last Session was by his Majesties commaundement delivered by the Clerk of the upper house to the Speaker, to be by him published in the lower house, which answere was in parchment and is inrolled in the Clerk of the parliaments journall book 19 Novemb:[256]

The instrument of the union conteyning the Articles agreed uppon

---

[255] Briefly noted in *Bowyer*, p. 185. The King also spoke at length, see *ibid.*; *CJ*, i. 314–15.

[256] *CJ*, i. 316–18.

by the Commissioners to be presented to the Parliament, was by speciall messengers sent downe from the Lords to the lower house to be there read and is entred in the Clerks journall book 21 Novemb: 1606[257]

Burgesses. Referred to Comittees and ruled in the house uppon question according to the opinion of the Committes, that whereas any member of the house is by the kinges letters pattents appointed an Officer for life in Ireland there ought a newe to be chosen in his roome which was the case of **Sir Humfrey Wynch** chosen chief Baron of Ireland, **Sir Thomas Ridgway** chosen Treasurer **Sir Oliver St John** Maister of the Ordinance in Ireland But where the ymployment out of the Realme is at the kings pleasure as in the case [**f.93v**] of Ambassadour it is otherwise and in that case a newe ought not to be chosen. This was the case of **Sir Georg Carew** in France **Sir Charles Cornewalleis** in Spayne, **Sir Thomas Edmonds** with the Archduke who after their ambassage ended did returne to theire service in the house 19 Nov: 1606 & 22 Novem: 1606.[258]

Question Burgesses. A question was put whether **Mr. Hubbert** chosen Kings Attorney & called by writt into the upper house should be recalled which question was put whether there should be a newe choyce. The house hereuppon grewe into confusion, and then another question made whether there should any more questions be thereof made for that time which was ruled No, 22 Nov: 1606

Hereuppon Mr. Attorney finding that uppon debate thereof, the opinion of the house was like to sway that he ought still to serve amongst them, Did of his owne accord without any expresse order in the case come into the house and serve there In debate of which matter it was remembred that Onslowe beeing chosen Sollicitor and called by writ into the upper house was never the lesse chosen Speaker as continuing still a member in the lower house the Speaker being dead betweene two Sessions And that Mr. Jeffreis chosen Queenes Serjeant & called by writt into the upper house was demaunded by the lower to serve amongst them bycause they were first possessed of him and did returne to them And though there were now president in the case of the Attorney Generall yet the reason was all one. 22 Nov: 1606[259]

The Instrument of the union returned to the Lordes after a Copie had beene taken for the use of the house bycause it was the authenticall instrument under the seales of the Commissioners 24 Novem: 1606[260]

[**f.94**] Clark. **Sir Tho: Lake** entreth into a statute of 5000[li] to performe certen payments according to an Act passed which statute

[257] *Ibid.* i. 318–23.
[258] *Ibid.* i. 315–16, 323–4; *Bowyer*, pp. 186, 188; Mountagu Diary, p. 123.
[259] i.e. Sir Henry Hobart, MP for Norwich; see *Bowyer*, pp. 188–9; Mountagu Diary, p. 123.
[260] *CJ*, i. 324; Mountagu Diary, p. 123.

was left with the Clark of the Parliament and therewithall certen Indentures of defesance which uppon the parties letter to Mr. Speaker that the payments were performed read in the house, were by order of the house delivered back to be cancelled 26 Novem: Sir Hugh Losse his case.[261]

Sir Ed: Hobby was the only man of the Commissioners for the Union that refused to set his seale thereto it was moved that he might shewe the reason of his refusall himself answered the motion and amongest other thinges said *Licet uniquiq' frui abundantia cordis sui,* and it was not thought fit he should yeild his reason For where the major parte have overruled it, the rest are wrapped up in silence as in a voyder and committed to oblivion 27 Nov: 1606.[262]

Conference. The warinesse of the house not to yeeld to conference with the Lords till they had first debated the matter emongest themselves & so prepared themselves for the conference 28 Nov: 1606.[263]

Attendance. A speciall Order that no lawyer depart the Towne without leave of the house 29 Nov: 1606.[264]

Serjeant Poore. **Sir Hen: Billingsley** one of the Collectors for the poore dying uppon a mocion made, a newe was chosen & ordered that the Serjeant should goe to his executors for the money receaved 1° Decem:[265]

Committee. A Committee touching the Union beinge appointed in the house and adjourned from the afternoone before to the morning following in the house The Speaker the next day [**f.94v**] beeing sic, it was moved that the house would geve leave to the Committee which was done, the speaker rising out of his chaier and setting by and one appointed by the Committees taking the place of the Clark 17 Decemb: 1606.[266]

This Course was held inconvenient and the motion denied 27 Junij 1607 But in the last Session of this Parliament it was a common practise.[267]

Adjournament Message. Message brought from the Lords signifying that his Majestie had declared his pleasure to them that the Parliament should be adjourned till within Three dayes of the end of the next Terme whereuppon the Speaker adjourneth it accordingly.

---

[261] *CJ*, i. 325. The Act in question was 3 Jac. I, Private Acts cap. 12.

[262] *CJ*, i. 325; *Bowyer*, p. 194.

[263] This was a result of the Lords' request for a preliminary conference on the union. *CJ*, i. 326.

[264] *Ibid.* i. 326.

[265] *Ibid.* 326–7.

[266] *Ibid.* 331; *Bowyer*, pp. 208–9.

[267] This ruling is not recorded elsewhere, but may have sprung from the debate over the Hostile Laws bill on 26 June, see *CJ*, i. 387–8, 1054; *Bowyer*, p. 351.

Nota adjourned uppon a message from the Lords signifying his Majesties pleasure. Mr. Ewens his note.[268]

Speaker. Memorandum that the Speaker did practise at the bars the beginning of hillary Terme *quod non fuit conveniens* For the Session still continued.

Priviledg. Mr. Davies one of the Mr. Speakers Clarks was ordered in the Court of wards to joyne in commission as assignee of a ward in suite then ready for Commission betwene other parties whereuppon Mr. Speaker writeth his letter to the Attorney of the Wardes shewing that by generall warrant of the Common house of parliament he was to informe touching the priviledge of that house, and thereuppon signifieth that priviledg was in this case due to his servant, though that the time the Court was adjourned, the Session still continuing 2 Febr: 1606 which was 6 or 7 daies before the house sate uppon the last adjournement. See the forme of the letter there. **[f.95]**[269]

Speaker Priviledg habeas corpus. See the forme of Mr. Speakers warrant to the Clerk of the Crowne to make an *habeas corpus* where any party priviledged is under arrest to bring him to the house 10 Febr: 1606.

See also the forme of the *habeas corpus* there, which note is returnable *coram norbis in prescenti Parliamento nostro, ad faciendum et recipiendum quod per nos in dicto parliamento nostro consideratum et ordinatum fuerit: una cum causa.*[270]

Committee. Ordred uppon motion that the adjournment of every Committee amongest themselves should be the next day published in the house 11° Febr 1606.[271]

Serjeant. One committed to the custody of the Serjeant for a moneth by the speciall leave of the house is permitted to goe at large in the custody of one of the Serjeants men. 12 Febr. 1606.[272]

Speaking misdemeanour. **Sir Chr: Pigott** crieth out sitting still in his place, & being covered, to have certen articles read, his rude behaviour beeing observed he was demaunded to utter his minde in decent order whereuppon arising he spake much and uncivily against the Scottes yet nothing was further said unto him that day 13 Febr. 1606.[273] But afterwards he was committed by the house to the Tower and another chosen in his place.[274]

[268] *CJ*, i. 331. As Under-Clerk of the Parliament, Ralph Ewens was the senior clerk in the Commons.

[269] *Ibid.* i. 331, which names the clerk as Nicholas Davye.

[270] *Ibid.* i. 332, privilege claimed by **Sir Michael Sondes** on behalf of his servant Thomas Finch.

[271] *Ibid.* i. 333.

[272] The attorney Robert Bateman, detained the previous day on a privilege complaint. *Ibid.* i. 333.

[273] This is confirmed by *ibid.* i. 333; Mountagu Diary, p. 129.

[274] *CJ*, i. 335–6; Mountagu Diary, pp. 130–1.

Priviledg. One Mr. Finch an Attorney of the common pleas beeing arrested claymed priviledg as one of **Sir Michaell Sandes** his servantes and Sollicitor of his busines It was questioned whether a Sollicitor of causes to one of the house not beeing his meniall servant should be priviledged, It was remembred that a Sollicitor of the Baron of Walthams[275] & the like of one Mr. Hurleston[276] had priviledge 43 Eliz: But in this case Sir Mich: Sands protested [**f.95v**] to the house that Fynch lay in his house & had wages of him, 13 Febr: 1606.

All menial and necessary servants to have priviledg 14 Febr: 1606
Quere whether it extendeth to meniall and necessary servantes in the Countrey or to such as attend the person here.[277]

It was delivered as a rule that only the resolution of the house uppon a bill depending was a judgment of the house, Other resolucions uppon motions were but opinions. In the case of naturalization of the Antenati 21 Febr:[278]

Priviledg. A letter from Mr. Speaker to the shrief of Southampton who had made a seizure of some of the goods of **Sir William Kingsmill** geving him to understand that aswell the goods as the persons of the members of the house are to be priviledged and advising him to make restitution 26 Febr: 1606.[279]

Misdemeanour King. **Sir Chr: Pigot** maketh peticion to the house for his enlargement, great dispute whether the house should move his Majesty in it, Seeing he was committed by them 27 Febr: Nothing being resolved his Majesty tooke notice of the matter and did leave him to be dealt withall as they would. By order of the house Mr. Speaker wrote his letter to the lievetenant of the Tower to enlarge him 28 Febr. [**f.96**][280]

Attendance. Many beeing gone without leave much debate was what course to be taken to recall them resolved the Serjeant or his Deputy should be sent for them, and the Offenders to pay Officers fees uppon their returne & to be held contemners of the authority of the house. It was signified by his Majestie that the contempt of one that represented a shire, a City or a borough in departinge without licence was greater

---

[275] D'Ewes, *Eliz.* pp. 642–3; Baron of Waltham was a courtesy title held by Thomas Langton, MP for Newton-in-Makerfield in 1601.

[276] Anthony Curwin, servant to William Huddleston, MP for Cumberland in 1601. D'Ewes, *Eliz.* p. 686 does not specifically state that Curwin was an attorney.

[277] *CJ*, i. 334; *Bowyer*, pp. 209–10; Mountagu Diary, p. 130 which all state that the Commons' judgement on this case was handed down on 13 February.

[278] This helps to explain the gnomic order recorded in *CJ*, i. 339: the Commons doubtless hoped the ruling would allow them to postpone a conference with the Lords, who were pressing them on the vexed question of naturalization [see Mountagu Diary, p. 132], but allowed themselves room to revoke the decision if it proved controversial.

[279] *CJ*, i. 343.

[280] For the text see *ibid.* i. 344.

than if a lord should departe without leave, and he offred the assistance of his proclamacion to recall them if need should require, 27 Febr: 1606.[281]

Motion. Peticion exhibited by merchants conteyning complayntes of great wronges offred unto them by the Spaniards, The Consideracion for redresse was referred to Comittees 25. 28 Febr: 1606.[282]

deficiente lege recurrendum est ad consuetudinem deficiente consuetudine recurrendum est ad rationem.

Message. Message sent downe from the Lords in writing and read by their messengers Being desired to leave their writing they said they had noe such Commission, But beeing desired to read the same agayne distinctly that the Clerk might wright it out they did so. 2 Martij.[283]

Committees Motions. A Committee appointeth to consider of some course for the repayre and releef of the great losses & calamities by meanes of the late great inundacion in Somersetshire.[284]

Committees Billes. Ordred that Committees which amend the bill should likewise amend the brief in the same poinctes.[285]

Attendance Speaker. Letters written by Mr. Speaker by order of the house to some Lawyers which departed without leave to returne speedily 3 Martij 1606. **Mr. Hyde Mr. Tucker Mr. Digges** &c. [**f.96v**][286]

Billes. When a proviso is offred to a bill ingrossed which is alwaies in parchment, after it hath beene thrice read, the question must be put whether it shalbe added to the bill, And the question mush be put agayne for the passage of the bill with the proviso. Bill against Drunkenes. 3 Martij 1606.

Sir Ed: Hobby beeing sent as a messenger to the Lordes beginneth his message with theis wordes, The knights Citizens Burgesses and Barons of the Commons Court of Parliament, when he returned to them to receave his answer they tooke excepcions at those wordes & desire him to expound himself which he refuseth to doe, answering that his Commission was only to deliver a message, which he had done & to receave their answere which he was ready to doe. 4 Martij 1606.

The Lordes in sending their answers to the message omitted not to let the house knowe that they conceaved an error in the forme of delivering the last message, which they rather held to be *lapsus lingue* then otherwise For they cannot admitt that any Baron of Parliament

---

[281] *Ibid.* i. 343–4.

[282] *Ibid.* i. 340–2, 344.

[283] *Ibid.* i. 345–6; Mountagu Diary, p. 135.

[284] *CJ*, i. 346. The motion was made by Speaker Phelips, whose own estates lay in Somerset.

[285] *Ibid.* i. 346. This was presumably a reference to the amendments for the newly amended drunkenness bill, which was given a third reading directly thereafter.

[286] *Ibid.* i. 346.

hath any place in the lower house, And the lower house they will not acknowledge to be a Court without them For they both make but one Court. 4 Martij.

To which an answere was returned in writing that those which served for the Cinque ports are called Barons in the sommons of parliament *eligatis duos Barones* and likewise in the statute 6 H.6 mention is there made of those Barons without other addicion. Therefore they might justify the messenger in that poinct though he had noe expresse Commission to use that worde, But the lords needed not to feare that they intended to incroche uppon their dignity considering they placed the name Baron after Burgesses And touching the word Court doubt not but [**f.97**] the Commons house is a Court of itself and that of record, But beeing a question fallen incidentally they will noe more dispute but geve answere to the other parte of the message. 5 Martij.[287]

Councell at barre which speake against the Bill are to beginne and such as maynteyne the bill to answer 5 Martij

This was so ruled notwithstanding the Committees had reported against the bill 4to Martij 1607 the Marshalsey bill.[288]

In the middest of the dispute touching the bill against Inmates, Messingers which came from the Lordes were receaved & after that done the dispute was proceeded in & the Bill rejected 11° Martij.[289]

Noe man to depart without paying the ordinary fee to the Clark vjs. viijd., quod nota, For anciently but 2s. 6d. was due for a common burgesse 12 Martij.[290]

When any conference is with the Lordes of any great matter it is the course to appoint some in particuler to take notes & make report 12 Martij.[291]

Conferences. Committees appointed to consider of a more convenient manner of conference with the lords then nowe is used to stand & that bare hedded so long together which was painfull, And complaynt was made that conferences were growne too usuall which was not so safe for the house. 12 martij 1606[292]

Priviledg. A horse of **Mr. James** of Bristowe taken out of his Inne for a post horse the postmaisters man being told he was a burgesses horse, who was therefore committed to the Serjeants custody. 13 Martij.[293]

[287] *Ibid.* i. 348–9; *Bowyer*, pp. 212–14; Mountagu Diary, p. 137.
[288] This motion was in fact raised during the hearing of counsel for the bill for St Saviour's, Southwark. *CJ*, i. 349; *Bowyer*, pp. 216–17.
[289] *CJ*, i. 351.
[290] *Ibid.* i. 351.
[291] This order was presumably cited in making the motion recorded in *ibid.* i. 352.
[292] *Ibid.* i. 352.
[293] *Ibid.* i. 352.

Committees for more convenient a matter of conference report that by presidents they finde that in 6 Ed.3 both the houses sate together, And that after division of [**f.97v**] the houses uppon any occasion of conference the Lordes came in the lower house & the conference was there And that in reason those that are equall in Commission should not be as inferiour during that time And that the payne (especially in hott wether was intollerable. The house hoping the Lords would take notice of this complaint & redress did nothing more therein. 14 Martij. It was afterwards complayned of to the Lords, but noe redresse nor answere.[294]

Mr. Speaker writeth his letter to the Justices of Assise of Essex to excuse the attendance at the Assises of **Sir Gamaliel Capell** shrief of that shire, by reason of his necessary attendance in parliament. see the letter 14 Martij 1606.[295]

Speaker. The Speaker sent word he was sick and desired to be spared for 3 daies, prayer in his absence said by the Clerk. Notwithstanding the next day they mett & one uppon his mocion had licence to departe which was rather by connivence then by right They resolved not to meete till 4 daies after At which time they mett agayne & prayer said by the Clerk, And the Company beeing informed of Mr. Speaker his sicknes put of their next meeting till 2 daies after that, when meeting agayne, But the Speaker not coming a motion was made **by Sir John Heigham** for some pitie to be shewen to a prisoner in the Serjeants custody, to be at liberty for a time by way of connivence, It was thought reasonable, And **Mr. Fuller** moved they might proceed to conferre touching the wronges offred by the Spaniards to our merchantes which beeing [**f.98**] but upon a motion might be done in the absence of the Speaker and was done accordingly 20 Martij.[296]

There was much debate what was to be done during the sicknes of a Speaker, Some were of opinion that we might choose a Speaker from day to day only to moderate & put things to the question, & that there were presidents for it which was denyed by others, though he were not one hed but one of our fellowes yet he was appointed to that office by the King & could not be appointed by us. 'Twas said on the other side that there was a time when both the houses sate together that there was noe particuler speaker for the Commons But that the Chancelor was speaker for both houses At last there was a Committee appointed to serch presidentes and to report what was free to be in future times But the Speaker comming the next day the Committee made noe report. 23 Martij.[297]

[294] *Ibid.* i. 352; *Bowyer*, pp. 233–4.
[295] *CJ*, i. 353.
[296] Heigham and Fuller actually made their motions on 23 March. *Ibid.* i. 353–4.
[297] *Ibid.* i. 353–4; *Bowyer*, pp. 240–2; Mountagu Diary, p. 139.

The day of the kinges Coronacion happening during this Session, It was moved the day before that the morning of the next day they should meete in the house & from thence goe altogether to the sermon in Westminster which in such cases is usuall. 23 Martij.[298]

The bill for confirmacion of the kings letters pattents to Ro: Batherst esquier beeing ready for the question to passe uppon mocion by **Sir Nathan: Bacon** that it concerned **Sir Chr. Haydon** whome he undertooke to geve notice thereof, was for the time deferred And about 8 daies after uppon relacion by him that Sir Chr: Haydon was satisfied, the Bill was put the question for passage without further opening &c. did passe. 24 Martij 1606.[299]

Sir John Parker speaking against the unconscionable writing in Courtes of equity, said that Sir Tho. Tasborough paid 60[li] for one copie, Serjeant Heale 50[li] for another & that my lord in a sute depending two yeares payd for 60000[300] sheetes of paper & prayed that some consideracion might be had – 27 Martij[301]

Both the houses by his Majesties speciall appointment meete in the great chamber in the Whitehall, where his Majestie sitting under a Cloth of estate maketh a large speach unto them which is inserted into the Clarks book 31 Martij. After the speach ended which was made in the afternoone the Commons returned to their house, and Mr. Speaker by direction from his Majestie did adjourne the Court till the xx[th] of Aprill.[302]

Priviledg. In this vacacion Mr. Speaker beeing warranted by a former generall order for priviledge directed his letters in excuse of **Sir Ed. Ludlowe** & his sonne touching their attendance at the execucion of a Commission out of the Chauncery for examining of witnesses. The letter was directed to the Commissioners. 31 Martij 1607 dated in the time of vacacion.[303]

Councell. Conceaved for a generall rule that Councell ought not to be heard at the bar in mayntenance of a bill except it be opposed by Councell, the Bill of drayning the Fens in the Ile of Ely. 20 Aprill.[304]

Clark Billes. After a recesse for a time uppon the meeting agayne a note was read made by the Clark conteyning the rate of such [**f.99**] billes as then remayned in the house whether passed & not sent up

---

[298] *CJ*, i. 354.

[299] Despite the dates given, the bill was reported on 26 March. *Ibid.* i. 354.

[300] It is probable that this number should read 6000 rather than 60000.

[301] *CJ*, i. 355–6.

[302] *Ibid.* i. 357–63.

[303] *Ibid.* i. 363.

[304] *Ibid.*, i. 364. Counsel both for and against the bill were eventually heard on 9 May. *Ibid.* i. 371–2.

ingrossed committed dashed rejected or sleeping which was a good course. 20 Apr: 1607.

motion Adjornment. Court adjorned by reason of the small nomber.[305]

Councell billes. Councell heard uppon the second reading of a bill aswell as uppon the passage.

Committee Bll. The Bill against the Marshalsey was committed and reported and councell heard It was thereuppon recommitted & other Committees added who altred the former proceeding. It was argued that the former proceedings were wayved and the later good. 30 Apr: 1607.[306]

The opinion of the house touching the poinct of naturalization was contrary to that which had beene delivered by the Judges whereuppon much dispute grewe howe they might have their opinion of force against that of the Judges, & to remayne to posterity It was thought that a memoriall made thereof by the Clerk in his book would litle avayle in another age, and they were assured they should never passe a bill thereof So as whatsoever had beene said therein and the reasons delivered were noe where recorded.[307]

Another speach by his Majestie 2° Maij.[308]

Priviledg. A *subpena* out of the Exchecquer served uppon **Sir Ric: Pawlett** *ad respondedum certis articulis tibi tunc et ibidem ex parte nostra obijciendis*. Fanshawe. priviledge was allowed 3° Maij 1607 & the parties offending sent for, And a letter written by Mr. Speaker to the Lo: Chief Baron signifying the priviledg & order of the house & praying noe further proces might be awarded. [**f.99v**][309]

Priviledg. **Sir Tho: Biggs** and **Sir Tho: Lowe** members of the house were served to appeare at the Kings Bench barre as Jurors in an Attaynt They had the priviledge of the house allowed them and the Serjeant sent with his mace to declare the order of the house to the Secondary of the kings bench, the Court then sitting, *quod nota*, 6 Maij 1607.[310]

Ruled that the whole house might by a Committee Mr. Speaker beeing absent or not sitting in his chayer. In the dispute of the Bill touching hostile lawes. 7 Maij 1607[311]

---

[305] *Bowyer*, p. 253 puts the number at 53. Mountagu Diary p. 141 ascribes the absences to the forthcoming St. George's feast at Windsor.

[306] i.e. A recommittal of a bill overrides the conclusions reached by the original committee. *CJ*, i. 365.

[307] This refers to the debates of 28 April to 1 May, which are recorded only perfunctorily in *CJ*, i. 364–5. For the fullest reports, see *Bowyer*, pp. 255–86.

[308] *CJ*, i. 366–8; *Bowyer*, pp. 287–8.

[309] 3 May was a Sunday; the case was aired on the following day. *CJ*, i. 368.

[310] *Ibid.* i. 369.

[311] *Ibid.* i. 371.

The house was much greeved that his Majesty in his last speach had taxed divers of the house, though not naming them with indiscreete and violent behaviour. Moved by some that the gentlemen blamed might pray accesse to his Majesty to explane themselves. By others that the cleering of the gentlemen (which was intended to be **Mr. Yelverton**) might passe by voyce, That it were fitt to make knowne to his Majestie the desire of the house in theis 3 poinctes That his Majestie would be pleased not to receave informacion by private suggestion of matters done within the house but from the house it self That the parties blamed might cleere themselves in his Majesties presence That his Majestie would be pleased to signify his pleasure, that such as speake in parliament shall have the ancient liberty of speach without feare of controll.

The next day Mr. Speaker delivereth to the house that his Majestie tooke notice of the greef conceaved, and mervayled that the house should be jealous of him that he had any meaning to infringe the liberty of speach in the house, he for his parte thought him not worthy of his place that would not speak freely what he thought (so it were bounded with modesty and discrecion, Further mocions [**f.100**] were made, that his Majestie might be moved to discover the party to us that had misinformed him and to deliver him to be censured by the house But noe more done.

Mr. Lewknor spake well in this busenes.[312]

Ordred uppon motion that upon rising of the house noe man should goe forth before Mr. Speaker.[313]

Serjeant priviledg. A warrant from the Speaker directed to the Serjeant to apprehend one which had served a *subpoena* uppon **Sir Wm Cook** which is not needfull but he may doe it by shewing his mace, there beeing an order to pprehende the parties 8 Maij. *Quere* but a warrant hath beene usuall.[314]

Before Councell be heard against a bill the bill ought to be read which order was neglected when **Mr. Gerrard** spake against the bill of All Soules colledge and noted to be disorderly. 8 Maij 1607

When Councell of both sides is appointed & one of them fayleth uppon great debate whether one might be heard It was resolved he might. **Mr. Gerrard** in the bill of all soules Colledge. 8 Maij 1607[315]

Priviledg. A *subpoena* out of the Star Chamber *ad comparendum coram nobis et consilio nostro*, served uppon **Sir Edmond Ludlowe** at Mr. Attorney his suite for the king, which made it disputable whether he

---

[312] This alludes to the debates of 6–7 May; *ibid.* i. 370–1; *Bowyer*, pp. 376–81; Mountagu Diary, p. 144. No version of Lewkenor's speech appears to survive.

[313] *CJ*, i. 371 (7 May).

[314] *Ibid.*

[315] *Ibid.* i. 371, 1042.

should have priviledge, And it was referred to the Committee for priviledges.[316]

<u>Billes</u>. The Bill of Clothing beeing ingrossed and read, the third time excepcion was taken to the last proviso thereof whereuppon after much debate it was recommitted, the next day it was returned agayne by the Comittees with their opinions, That they [**f.100v**] held it fitt that the last proviso should be struck out whereuppon question grewe howe the proviso wold be put to the question alone without dashinge the whole bill At last resolved the Proviso to be putt to the question alone which beeing disapproved it was ordered it should be rased out of the bill, which was presently done at the borde by the Clerk & the bill put the question & so passed, *quod nota bene.* 17 May 1607.[317]

The like in the bill touching wherrymen 18 Maij.[318]

Uppon a peticion exhibited to the house by the Merchants, of great wronges offred them by the Spaniards, the matter beeing referred to Comittees and found by them that the complaintes were just, they propounded a remedy by preferring a peticion from the whole parliament wherein to desire the Lords too joyne, that letters of mart might be granted, Where note that in such cases of publique greevance the parlament doth sollicite the king for redress without a bill depending only upon peticion made to them. 13 Maij 1607.[319]

Informed that **Mr. Rich: Martyn** stood outlawed at the sute of one Palmer in debte, and that one Allen Palmer Attorney warned one Martyn that he would proceed to a triall, The party & Attorney ordered to be sent for by the Serjeant.[320]

An attachment was served out of the Chancery uppon **Mr. Bellingham** the plaintiff beeing in the Countrey & not easily to be found, A letter was written by Mr. Speaker to one of the six Clarks the plaintiffs Attorney not to proceed further thereuppon 13 Maij. the offender sent for by the Serjeant, 6 Junij. [**f.101**][321]

Sir John Boys and **Mr. Brock** both of the house and Lawyers are reteyned to be of Councell and to attend a Committee in a private cause in the upper house, which did not presume so to doe without leave of the house, It was remembred that 27 Eliz. Mr. Speaker himself had leave to attend the upper house, beeing then one of the members of the lower house in a case for my Lord Darcies,[322] and that Mr.

---

[316] 8 May. *Ibid.* i. 371.
[317] This debate actually took place on 11–12 May, *ibid.* i. 372–3; *Bowyer*, pp. 291–2.
[318] *CJ*, i. 375.
[319] *Ibid.* i. 373, 1044.
[320] 13 May. *Ibid.* i. 373.
[321] *CJ*, i. 373, 379. Although the Journal names him as Francis Bullingham, this was in fact Richard Bellingham, MP for Bletchingley.
[322] This does not appear to have been recorded at the time. Hasler, iii. 216.

Sollicitor & Mr. Recorder had like leave to attend the upper in a title of honour for the Lord Lespencer the last session[323] whereuppon leave was granted the 15 Maij 1607 But note that the Title of honour is decidable only in the upper house, and not to be medled withall in the neither house And therefore more reason to admitt them to be of Councell in that case werein they cannot be Judges then in any case which is to passe both houses.[324]

His Majestie sendeth a message to the house by Mr. Speaker, that he did take notice of slanderous reportes spread abrode touching violent and undue proceeding in the Borders with partiality to the Scots in the person of Barrowe, for cleering of which scandall his Majesty wished them to heare the relacion of one Sir William Seaton a Scottish gent, who was a principal Actor in those businesses The house yeilded to the motion and it was disputed where he should stand whether without the barre or within At last in respect he came sent by his Majestie & in defence, of the iustice of the kingdome of Scotland it was thought fit he should be fetcht in with the mace, he beeing then in the outer roome, and that he should stand a yard or thereaboutes within the barre which was [**f.101v**] done, and he spake in that place about half an hower relating the particuler of the proceedinges, wherein he gave the house good satisfaction 19 Maij 1607.[325]

Committees may meete notwithstanding an adjournment for a few dayes except speciall order be to the contrary 20 Maij 1607.[326]

The Speaker directeth his letter to the Lord President at York to stay a sute there commenced against of **Mr. Talbot Bowes** whome the cause concerneth in interest 20 Maij 1607, which letter was written in the vacancy of an adjournement.[327]

Great offence taken to the Speaker for adjournment of the house, so fewe beeing present and that of his own head, his protestation, noe purpose of wrong to the house And that he had power by authority from his Majesty which may adjourne it at his pleasure He also declareth that his Majestie had conceaved offence of a brute that was spread, that the house was adjourned to circumvent them, That at the next meeting fewe might be present but such as his Majestie was sure would yeild to his pleasure. 27 Maij 1606. [*sic?*][328]

[323] Spencer v. Abergavenny, 24 March 1606. *CJ*, i. 288.

[324] *Ibid.* i. 373.

[325] *Ibid.* i. 375; *Bowyer*, pp. 293–7.

[326] Which clarifies the order in *CJ*, i. 375: 'no committees should sit until their next meeting'.

[327] *Ibid.* i. 375.

[328] *Bowyer*, pp. 297–8 explains that some suspected this adjournment was intended to defuse the Commons' objections to officially sponsored amendments to the Hostile Laws bill.

A Committee appointed to consider what to be done to have better attendance, resolved to have the house called, and to sett fines uppon the absents, and search to be made whether fines heretofore uppon like occasion imposed, have beene extreated & levyed And that a bill in the house for better attendance of the members should be proceeded in 28 Maij 1607. [**f.102**]³²⁹

Mr. Speaker sate from Nine till eleven and did rise with out any bill beeing read or motion made during which time there sate a Committee in the Court of Wardes touching the Bill of hostile lawes. 1° Junij 1607.³³⁰

Mr. Speaker informed the house that he had receaved a letter from his Majestie touching the hostile laws which he read twice by commandement of the house. The letter in the Clarks book 2° Junij.³³¹

A paper delivered to Mr. Speaker conteyning the lawe and custom of Scotland touching the producing of witnesses in criminall causes, which paper was read and is in the Clarks book. 3 Junij 1607.³³²

A message delivered from his Majesty to the Committee for the bill of hostile lawes 4 Junij.

Reports. Every thing agreed uppon by a Committee must be reported, but not every thing spoken. 4 Junij.

Billes. In the Bill of hostile lawes beeing returned from the Committees beeing a matter of that importance the whole bill was first read & the alteracions by themselves which was done uppon speciall order. 4 Junij.³³³

Messengers admitted from the Lords in the middest of dispute as it falleth out often. 8 Junij.³³⁴

Mr. Speaker uppon motion and by order of the house writeth his letter to the Tenants of land which one Holdich [**f.102v**] claymed to be subject to his charge, for the charging of which Holdich hath a bill in the house perswading the tenants too make composition with him considering the equity of the case, and the poverty of the peticioner. 9 Junij.³³⁵

Calling of the house. The manner of calling the house is thus, The Clark readeth the names of the Burgesses according as they are sett downe by the Clark of the Crowne at the beginning of the parliament

---

³²⁹ Second reading. The question had been considered upon a recommendation from the King on 27 February, and the bill had received its first reading on 4 March. *CJ*, i. 343–4, 347, 376.

³³⁰ *Ibid.* i. 377. The union debate is briefly recorded in *Bowyer*, pp. 307–8.

³³¹ *CJ*, i. 377–8.

³³² Actually entered on 4 June. *Ibid.* i. 378–9.

³³³ The notes for 4 June are all recorded in *ibid.* i. 379.

³³⁴ *Ibid.* i. 380.

³³⁵ The text of the letter is entered in *ibid.* i. 380–1.

in a book which followeth the order of the alphabet of the Shires
Attendance. The Speaker & Clark & all other sitting in their places as
at other times Every man as he is called by his name, if he be present
riseth up & answereth, yf he be absent he is excused by some in the
house, & his absence and excuse noted by one of theis wordes according
to the truth of his case in the margent of the book.

Licenciatur which is when he hath a licence to departe	*excusatur ex gratia* which is when he hath done speciall service & chanceth to be absent at that tyme.	
Ægrotat speciale servic regis	*Vicecomes* Maior	The calling in of the house usually in the afternoone.

Yf noe man excuse him he is noted *deficit* The names of the defaultes
are usually presented the next day to the house. 19 Junij *post meridiem*.[336]

Poore. Certen of the house appointed to take the accompt of such
as are appointed collectors for the poore 9 Junij *post meridiem*. [**f.103**][337]

Priviledg. A triall of a cause at the Exchequer barre stayed by letter
from Mr. Speaker wherein **Sir Robert Johnson** was deft at the sute
of Sir Robert Brett. x° Junij.[338]

Priviledg. In a writt of partition depending in the Common pleas
betwene the Lary Lucie plt and **Sir Robert Oxenbridg** one of the
house deft, After default made by Sir Robert, a distresse was awarrded
and xx^{li} issues retorned against him uppon motion made for priviledge
to be granted in this case. After some debate it was ordred that if the
issues were not discharged before the next day at night the Attorney
Anthony Dawly, the sollicitor one Jo Branion and one John Pritchard
the undershrief should answere the contempt at the barre. 16 Junij
1607.[339]

Libertie of speach. Kings authority. It was resolved by the house that
a petition should be exhibited to his Majesty praying that the lawes
against jesuites priests and Recusantes might be putt in execucion, as
also for redresse of non residency & unlerned and idle ministers &c.
Committees beeing appointed to frame a peticion it was by them

---

[336] [*Sic*] 9 June pm. *CJ*, i. 381.
[337] *Ibid.* i. 381.
[338] *Ibid.*
[339] *Ibid.* i. 383–4.

agreed uppon and brought to the house and beeing pressed too be read, the Speaker informed the house that his Majestie had taken notice of the peticion & of the poinctes thereof and that it conteyned matter belonging meerely to his Care, And that it should be needlesse to present it unto him. Whereuppon 'twas said, to deny free proceeding in any matter depending in the house was a great wound to the libertie of the house, and as it were an arrest uppon the whole house. Mr. Speaker said there were many presidentes in the late Queenes time of restraynt of proceeding by her Commaundement from medling in peticions of divers kindes and read some presidentes out of the Parliament books whereupon a Committee was appointed to serch presidents touching this poinct of restraynt by message As also to consider & [**f.103v**] report their opinions whether that it were fitt a memoriall should be made in the Clarkes book of the letter lately sent to the Speaker and read in the house touching the remaunding of malefactors It was further desired that Mr. Speaker at his next accesse to his Majestie should declare to his Majestie the great grief that the house conceaved that they were restrayned in proceeding with the peticion. 16 Junij 1607.[340]

The King yeilded the peticion should be read 18 Junij 1607 which was done, And upon debate it was agreed to sleepe 18 Junij *vide post*.[341]

Divers presidentes were produced at a conference with the Lordes by the Lords themselves that uppon complaint of wrongs offred to merchants by forraine princes and thereupon a petition by the Commons exhibited to the King, such wronges have beene undertaken by the Kinges to be redressed. 17 Junij. *Quere* of **Mr. Fuller** for tbe presidents.[342]

Kings authority. Ordred to be sett downe as a memoriall in the Clarks book that his Majestie by message declared that he had noe meaning to infringe the freedome or priviledges of the house by any message But that rather his Majesties desire was the house should enjoy them with all liberty 18 Junij 1607.

Entries in the Clarks book. Kings authority. Committees to consider whether it were fit that a letter from his Majesty conteyning a sharp reproof of the house touching the matter of remaunding malefactors should be entred in the Clarks book, report that they held it not fitt whereupon it was so ordred. 18 Junij 1607.[343]

In dispute touching the peticion against recusants t'was said that in England there were [**f.104**]

[340] Cotton and Robert Bowyer were ordered to conduct a search for precedents on this point. *Ibid.* i. 384; *Bowyer*, pp. 330–3.

[341] *CJ*, i. 384–5.

[342] *Ibid.* i. 384; *Bowyer*, pp. 333–9.

[343] *CJ*, i. 385; *Bowyer*, p. 343.

8000 parish churches
not 2000 resident preaching ministers
not 1000 that preach once a moneth
not 50 single beneficed
300 deprived suspended or silenced
400 Jesuits & seminaries in England
40 simple people converted in one yere by one Jesuite
300 convicted Recusantes in a shire at the Queenes death nowe 800[344]

A Committee is appointed to consider what entries have beene made by the Clark in his journall book ever since the parliament began touching the priviledges of the house 19 Junij 1607.[345]

Order geven to stay a triall in the Common pleas wherein Mr. Stone and the house was plt & one Marsh deft. 20 Junij 1607.[346]

Clark Billes. A Bill for better execucion of the Commission of Sewers within the Countie of Somerset though it concern a whole shire, noted by the Clark to be a private bill and whereuppon fees are due, So though it concerne 5 or 6 sheeres. 22 Junij 1607.[347]

The bill for amendment of high waies in Sussex Surrey and Kent was by the whole house adjudged to be a private bill and ordred to pay fees. 18 Junij 1607.[348]

A letter by order of the house written by Mr. Speaker to certen gentlemen of the house to mediate an end betwene Mr. Essex and his Creditors, and thereuppon to frame a bill against the next Session for the sale of landes for theire satisfaccion. 22 Junij 1607. [**f.104v**][349]

Billes. Uppon the third reading of a private bill of Sir William Selbies, an error was found in the bill and thereuppon the question deferred for that time. 22 Junij 1607.[350]

Billes. In the Bill concerning hostile lawes which passed from the lower house to the Lords beeing returned by the Lords there was a proviso added & some amendments desired to be made Uppon committment thereof the proviso was by the Committees & by the house uppon their report thought fitt to stand, But if the bill should be so amended as the Lords desired, it would much alter the sence of the house. Whereuppon greate doubte arising what in this case was to be

---

[344] This is almost a *verbatim* copy of *CJ*, i. 385.
[345] *Ibid.* i. 385–6.
[346] *Ibid.* i. 386. The parties were Christopher Stone, MP for Bath and Edmund March.
[347] First reading. *Ibid.* i. 386.
[348] Presumably the wrong date. This bill was first read on 9 June, second read and committed on 10 June and reported and engrossed on 23 June. *Ibid.* i. 381. 387.
[349] *Ibid.* i. 386–7.
[350] *Ibid.* i. 387.

done, a president was vouched that the amendments desired by the Lords might be amended and altered by the Commons. Some other said it stood with order to add a proviso thereby to help the mischeef which may arise by suffring the amendments to passe, but that the amendments might not be alt'red. At last it was thought the safest course in a matter of this consequence to pray a conference with the Lords/ which was done/ and Commission given to the messengers to conferre presently if the Lords desired it which fell out accordingly And thereuppon the bill was sent up to them 29 Junij 1607. The Lordes agreed & the amendments were altered and inserted after they had beene thrice read. 30 Junij.[351]

Priviledg. A Waterman yet a dayly attendant uppon **Sir Henry Nevill** of Kent had priviledge. 30 Junij 1607. [**f.105**][352]

Billes. In the Bill of hostile lawes which passed from the lower house a proviso was added by the Lords in which proviso it was thought fit by the Commons an amendment should be, The word thought fit to be amended was in paper annexed to the proviso with direction to the palce And the Bill was put to the question for passage with those alteracions & amendments & passed And was sent up and passed in also the Lords without any further intercourse betwene the houses. 30 Junij 1607.[353]

Billes. When amendmentes or provisoes come from the Lords, the use is to read them twice, and committ the consideracion to the former Committees for the bill. 30 Junij 1607.

Billes. A report from a Committee touching a Bill referred to them but the readinge deferred till the next day, 30 Junij The amendments desired by the Lords and the proviso to be added to the Bill of Clothing was the thing reported and deferred to be read 3 Julij it passed uppon a third reading.[354]

A proviso sent downe by the Lords to be added to the Bill of Southwark uppon twice reading put to the question for Commitment, and ordred not to be committed. The same proviso uppon a third reading much argued *pro et contra*, and putt to the question for passage did passe. 2 Julij 1607.[355]

Bill. The Bill for increase & preservacion of timber uppon the first reading beeing found apparantly inconvenient was disputed 2 July 1607. This is not usuall but yet hath also beene done at other times. [**f.105v**][356]

---

[351] *Ibid.* i. 388–9; *Bowyer*, pp. 358–63.
[352] *CJ*, i. 388.
[353] **Lawrence Hyde** moved to add the word 'oath'. *Ibid.* i. 388–9; *Bowyer*, p. 362.
[354] The dates mentioned in *CJ*, i. 389 are 1–2 July.
[355] This was actually the bill to confirm a clause in the charter of Southampton. *Ibid.* i. 390.
[356] *Ibid.* i. 390.

The Committee appointed to consider the entries made by the Clark make report that they had taken into their consideracion Three thinges whereof the entries principally consisted Matter of priviledge Matter of order and Matter of message and entercourse betwene both the houses, And conceaved that as in this parliament there had as many and as weighty matters come in question as ever in any former parliament So it were fitt some extraordinary care should be taken in keeping a memoriall of them For the present they had sett downe in writing what course they thought fitt to be held, with a desire it might be read & entred which was to this effect, that the Clark should perfect his journall for the Three first Sessions, that noe matter concerning priviledge order message or conference should be esteemed to be of Record, or of force till it had beene perused and perfitted by a Committee to be appointed the next Session and approved by the house And that from henceforth the Committee doe every saterday in the afternoone peruse and perfect the book of entries in all the said poincts And that some course be taken for reward to the Clark. 3 Julij.[357]

Collection. Committee appointed to consider of the distribution of the money collected by the Collectors for the benevolence of the house 3 Julij.

The some came to about 42^{li} And yet 87 knightes and burgesses did not pay distributed in this sort To the Clark of the parliament 10^{li} The Serjeant xij^{li} Mr. Speakers officers vj^{li} Fower of Mr. Ewens [**f.106**] his Clarks 4^{li} Fower of Mr. Serjeants men vj^{li} Usher of the Court of Wardes and usher of the Exchequer for attending at Committees 4^{s} a peece &c. to be paid the next day in the Court of Wardes.[358]

Mr. Speaker informeth the house that it was his Majesties pleasure himself and the whole house shall attend in the higher house in the afternoone at 2 of the Clock and put them in minde that uppon such occasion it hath beene the manner First to assemble in this house & goe up with the Speaker which was nowe so ordred. Mr. Speaker, the Clark & Serjeant dined in the Committee Chamber Presently after dinner Mr, Speaker was sent for to Whitehall to the King about the Bill of Clothing Mr. Speaker returning to the house about fower of the Clock, he with the Commons were sent for to attend his Majestie in the higher house, where Mr. Speaker made a speach, the Lord Chancelor answered him The King made a speach, Then was the royall assent geven to billes as they were read, The title of the Bill read by the Clerk of the Crowne of the Chancery, and the royall assent or disassent read by the Clerk of the Parliament in this sort &c.[359]

---

[357] *Ibid.* i. 390. The reporter was **Sir Edwin Sandys**, see *Bowyer*, pp. 367–8.
[358] *Ibid.* i. 390–1.
[359] *Ibid.* i. 391–2.

Sir Edward Mountagu's Diary of the 1607 Session
[Northants. RO, Montagu MS 30:]

A jornall of the Sessions for Parliament begun the 18 of
November 1606 4° Ja:

Tuesday 18 Novemb.

19 No. cottd	bb: An act to make good the
28 reported	grants of all assurancs made by
2 decemb dashed	corporations notwithstanding the
	misnaming of the corporation.

Mr. Speaker told us his majesties pleasure was we should attend in
the higher house that after noone at ij of the clock: which we did: wher
the Lord Chancelor by his majesties command deliverd a speech: ~~And
after his majestie used~~ And the answer to the grevances was red And
after that his majestie made a speach: especially aboute the union.[360]

Wedensday 19 No:
The former bill reed ageyne & a committee chosen about priveleges.
   The answer to the grevances was by his majesties direction sent to
Mr. Speaker which we read.

Thursday 20 [November]
A message from the Lords who sent us the Instrument of the Union
agreed one by the commissioners. It was somwhat late[361] before yt cam
downe so the reeding of yt was deferred to the next day.

Friday 21 [November]
The Instrument of the union was reede.[362]

Saterday 22 [November]
The committees for preveleges my selfe being one made there reports
of these things

---

[360] The speeches are noted in *CJ*, i. 314–15; *Bowyer*, pp. 185–6. The answer to the
grievances is printed in *CJ*, i. 316–18.
[361] 11am according to *CJ*, i. 318.
[362] For which see *ibid.* i. 318–23.

For Sir Humphry Winches place made cheffe baron of Ireland: we had a presedent for yt the last session

Sir James Lees case made cheffe Justice there: that a new one was chosen for him & we thought yt fitt agayne which the house allowed of:

And Sir Tho: Rigeway Sir Oliver St Jhon sent likewise ?over into Ireland & ~~having~~ there their service being [?required] that they could not attend here we thought [?to choose] new for them. This agreed to likewise.

For the case of Imbassadors: yt was last ?so ruled & so many presedents that ther returne being uncertyne & at his majesties will that no new should be chosen for them.

For Mr. Atturney his case whether to be demaunded oute of the heyher house in that there was some difference we never found president that the Atturney had served in the house: but there was many presedents of the Sollicitor & the Kings Serjeant that though they had writs to attend in the higher house being returned members of the Comon house they served therein And the same reason held for the Atturney as did for them, there was one forme of the writt & no more necessity in his service in the higher house then of theres:[363]

This was much debated in the house at length resolved that yt should rest till further time ~~of debate~~.

Monday, 24 [November]
Mr. Atturney cam into the house with Mr. Speaker *quod nota*.[364]

Sir Anthony Cope moved that the Instrument of the union might be sent to the Lords with the message that yt had bene reed & divers coppys taken of yt: So **Mr. Secretary Harbet** accompand with divers of the house caried yt:

Sir Will: Maurice deliverd in a bill for the name of greate brittyne.

A message from the Lords that they having recyved the Instrument of the Union & considering how gravely & judicially we had proceeded in the reading of yt & taking a coppy & so returning yt to them: desired that seeing yt wer a matter of that Importance so much concerning the whole realme And that ther house & ours made but one ~~house~~ courte of parliament that all other occasions sett aside we would geve them conference [tomor]row in the after noone ij of the clock in the paynted chamber there number – 40.[365]

After Mr. Speaker had delivred this message there was a great silence in the house so that Mr. Speaker was fayne to rise & know the houses pleasure.

---

[363] *Ibid.* i. 324; *Bowyer*, pp. 188–9; Cotton Diary, p. 104.
[364] Following the question raised about his attendance on 22 November.
[365] *CJ*, i. 324.

?Thus ?was conference made some ?staggeyng because we had nothing to confer of but to geve the Lords meeting & to heare what they would propound we would be ready & so appoynted 80. And so the message was sent them that we would according to there Lo: desire geve them meeting & heere what they would propound & so report to the house & so to proceede further.[366]

25 Novemb:

In the morning I was not ther: there being divers pryvate bills read.[367]

In that afternoone we attended the lords who would have bene glad that we had come with a large commission than only to have heard & therefo.

The propounded things concerning the manner of proceeding in the union beeing that we might have a larged commission that the things propounded might be debated from poynct to poynct.[368]

26 Novemb:

An Act to explane the act the last Session of free trade not to make voyd the letters patents for exetor.[369]

An act for the better inabling of Jhon Eveling esq. to sell land for payment of his debts.[370]

An act for the sale of some of the lands of Tho Momperson esq. for the payment of his debts.

An act for the better continuance of the fame & memory of noble & worthy persons deceased.

Mr. Recorder made reporte of the Lords speaches at the meeteing many propositions was propounded what course might be taken in those affayres but nothing agreed one for that day but referred till to morrow.

27 November

We fell into debate what answer to returne to the Lords.

At length agreed uppon what we should send a message to the Lords that for the Hostele Lawes & matter of commerce we would take in debate leaving the border matter & naturalising to ther Lordships.[371]

---

[366] Bowyer noted that Mountagu considered that because the Commons' answer failed to endorse the Lords' message they should have returned answer by their own messengers. *Bowyer*, p. 191.

[367] Three private bills, the free trade bill and the bill for the fame of noble persons received first readings on this day. *CJ*, i. 324.

[368] Reports (made the following morning) are to be found in *ibid.* i. 325; *Bowyer*, 191–2.

[369] 3 Jac. I, cap. 6 abrogated the charters of all companies trading with France and Spain. *SR*, iv. 1083.

[370] i.e. John Evelyn. *CJ*, i. 325.

[371] *Ibid.* i. 1005; *Bowyer*, pp. 195–7.

The Lords sent us word and we should have ther answer to morrow.

28 Novemb[er]

An act to direct some proceedings in causes & courtes ecclesiastical.[372]

A message from the Lords repeating the effecte of our message: And that if uppon our second thought we thought not fitt leaving us to proceed as we thought but would have be [i.e. been] glad there might have bene a community in this betwene us considering the matters concerned all of us in our persons blood & fortunes.

We returned they should presently heere from us whereuppon we sent them word that we never intended to deny a conference but that we purposed to debate those things which we fittest for our capacety in this house amongst our selves & leaving the higher matters of state to be likewise debated by them & then to have word in conference. But for the expediting of the busines we would fall into debate of all the matters amongst our selves desering that ther Lo: would do the like & then when we wer ready we would send to there Lo: for conference This message pleased the Lords.[373]

29 Novemb:

Sir Fra: Barington deliverd in a bill agreed with old bill the last sessions agaynst the Canons.[374]

We fell into debate what course to take in the proceeding of the union. A committee of most the house was chosen & appoynted to meete in the house one Monday in th'afternoone.[375]

Monday the first decemb

Nothing donne to my remembrance.[376]

2: Decemb:

19 Feb co'ttd	bb An act to restryne the uttering
6 march passed	of beere and Ale to Alehouseys
	not licensed.[377]

---

[372] This bill dealt with the *ex officio* oath, one of the issues Mountagu raised in his speech of 23 March 1604 on this subject, for which see above and *Bowyer*, pp. 199–200.

[373] *CJ*, i. 326; *Bowyer*, p. 198.

[374] 'To retrain the execution of Canons ecclesiastical not confirmed by Parliament' *CJ*, i. 326. This was another of the measures recommended by Mountagu on 23 March 1604.

[375] *Ibid.* i. 326; *Bowyer*, pp. 198–9.

[376] **Sir Hugh Beeston** was appointed one of the collectors of the benevolence, and the House adjourned early in preparation for the afternoon's Grand Committee on the Instrument of Union. *CJ*, i. 326–7.

[377] Enacted as 4 Jac. I, cap. 4. *SR*, iv. 1141–2.

10 decemb co'tte
15 Feb Ingrossd
5 march passed

bb An act to restryne Canons not confirmed by act of parliament

3 decemb[er] nothing[378]

4 december
co'ttd
12 May passed

b An act for naturalising Doctor Barrow[379] his wife & children.

co'ttd

b An act for the releffe of Mary Cavendish the wiffe of Will Candish late deceessed.

5 december
8 decemb co'tted
    passed

bb An act agaynst the odious & loathsom sinne of drunkennese.

6 decemb
8 decemb co'ttd:

b An act to avoyd the infinite nomber of buildings in and aboute London & agaynst Inmates

8 December
co'ttd:
11 May passed

bb An act for reformacion of abuses committed in the: court of marshalsey & for limitacion of the Jurisdiction of the same.

9 Decemb
16 decem dashed

bb An act to prevent causes of devorce and separation betwene man & wife.

co'ttd

bb An act for exposition of a branch of the statute 18 Eliz. aboute bastards[380]

cott:
1 May passed

bb An act for explanation of the statute the first of this parliament

---

[378] Interim report on the Union committee, two bills read and one reported, complaint about border abuses. *Ibid.* i. 327; *Bowyer*, pp. 199–200.

[379] Peter Baro, MD. The measure was enacted as HLRO, 4 James I, OA 30.

[380] 18 Eliz. I, cap. 3, 'An Act for the setting of the poor on work'. *SR*, iv. 610–13.

touching Tanners.[381]

10 decemb

The Lords sent us a message to have a conference aboute the two first parts of the union which had bene debated severally amongst our selves.[382] We assented to meet them of Saterday next.

11 december

L bb   An act for the better satisfiing of
                                       due debts
b   An act for the explanation of the
                                       statute of Tonnage & poundage
                                       made the first session of this par-
                                       liament.[383]

12: ~~& 13~~ *[December]*

I was at a comittees [*sic*] in the morning for marshalling the conference with the Lords & that day was brought from the Lords 3 bills.

LL b   one for the passing of the vic-
twise red that day & the next   arage or parsonage of Chesson
dae passed   to the Erle of Salisbury & for the
                                       vicarege or parsonage of Orsney
                                       to the bishop of London in
                                       recompence.[384]

LL b   An act for confirmation of the
15 decemb cott   Kings letters patents to Robert
passed   Bathurst of the manor of Lea-
                                       chlade in Glocester shire.[385]

LL b   The like for the mannor of Bard-
15 decemb cottd   esly in Glocester shire to Bou-
passed   chers.[386]
13 decemb cottd   b An act for to confirme the
a new bill put in   Kings letters patents to Sir Roger

[381] 1 Jac. I, cap. 22. *SR*, iv. 1039–48.
[382] The two parts in question were hostile laws and commerce; *CJ*, i. 329; *Bowyer*, p. 204.
[383] Briefly detailed in *Bowyer*, pp. 204–5. The 1604 bill was 1 Jac. I, cap. 33. *SR*, iv. 1062–4.
[384] Enacted as HLRO, 4 James I, OA 18.
[385] Enacted as HLRO, 4 James I, OA 20.
[386] Enacted as HLRO, 4 James I, OA 21.

Aston for the mannor of Some.[387]

Saterday 13 decemb
I was as before in conference aboute ordering the buisines with the Lords. That after noone we conferred with the Lords.

Monday 15 decemb

b An act aboute assurance of land to the heyrs of George Clifton esq. maried to Sir Anthony Torrolds daughter.

cottd

b An act to enable Henry Boughton to sell lands for payment of his debts. comted with the above.

Tuesday 16 december
conferd with the Lords in the after noone.

Wedensd. 17 [December]
conferred with the Lords both fornoone & afternoone.

Thusday 18 december
A message from the Lords signifiing his majesties pleasure to ?rejorne this courte till Tuesday the xth of february next.[388]

Tuesday 10 Feb:
We mett agayne & then Mr. Speaker made knowen unto us that Sir Michaell Sonds had a man called finsh[389] was arrest & in execution: whereuppon ordered that the Serjeant & procurer ~~was sent~~ should be sent for.

Then **Mr. James** a burgesse made knowen how that in this Cessation he had bene like wise arrested & forced to compound: It was likewise ordered that the Attorney & sergant should be sent for.

The Speaker related what had bene donne the last Sitting for bills passed; bills in committee & bills once reede.

After that he read a note of remembraunces of the conference for the two first points of the union: put off till the next day to be considered of.

---

[387] Soham, Cambridgeshire.
[388] *CJ*, i. 331; Cotton Diary, pp. 105–6.
[389] Thomas Finch. *CJ*, i. 332.

Wedensday 11 [February]

Mr. Speaker remembred the house to fall into consideracion of the remembrances: but being moved that yt might stay till the terme was ended that we might have the lawyers: yt was put of till Friday.

Bateman the Atturney & Hutchens the sergent that arrested **Mr. James** we heard & committed to the Serjeant for a moneth & so during the pleasure of the house.[390]

Thursday 12 [February]

13 Feb: cottd 18 Feb Ingrossd 25 Feb dashed: I 53 No: 88	b An act for confirmation of the Kings letters patent to Sir Roger Aston for the manor of Soame in Cambrigeshire
13 Feb: ~~dashed~~ rejected	An act for reformation of abuses & due execution of Justice in the courte of Marshalsey within the Virge.
18 Feb cottd 5 march Ingss. 9 march passed	bb An act for some addicion to be made to the statut of 8 H 6 for forcible entries.[391]

Friday 13 Feb:

Mr. Speaker offered to the house the examenacion of the conference to be read: aboute which some dispute did grow.

And one **Sir Christopher Pigott** the knight for Buckingham shire rising once or twice reade all one told him that if he spake he should rest up & not sitt still: whereuppon he rose & made a very offensive speach agaynste the Scotts: much to the dislike & greffe of the whole house yet by reason of the outeragiousnes of the speach both in words & actions they wer rather driven into an astoneshment then to answer or say anything to [*sic* so] yt was passd over with silence.[392]

And we fell into the busines: the house not allowing the paper of remembrances to be any record but to be delivered to **Mr. recorder**[393] agayne that brought yt in & he to reporte. So Mr. Atturney & he reported & the next day appoynted to fall into debate.

Then the Serjant & the procurer of **Sir Micheal Sonds** his man to be arrested we hard Sir Michaell Sonds his man had privelege &

---

[390] Robert Bateman and Peter Hutchins. *Ibid.* i. 333.

[391] 8 Hen. VI, cap. 9. *SR*, ii. 244–6.

[392] *Ibid.* i. 333.

[393] i.e. The diarist's brother **Sir Henry Mountagu**, Recorder of London.

the serjeant & procurer but because that Finch was once attorney at common place[394] sworne which is not usuall & therefore to be pre-supposte that he could belong to none of the parleamente house.[395]

Saterday 14 [February]

We fell into debate of the matter of naturalisacion.

Mr. Fuller spake saying yt was hurtfull to both realmes especially to England & that things ?of this nature could not passe nor binde the subjecte without an act of parliament.[396]

~~assone as this speach was ended Mr. Speaker told us that ther was a message~~

Assoone as **Mr. Fuller** had ended **Mr. Wentworth** stept up but Mr. Speaker told us there was a message from the Lords who we called in.

Th'effect was to desire a conference both of the ij former poyncts formerly debated as also of the matter of naturalising.

~~Yt was ruled that~~

The day to be Monday next the wonted place & the former committee.

Yt was ruled after some debate that we would send messengers of our owne for with which we did which in effect was had that as yet we wer not ~~yet ready to give them answer~~ resolved what answer to make their lordship but as soone as we wer they should heare from us.[397]

Monday 16 Feb:

Sir George More remembred the house of **Sir Christopher Pigott's** speache & some course to be taken: That he being absent might be sent for & that a co'ttee might be chosen to sett downe the words wherewith to charge him. They tooke order presently & sent the serjeant for him:-but for the other poyncte there was much debate: whether fitt to charge him with particuler or ellst in generall (while we wer thus in debate he came into the house the Serjeant missing him assoone as he was spied Mr. Speaker willed him to withdraw him selfe & not departe.)

The words we thought so odious & so unpleasing that yt could not but breed offence in the repeticion & therefore concluded that he should be charged in generall for his speach To heare how he would extenuate yt & so proceede to Judgmente He was called in but gave

---

[394] i.e. The court of Common Pleas.
[395] *CJ*, i. 334; *Bowyer*, pp. 209–10; Cotton Diary, p. 107.
[396] *CJ*, i. 334–5.
[397] *Ibid.* i. 335.

no greate satisfaction in his extenuation which was he ment yt but of the Scotts that would have killed the King & not of the nation in generall.

Concluded for his punishment that he should go to the tower during the pleasure of the house to be removed from his place of service & a new writt to go forth to elect a new knight.[398]

Tuesday 17 Feb
23 Feb cott   bb An act for the true making of
12 May passed   wollen cloaths.[399]

bb An act to geve costs to deft: upon a non suite of the play:[400] or verdect agaynst him.

20 Feb. cottd   b An act for the better inabling
                                     of Herbert Pelham esq. to sell
                                     the mannor of Swinsted in the
                                     county of Lincolne.

We fell into the poynte of naturalising:[401]

Wedensdey 18 Feb:
Debate of naturalising

Sir Roger Owen moved these cautions
First to relinquish all there freedome & privileges in Fraunce.
Secondly the renowncing of the French to have freedome with them.
3 to be under our government of our church in the rites & ceremonies of religion.
4 to be subject to our lawes.
5 we for a time to have the precedency & preferment.[402]

Wednesday [sic Thursday] 19
Hutchins the Serjeant made a submission & ordred that he should be released.[403]
Naturalising.[404]

---

[398] *Ibid.* i. 335–6.
[399] Enacted as 4 Jac. I, cap. 2. *SR*, iv. 1137–40.
[400] The abbreviations denote 'defendant' and 'plaintiff'.
[401] *CJ*, i. 336–7, 1015.
[402] Owen was the last of several speakers. *Ibid.* i. 337, 1016.
[403] The man who had arrested the MP Richard James. See above 10–11 February.
[404] *CJ*, i. 338, 1016–18; PRO, SP14/26/54.

Thursday [Friday] 20 Feb.

21 Feb. cottd	b An act for further assurance to
25 Ingrossd	the purchasers of Sir Jonathan
28 Feb passd:	Trelany his lands.[405]

A message from the Lords to hasten the conference we returned answer by there messengers that we wer not yet ready but assoone as we wer they should heare from us.[406]

Naturalisation.[407]

Friday [sic Saturday] 21 Feb

25 cottd:	b An act for confirmation of an
12 May Ingrossd	act 32 H.8 aboute Church-wardens in St. Saviour in South-worke.[408]

24 feb cottd	b An act to inable the com-mittees of Ro: Tompson esq.
12 march Ingrossd	lunaticke to dispose of lands for
14 passed:	Joyntur.[409]

Naturalising.[410]

The committees for the union matter to meete that after noone to meete & to dispute of yt shortly & not by way of long discourse which was done.

Saterday 22 [sic 21] Feb

26 Feb rejected	bb An act for the utter abol-ishing & prohibiting of logwood and blockwood to be used in England.

Ordered that the committees for union should meete agayne & so reharse there opinion to the house. Which was donne & at committee by a generall voyce some few excepted that there opinion was that the Scots are not by the laws of the realme naturalised.

[405] Enacted as HLRO, 4 James I, OA 24.
[406] *CJ*, i. 338–9.
[407] *Ibid.* i. 1018–19.
[408] For which see HLRO, Main Papers (Parchment Collection) Box 1E, 27 May 1607. It enlarged upon 32 Hen. VIII, OA 49.
[409] Enacted as HLRO, 4 James I, OA 27.
[410] *CJ*, i. 1019–20.

Monday 23 Feb.

25 Feb cottd	b An act to converte the prebend
2 March Ingrossed	of Cutton in Devon being *sine*
5 March passed	*cura* to the mayntenance of a free schoole[411]

26 Feb. cottd	bb An act to avoyde the distruction of wheate & other grayne by making of starch

26 Feb. cottd	b An act for naturalising of Jhon
13 Ingssed	Ramsden gent.[412]
passed:	

A reporte what was donne and agreed by the committees on Saterday wheruppon message was sent unto the Lords that for the first poynt of naturalising we wer ready to confer with ther lordships at ther pleasure after this day.[413]

They appoynted Wedensday next.

Tuesday 24 [February]

9 May cottd	b An act for the drayning of the fenns & low ground in the Isle of Ely & other counties conteyning 3 hundred thousand acer.[414]

The rest of the day spent in nominating cottees to speake to morrow with the Lords.[415]

Wedensday 25 Feb

28 Feb cottd	b An act for the founding a free schoole in Northleach in the county of Gloster.[416]

[411] HLRO, Main Papers, 9 Mar. 1607.
[412] HLRO, 4 James I, OA 33.
[413] *CJ*, i. 339, 1020.
[414] *Ibid.* i. 340 mentions 30,000 acres; the final Act mentions only 6,000: 4 Jac. I, cap. 13; *SR*, iv. 1152.
[415] *CJ*, i. 340.
[416] 4 Jac. I, cap. 7. *SR*, iv. 1144–6.

Then we fell into the matter of naturalising.[417]

Thursday 26 Feb.
bb An act to make Joyntresses *apres* possibility of Issue extinct subject to waste as tenant in dower or for life.[418]

4 March cottd
5 March Ingrossd
9 March passd

bb An act agaynst non-residency & plurality of benefices

bb An act for better satisfiing of due debtes.[419]

This afternone we hard the Judges in poynte of naturalisation.

Friday 27 Feb.
4 March cottd
27 Ingrossd
1 May: passd

bb An act for better provision of meadow & pasture for mayntenance of Tillage in divers Townes in the county of Hereford.[420]

Saterday 28 Feb.
A message from his majestie to take some order for the better attendance of the members of the house ordered that the house should be called on Monday come sevennight & all that wer absent to be sent for by the Serjeant.[421]

Monday 2 March
cottd 11 March
Then a sleepe

b An act touching Iron millnes neere the city of London & for preservation of woods neere certeyne places.[422]

bb An act for the more assured execution of Justice in Ecclesiasticall courts:

[417] There was also a lengthy complaint about Spanish interference with English trade. *CJ*, i. 340–2.
[418] Second reading. *Ibid.* i. 342.
[419] Second reading. *Ibid.* i. 343.
[420] Enacted as 4 Jac. I, cap. 11. *SR*, iv. 1149–51.
[421] *CJ*, i. 344 and Cotton Diary p. 107 date this to 27 February.
[422] Draft bill in BL, Add. 34218, fols 94–5.

bb An act for avoyding of Idlenes & reforming abuses in Tipling howses:

The reporte of the Judges opinion.

A message from the Lords that they have a purpose to send presently to & therfor desired us to sitt a while.

The message from the Lords. That forasmuch as yt was not unknown unto us that in the greate matter of unione they had held a uneformitie with us, & that the greatest poynte was yet to come undebated of saving in one braunch therof wherein they have no way expressed there opinion: And therefore before any further proceeding we would determine of some shorte meeting to confer of naturalisation in generall to the intent that at the next meeting each house might know each others mindes & then to draw to some resolucion.

This message was dictated owte of a peece of paper by there messenger being Serjeant Crooke.

Mr. Speaker desired of him the paper he answered they wer but shorte notes from his owne remembrance, but yf the house doubted of any thing he would be ready to geve further satisfaction. The messenger withdrawen Mr. Speaker desired that his memory might not be charged with that message which seemed to be so carefully deliverd that yt was sett downe in writing whereuppon yt was agreed to call them in agayne & Serjeant Crooke to dictate yt so leysurely as our clarke might wright yt after him which was donne.

Then we returned answer that they should after this day here from us. A committee was selected oute of the greate committee to consider of this motion.[423]

Tuesday 3 March
13 mar cottd

b An act to repeale a braunch of statute made 1 Ja: concerning wherrymen & watermen.[424]

9 March cottd
14 Marc Ingrossd
2 May passed

bb An act for explanation of the statute 13 Ell: concerning subscription.[425]

Mr. Speaker made a motion for some charitable course to be taken

[423] *CJ*, i. 345–6.

[424] 1 Jac. I, cap. 16. *SR*, iv. 1034.

[425] 13 Eliz. I, cap. 12, 'An Act to reform certain disorders touching ministers of the church'. *SR*, iv. 546–7.

for the releving of those counties lately surrounded whereuppon a committee was chosen.[426]

The committee chosen to make answer to the lords brought there opinion in writing: to this effect That for asmuch as there lo had sent unto us to geve them a meeting & confer in the poynct of naturalisation in generall: for the *post nati* we had already debated & for the conveniency we would prepare our selves as soone as might be to attend that service with them.

They returned by our messenger that they had sent unto us to confer of naturalisation in generall how we understood yt they left to our wysdomes they meaning to make no other explanation & withall desired us with convenient speede to prepare our selves for the conference.

Hereuppon we appoynted the committees to meet agayne for to consider an answer of this which was that for the first parte there lordships had hard our opinions: And for the second there lordship would be pleased to open them selves we would be ready to confer ~~this was delivered in by writing: by Sir Edward Hobby.~~[427]

A message from the Lords with ij bills

6 march read	bb Agaynst dividing of tenements Inmates, undersetters & other
11 march rejected	unlawfull houses in and aboute London & Westminster & 3 miles thereof.
LL:	bb An act to restryne the multitude of inconvenient building
27 Aprill cottd	about London & Westmr. & the suburbs of the same.

Wednesday 4 March
bb An act for the better attendance of the commons house of parliament.

6 march cottd	b An act betwene warren &
30 march passed	waller the same that was last session.[428]

Sir Edw: Hobby sent with the message to the Lords aboute the

---

[426] The floods had affected Somerset, where Phelips' own estates lay. *CJ*, i. 346; Cotton Diary, p. 108.

[427] This report was made by **Sir Edward Hoby**. *CJ*, i. 346–7.

[428] Enacted as HLRO, 4 James I, OA 28.

conference: in delivery whereof he used these words that Knights citisens burgesses & Barons of the Commons courte of parliament:-

To this the Lords tooke exception & sent us words to stay a while & that they would send unto us messengers of there owne.

We sate tell one of the clocke & then Serjeant Crooke came with the message That the strength of both houses consisted in nothing more then in the rightes & priveleges that pertayned to each house: & whereas there was delivered unto them a message for the Knights citesens burgesses & barons of the commons courte of parliament: first they knew of none that could sitt in that house A baron of parliament though that there was some such eyther by Appellation or denomination as the barons of cinq portes: & for the word courte both howses made but one courte: but they tooke this to be but *lapsis linguae* of the messenger & therefore leave that: & if so we pleased they would geve us meeting on Saterday next.[429]

We returned answer that yt was late & that to morrow they should have answer.

That afternoone there was conference by the committee what answere to make: which was reported by **Mr. Marten.**[430]

Thursday 5 March:

Mr. Martin was sent to the Lords for the word baron yt was usuall our bookes full & the statute of 9 H8: stand [*sic* stated] yt playnly For the word courte the messenger did not remember he used that word but if he did yt might well beborne but leaving question of words they would geve conference at the day & place appoynted: **Mr. Martinn** brought word that the Lords would leave contention of words for that time: but my Lord Chancelor desired leave of the lords & commons: that he might remember there was no such statute of 9 H8: but 6 of H8 & therefore that hereafter we would nott geve creditt to the abridgment withowte seing the statute at large.[431]

Friday 6 March:

2 May cottd

bb An act for the more speedy payment of the Kings debts & to provide that the subjects may more spedily be payd there debts due to them.

---

[429] *CJ*, i. 348; *Bowyer*, pp. 212–14; Cotton Diary, pp. 108–9.
[430] On the following morning. *CJ*, i. 348.
[431] *Ibid.* i. 348–99; *Bowyer*, p. 216; Cotton Diary, p. 109.

Saterday 7 March:

13 march Ingssd   b. An act for naturalising
2 May passed   Demistres[432]

Sir Edwin Sands made reporte how the the [*sic*] cottees had ordered
the matters for conference that after noone:[433]
    We conferd.

Monday 9 March:
    Yt was late ere I cam but nothing of moment.
    Only the calling of house was put of till Saterday next.

bb: An act aswell for the case & good of Jurors as the publike benefites
unto sutors together with together with the preventing and reforming of
many Inconveniences & enormeties dayly committed by undersheriffs &
bayliffs.[434]

Tuesday 10 March

13 May rejected   bb An act conserning measuring
                                   assising & marking of timber
                                   used in building.

Wedensdey 11 March
    A message from the Lords to put of the converence till Saterday.

28 Aprill cottd   b An act aboute one Holdich for
                                   reversing a fine.[435]

Thursdey 12 March
bb. An act for better ordering & directing of common ballances in
market townes.

Friday 13 March:
    There was one committed to the serjeant for taking **Mr. James** the
burgesse of bristow his horsse to ride post.[436]

---

[432] James Desmaistres. HLRO, 4 James I, OA 31.
[433] *CJ*, i. 350.
[434] No such bill is recorded as being read on this day. *Ibid.* i. 350–1, 1028–9.
[435] The background to the dispute is rehearsed in *ibid.* i. 380–1.
[436] *CJ*, i. 352; Cotton Diary, p. 109.

Saterday 14 March
We conferd with the lords: butt brake of upon the difference of *post* &
antenatis.[437]

Monday 16:
This day Mr. Speaker fell sick & come not to the house till Tuesday
the 24 of March: & then he taried not but rejorned the courte till
Thursday:-The parliament men that wer in the house went to a sermon
to Westminster:[438]

Thursdey 26 March 1607
   Mr. Holt made reporte of the first days conference with the Lordes
which was Saturday was fortenight & **Mr. Recorder** made reporte of
the last days conference which was Saterdaye was sevennight: & how
yt went not forward by reason that the Lords would make a difference
betwene *postnatis* and *antenatis*: & we wer commaunded that yt they did
so we should but heare them.[439]
   A message from the Lords: 2 bills.
LL:

[27 March] read[440]	b An act touching the drowned
28 cotted	marshes of Lessens & Fant in the
31 passed	county of Kent[441]
LL:	
27 read	b An act whereby Rich Sackvile
28 cotted	esq. is inabled to surrender the
31 March passed	office of cheffe butlership of
	England & Wales notwith-
	standinge his minority:[442]

The house this day was divided for the hearing of the counsell of the
marshalsey. The I wer: 110: The no: 89 so they wer hard:[443]

Friday 27 March:
   A message from the Lords to desire our patience to sitt a while &
they would send unto us.

[437] The conference took place at 2pm in the Painted Chamber. *Bowyer,* pp. 235–40.
[438] The day being the fourth anniversary of the King's accession. *CJ,* i. 354.
[439] i.e. The conferences on 7 and 14 March. *Ibid.* i. 354, 1032.
[440] The first reading of this bill is not recorded in the Journal; it otherwise proceeded
in tandem with Sackvile's bill. *Ibid.* i. 355–7.
[441] Lesnes and Fants. 4 Jac. I, cap. 8. *SR,* iv. 1146–7.
[442] HLRO, 4 James I, OA 17.
[443] *CJ,* i. 354–5.

There message was to move a new meeting agayne aboute the matters whereaboute we brake of at the last day:

We sent them word we would advyse of there Lordship motion & when we wer resolved they should here from us by messenger of our owne.[444]

Saterday 28 March

A messag from the Lord: a bill.

LL:

31 March read	An act to make liable the lands & tenements of Will Cardinall deceassed to a decree of 500[l.] decreed in the courte of White Hall[445]
6 May rejected	

Monday 29 [sic 30] March

30 Aprill cottd	b A private bill aboute the assurance of the manor of Mott in kent to **Sir Will Selby**:[446]
8 May rejected	b: An act to restryne the fruicterers of London from going abroad to sell there fruict on the Sabbath day & for the better goverment of such as sell fruict in London & within 3 miles of the same.

Mr. Speaker signified his majesties pleasure to speake with us before we brake up the sitting: Therefore none to departe till to morrow at two of the clock at which time we should have accesse to his majestie in the meane season to stay further speach of the matter in debate which was aboute conferring with the lords.[447]

A message from the Lords j bill.

LL:

31 March read	An act for confirmation of certaine lands to All Soules college in Osford & to Sir Will Smith knight.[448]
cottd	
8 May passed:	

---

[444] *Ibid.* i. 356; *Bowyer*, pp. 242-4.

[445] i.e. The court of Requests.

[446] Ightham Mote, Kent. The bill seems to have been intended to extinguish the reversionary claim held by Stephen Allen, whose father had sold the manor to Selby while he was still underage, and hence unable to waive his rights.

[447] *CJ*, i. 357.

[448] Enacted as HLRO, 4 James I OA 22.

Tuesday 31 March:
A message from the Lords j bill.
LL:

15 May cottd	An act for confirmation of letters patents to be made uppon composition with his majestie his Heyres & Successors for 7 yeares ~~time~~

Mr. Speaker signified his majesties pleasure to be that we should attend in the courte in the greate chamber & to rejorne the courte till 4 of the clock in the After noone.

At two of the clocke we attended in the greate chamber which was prepared like to the parliament house, The bishops of one side the Lords of the other & we at the end.

His majestie used a long speach of 2 howres long or very neere & performed yt most excellently:

Then we went to the house which by his majesties direction was rejorned till Monday the 20th of Aprill:/[449]

Monday 20th Aprill
We mett but being very few then nothing donne.[450]

Tuesday 21th Aprell
The house was still so thinn & Sct. Georgs feast drawing on we ~~advised to~~ we adjerned the courte till Monday:

The Lords sent us a bill.
LL:

29 Aprell read	b, An act for securing & confirming of lands & tenements devised & geven to the Maior & comminalty of London.[451]
4 May cottd.	
9 May passed	

Monday 27 Aprill
The bill of fenns read & counsell appoynted to be herd one Wedensday:

A motion to fall into consideracion of the matter of the union: which was appoynted to morrow at 9 a clock.

---

[449] *CJ*, i. 357–63; *Bowyer*, pp. 252–3.
[450] *Bowyer*, p. 253 states that one MP counted 53 members present.
[451] Enacted as HLRO, 4 James I OA 23.

Tuesday 28: Aprill

1 May cottd	b: An act for explanation of the
8 May passed	statute made 3 Jacobi for bring-
	ing in water to the north parts
	of London[452]

At 9 of the clock **Sir Edwin Sands** entred into the matter of the union some notes wherof see in a paper by yt selfe.[453]

Wedensday 29 Aprill

1 May cottd	b An act for confirmation of
	some parte of a charter graunted
	by H:6: to the Maior & burgesses
	of the towne of Southampton[454]

Matter of the union debated uppon **Sir Edwin Sands** motion debated [*sic*][455]

Thursday 30 Aprill

b An Act to repeall a branch of a statute made 1 Jacob: agaynst forreyne Curriers.[456]

The matter of the union uppon **Sir Ed: Sa:** debated.[457]

Friday 1 May:

1 May cottd	b An act for naturalising of
	Thomas Anwood.[458]
May cottd	bb An act to reform the mis-
	demenors mariners & saylors
	after they have bene hired.[459]

We fell into debate aboute the former matter of the union.[460]

After som few had spoken Mr. Speaker told us that he had receyved letters to signifie his majesties pleasure to us which was that he hard

---

[452] 3 Jac. I, cap. 18. *SR*, iv. 1092–3.
[453] This paper has not been found. See *CJ*, i. 364, 1035–6; *Bowyer*, pp. 255–63.
[454] Enacted as 4 Jac. I, cap. 10. *SR*, 1148–9.
[455] *CJ*, i. 365, 1037; *Bowyer*, pp. 263–74.
[456] Presumably part of the Tanners' Act, 1 Jac. I, cap. 22. *SR*, iv. 1039–48.
[457] *CJ*, i. 365, 1038; *Bowyer*, pp. 274–84.
[458] *CJ*, i. 365 says Thomas Annoot.
[459] HLRO, Main Papers, 11 June 1607.
[460] *CJ*, i. 366, 1039; *Bowyer*, pp. 284–6.

there was some speaches of his late speach & therefore we should forbeare till we had attended him which he appoynted to morrow at two of the clock in the greate chamber: at the courte.[461]

Saterday 2 May:
Some bills cottd & passed, the counsell for the marshalsey bill was brought in & one of them moved that the lawyers of the house might [be] sent for so after som speach they wer withdrawn & the house devided whether the consell shold be hard that day: I wer: 73: No 81 & so put of.[462]

That afternone we attended his majestie who made a speach devided into 3 parts.

> First to Interprett the meaning of his speach.
> Second to answer som objections.
> Thirdly to sett us in som way of proceeding[463]

Monday 4 May

15 May rejected	bb An act for the utter abolishing of logwood & blockwood & for the prohibiting of yt to be imported into the kingdome used within the same.
7 May cottd	bb An act for the punishment of the parents of bastard children & the discharge of the parishes where they ar borne & to prevent the unnaturall murder of such children cottd by the mothers.

Mr. Speaker told us though yt was not the manner to reporte his majesties speach because all the house attended yet yet [*sic*] he would remember us of two parts of yt in his last part namely:-caution & direction;
and by his majesties direction he presented a bill Intituled

presently read 7 May cottd	bb An act for the continuance & preservation of the blessed union of the Realmes of Eng: & Scot:

[461] *CJ*, i. 366.
[462] *Ibid.* i. 366.
[463] *Ibid.* i. 366–8; *Bowyer*, pp. 287–8.

and for the abolishing & taking
away of all the Hostile lawes
statutes & customs that might
hinder the same.[464]

This bill being read many of the house offred to go forth amongst the
rest **Mr. Atturney generall** but the house cried to shut the doore &
to stay them & to bring they key which was donne then the counsell
for the marshalls bill was called in but at there comming in **Mr.
Atturney** went forth thereby much difference arose & the counsell
being withdrawen yt was debated whether **Mr. Atturney** should be
sent for the house was devide about yt
    the I: 123: the No: 110 so he was not sent for.[465]

More for Tuesday 5 May[466]

Wednesday 6 May:
The bill for Hostile lawes being read: **Mr. Samuell Lewknor** made
a motion consisting of 3 parts. First that Mr. Speaker or some else
might be sent to move his majestie that he would not beleve reportes
untill they wer confirmed by Mr. Speaker. Secondly that the gentlemen
wronged by those reportes might have accesse to his majestie to
geve him satisfaccion. Thirdly that because we have receyved some
discoragement that agayne his majestie would geve us leave to use
freedome of speach.[467]
    This held debate the wholl morning & put of till the next day:-

Thursday 7 May:
They fell into debate of the former matter. Then Mr. Speaker delivered
that his majestie had taken notice of the motion yesterday made
consisting of 3 partes. For the 2 first he did assent unto yf leaving yt
what course to take therein. For the 3: he marvyled that any shold be
so Jelous: for duty modesty & decency observed he should never be
offended with any that should speake freely to the matter in hand.[468]

---

[464] *Bowyer*, pp. 289–90. Enacted (after much controversy) as 4 Jac. I. cap. 1. *SR*, iv.
1134–6.
    [465] *CJ*, i. 368.
    [466] When counsel for the Marshalsea bill was heard. *Ibid.* i. 369; *Bowyer*, pp. 290–1.
    [467] In his speech of 2 May the King had complained of 'speeches against duty, almost
against allegiance' in the Union debates in the Commons. *CJ*, i. 367. For the debate of
6 May see *ibid.* i. 370, 1041; Cotton Diary, p. 112.
    [468] *CJ*, i. 370–1; *Bowyer*, pp. 376–81.

Friday 8 May:
passing of bills.

Saterday 9 May
passings & committments.

Monday 11 May
passings & committments.[469]

Tuesday 12 [May]
cottd

b A bill read for assurance of lands betwene the Lord Bruce & captayne Dyle.[470]

A message from the Lords a bill

LL:

b An act of restitution in blood of the sonns and daughters of Edward Winsor.[471]

cottd

bb An act to reforme the abuses of wide & waste writings in English copies.

Wednesd 13: [May]
15 cottd

bb An act for amortising of lands to poore churches & for better serving of the Cure.

Sir Edw: Sands made reporte of the greevances agaynst Spayne.[472]

Thursday 14 [May] Ascension day
We sate not

Friday 15 [May]
cottd

bb An act agaynst dividing of tenements & inmates in & aboute the cities & universities & corporate townes or within 3 miles of the same.

---

[469] *CJ*, i. 371–3. The debate on the hostile laws bill continued until a conference with the Lords on 11 May. *Bowyer*, pp. 381–7.

[470] Edward, Lord Bruce and Michael Doyley. Enacted as HLRO, 4 James I, OA 19.

[471] Enacted as 4 James I, OA 25.

[472] *CJ*, 373, 1044; PRO, SP14/27/19; Cotton Diary, p. 114.

The bill was the selfe same that we rejected before which came from the lords[473] only this was generall & that for London whereaboute much speach was yet put to the question for committment the house was divided the I: 79: the No: 59: & so cottd

the bill was felony & cottd	bb An act for the suppressing & utter abolishing of Logwood and blockwood within the realme of England.

[Satur]day 16 May
was passed & new committed
bb An act for restrynt of going into forreyne countries and restryning transporting of Gold oute the Kings dominions.

Monday 18 [May]
bb An act for avyding of privy & secret outlawries in privilegd places & sanctuary:

bb An act for reformation of abuses for suing for titles in Ecclesiasticall courtes.

A message from the Lords who sent this bill

LL	b An act for the establishment of divers possessions & hereditaments of Ferninando late Erle of Darby.[474]

Tuesday 19: [May]
Mr. Speaker delivered a message from his majestie that there is a fame going abroade which is [*sic*] majestie is greeved at not with this house or any member of the same/ The fame is of an execution upon the Laird of Barroow/ that this dame might be stopped his majesties pleasure is that we should heare Sir Will: Seten which we did & he stood ij yard within the barr.[475]

Wedensday 20 [May]
About this day there was a Sessation by reason of Whittsontide till aboute the 3 of June/

---

[473] See above, Tuesday 3 March.
[474] Enacted as HLRO, 4 James I, OA 16.
[475] *CJ*, i. 375; *Bowyer*, pp. 293-4; *Cotton Diary*, p. 115.

Saterday 23 of ~~June~~ May
being Whitson even I was sent downe by the Lords aboute opposing the tumults & insurrections in Northampton shire.[476]

I returned not from thence till the 25 of June: which was Thursday

Friday the 26: [June]
I came into the house but after this time I tooke no notes of things donne in the house/ only these things I thought fitt to remember.

The bill for Hostile laws was made a new bill by our house this was sent downe from the lords with amendment the which the house stood uppon but at lenght committed & ordered that there should be a conference with the Lords to amend there amendments some presidents wer found oute for that & so agreed to/ & the Lords amendment we amended.

There wer bills come from the Lords but they passed not & therefore I mention not them.

Saterday the 4 July
The King ended this Session & proroged yt till Monday the xvj of October 1607.[477]

---

[476] For which see the narrative in J. E. Martin, *Feudalism to Capitalism* (New Jersey, 1983), pp. 161–80.
[477] The next session eventually convened on 30 January 1610.

WAR OR PEACE?
JACOBEAN POLITICS AND THE PARLIAMENT OF 1621*

Brennan Pursell

When the Parliament of 1621 convened, it had been seven years since the dissolution of the so-called 'Addled Parliament' of 1614, which had foundered on a fundamental disagreement between King James I and the House of Commons about the legality of impositions. The Parliament of 1621 faced more than unresolved domestic issues; it met under the shadow of the gravest international crisis of the early modern era. The defenestration of Prague in 1618 had marked the beginning of the Bohemian rebellion and the Thirty Years' War, and in the following summer James's son-in-law, Elector Palatine Friedrich V, accepted the Bohemian crown from the rebels, who had just deposed their Habsburg monarch, Ferdinand of Styria. Two days later Ferdinand was elected Holy Roman Emperor, and he was determined to retake the Bohemian throne from the new Palatine occupant. In the autumn of 1620, the emperor's Spanish cousins aided his cause by dispatching a large portion of the Spanish Army of the Netherlands to invade the Lower Palatinate, Friedrich's rich patrimonial estates on the Rhine. A couple of months later, on 8 November 1620, the Bohemian rebels were vanquished at the Battle of White Mountain outside Prague, and Friedrich and his wife, James's only daughter, the princess Elizabeth, fled for their lives. Until this point James had refused to mobilize his military forces in favour of Friedrich's gamble for the Bohemian throne.[1] Instead, the king's ambassadors had proclaimed his innocence in the affair to the whole of Europe and had extended his offer to mediate a solution to the conflict. Many people in England and on the continent felt that James had abandoned his daughter and son-in-law and the

* I would like to thank Professor Mary Gaylord for her time, patience, and assistance in the translation of these two letters. Research was made possible by a grant from the *Real Colegio Complutense*, Cambridge, Massachusetts.

[1] In the autumn of 1620 Sir Horace Vere led a small force of only 2,250 volunteers to the Lower Palatinate to assist in its defence. Elmar Weiss, *Die Unterstützung Friedrichs V. von der Pfalz durch Jakob I. und Karl I. von England im Dreißigjährigen Krieg (1618–1632)* (Stuttgart, 1966), pp. 24–5. This force was intended to deter war, not to precipitate it. Neither the English nor the union forces engaged the Spanish troops in a serious battle during this time. Anna Egler, *Die Spanier in der Linksrheinischen Pfalz, 1620–1632* (Mainz, 1971), p. 48.

Protestant religion as well in the face of Habsburg might, but James remained firmly committed to peace. Instead of turning against Spain, during the invasion of the Palatinate he dispatched six royal warships and twelve outfitted merchant vessels under the command of Sir Robert Mansell to the Mediterranean to join a Spanish fleet of the same size for a joint attack on the pirates of Algiers.[2]

Anti-Spanish war-like sentiments in the Parliament of 1621 came to the fore only gradually. In the opening weeks of the first sitting the Commons voted James two subsidies, an unprecedented gesture that belied an eager willingness to support the defence of the Palatinate. Only a few months later, on the day before Parliament was adjourned, did the house enthusiastically proclaim its readiness to contribute to a military campaign on behalf of James's children. As the summer began, things had been relatively quiet in the Palatinate, but in August all signs of peace vanished. Friedrich's confederates resumed fighting in Bohemia and Moravia, and the Vere's small force in the Lower Palatinate invaded the neighbouring lands of the bishop of Speyer, supposedly in search of supplies. Immediately the Spanish army resumed its offensive, and in October imperial forces invaded Friedrich's Upper Palatinate, just west of Bohemia. Worst of all, Sir John Digby's diplomatic mission to the emperor to procure Friedrich's full restitution failed utterly. Because of the resumption of hostilities, James's requests for mercy for his son-in-law had been mocked.[3] Digby, furious and belligerent, returned to England in November, and immediately James came under increased pressure to restore the Palatinate and redeem his besmirched honour by force of arms. When the king called for Parliament to reconvene for a second sitting, there was wide-spread hope and expectation for a declaration of war.

Indeed, this state of affairs might have led to war between England and Spain if not for the efforts of James I and the Spanish ambassador, Count Gondomar, who of all ambassadors at the English court was on the most intimate terms with the king. Since the beginning of Gondomar's embassy in 1613, he had successfully ingratiated himself with the king, his son, his favourite, his ministers, and members of his council, and various members of the nobility. James took pleasure in Gondomar's company. Both were well educated and enjoyed hunting and good conversation.[4] Politics aside, the two might have become

---

[2] See David Delison Hebb, *Piracy and the English Government, 1616–1642* (Aldershot, 1994) for an account of this expedition.

[3] Robert Zaller, ' "Interest of State": James I and the Palatinate', *Albion* vi (1974), pp. 144–75.

[4] See Charles H. Carter, 'Gondomar: Ambassador to James I', *HJ* vii (1964), pp. 189–208, and *idem, The Secret Diplomacy of the Habsburgs, 1598–1625* (New York, 1964), pp. 120–33. Also see Garrett Mattingly, *Renaissance Diplomacy* (Boston, 1955), pp. 255–68. An out-

intimates, but for a king and another king's ambassador politics were inescapable. This meant that all that was said between them, no matter how secretive, was ultimately subject to a fundamental doubt. Both had a variety of reasons for keeping the present peace, and certainly neither wanted to see their nations go to war over the reckless activities of the Elector Palatine. After Digby's return, Gondomar wrote that he had never seen the king in such a difficult position before; he knew that the situation was critical.[5] The two letters below describe how he and James acted to protect the Anglo-Spanish peace from the belligerent desires of an angry Parliament.

The first letter provides examples of the secretive, intimate nature of Jacobean diplomacy and its potential for theatricality. The king was the author of his own foreign policy, which he shrouded in mystery. Neither the members of his privy council nor some of his closest servants knew about some of his plans, but he included Gondomar in some of the greatest secrets of state. For example, James informed only his son, Prince Charles, his favourite, the Marquis of Buckingham, and his friend, Gondomar, in a scheme to dissolve the 1621 Parliament before it reconvened for a second sitting.[6]

The second letter mainly relates Gondomar's narrative of the second sitting of the Parliament of 1621 and the role he played in its dissolution. Though he was not present in Parliament, the level of detail in his report shows that he was informed by people who did attend. To him, the House of Commons was bellicose and virulently anti-Catholic, and the only one holding them back from war was the king.[7] It appeared

dated view is that Gondomar controlled James. See S. R. Gardiner, *History of England from the Accession of James I to the Outbreak of the Civil War* (10 vols, 1883), iii and iv; F. H. Lyon, *Diego de Sarmiento de Acuña, Conde de Gondomar* (Oxford, 1910); and Don Wenceslao Ramirez de Villa-Urrutia, *La Embajada del Conde de Gondomar á Inglaterra en 1613* (Madrid, 1913). Francisco Javier Sanchez Canton, *Don Diego Sarmiento de Acuña, Conde de Gondomar, 1567–1626* (Madrid, 1935), relies more on primary sources than either Lyon or Villa-Urrutia but has more to relate about Gondomar's personal state of mind than about his negotiations in England and Spain. José María Castroviejo and Francisco de P. Fernández de Cordoba, *El Conde de Gondomar, un Azor entre Ocasos* (Madrid, 1967), is a general biography based almost entirely on printed sources and offers no citations.

[5] Ministerio de Educación y Cultura de España, Archivo General de Simancas, Estado, Libro 374, fol. 304: 26 Oct./5 Nov. 1621, Gondomar to Infanta Isabella. Gondomar, not given to exaggeration, rarely used this kind of superlative.

[6] This fact demands an alteration in the interpretation of this dissolution. The king's famous outburst against the Commons over their invasion of his royal prerogatives was a mere screen for his political and diplomatic goals. See Brennan C. Pursell, 'James I, Gondomar, and the Dissolution of the Parliament of 1621', *History* lxxxviii (2000), pp. 428–45. Also see Chris R. Kyle, 'Prince Charles in the Parliaments of 1621 and 1624', *HJ* xli (1998), pp. 603–24, which the preceding article modifies slightly.

[7] The degree of belligerence in this Parliament has been the subject of an interesting debate. See Thomas Cogswell, 'Phaeton's Chariot: The Parliament-men and the Continental Crisis in 1621', and Conrad Russell, 'Sir Thomas Wentworth and anti-Spanish

to Gondomar that English Puritans, supported by the Dutch, were considering a rebellion against James I, because of his refusal to declare war on Spain in favour of the Palatinate.

Both letters show how James successfully convinced the count of his good will for Spain and his desire for an Anglo-Spanish alliance above all other considerations domestic and foreign. Prince Charles, Buckingham, and Digby assisted in the effort, though the latter also pushed for war on the Elector Palatine's behalf. James informed the count of his frustration with the Palatine crisis and his commitment to peace with Spain. He was wary of the House of Commons being overly swayed by a minority of those of a Puritan persuasion.

For political historians, ambassadorial reports are indispensable sources, though their verisimilitude and reliability are at best irregular. Gondomar's are more informative than analytical and tend to focus on the people with whom he spoke. They reflect his endeavour to be his king's eyes and ears in England. In general it is safe to take at face value his accounts of events and exchanges at which he was either an eye witness or a participant. In those instances, these letters function as direct, independent sources; for many conversations, Gondomar's first-hand relation is the only extant account. But when describing activities at which he had not been present, then the nature of the source changes dramatically. In order to report secondary information, he had to rely on a written or oral source of information that no longer survives in most cases. These letters then serve as indirect, independent sources. The degree of reliability, however, can vary greatly. In his reports Gondomar was careful to differentiate between what had merely been said somewhere, what he himself had heard, what might be the case, and what was certain. While much of the information these letters provide is correct, some is less than accurate, some mistaken, and some utterly false. Gondomar's interpretations of what was said and of the surrounding political circumstances should be taken with more than a grain of salt. In the following transcriptions, neither spelling nor diacritics have been modernized. Though the letters 'u' and 'v' appear identical in the manuscript, I have differentiated them in accordance with modern Spanish, and all abbreviations were extended. Punctuation has been altered in the translations in accordance with the meaning of the text. Because these documents have more historical significance than literary merit, the sole attempt has been to render the content, and not the style, into meaningful English as accurately and literally as possible. To counteract the strings of dangling modifiers in the Spanish,

Sentiment, 1621–1624', *The Political World of Thomas Wentworth, Earl of Strafford, 1621–1641*, ed. J. F. Merritt (Cambridge, 1996), pp. 24–46, 47–62.

I have inserted antecedents where appropriate. The rambling syntax of the sentences, however, has been left untouched.

8/18 November 1621, Gondomar to Infanta Isabella[8]
†
Señora

Jueves a 11 de este mes escrivi a Vuestra Alteza como avia llegado aqui el Baron Digby el día antes, y avia estado con el Rey, y despues conmigo, y lo que avia pasado sobre la quenta que dio al Rey, y al consejo de su negociacion.

El dia siguiente por la mañana a instancía suya bolvio el Rey a juntar el consejo, donde el Baron Digby tornó a ponderar con mayor pasion y exsageracion la poca estimacion que el Emperador y el Duque de Baviera avian hecho de este Rey, y el engaño de averle dado cartas para Vuestra Alteza y rebocadolas despues, y ylle tomando entretanto los estados al Palatino, como se huviera hecho, sin averle dexado un palmo de tierra, si el Digby no huviera acudido al remedio dello, y puesto las cosas de manera, que el Emperador y el Duque de Baviera se acordarian del Rey de Inglaterra, torciendose la oreja muchas vezes, y con mucho dolor de no aver acetado los medios y proposiciones que el les avia offrezido, y suplicado de rodillas, y con lagrimas en los ojos en nombre de este Rey, y por el bien y paz de la christiandad.

Que agora con la gente de Mansfelt,[9] que el dixo eran doze mil infantes y mas de quatro mil cavallos, y con la del Oracio Ver,[10] y la que de muchas partes de Alemania, y del Pais[11] se les yva juntando, era un muy poderoso y numeroso exercito, con el qual se recuperaria sin duda no solamente todo lo ocupado en el Palatinato inferior, pero hecho esto, yendo con estas armas al Palatinato superior, no allarian resistencia, y avria buelto este Rey por su honrra, como tan gran Rey, y como

[8] Ministerio de Educación y Cultura de España, Archivo General de Simancas, Estado, Libro 374, fols 307–14. This document is not transcribed in full. The Infanta Isabella was the ruler of the Spanish Netherlands following the death of her husband, Archduke Albert, on 15 July 1621. By order of the King of Spain, Felipe IV, and the Spanish Council of State, Gondomar kept the Infanta abreast of developments in England during the Palatine war. For a reference to this order see Biblioteca Real, Madrid, MS II/2108, fol. 112: 2 January 1622, Gondomar to Felipe IV.

[9] Ernst, Count of Mansfeld, was a mercenary general commissioned by Elector Palatine Friedrich V during the first stages of the Thirty Years' War.

[10] Sir Horace Vere was the general of the roughly 2,200 English volunteers defending the Lower Palatinate.

[11] Because this word is capitalized, I take it to be an abbreviation for 'Países Bajos'.

Cavallero, restituyendo a su hierno y a su hija en su docte y patrimonio sin tener que andar rogando a nadie, ni haziendo sumisiones, ni indignidades, de mas de que ya esto era forçoso, pues aviendo provado todos los remedios humanos de ruegos, y suplicaciones, no avian servido de mas, que perder este Rey reputacion y tiempo, y aun dinero, pues a el solo le avia dado ochenta mil ducados, que gastó en la jornada con el socorro que dió a Oracio Ver; que el avia amado siempre la paz y ayudado a los medios para ella en tanto que tuvó por posible que con ellos se consiguiria, y que testigos avia [*sic*] presentes de que avia sido mormurado, y tenido por pinsionario de España, y enemigo declarado del Palatino; que el era solo parcial y pinsionario de la razon y del servicio de su Rey, y que assi mientras vio que el Palatino no tenia razon en sus andanças y empresas de querer lo ageno, siguio la opinion y prudencia de su buen Rey y señor en no aprovallo, ni ayudallo....

[A summary of the emended passage is to be found in the English translation.]

Yo estaba determinado de veer al Rey aquel mismo dia viernes a la tarde, y aviendo sabido la resolucion que se avia tomado aquella mañana, y todo lo que se avia tratado, me parezió combiniente estarme quedo, porque ni el Rey ni nadie pudiesen pensar que me avia inquietado la novedad; vinó a boca de noche el Marqu‹es› de Boquingan a veerme y diome cuenta dello, hablandome com‹o› hombre de bien, y como buen cavallero, diziendome la aflicion del Rey, y el disignio de los malos en empeñalle a sus fines, que el Baron Digby se queria hazer inmortal con el pueblo y los puritanos, por restaurador del Palatinato, y de la religion protestante en Alemania, pero que no me diese cuidado, porque el Rey le avia mandado que me dixese que no se haria nada, ni vendria finalmente en cosa sin que yo lo supiese y sin mi parecer jurandome que el Rey no se fiaba enteramente mas que del y de mi, porque sabia que no teniamos otros fines, sino solo el bien publico y la paz, y que en todos los demas consejeros suyos allaba disignios y affectos particulares, que el Rey deseaba mucho habla‹r› conmigo, y que assi me pedia fuese el dia siguiente sabado a la una, porque huviese tiempo para hablarle despacio.

[A summary of the emended passage is to be found in the English translation.]

Despues me apartó el Rey solo a una bentana, y me dixo que le tuviese lastima, porque si supiera bien lo que le dezian y oia, eran cosas que no las podia sufrir el mas miserable hombre del mund‹o›, haziendole

todos un argumento, que, o, deseaba la perdicion de su hija y nietos,
o, no, si la deseaba, lo declarase, y que el Principe y ella no eran sus
hijos, ni sus nietos, pero que si lo era‹n›, y la Palatina su hija unica la
ayudase a recuperar y conservar el estado con que se cassó, pues todos
sus Reynos le querian ayudar a ello, y se lo offrezian, y reconociendo
del quanto deseaba no disgustar al Rey mi Amo, aun en esta defensa
natural, le dezian que esto lo hiziese sin que se pudiese ofender, y que
el mismo Digby le havia hablado en ello con notable respecto, que esto
era cierto, y que tambien le hazia otro argumento, a que el no allaba
respuesta; diziendo que el le avia embiado con cartas del Rey de
España, y del Señor Archiduque, que aya gloria, para que el Emperador
admitiese en su gracia y obediencia al Palatino, y le restituyese el
estado, haziendo la sumision devida, que el Baron propusó todo esto
al Emperador, y que este Rey haria con su hierno que viniese en todo
lo demas que su Majestad Cesarea quisiese; que el Emperador no quiso
admitir tratado, ni platica dello, ni de rebocar ni suspender la execucion
del bando Imperial contra el Palatino, ni admitir cesacion de armas,
ni lebantar el sitio del lugar de que este Rey tenia tomada la posesion
por el dote de su hija, y para su viudez, que viendo negadas todas sus
demandas, dezia el Baron que avia propuesto al Emperador que este
Rey se contentaria de que sus Majestades Cesarea y Catolica tomasen
ensi los Palatinatos, y los tuviesen hasta resolver lo que se podia hazer
en ello, pero que el no podia venir en que el Duque de Baviera se
apoderase del Palatinato superior, pues se veia lo que avia hecho con
la Austria, y que visto que tampoco esto se admitia, sino que todo se
perdia, fue forçado a lo que hizo, antes que se acabase de perder, y
bolviendo aqui con tan mal despacho en todo era menester escusar su
mala negociacion con hechar la culpa a alguno, y que assi por la
verdad y por la conviniencia, avia querido culpar al Duque de Baviera,
y a los ministros que le favorezian con el Emperador, por poder con
esto salbar mejor la amistad y buena correspondencia de este Rey con
Vuestra Alteza y el Rey de España, y quitar el odio que causara en el
pueblo lo contrario (como se via) pues con ser esto assi, viendo su mal
despacho, veya yo quales estaban estas gentes contra España, con que
el tenia por gran favor de Dios, que no se huviese ocupado a francandal,
porque entendia que el pueblo y los puritanos huvieran tomado alguna
resolucion desatinada contra el y contra mi, sin que tuviera remedio,
porque les parezia que todo se avia perdido en Alemania por no averlo
el socorrido, y por averselo estorbado yo, que viese lo que me parezia
que se podia hazer, que lo del parlamento no me diese cuidado, porque
el se yva a Niumarquete, y llebaba consigo al Marques de Boquingan,
y dexaba aqui al Principe con una comision secreta que solos los tres
la sabian, y yo, con que seriamos quatro, y era que si el parlamento se
quisiese meter en qualquiera otra cosa mas que en concedelle servicio

de dinero para socorro del Palatinato, el Principe le disolviese, pues agora no se juntaba para mas de solo esto, y que el queria estar lejos, para que se executase antes que pudiesen yr a el con quexas para el remedio; y con esto llamó al Marques de Boquingan que estaba apartado con el Principe y con Digby, y dixole lo que me avia dicho debajo de secreto; y el Marques añidi‹ó›, yo he dicho a mi Amo que el dinero que nos dieren no le demos a su hierno, sino que nos juntemos con España, y le gastemos contra el enemigo comun, de que el Rey se rió mucho, asiendome de los brazos, y diziendome que a quien pensaba yo que aquel mal hombre llamaba el enemigo comun, que yo pensaria que era el Turco, y que no eran sino los señores estados de Olanda.

Dixele que hablasemos un poco en el Baron Digby, y en donde pensaba el Rey señalarle puestos para las estatuas que le querian hazer los Puritanos en Inglaterra, ponderó con suspiro que assi era, pero que tambien queria el Baron que sobre las muchas mercedes que le avia hecho, y algunas a mi instancia, le hiziese mas agora, que me pedia que yo pasase y disimulase, porque le dariamos mayor bentaja y autoridad con el pueblo, si yo me mostrase ofendido, y el Marques de Boquingan lo aprobó mucho, pidiendome lo mismo, y vi este dia al Principe aprobar mucho las acciones del Digby, y he sabido que pribadamente en su camara lo haze assi.

Con esto llamo el Rey al Principe y al Baron Digby, y estuvimos un gran rato a la chiminea hasta que anochecío, hablando en las cosas que se offrezian dentro y fuera del Reyno, y diziendo el Rey los avisos que tenia de todas partes, con que me despedi, aviendo andado el Rey a ratos en pie y paseandose, y yo sentado por no poder estar de otra manera; salieron conmigo el Marques de Boquingan, y el Baron Digby, y aviendo hecho yo mucha instancia con el Marques para que se quedase, me dixo al oido que el Digby le avia hecho señas que no pasase adelante, porque devia de desear hablarme a solas, que el estaba cierto de que no me mataria, porque avia visto que en mi presencia no era tan valiente, con que yo le dixe al Marques que me yva la honrra en no llevar padrino, pues el otro no le tenia, y assi se quedó, y el Baron y yo nos entramos en una galeria solos; y lo primero que me dixo fue, que de dia y de noche encomendaba a Dios mi salud, como se me luze, pues me ando muriendo, y añidio, que siendo lo que yo deseaba el bien y augmento de la religion Catolica y la verdadera amistad y union de nuestros Amos, esperaba que Dios avia ordenado esta ocasion, para perfficionarlo, que el me juraba (como me juró con grandes juramentos) que nunca avia tenido mas afficion, de que esto se consiguiese a entera satisfacion de su Majestad Catolica, que agora, que yo estuviese muy contento, porque todo se avia de hazer muy bien, que por amor de Dios me pedia no le tuviese por mal hombre, ni por ingrato a tantos benefficios rezibidos, tornandome a hazer grandes protestas y juramentos de que no avia hablado palabra que fuese en ofensa ni desservicio de su Majestad, ni de Vuestra Alteza, ni de ministro de España antes muchas alabanças, y que por poder hazer esto mejor sin que el pueblo se lebantase contra el y le ahorcase, hechaba la culpa de toda su mala negociacion al Duque de Baviera, y a los valedores que tenia cerca del Emperador, pudiendo hecharla a los ministros de España, contandome en esto algunas particularidades que le dixeron y entendió, de que el Palatinato se restituiria al Palatino, con que este Rey hiziese que los estados de Olanda se restituyesen a su Majestad, y que de esta manera tendria cada uno lo suyo, y de otra no avia que pensar de restitucion del Palatinato, encareziendo siempre mucho su mal despacho en los negocios a que fue, y diziendome otras cosas que le avian dicho, que yo no creo, y por eso no embaraço con ellas a Vuestra Alteza y que no se le podia pedir a ninguno que se dexase matar, y que si yo no pretendia esto del, no me podia quexar.

Respondile a esto mesurada y brevemente lo mejor que supe escusando el alargar el discurso con mis males, y con tener necesidad de venirme a casa, y ni a el, ni al Rey, ni a nadie he querido dezir todas las razones que ay en justificacion de lo que el Emperador y el Duque de Baviera han hecho, pareciendome que en algunas cosas es combiniente, que ellos mismos lo digan y vengan las relaciones de Alemania, y que el Rey nuestro señor y Vuestra Alteza queden libres y arbitros tenidos por tales para mediar y componer lo que se offrezia; con que me despedi, y pareziome tambien conviniente no porfiar, ni poner la cosa en disputa entre mi, y el Baron Digby ni desesperalle, ni dalle con esto mas amigos de los que el ha ganado, recatandome de la razon, porque con ella allado he visto perder grandes negocios por no hazer distincion de tiempos y de personas, y assi embiandome el dia siguiente el Marques de Boquingan a pedir con su secretario que yo visitase al Baron Digby, pues me avia visto el (con ser recien venido) dos vezes, le dixe que lo haria, pues me lo aconsejaba, y sin esto pensaba veerle, pero holgue de podello hazer, hechando cargo al Marques, y al Rey en ello; con que le vi, y el Marques de Boquingan me dio muchas gracias de parte del Rey y de la suya, convidandome a cenar, y al Baron tambien, pero de esto me escusé, por no estar verdaderamente para ello; que es el estado que oy tiene todo esto.

Entiendo que el Baron Digby ha hecho desservicio a su Rey, pues si sin embargo de la venida de Mansfelt el Palatinato inferior se acabase de ganar, ya se vee quan profanado quedará su triunfo, y si no, ha empeñado a este Rey en una gran costa y embaraço con mucha duda de buen suceso por este camino, y desobligado al Emperador en todos acontecimientos para la piedad y clemencia que el Palatino ha menester use con el su Majestad Cesarea, sin embargo de que oy es grandissimo el contento que aqui tienen generalmente los mas de esto que el Baron Digby ha hecho, y le dan grandes alabanças, viendo que ha sido causa de esta junta de parlamento, pensando que en el se resolvera el rompimiento de la paz con España, y assi todas las proposiciones y deseo de esta gente, son, que su Rey embie veinte mil Infantes y cinco mil cavallos a Flandes por la inclusa, o, por otra parte y ocupe alli las plazas y fuerças que pueda con este exercito, y con la union y asistencia de los Olandeses por la mar, y dizen que de otra manera se perdera toda la gente y dinero que de aqui se embiare de socorro a Idelbergh y juntamente el tiempo de podello remediar, hechando Inglaterra sobresi una pinsion grande y perpetua para una guerra en Alemania, sin utilidad ni probecho de Inglaterra, y afirmanme que esta sera la voz de la mayor parte del parlamento, y que haran fuerça en no conceder servicio sin que la guerra se declare primero con España, y que para estos veinte mil Infantes y cinco mil cavallos ocupados en Flandes, y para treinta galeones, daran luego quanto sea menester, pero entiendo que el Rey no vendra en ello, sino es forçado, y el Baron Digby lo reconoze assi, porque sé que ha dicho a un confidente suyo, que el Rey no estima los grandes servicios que el le ha hecho, antes teme que por ellos ha de morir preso en la torre como si fuera traydor, aunque el Principe se quiere mostrar valeroso contra lo pazifico de su padre, y tiene algunos movimientos estos dias de esto, pero es muy obediente al Rey.[12]

TRANSLATION
†
Madame

On Thursday, the eleventh of this month, I wrote to Your Highness about how Baron Digby had arrived here on the day before, and how he had been with the king and afterwards with me, and [about] what the response had been to the report on his negotiations that he gave the king and the council.

On the next day in the morning, at his instance, the king met the council again, where Baron Digby once again gravely related with great passion and emphasis the low esteem that the emperor and the

[12] The letter continues with Gondomar's advice about what measures should be taken next in the Palatine crisis. Neither the Infanta nor the King of Spain followed it.

Duke of Bavaria had had for this king[13] and the deception of having given him letters for Your Highness and having them revoked afterwards, and meanwhile proceeding to take the estates of the [Elector] Palatine,[14] as would have been done, without having left him a handbreath of land, if Digby had not come to the rescue with a remedy for it and had arranged things so that the emperor and the Duke of Bavaria would come to an agreement with the King of England, bending his ear many times, and with great pain at not having accepted the means and propositions that [Digby] had offered them, [he] begged on his knees, and with tears in his eyes in the name of this king, and for the well-being and peace of Christendom.

That now, with Mansfeld's men, which, [Digby] said, were 12,000 infantry and more than 4,000 cavalry, and with those of Horacio Vere, and those who were coming to join them from many parts of Germany and the Low Countries, it was a very powerful and large army. With such a one, doubtlessly not only all the occupied parts of the Lower Palatinate would be recovered, but, having done this, going with these arms to the Upper Palatinate, they would not encounter resistance, and this king would regain his honor, as such a great king, and as a gentleman, restoring his son-in-law and his daughter to their dowry and patrimony without having to go begging to anyone, nor making submissions, nor indignities, more than that which was already forced, since having tried all human remedies of requests and supplications, none had served any purpose but to cost this king prestige and time and even money, since to [Digby] alone, [James] had given 80,000 ducats, which [Digby] spent on the journey with the aid that he gave to Horacio Vere; [Digby said] that he had always loved peace and helped the means to it inasmuch as he thought it possible that to obtain it with them, and that he had present witnesses [for the fact] that he had been whispered and held for a pensionary of Spain and a declared enemy of the Palatine; [Digby said] that he was only biased and a pensionary of reason and in the service of his king, and that thus while he saw that the Palatine was wrong in his doings and undertakings to want something else; he himself followed the opinion and the prudence of his good king and lord in not approving it nor helping to bring it about...

[In the rest of this passage and in the next paragraphs, Gondomar

[13] James I.
[14] Friedrich V, the Elector Palatine and dispossessed King of Bohemia. Through his marriage to Elizabeth Stuart, he was also the son-in-law of James I. Gondomar refers to Friedrich as both the 'Count', the 'Elector', and the 'Prince' Palatine.

relates how Digby described the precarious state of the Palatinate and made a declaration that only Felipe IV, the Infanta Isabella, and James I could find a peaceful solution to this crisis. The council members then all agreed that more help must be sent to the Elector Palatine at once. Some were inclined to attack Flanders, but the king refused on the grounds that he was only committed to defending and restoring the Palatinate within its borders. It was resolved that £40,000 would be sent to the Palatine forces and that Parliament would be recalled for 20/30 November.]

I was determined to see the king on that same day, Friday, in the afternoon, and having known the resolution that had been taken that morning, and all that had been discussed, it seemed convenient to me to be still, so that neither the king nor anyone could think that the news had disturbed me; in the early evening the Marquis of Buckingham came to see me and gave me an account of it, talking to me as a worthy man, and as a good gentleman, telling me of the king's grief, and of the ill-intentioned people's design to force him toward their ends; that Baron Digby wanted to make himself immortal with the people and the Puritans as the restorer of the Palatinate and of the Protestant religion in Germany; but that I should not be worried, because the king had sent [Buckingham] to tell me that nothing would be done, nor would [James] decide finally on a matter without my knowing it and without my opinion, swearing to me that the king did not trust entirely anyone more than [Buckingham] and me, because he knew that we did not have any other ends than the public good and peace, and that in all his other councillors [James] found particular designs and inclinations; [Buckingham added] that the king greatly desired to speak with me, and that thus he asked me to come on the following day, Saturday, at one o'clock, in order that there would be time to speak to him at length.

[In the next paragraphs, Gondomar reports how, despite his ill health, he met the king, Prince Charles, and Buckingham in private. James announced that Digby would enter and make a speech and then the former would talk to Gondomar in private. Digby came in and made an oration about the English desire for peace with Spain and about the Duke of Bavaria's perfidy in the negotiations for peace in the Palatinate. Gondomar made a cool rebuttal and then asked Digby that they not quarrel like Arminians and Gomarists. Gondomar swore to help James in his efforts to restore his undeserving son-in-law to the emperor's grace and to protect the peace and friendship between England and Spain. James applauded and asked that Felipe IV and the Infanta Isabella continue their intercession with the emperor.]

Afterwards the king alone took me aside to a window, and he told me to feel sorry for him, because if I knew well that what they were saying and what he was hearing, they were things that the most wretched man in the world could not endure, making everything into one argument: that either he desired the perdition of his daughter and grandchildren or, if not, if he desired this, he might declare it, and that the prince and she were not his children, nor were his grandchildren, but that if they were, and the [Electress] Palatine was his only daughter, he would help her to recover and conserve the estate with which she married, since all his kingdoms wanted him to help her, and they were offering it; and, recognizing how much he did not want to displease the king, my master,[15] even in this natural defence, they were telling him that he might do this without offending [Felipe IV]; and that the same Digby had spoken to [James] about this with noteworthy respect, that this was certain; and that also [Digby] was making another argument, to which [James] was not finding a reply, saying that he had sent [Digby] with letters from the King of Spain and from the Lord Archduke,[16] may he rest in peace,[17] in order that the emperor admit the [Elector] Palatine into his grace and obedience and restore him to his estate, making the due submission; that the Baron proposed all this to the emperor, and that this king would arrange that his son-in-law would go along with all other things that His Imperial Majesty would want; that the emperor refused to accept a treaty or a conversation about it, to revoke or to suspend the execution of the imperial ban against the [Elector] Palatine, to admit a cessation of arms, or to raise the siege of the place of which this king was taking possession as his daughter's dowry and for her widowhood;[18] that seeing all his demands refused, the baron was saying that he had proposed to the emperor that this king would be content if Their Imperial and Catholic Majesties would take the Palatinates between themselves and would hold them until resolving what could be done in that [business]; but that he could not accept that the Duke of Bavaria would take over the Upper Palatinate, since it was evident what he had done with Austria;[19] and that having seen that this would not be admitted either, but that all would be lost, [Digby] was forced [to do] what he did, before it had been lost; and returning here with such a bad report on all fronts, it was necessary to excuse his bad negotiations by casting the blame on someone, and that therefore because of the truth and for convenience,

[15] Felipe IV.

[16] Archduke Albert. See n. 2.

[17] Literally, 'may he have glory'.

[18] Frankenthal.

[19] Maximilian I had occupied Upper Austria as a pledge for his expenses in the war on the emperor's behalf against the rebellions in Bohemia, Austria, and Germany.

he had wanted to blame the Duke of Bavaria and those ministers who
favored him with the emperor, in order to be better able, with this, to
save the friendship and good correspondence of this king with Your
Highness and the King of Spain, and to prevent the hate that the
contrary would cause in the people (as it was going) since, with this
being the case, seeing his bad report, I could see how these people
were against Spain; with which [James] considered as a great favour
from God that Frankenthal had not been occupied, because he understood that the people and the puritans would have taken some extreme
resolution against him and against me that would have had no remedy,
because it appeared to them that all had been lost in Germany for not
having had assistance and because I had obstructed it; that [James]
saw what appeared to me that could be done; that the business of the
Parliament ought not to worry me, because he was going to Newmarket,
and was bringing the Marquis of Buckingham with him, and was
leaving the prince here, with a secret commission that the three alone
knew, and I, making four; and it was that if the Parliament wanted to
meddle in any other matter apart from granting him a supply of money
for the assistance of the Palatinate, the prince would dissolve it,[20] since
now it was not meeting for more than this [purpose] alone; and that
[the king] wanted to be away, in order that it be executed before they
could go to him with complaints for a remedy; and with this he called
to the Marquis of Buckingham who was aside with the prince and with
Digby and told him what he had told me under secrecy; and the
Marquis added, 'I have told my master that we should not give the
money that they give us to his son-in-law, but that we should join
ourselves with Spain and spend it against the common enemy', at
which the King laughed a lot, taking me by the arms, and asking me
which bad man I thought he was calling 'the common enemy', that I
would think that it was the Turk, and that it was not they, but the
Estates of Holland.

I asked him if we might talk a bit about Baron Digby, and about where
the king was thinking to point out to him standing places for the statues
that the Puritans wanted to make of him in England; he pondered with
a sigh, saying that it was this way, but that the Baron would want that
above the many favours that [James] had done him, and some at my
insistence, he would do him more now; he asked me to tolerate it and
dissimulate, because we would give him greater advantage and authority
with the public if I showed myself offended, and the Marquis of

[20] Because Prince Charles did not have to power to dissolve Parliament, this passage
shows that Gondomar misheard or otherwise misunderstood the king's words. James had
probably said that Charles would give his father a signal for the dissolution.

Buckingham approved this greatly, asking me the same, and I saw this day that the prince approved Digby's actions very much, and I have known that privately in his chamber [Charles] acts this way.

With this the king called to the prince and to Baron Digby, and we stayed a long time by the fireplace until it grew dark, talking about current affairs in and outside the kingdom, and the king telling about the notifications that he had from everywhere, after which I took my leave, the king having been standing for a while on foot and strolling about, and I seated for not being able to stand in any way; the Marquis of Buckingham and Baron Digby left with me, and after I pled with the marquis that he remain, he whispered in my ear that Digby had made signals to [Buckingham] that he not come along, because Digby must have wanted to speak to me alone. [Buckingham added] that he was certain that [Digby] would not kill me, because [Buckingham] had seen that, in my presence, [Digby] was not so valiant; at which I told the marquis that it was a point of honour with me, not to bring along a second in a duel, since [Digby] did not have one, and thus [Buckingham] stayed behind, and the Baron and I entered a gallery alone, and the first thing that he told me was that day and night he was commending my health to God, in so far as I showed it, because I was at death's door, and he added that since I desired the well-being and the augmentation of the Catholic religion and the true friendship and union of our masters, he hoped that God had ordered this occasion in order to improve them; that he would swear to me (as he did swear with great oaths) that never had he been so keen than for this to succeed to the full satisfaction of His Catholic Majesty; that now, so that I may be very content, because everything had been done very well, that for the love of God he was asking me not to consider him a bad man, nor as ungrateful for the many benefits he had received, once again making me grand protests and oaths that he had not spoken a word that may be an offense or a disservice to His Majesty,[21] or to Your Highness, or to a minister of Spain, rather great praises; and that in order to be able to do this better, without the people rising up against him and hanging him, he would blame the whole of his bad negotiations on the Duke of Bavaria and on the supporters that he had around the emperor, although he could have blamed the ministers of Spain; he told me some particulars about this that they told him and he understood that the Palatinate would be restored to the [Elector] Palatine, provided that this king would arrange that the states of Holland would be restored to His Majesty,[22] and that in this way, each

---

[21] Felipe IV.
[22] Felipe IV.

would have his own, and in any other way, the restitution of the
Palatinate was unthinkable, always stressing his bad report of the
negotiations to which he went, and telling me other things that they
had told him, which I do not believe, and because of this I will not
burden Your Highness with them; and [he added] that it was not
possible for him to order anyone to be killed, and that if I was not
attempting this with him, I was in no position to complain.

I responded to him about this moderately and briefly in the best way
that I knew, excusing myself from continuing the conversation because
of my maladies and with the need to return to my house, and [I said
that] neither to him, nor to the king, nor to anyone did I want to tell
all the reasons that there are in justification of what the emperor and
the Duke of Bavaria have done, because it seems to me that in some
things it is convenient that they themselves tell it and the reports may
come from Germany, and that the king our lord and Your Highness
remain free and kept as arbitrators for such things, in order to mediate
and compose what is offered; with which I took my leave, and it also
seemed convenient to me not to persist nor to make a dispute about
the matter between myself and the Baron Digby, nor to exasperate
him, nor to give him with this more friends than those that he has
won, acting cautiously with reason, because with it [left] at the side I
have seen great matters lost by not making the distinction among times
and persons; and thus on the following day the Marquis of Buckingham
sending me his secretary to ask that I visit Baron Digby, since he (being
recently returned) had seen me twice, I told [the secretary] that I would
do it, since [Buckingham] was advising me, and without this I meant
to see [Digby], but I was delayed in being able to do it, making the
marquis and the king responsible in this; and so I saw him, and the
Marquis of Buckingham gave me many thanks on his part and on the
king's inviting me to dinner, and the baron too, but I excused myself
from this, for not being truly in shape for it; this is the state [in] which
this is today.

I understand that Baron Digby has done a disservice to his king, since,
in spite of from Mansfeld's coming, the Lower Palatinate should have
just been won, already one can see that [Digby's] triumph would be
profane, and if not, he has pledged this king in a great expense and
trouble with much doubt about a good outcome by this way; and
having released the emperor from an obligation in all events for the
mercy and clemency that the Palatine needs [and which] His Imperial
Majesty may use with him, nevertheless today those who are generally
content with what Digby has done are very pleased indeed; and they
give him great praises, seeing that he has been the cause of this meeting

of Parliament, thinking that, in it, the breaking of the peace with Spain will be resolved and so all the propositions and the desire of this people, which are: that the king send 20,000 infantry and 5,000 cavalry to Flanders by way of Sluis, or through another area, and occupy there the places and forces that he can with this army, and with the union and assistance of the Dutch by the sea; and they say that by any other means all the people and money will be lost that might be sent from here as aid to Heidelberg and with them the time to be able to remedy it, casting on England a great and perpetual financial commitment for a war in Germany, without use or profit for England, and they confirm to me that this will be the voice of the greater part of the Parliament; and that they will show their strength in not conceding supply unless the war with Spain be declared first, and that for these 20,000 infantry and 5,000 cavalry busy with Flanders, and for thirty galleons, they will give right away however much may be necessary; but I understand that the king will not come to this, unless he is forced, and Baron Digby recognizes it so, because I know that he has told a confidant of his that the king does not esteem the great services that [Digby] has done for him, rather [Digby] fears that in exchange for them, he will have to die a prisoner in the tower as if he were a traitor, although the prince would like to display his valour against his father's pacifism, and [the prince] supports some movements these days for this, but he is very obedient to the king.

[The letter ends with Gondomar's report about the escalating anti-Catholicism of the populace. He advised the Infanta to stop Mansfeld as soon as possible and at any cost. As a postscript, he said that he was told that of the £40,000 that the Council allotted for the Palatinate, £10,000 would go to repaying Digby's expenses, and the remaining £30,000 would take a long time in getting to the Palatinate, because the bills of credit had to be remitted at the Frankfurt fair, which was more than three months away.]

6/16 December 1621, Gondomar to Infanta Isabella[23]
†
Señora

A primero de este mes[24] di cuenta a Vuestra Alteza de como aqui se avia juntado el parlamento, y lo que se avia propuesto en el en nombre de este Rey por algunos de sus ministros.

[23] Ministerio de Educación y Cultura de España, Archivo General de Simancas, Estado, Libro 374, fols 369–73.
[24] 21 Nov./1 Dec. 1621.

Fuese continuando el hablar en la guerra y la contribucion de socorros para ella; y el brazo y casa inferior (que assi llaman aqui a los procuradores de las Provincías, Ciudades, Villas, y tierras del Reyno que son quatro cientas y setenta personas) han procedido con tal violencia y sedicion contra la religion Catolica y casamiento con España; que en lo uno y en lo otro han dicho notables desatinos, tomando por pretesto la conservacion de su religion, y la ruina que se le ha seguido y sigue de no aver el Rey confirmado las leyes que han hecho contra los Catolicos, ni executadose las que estaban hechas antes; con que los Catolicos avian crecido en tanto numero y de todos estados, que los protestantes y su verdadero Evangelio devian temer una gran ruina si se dilataba el remedio, pues los papistas atrevidamente dezian que se veria presto Rey Catolico en Inglaterra, y que los protestantes tendrian necesidad de pedir toleracion de su religion con mucha duda de que se les concediese, por que lo mas cierto seria tratallos y hazer con ellos lo que se hazia agora en francia, que el daño de todo consistia en el tratado de casamiento de este Principe en España, pues con ello, y con esta sombra yvan el Papa y su hijo mas amado, haziendo los progresos y ventajas que se veian en favor de su ydolatria; que el remedio era suplicar al Rey casase al Principe con muger de su religion, y que executase todas las leyes antiguas contra los Catolicos, y las que agora se avian añidido y hecho de nuevo, y acordaron de concedelle luego un susidio (que assi llaman aqui este servicio que monta cerca de quatro cientos mil ducados, para que tienen ya forma de repartimiento general asentada, y le hazen con facilidad) y que estos quatro cientos mil ducados fuesen luego en letras para socorro de la gente de guerra que está en el Palatinato en servicio del Palatino, incluiendo por condicion en esta concesion que los Catolicos pagasen doblado, y fuesen avidos por estrangeros desunidos y apartados del comercio del estado, pues no se conformaban con las leyes, y govierno del, y que juntamente se suplicase al Rey declarase el enemigo contra quien se hazia esta guerra, y lo proclamase, y publicase, para que conforme a ello, se le diesen los socorros y asistencia; que le darian quanta fues‹e› menester conforme a la calidad y poder del enemigo, hasta trein‹to› susidios, si fuese necesario, que son doze millones de ducados, y que bien se sabia que el Emperador y el Duque de Baviera no eran el enemigo verdadero, sino supuestos y fingidos; y que el verdader‹o› era el que los socorria con dinero, y que assi lo sustancial, y lo convinien‹te› era, hazer la guerra a donde estaba la bolsa para atajar los daños y divertillos; y que mientras assi no se hiziese, era perder tiempo y gastar gente y dinero banamente en quanto se embiase al Palatinato; que un gran exercito embiado a Flandes y una gran armada embiada a las Indias, o, a España, era el unico remedio, y el juntarse y unirse para esto muy estrechamente con los

Olandeses, pues aunque era cierto que Inglaterra avia rezibido dellos muchos daños y ofensas; las cosas estaban en termino que era forçoso disimular esto para no perder la religion, y el estado, y venir a manos de quien se sabia que queria señorear todo lo temporal con nombre de dar al Papa lo spiritual; y que no avría duda en que los Olandeses entregarian luego a este Rey la inclusa, y Flesingas, y las demas plazas que quisiese de aquellas Provincias, que assi lo dezian y offrezian los diputados que agora avian venido aqui dellas.

Todas estas proposiciones asentó y acordó el parlamento de esta casa inferior del tercero estado, poniendo las en una peticion para el Rey, y resolvieron que se la llevasen doze del parlamento, a que llamaron los doze Apostoles, y les dieron orden que díesen y leyesen la peticion al Rey, y le pidiesen la respuesta y declaracion a todos los puntos della, por escrito, y que con la que les diese se bolviesen luego, y nombraron por uno de estos doze a Don Ricardo Guaston, que es del consejo de estado, y chanciller de la hazienda, y uno de los procuradores del Reyno en esta casa inferior, cavallero muy honrrado, y que no concurrio en estos desatino‹s›, pero pasados por mayor parte, huvo de cumplir el nombramiento que hizieron del con los demas, y lo que le mandaron, que fue que todos se partiesen martes .14. de este mes[25] a Niumarquete donde el Rey está, y assi lo hizieron.

Yo avia escrito al Rey y al Marques de Boquingan quatro dias antes la sedicion y maldad que pasaba en este parlamento, y que sino estuviera tan seguro de la palabra y bondad del Rey, que lo castigaria y remediaria con la brevedad y exemplo que convenia, me huviera salido de sus Reynos sin aguardar a tercero dia, deviendo hazello assi, cumpliendo con mi obligacion si el no fuera Rey de estas gentes, pues al presente, yo no tenia aqui exercito con que castigarlos.

El Rey embió luego una carta al parlamento que llegó a manos del secretario de Estado Don Jorge Calvert el mismo Martes .14. de este mes a las diez horas antes de medio dia en cuya mañana se avian partido los doze comisarios, a donde el Rey estaba; y a esta hora de las diez abrió el secretario el pliego en el mismo parlamento, y dio la carta del Rey al hablador del parlamento, que assi llaman aqui al electo para esto, y le ponen en una silla eminente y es de ordinario un Doctor grave y eloquente, y el sobre escrito de la carta era para este, diziendo a nuestro fiel y bien amado el hablador de la casa comun del parlamento, que la tomó y leyo en alta voz y lo que contenia era dezirle el Rey que avia entendido por diversas relaciones con muy gran

<hr>

[25] 4/14 Dec. 1621.

dolor suyo que la distancia y apartamiento de su persona al presente
de su alta Corte de parlamento causada por su falta de salud avia dado
atrevimiento a algunos spiritus furiosos y populares en la casa comun
de disputar y arguir publicamente en negocíos mucho mas altos de su
entendimiento y capacidad en grande desonor suyo, y queriendo baxar
y deshazer su prerrogatiba real, y que el hablador les hiziese saber a
todos los de la casa, que la boluntad del Rey era, que ninguna persona
desde entonzes en adelante presumiese entremeterse en alguna cosa
tocante a su govierno real, o, a materias de estado, y particularmente
de hablar en el matrimonio de su hijo Carlos con la hija de España,
ni tocar en el honor y respecto que se devia a aquel Rey, o, algunos
otros sus amigos y confederados, y de no se entremeter tampoco en los
particulares de algunos hombres que tenian sus procesos en las Cortes
ordinarias de justicia, y que por quanto avia oido que querian embiar
un mensage al cavallero Edduin Sans, para saber dellas razones que el
Rey tuvo para prendelle, que el hablador les dixese en su nombre, que
la prision no avia sido por ninguna cosa tocante al parlamento, y que
por sacallos de toda duda y question sobre materias de esta naturaleza,
les dixese resolutamente en su real nombre que su autoridad era
bastante para castigar el mal comportamiento assi despues de pasado
el parlamento, como mientras duraba y asistian en el, lo qual no
pensaba disimular si huviese alguna ocasion de insolencia entre los que
estaban dentro, y si tornaban a hablar en los dichos puntos, o, trataban
de embiarle sobre ellos alguna peticion sin reformallos antes que le
fuese presentada, que el les declaraba que no les haria la honrra de
oilla, ni admitilla; y que porque avia entendido que el parlamento
deseaba que el hiziese una sesion antes de Navidad para confirmar
algunas leyes; que el hablador les dixese que si esto no se hiziese, y el
parlamento se rompiese sin ello, seria la falta dellos, porque si ellos
quisiesen acordar entre si en este tiempo las tales leyes, que fuesen
realmente buenas para la republica, el Rey daría muy boluntariamente
su consentimiento, por lo qual constaria que si no se hiziesen buenas
leyes para bien del pueblo; el vituperio que daria solamente sobre tales
spiritus turbulentos, que preferian su interes y fines particulares al bien
del Reyno y publico; con lo qual le dezia a Dios, que fue el fin de la
carta, hecha en Niumarquete a .13. de este mes a nuestra quenta.[26]

Leyda esta carta quedaron tan aturdidos los malos, como alentados los
pocos buenos que alli avía, pero la mayor parte se lebantó, diziendo
que no avia que hablar ni que tratar, sino yrse, y dexarlo todo, y
instando otros en que se estuviesen y confiriesen sobre la materia, dixo
uno que el negocio era gravissimo, y jamas visto, ni oido otro tal, ni

[26] 3/13 Dec. 1621.

carta como aquella en aquella casa, y que assi podria ser que de repente y sin madura consideracion se dixese alguna disparate, y si hiziese algun grande herror, que por esto era bien lebantarse y yrse sin hablar por entonzes mas en ello, ni juntarse tampoco aquel dia, sino dexallo para el siguiente, que fue ayer Miercoles,[27] y que todos tuviesen pensado (aviendo dormido sobre ello) lo que convenia hazer, con que se lebantaron, embiando por la posta a alcançar los doze comisarios, que avian ydo, para que se bolviesen sin llegar a hablar al Rey, y assi los alcançaron, y se bolvieron.

Juntaronse ayer miercoles por la mañana, y Eduardo Cuque letrado, que ha sido justicia mayor de este Reyno, y es agora consejero de estado, y uno de los asistentes de esta casa, començó a hablar diziendo que el dia antes quando avia visto la carta del Rey avia quedado afligidissimo, pero que al presente se allaba muy consolado, porque avia considerado, que en todo la carta no hablaba el Rey palabra en materia de religion, con que se veia que no se avia disgustado de lo que avian tratado tocante a ella, y que assi podian constantemente procurar de defendella por todos los medios que avian propuesto deshaziendo sus enemigos, pues todo el peligro que corrian en tratar esto constantemente, era ser ahorcados por leales y por buena causa, muerte mas dulze y honrrosa, que morir al palo quemados, como moririan si los filisteos no circuncisos vencian, que era los papistas, y tambien se podia y devia creer que en los demas puntos contenidos en la peticion, el Rey estaba mal informado, y que estando lo bien, los aprovaria, y se lo agradeceria pues no avia en ellos cosa en que el parlamento no tuviese autoridad para tratarlo, de que avia muchos exemplos antiguos en cassos semejantes, y que por todas estas razones, y por la autoridad y defensa de los previlegios del parlamento, le parecia que se tornasen a nombrar veinte comisarios, que ajustasen la peticion y proposiciones della, y con la sumision y humildad devida tornasen a representar y suplicar al Rey lo contenido.

La mayor parte gritó aprobando esto, y resolviendo que assi se hiziese, y que hasta tanto que el Rey respondiese derechamente a ello, no se tratase de ninguna otra cosa, y que de la carte del Rey, y de la peticion y proposiciones del parlamento, se sacasen y diesen copias a todos los que las quisiesen, para que se viese su justificacion; con que ha parado el proseguirse en el despacho de los quatro cientos mil ducados.

Este es el estado en que oy está esto, que es de gran confusion y dificultad, pues obliga y fuerça al Rey, o, a romper el parlamento, o,

<hr />

[27] 5/15 Dec. 1621.

a entregarse a ellos, y romper con todo lo demas; y los comisarios de Olanda que han venido aqui, no cesan de dia ni de noche por todos los medios que pueden de ayudar a esta turbacion, y persuadir al Rey que se incline a ello, y para esto tienen muchos amigos y valedores, y los pagan muy largamente.

Procurase tambien por la buena parte hazer contra ello todo lo que se puede con Dios y con los hombres; el Rey no ha dado hasta agora Audiencia a estos diputados de Olanda, pero lo que dizen a los ministros a quien han visto, es, que vienen a ponerse a los pies de este Rey, para que haga dellos lo que quisiere, y que pisados y maltratados, y de qualquiera manera, quiera los, o no los quiera le han de ser fieles y obedientes, estendiendo esto con notable sumision, y deseo de obligar a que se haga lo que pretenden.

Aqui ha llegado un despacho de muchas cartas, tomadas por el Conde de Mansfelt, a correos de Alemania y de Italia; han pasado a Niumarquete, donde el Rey está, y assi no he podido hasta agora veellas, ni saber particularmente todo lo que contienen, pero la mayor sustancia me dizen que es, que el Emperador embiaba a un religioso, que se llama el padre fray Jacinto, para que ai informase a Vuestra Alteza y en España a su Majestad de la razones que ay, para que el Emperador dé al Duque de Baviera el electorato que tenia el Conde Palatino, y que si las razones de religion, de estado, y de agradecimiento, que representare, no bastaren; se declare en que el Emperador está prendado, y ha dado su palabra al Duque de Baviera de dalle el electorato y que assi no puede escusarse de hazello, que es cosa que aqui da harto cuidado, aunque ha puesto nueva obligacion y estimacion en este Rey en afirmarse mas con esto, de que Vuestra Alteza y su Majestad Catolica por su intercesion y consideracion no desean la total ruina de su hierno, aunque el no lo merezca, y mas con lo que escriven agora de la Aya, que buelve a estar obstinado en no querer hazer la sumision al Emperador, ni nada de lo que este Rey ha offrezido en su nombre que hara, con que el Baron Digby, aunque ha sido el instrumento fatal de todas las turbaciones que aqui ay oy, va hechando ya la culpa al Palatino solo, y es cierto que agora habla con grandissimo respecto de España y de Vuestra Alteza y del Señor Archiduque que aya gloria, y hablando de su Alteza el otro dia en el parlamento, dixo que avia sido de los mas prudentes y exemplares Principes que avia avido en el mundo, y que el no podia nombralle, sin dalle tales atributos, porque se le devian.

Todo lo que hasta agora se ha cobrado aqui de las treinta mil libras, con que avisé a Vuestra Alteza socorria este Rey al Palatino, y lo que se le ha librado a quenta dellas, mandara Vuestra Alteza veer por la memoria que va con esta y como van a distribucion del Embax.or que este Rey tiene en la Aya, donde me dizen que se consumira en lo que los Palatinos deven y gastan, sin llegar nada al socorro de los que estan en el Palatinato. Guarde Dios la serenísima persona de Vuestra Alteza ett. Londres .16. de diciembre 1621.

Aora rezibo una carta del Marques de Boquingan con correo a toda diligencia escrita a noche en Niumarquete a donde el Rey está, en que me dize que el Rey está constantissimo, y embiame copia de lo que el Rey escrivio al parlamento, y dizeme que dentro de dos otres dias espera poderme avisar de mas.

He sabido tambien agora por via cierta, que los diputados de Olanda, y de la Rochela estuvieron ayer juntos seis horas, y resolvieron quatro puntos; el primero procurar con el parlamento, y por todos los demas medios humanos y posibles, que este Rey rompa el tratado de casamiento, y la paz con España; el segundo que en casso que no se pueda conseguir esto, que se procure que publica, o, secretamente socorro a los Olandeses, y a los Uganotes de Francia; el tercero que no pudiendose tampoco conseguir esto, se procure matar al Conde de Gondomar, levantando el pueblo contra el por causa de la religion, o, buscar otra forma publica, o, secreta, con que acavalle, porque el es causa de todo lo que el Rey haze y dexa de hazer en defensa de su religion, y que era cierto que el Marques de Boquingan se conserbaba con el Rey por la amistad y traza y disposicion del Conde, y que quitado el Conde, naturalmente el Marque caeria. Lo quarto y ultimo que acordaron fue, que si estas cosas no se pudieren conseguir, se encamine como vengan aqui el Principe Palatino y su muger y sus hijos, y asistidos de los Puritanos Ingleses y socorros de Olanda y Francia se apoderen del Reyno; que sera facil estando el Rey y el Principe tan malquistos, y queriendo como quieren mudar la religion, y entregar el Reyno al Papa y al Rey de España, en esto es cierto que quedaron ayer de acuerdo, pero no permitira Dios que puedan cumplir nada dello, ni lo que toca al Conde de Gondomar, aunque es lo de menor importancia.

TRANSLATION
†
Madame

On the first of this month[28] I recounted to your Highness how Parliament had met here and what was proposed in it in the name of this king by some of his ministers.

The discussion of the war and of the contributions for assistance in it continued; and the power, the House of Commons, (so they are called here, the representatives of the provinces, cities, towns, and lands of the kingdom, which make 470 people) have proceeded with such violence and sedition against the Catholic religion and the marriage with Spain, that in the one and the other, they have said amazingly wild things, taking as a pretext the conservation of their religion; and the damage that has come and continues from the king's not having confirmed the laws that they made against the Catholics, nor having executed those that they made earlier; since the Catholics had grown to a great number and of all social ranks, the Protestants and their true Gospel ought to fear a great ruin if the remedy were delayed, since the papists were saying audaciously that a Catholic king would be soon seen in England and that the Protestants would have to ask for toleration of their religion with much doubt that it would be conceded to them, because the most certain thing would be that he would treat them and do with them what is now being done with them in France.[29] [It was said in Parliament] that the harm in everything consisted in the marriage negotiations for this prince and Spain, since with it, and with this shadow, the Pope and his most beloved son[30] were making progress and advantages that appeared in favour of idolatry. [It was said in Parliament] that the remedy was to beg the king to marry the prince to a woman of their religion and to execute all the old laws against Catholics and those that had now been added and renewed; and they agreed to grant him a subsidy (so it is called here, this service that raises around 400,000 ducats, for which they have already a form of general distribution, and they will finish it easily) and these 400,000 ducats would be in letters for aid for the troops that are in the Palatinate in the service of the [Elector] Palatine, including as a condition in this grant that the Catholics pay double, and [that] they be held as separate foreigners and be excluded from the state's commerce, since they were not conforming with the laws, and the government. [Parliament agreed]

[28] 21 Nov./1 Dec. 1621.

[29] In the summer of 1620 Louis XIII led an army into southwestern France to force Protestants to restore all church properties seized since 1569 to the Catholic church.

[30] The King of Spain.

also to ask the king to declare the enemy against whom the war was being made, and to proclaim it and publish it, so that, in conformity with it, the aid and assistance be given to him. [They said] that they would give as much as may be necessary, in accordance with the quality and power of the enemy, up to thirty subsidies, if it were necessary, which make 12 million ducats, and that it was well known that the emperor and the Duke of Bavaria were not the true enemy, but supposed and feigned [to be], and that the true [enemy] was the one who was helping them with money, and that therefore it was necessary and convenient to make war where the purse was, in order to discontinue the damages and to divert them; and that while such was not being done, it was to lose time and waste men and money in vain in as it was sent to the Palatinate; that a great army sent to Flanders and a great fleet sent to the Indies or to Spain was the only remedy, and to join and unite themselves for this with the Dutch very closely, since although it was certain that England had received much harm and offence from them, the affairs were at the point where it was necessary to dissemble this, in order not to lose the religion and the state and to come into the hands of the one, it was known, who wanted to dominate the temporal world in the name of giving the spiritual to the pope; and that there would be no doubt that the Dutch would then hand over to this king the Sluis and Flushing, and the other places that he may desire in those provinces, which was what the deputies who had now come from there were saying and offering.

The House of Commons assented and agreed on these propositions, putting them in a petition to the king, and they resolved that it be carried by twelve of the Parliament, whom they called the Twelve Apostles, and [the Commons] ordered them to give and read the petition to the king and ask him for a response and declaration on all its points in writing, and that they should then return with the reply that the king gave them. They named as one of the twelve Sir Richard Weston, who is one of the privy council and chancellor of the exchequer and one of the representatives of the kingdom in the lower house, a much honoured gentleman. He did not concur with these crazy actions, but as they were passed by the majority, he had to comply with the nomination that they made for him with the others, and that which they sent him, which was that all depart on Tuesday, the 14th of this month,[31] for Newmarket, where the king is. And so they did it.

I had written to the king and to the Marquis of Buckingham, four days before the sedition and wickedness that was occurring in this Parliament,

---

[31] 4/14 Dec. 1621.

that if I had not been not so sure of the word and goodness of the king that he would punish and remedy [the Parliament] with the speed and example that was convenient,[32] I would have left his kingdoms without waiting three days, having to act in this way, fulfilling my obligation as if he were not king of these people, since at present, I did not have here an army with which to punish them.[33]

The king then sent a letter to Parliament, which reached the hands of the secretary of state, Sir George Calvert, on the same Tuesday, the fourteenth of this month, at ten o'clock before mid-day, in the morning on which the twelve commissioners had departed for where the king was; and at this hour of ten o'clock the secretary opened the document right there in Parliament and gave the king's letter to the Speaker of the Parliament (so they call here the man elected for this, and they put him in an eminent seat, and he is normally a grave and eloquent doctor [of law]), and the address of the letter was for this man, saying, 'to our loyal and well loved speaker of the House of Commons of the Parliament'. He took it and read it outloud, and that which it contained was that the king was saying that he had understood through various reports to his very great regret that the distance and separation of his person for the present from his high court of Parliament, which was caused by his bad health, had given audacity to some furious and popular spirits in the House of Commons to dispute and argue publicly in affairs much higher than their understanding and capacity to his great dishonour, and desiring to reduce and undo his royal prerogative, and that the Speaker would make known to all of the House that the will of the king was that no one from that time on may presume to meddle in any affair touching his royal government or matters of state, and particularly to speak about the marriage of his son, Charles, with the daughter of Spain, nor touch upon the honour and respect that was owed to that king, or his other friends and confederates, nor to meddle either in the particularities of some men who were being held for trial in the ordinary courts of justice; and [the king said] that for as much as he had heard, they wanted

---

[32] Here Gondomar refers to the king's plan to dissolve Parliament.

[33] Gardiner says that James had invited Gondomar to join him at Newmarket, and cites this letter, but there is no such invitation in this version. See *History of England*, iv. 248. Gardiner seems to take Gondomar's joke as insolence. According to Gardiner, Gondomar wrote that his leaving the kingdom 'would have been my duty to do, as you would have ceased to be a king here, and as I have no army here at present to punish these people myself', p. 249. Gardiner should have translated '*si no fuera Rey*' as a counterfactual phrase and not as a potential condition. James and Gondomar had repeatedly discussed, in seriousness and in jest, the rebelliousness of the English, and it was common for Gondomar to use such counterfactuals in his correspondence.

to send a message to Sir Edwin Sandys to learn the reasons that the
king had for arresting him; [the king said] that the speaker may tell
them in [the king's] name, that the imprisonment had not been for
any reason concerning Parliament, and that in order to relieve them
from all doubt and question about matters of this nature, [the Speaker]
would tell them resolutely in [the king's] royal name that his authority
was enough to punish bad behavior in this way after the end of
Parliament, and while it sat and they were attending it, which he never
thought to dissemble if there were some occasion of insolence among
those who were present, and if they were to speak again about the said
points or to try to send him another petition about them without
reforming them before it was presented to him, that he was declaring
to them that he would not do them the honour of hearing it or of
receiving it; and that because he had understood that the Parliament
desired him to allow a sitting before Christmas in order to confirm
some laws, that the speaker would tell them that if this were not done,
and the Parliament was broken without it, it would be their fault,
because if they wanted to agree among themselves at this time upon
such laws, which were really good for the commonwealth, the king
would give his consent very voluntarily, therefore it would be certain
that if the good laws were not made for the good of the people, the
vituperation that he would give [would be] solely over such turbulent
spirits that were preferring their interests and particular ends to the
good of the kingdom and the public; with which he said goodbye,
which was the end of the letter, written at Newmarket, on the thirteenth
of this month by our count.[34]

When his letter was read, the bad [Members] were as stunned, as the
few good ones that were there were encouraged, but the majority rose,
saying that there was nothing to discuss or negotiate, [and there was
nothing to do] but to go away and leave everything; and when others
urged to remain and confer about the matter, one said that the affair
was very serious, and no other such had been seen or heard of, nor a
letter like that one in that House; and [he said] that thus it could be
that suddenly and without mature consideration some rubbish may
have been said, and if some grave error were made, that because of
this it was well that they rise and leave without speaking about it any
more for the time being, nor should they meet that day, but leave the
affair for the following [day], which was yesterday, Wednesday; and
[he said] that everyone (having slept on it) would have to have thought
about what was convenient to do; with which they rose, sending by
post to reach the twelve commissioners that had gone, so that they

[34] 3/13 Dec. 1621.

might return without succeeding to speak to the king, and thus they reached them, and they returned.

They met yesterday, Wednesday, in the morning, and the learned [Sir] Edward Coke (who has been a chief justice of this kingdom and is now a privy councillor and one of the attendants of this house) began to speak, saying that on the day before, when he had seen the king's letter, he had been left most upset, but that at present he found himself much consoled, because he had considered that in the whole letter, the king was not saying a word on the matter of religion, with which it appeared that he had not been displeased with what they had dealt with regarding it, and that thus they could try to defend it by all the means that they had proposed to undo their enemies, since all the risk they were running in deliberating this constantly was to be men hanged for their loyalty and for a good cause, a sweeter and more honourable death, than to die burnt at the stake, as they would die if the uncircumcised Philistines (who were the Papists) were to conquer, and also it was possible and one ought to believe that the king was misinformed in the remaining points contained in the petition, and that if he were well informed, he would approve them, and he would be thankful since there was nothing among [the remaining points] in which the Parliament would not have authority to discuss, of which there were many ancient examples in similar cases, and that for all these reasons, and for the authority and defence of the privileges of Parliament, it appeared to him that they may again name twenty commissioners, that they adjust the petition and its propositions, and with the appropriate submission and humility, may again represent its contents to the king and make their plea.

The majority shouted in approval, and resolving that it be done in this way, and that until that the king responded appropriately to it, they would deliberate on no other business; and [they resolved] that copies would be made from the king's letter and from the petition and the propositions of the Parliament and would be given to all those who wanted them, in order that their justification be seen, and with the result that progress has stopped in the dispatch of the 400,000 ducats.

This is the state in which things are today, which is of great confusion and difficulty, since it obligates and forces the king either to break Parliament or to surrender to them and break with everyone else; and the commissioners from Holland which have arrived here do not cease day and night by all the means that they have, to contribute to this confusion and to persuade the king to incline himself to [their cause], and for this they have many friends and protectors, and they pay them very lavishly.

It is also true that the well-inclined are trying to do all that is possible with God and with men against it; the king has not until now given an audience to these deputies from Holland, but what they tell his ministers, whom they have seen, is that they come to place themselves at the feet of this king, in order that he may do to them what he wants, and that even down-trodden and mistreated, and in anyway at all, whether he likes them or not, they will be loyal and obedient to him, reiterating this with notable submission and the desire to obligate [him] to do what they claim.

Here there has arrived a dispatch of many letters taken by the Count of Mansfeld in the post from Germany and Italy; they were sent to Newmarket, where the king is, and therefore I could not until now see them nor know in detail all that they contain, but they tell me that the gist of it is that the emperor was sending a religious, who is named Pater Hyancinth, so that he inform Your Highness and His Majesty in Spain of the reasons that there are that the emperor give to the Duke of Bavaria the electorate that the Count Palatine had, and that if the reasons of religion, state, and gratitude which he would represent would not be enough, it would be declared that the emperor is pledged and has given his word to the Duke of Bavaria to give him the electorate and that thus [the emperor] cannot get out of doing it, which is something that causes great concern; although [the emperor] has placed a new obligation and esteem on this king in aligning himself more with this position that Your Highness and His Catholic Majesty, by your intercession and consideration, do not desire the total ruin of his son-in-law, although he does not deserve it, and moreso now that they are writing from The Hague[35] that [the Elector Palatine] is once again obstinate in not wanting to make a submission to the emperor, nor [wanting to] do anything of what this king has offered to do in his name; with a result that Baron Digby, although he has been the fatal instrument of all these confusions that are here today, is already laying the blame on the [Elector] Palatine alone, and it is certain that [Digby] now speaks with the greatest respect for Spain and Your Highness and the Lord Archduke [Albert] – may he rest in peace[36] – and speaking of His Highness the other day in Parliament, [Digby] said that [the Archduke] was among the most prudent and exemplary princes that

---

[35] Friedrich V and his court-in-exile resided in The Hague as guests of the States-General of the United Provinces.
[36] Literally, 'may he have glory'.

there had been in the world, and that [Digby] could not say [Albert's] name without mentioning these attributes, because he deserved them.

All that has been collected here until now of the £30,000 (with which, as I informed Your Highness, this king would aid the Count Palatine) and that which has been issued to him toward that sum, Your Highness may order to see, by the memo that accompanies [this letter], and how the money is handed over for distribution by the ambassador that this king has in The Hague, where, they tell me, it will be consumed in what the Palatines owe and spend, without anything coming to the assistance of those who are in the Palatinate. May God keep the most serene person of Your Highness, etc., London, the 16th of December 1621.

Now I receive a letter from the Marquis of Buckingham by the post, written in all diligence last night at Newmarket where the king is, in which he tells me that the king is most constant, and sends me a copy of what the king wrote to Parliament, and tells me that within two more days he hopes to be able to inform me further.

I have also now learned for certain that the deputies from Holland and La Rochelle were together yesterday for six hours, and they resolved on four points; the first, to endeavor with the Parliament and through all further human and possible means that this king break the marriage negotiations and the peace with Spain; the second, that in case this cannot succeed, that aid be procured, publicly or secretly, for the Dutch and the Huguenots of France; the third, that should they not succeed in this either, they should arrange to kill the Count of Gondomar, raising the people against him for the cause of religion, or to search for another way, public or secret, to achieve this, because he is the cause of all that the king does and fails to do in the defense of his religion, and that it was certain that the Marquis of Buckingham was maintaining himself with the king by the friendship and design and disposition of the count, and that having gotten rid of the count, naturally the marquis would fall; the fourth and last thing that they agreed to was that if these things could not be carried out, they would arrange that the Prince Palatine and his wife and their children may come here, and, assisted by the English Puritans and [with] the aid of Holland and France, they may take over the kingdom, which will be easy, the king and prince being so disliked, and desiring as they do to change the religion and surrender the kingdom to the pope and the King of Spain; in this it is certain that [the deputies] reached an agreement yesterday, but God will not permit them to carry out any of it, nor that which affects the Count of Gondomar, although it is of lesser importance.

'IT WILL BE A SCANDAL TO SHOW WHAT WE HAVE DONE WITH SUCH A NUMBER:' HOUSE OF COMMONS COMMITTEE ATTENDANCE LISTS, 1606–1628

Chris R. Kyle

That committee membership has played a significant role in parliamentary history is beyond question. It formed an important part of the analysis of the importance of Members of Parliament in the Elizabethan *History of Parliament* volumes and appointments have frequently been used to illustrate the particular interest of Members in parliamentary issues and legislation.[1] However, much of the analysis has been undertaken in a simplistic fashion, derived solely from the Underclerk's record in the *Commons Journal* and subjected to little more than superficial scrutiny. Stuart historians have been slow to heed Lord Macaulay's advice that Victoria Tower is 'that dark repository in which the abortive statutes of many generations sleep a sleep rarely disturbed by the historian or antiquary', for it is in the House of Lords Record Office that the majority of committee lists survive.[2] And the existence of these attendance records allows us to expand and clarify previous analyses of Commons attendance. In particular, they show the minutiae of Parliament at work on a day-to-day basis as well as providing valuable biographical information. Viewed individually or taken as a whole, the documents also allow the development of broad and far-reaching conclusions about Parliament itself. The thirty-three committee lists transcribed below cover the period 1606–1628 and offer insights into local issues, such as the presentment to the parsonage of Radipoll,

---

[1] P. W. Hasler, ed., *The House of Commons, 1558–1603* (3 vols, London, 1981). See, in particular, Stephen D. White, *Sir Edward Coke and 'The Grievances of the Commonwealth', 1621–1628* (Chapel Hill, 1979), pp. 279–83; R. C. Munden, '"All the Privy Council Being Members of this House": A Note on the Constitutional Significance of Procedure in the House of Commons, 1589–1614', *PH* xii (1993), p. 118; Chris R. Kyle, 'Prince Charles in the Parliaments of 1621 and 1624', *HJ* xli (1998), pp. 617–18, 622–4. Further detailed analysis of early Stuart parliamentary committees is forthcoming in Chris R. Kyle, 'Attendance, Apathy and Order?: Parliamentary Committees in Early Stuart England', in Chris R. Kyle and Jason Peacey, eds, *Parliament at Work: Parliamentary Committees, Access and Lobbying Under the Tudors and Stuarts* (forthcoming, Boydell and Brewer).

[2] Lady Trevelyan, *The Works of Lord Macaulay* (8 vols, London, 1866), iii. 357–8.

Dorset, and matters which concerned the commonweal, for example, purveyance and debt collection.

The most obvious conclusion which can be drawn from the lists is that they illustrate that poor attendance was not only a problem suffered in the House but in committees as well. This corollary to the contemporary concern over low turnout in debate may not be unsuspected in itself, but it is surprising that the numbers are so low, especially on matters of commonwealth interest. For example, purveyance was a major issue throughout the early Stuart period and was one of the prerogative rights under discussion in the Great Contract (1610). Despite numerous speeches against the abuses of purveyors, the committee meeting on 10 March 1624 only attracted three MPs: Sir Gilbert Gerard, possibly one of the 'Middlesex men' who had introduced the bill in 1621; Sir William Fleetwood, one of the main agitators for the measure; and the Comptroller of the Household, Sir John Suckling.[3] On such an important issue, the attendance was startlingly small. A similar example is shown by the Export of Wool bill, to which only five MPs attended a 1624 committee meeting.[4] Even the 1621 measure to regulate the court of Chancery attracted only 11 of the 27 named to the committee. Admittedly, a number of senior Parliament-men in the House were present, including Sir Edward Coke, Edward Alford, Sir Henry Poole and Sir Francis Barrington, but nevertheless the number is still on the low side in a Parliament in which Chancery and other equity courts came under continual criticism, and the need for regulation was widely acknowledged.[5]

Furthermore the lists reveal that matters of seemingly minor local interest often attracted more committees than those commonweal issues referred to above. One probable reason for this is that much of the work on matters of national importance was undertaken in general debate on the floor of the House, while private bills were relegated to discussion in committee rooms. In this it echoes the claims of Thomas Norton that private matters were best dealt with in committees as they 'ever be eagerly followed and make factions'.[6] Factions or not, in comparison with public legislation, attendance on private bills was correspondingly higher. For example, the Chancery dispute between various members of the Edwards family attracted 15 MPs to the first committee meeting and a remarkable 23 to the second one. Interest

[3] See below p. 195.

[4] See below p. 224.

[5] See below p. 194 and Robert Zaller, *The Parliament of 1621: A Study in Constitutional Conflict* (Berkeley, 1971), pp. 90-97.

[6] BL, Harleian MS 253, fol. 4. Michael A. R. Graves, 'Managing Elizabethan Parliaments', in David M. Dean and Norman L. Jones, eds, *The Parliaments of Elizabethan England* (Oxford, 1990), p. 53.

had dropped for the last two committees when respectively only 6 and 7 MPs were present.[7] In 1626 the naturalization of a merchant, Thomas Southerne, and a physician, Samuel Bave, was debated by 19 MPs, while attendance was also high at meetings for the assurance of Goathland manor to Prince Charles (1624) and the bill for the restoration of Prees Manor, Lancashire, to members of the Wolferstone family (1624).[8] The measure in 1625 which affected the tenants of Macclesfield, Lancashire, was attended by 22 MPs at the first meeting, including all the MPs who sat for the county and its boroughs.[9]

In addition, the lists show that conclusions drawn about an MP's importance by his being named to multiple committees, and the relevance of particular named MPs to committees, needs to be considered afresh. The registers specifically illustrate that in many cases committee attendees were not individually named but turned up either as a representative for some generic group of other, for example 'knights and burgesses of clothing counties', 'all lawyers' or fell into none of the categories applicable to the bill. Indeed, one of the trends highlighted by committee attendance lists is that in a number of instances the majority of the committee was comprised of MPs who were not recorded individually in the Commons Journal. This point is highlighted by the Seamarks and Mariners bill of 1621 when none of the 12 MPs present at the meeting had been on the original committee list.[10] Similarly with the 1624 Lead Ore measure, the 7 MPs at the meeting had not been noted on the Underclerk's committee list.[11]

Thus certain broad-brush conclusions can be drawn from the documents. 1. There was widespread apathy in attending committee meetings. 2. The majority of work done in committees was carried out by a small number of MPs. 3. Many of the individual MPs at meetings were not individually named to the committee or even formed part of the generic group appointed. 4. The Underclerk's record in the Journal cannot be relied on as a source for indicating MPs' interests in attending the committee. 5. The work on public bills seems to have been conducted in the House whilst corresponding issues of local or private matters remained the preserve of committees.

Because of the disparity of the subjects covered by the documents, it has not been possible in a short introduction to discuss the implications of every committee attendance record. Further information on each list has been provided in the footnotes as a guide to the subject matter and for purposes of further reading. No doubt scattered in various

[7] See below pp. 204–5.
[8] See below pp. 229, 196–8, 206–7.
[9] See below pp. 227–8.
[10] See below pp. 188–9.
[11] See below p. 214.

archives are more notes on committee attendance. But the thirty-three herein are sufficient to emphasise Michael Graves' comment on Elizabethan Parliaments: 'an important precondition of parliamentary efficiency [was] that what mattered was not quantity but quality, and in particular experience, dedicated service and the legislative skills of the lawyers.'[12] Given the bold statistics of the attendance figures given below, that Jacobean and early Caroline Parliaments managed to enact any legislation at all is testimony to that dictum.

Nature of the Sources and Editorial Comment

The majority of the lists printed below are attached to draft bills in the Main Papers at the House of Lords Record Office. Because of their nature as scribbled lists which were clearly not intended to form part of a lasting parliamentary archive they are often difficult to read and interpret. Many are riddled with seemingly contradictory ticks, crosses and other marks, probably made by the chair of the committee. This has made the dating of many of the meetings problematical and I have erred on the side of caution when recording the day of meeting. Thus only meetings which can be definitely ascribed to a particular day have been dated. For reasons of clarity and cross-referencing MPs against the printed Journals and the *Return of Members*, the spelling of names has been modernised and the first names of Members simply noted as 'Mr' has been added wherever possible. The constituencies of MPs has been included where regional or patronage analysis may prove useful.

Select Abbreviations

Burg.	Burgesses
I. of W.	Isle of Wight
K&B	Knights and Burgesses
n.d.	No date

---

[12] Graves, 'Managing Elizabethan Parliaments', p. 43.

Texts of Committee Attendance Lists

An Act for the Relief of the Parson of Radipoll, in the County of Dorset.[13]
Secondly read and committed on 23 January 1606.
Weymouth Museum, MS S189/5

Members	5 June	Constituency
Sir Francis Hastings	✓	Somerset
Sir Thomas Freke		Dorset
Sir John Williams	✓	Dorset
Sir Jerome Horsey		Bossiney
Sir Daniel Dunne		Oxford University
John Hoskins		Hereford
James Bagg	✓	Plymouth
John Boden		Shaftesbury
Sir Robert Meller	✓	Bridport
Richard Martin	✓	Christchurch
Sir John Bennet	✓	Ripon
Edward Manne	✓	Poole
Sir Edward Greville		Warwickshire
Sir Edward Hext		Taunton
~~Sir Robert Napper~~		Wareham
Thomas Wentworth	✓	Oxford
Sir Roland Lytton	✓	Hertfordshire
Sir Gamaliel Capell		Essex
Sir Thomas Smythe		Dunwich
Dr Nicholas Steward		Cambridge University
~~Francis James~~		Wareham
John Spicer		Dorchester
William Spicer	✓	Warwick
Sir Christopher Parkins		Morpeth
Lawrence Hyde	✓	Marlborough
Total	**11**	

[13] *CJ*, i. 259. The bill does not appear to have been reported from the committee although a report in the Weymouth records incorrectly suggests that it was enacted: 'There was long discourse amongst the committees for the bill for erecting the said parsonage, and that in time, for they saw no way to ensure unto the said parson £4 by the year and to his successors, they concluded that there should be a house ensconced to the parsonage of the yearly value of £4 by the year which was accordingly done ... The parson himself was in London before the bill for the parsonage was past the Upper House. He sought to stop it but could not prevail.' Weymouth Museum, MS S189/5. I am grateful to Andrew Thrush for providing this information.

An Act for the Better Attendance of the Members of the House of Commons, 1610.[14]

Secondly read and committed on 18 April 1610.[15]

BL, Harl. MS 6806, fol. 270.

Members	n.d.	n.d.	Total	Constituency
Privy Council				
King's Counsel				
Sir Francis Hastings	✓		1	Somerset
William Waad				West Looe
Serjeant John Doddridge				Horsham
Sir Francis Bacon				Ipswich
Sir Edwin Sandys	✓	✓	2	Stockbridge
Serjeant Robert Barker				Colchester
Sir Edward Hoby				Rochester
Sir John Heigham				Suffolk
Sir George More	✓	✓	2	Guildford
Sir Edward Montagu	✓		1	Northamptonshire
~~Sir Robert Wingfield~~				
Sir Herbert Croft	✓	✓	2	Herefordshire
Sir Francis Goodwin	✓	✓	2	Buckingham
Sir William Strode				Plympton Erle
Sir Robert Knollys				Breconshire
Sir Robert Cotton				Huntingdonshire
Sir George Somers				Lyme Regis
~~Robert Bowyer~~				
Sir Nathaniel Bacon	✓	✓	2	Norfolk
Sir Roger Owen				Shropshire
Sir Robert Johnson				Monmouth Boroughs
Henry Yelverton				Northampton

[14] The Commons had always suffered from the problem of poor attendance and legislation to remedy the situation inevitably failed due to the vested interests of MPs. See Michael A. R. Graves, *Elizabethan Parliaments* (2nd edn, London, 1996), pp. 36–8; G. R. Elton, *The Parliament of England, 1559–1581* (Cambridge, 1986), p. 227; Vernon F. Snow, 'Attendance Trends and Absenteeism in the Long Parliament', *HLQ* xviii (1954–5), pp. 301–6.

[15] The bill was approved by the Commons on 26 June, although it was 'much disputed' and only passed after an ironically well-attended House divided, 126 yea and 106 noe. *CJ*, i. 443. It failed in the Lords, probably not because it sought to fine absent MPs but because it allowed the Speaker of the House or a committee of at least seven MPs to administer oaths. Elizabeth Read Foster, ed., *Proceedings in Parliament 1610* (2 vols, New Haven, 1966), i. 281–2.

Lawrence Hyde				Marlborough
Sir Anthony Cope				Oxfordshire
Sir Francis Barrington	?	✓	1 or 2	Essex
Edward Alford	✓	✓	2	Colchester
Sir George St Poll				Great Grimsby
Roger Puleston	✓		1	Flintshire
Francis Tate				Shrewsbury
Thomas Damet	✓		1	Great Yarmouth
Sir Thomas Holcroft		✓	1	Cheshire
Richard Martin				Christchurch
William Brock				St Ives
Thomas Crew				Lichfield
Sir Walter Cope				Westminster
Thomas Wentworth				Oxford
Sir William Bulstrode				Rutland
Sir James Perrot				Haverfordwest
Edward Duncombe				Tavistock
Sir John Holles				Nottinghamshire
Sir William Twysden	✓		1	Thetford
Dr Francis James				Wareham
Sir John Savile				Yorkshire
Samuel Lewknor				Bishop's Castle
Anthony Irby				Boston
Sir Richard Spencer				Brackley
Sir Charles Cornwallis				Norfolk
Sir Francis Leigh		✓	1	Oxford
Nicholas Fuller		✓	1	London
Total	**11 or 12**	**9**		

An Act for the True Making of Woollen Cloth, 1621.[16]

HLRO, Main Papers, 9 March 1621.

Secondly read and committed on 21 March 1621.

Members	n.d.	Constituency
Sir Robert Crane ·	✓	Suffolk
William Towerson		London
Henry Lord Clifford		Westmorland
Thomas Clench	✓	Suffolk
William Salusbury	✓	Merioneth
K&B Clothing Counties		
Burg. York		
Unnamed Members		
Sir Francis Barnham	✓	Maidstone
Robert Berkeley	✓	Worcester
Mr Wingfield, John or William	✓	Stamford or Lichfield
Sir Henry [illegible]	✓	
Edward Nicholas	✓	Winchelsea
Christopher Wray	✓	Great Grimsby
Mr [*Sic*] Sir Thomas Wise	✓	Bere Alston
Total	**9**	

[16] The bill continued the provisions of the acts 35 Eliz. I cap. 10, 43 Eliz. I cap. 10 and 4 James I cap. 10 on the manufacture of woollen cloth. It was not reported from committee in 1621 but an amended version was enacted in 1624 as 21 James I cap. 18.

An Act for the settling of certaine Manors and Lands of the Right Honourable Anthony Viscount Montagu towards the Payment of his Debts and raising of his Daughters Portions, 1621.[17]

HLRO, Main Papers, 22 February 1621.

Secondly read and committed on 15 March 1621.

Members	n.d.	Constituency
Sir Thomas Edmondes		Bewdley
Sir Edward Montagu		Northamptonshire
Sir Henry Poole	✓	Malmesbury
Sir Henry Curwen		Cumberland
Sir Richard Tichborne	✓	Winchester
Sir Jerome Horsey	✓	East Looe
James Lord Wriothesley		Callington
Sir William Spencer	✓	Northamptonshire
Sir Edwin Sandys	✓	Sandwich
Edward Wrightington		St Mawes
Sir George Dalston		Cumberland
Christopher Neville	✓	Sussex
Richard Harrison	✓	Wootton Bassett
Edward Alford		Colchester
Sir Miles Sandys	✓	Huntingdon
Sir Henry Vane		Carlisle
Henry Lord Clifford		Westmorland
John Wrenham	✓	Wootton Bassett
Sir Robert Lloyd		Minehead
Sir Thomas Lowe		London
Sir Talbot Bowes		Richmond
William Sotwell	✓	Ludgershall
Christopher Brooke		York
Thomas Crew		Northampton
Sir Humphrey May		Lancaster
Sir Henry Compton		East Grinstead
Total	**10**	

[17] It passed both Houses in 1621 but was not presented for the royal assent. In 1624 it was enacted as 21 James I OA 48.

An Act for the Explaining and Enlarging of a Statute made in the 8th Year of the Reign of the late Queen Elizabeth, intitled An Act concerning Seamarks and Mariners,1621.[18]

HLRO, Main Papers, 25 April 1621.

Secondly read and committed on 7 May 1621.
Added to the committee 12 May 1621.
Sir Francis Roe
Henry Rolle
Knights and Burgesses of Suffolk

Members	n.d.	Constituency
Sir Edward Coke		Liskeard
Sir Francis Darcy		Middlesex
Sir Henry Widderington		Northumberland
William Hakewill		Tregony
Sir Gilbert Houghton		Lancashire
Sir Guy Palmes		Rutland
Walter Pye		Brecon
Sir Edward Sackville		Sussex
William Mallory		Ripon
Sir Robert Killigrew		Newport
Sir Henry Poole		Malmesbury
Sir Richard Worsley		Newport, I. of W.
Henry Lovell		Bletchingley
Sir Charles Howard		New Windsor
Burg. York		
Burg. London		
Burg. Port Towns		
Barons Cinque Ports		
Added Members		
Sir Thomas Roe		Cirencester
Henry Rolle		Callington

[18] The bill was drafted by Deptford Trinity House and gave it control over all lighthouses apart from those on the Tyne. It sought to nullify the patent of Sir Edward Howard to build a lighthouse at Dungeness, and the grant to Sir John Meldrum and Sir William Erskine to erect a lighthouse at Winton Ness, Norfolk. The measure was opposed both by the King and George Villiers, Duke of Buckingham, and stood little chance of success in a Parliament adamantly opposed to monopolistic grants. G. G. Harris, ed., *Trinity House of Deptford Transactions, 1609–1635* (London Record Society, xix, 1983), pp. x–xi; 46.; *idem, The Trinity House of Deptford, 1514–1660* (London, 1969), p. 201.

K&B Suffolk		
Unnamed Members		
John Trefusis	✓	Truro
William Towerson	✓	London
Robert Bateman	✓	London
Robert Snelling	✓	Ipswich
John Lister	✓	Kingston-Upon-Hull
John Griffith	✓	Caernarvonshire
Benjamin Cooper	✓	Great Yarmouth
Sir Thomas Riddell	✓	Newcastle
William Nyell	✓	Dartmouth
Roger Mathew	✓	Dartmouth
Edward Nicholas	✓	Winchelsea
Robert Jermyn	✓	Penryn
Total	**12**	

An Act for the Free Trade and Traffic of Welsh Cloths, Cottons, Friezes, Linings and Plains in and through the Kingdom of England, 1621.[19]

HLRO, Main Papers, 24 April 1621.

Secondly read and committed on 2 March 1621.

Members	6 Mar.	25 Mar.	Total	Constituency
Privy Council				
Sir William Strode	✓		I	Plympton Erle
Sir Henry Poole				Malmesbury
Sir Carew Reynell				Cricklade
Sir John Trevor(s)				Bodmin or Denbighshire[20]
Sir John Hayward				Bridgnorth
Christopher Brooke				York
Sir Thomas Wentworth				Yorkshire
Sir Robert Phelips				Bath
Sir Samuel Sandys				Worcestershire
William Denny				Norwich
John Drake				Devon
Citizens of York				
Sir John Strangeways				Dorset
Mr Griffith, John or Nicholas	✓	✓	2	Caernarvonshire or Boroughs
Sir William Herbert		✓	I	Montgomeryshire
Sir Edwin Sandys				Sandwich
Sir Robert Floyd				Minehead
K&B Wales				
K&B Cheshire				
K&B Shropshire				
K&B Warwickshire				

[19] The bill passed both Houses in 1621 but was not presented for the royal assent. In 1624 it was enacted as 21 James I cap. 9. The act ended the monopoly of the Shrewsbury Drapers over the Welsh cloth trade and enabled other clothiers to buy Welsh cloth and transport it to London for sale. For a lengthy account of the bill's procedure and consequences see T. C. Mendenhall, *The Shrewsbury Drapers and the Welsh Wool Trade in the XVI and XVII Centuries* (London, 1953), pp. 168–84.

[20] It is likely that the Sir John Trevor junior, MP for Denbighshire, was appointed to this committee.

Unnamed Members				
Sir James Perrot	✓		I	Haverfordwest
Sir Henry Williams	✓		I	Breconshire
James Price	✓		I	Radnorshire
Lewis Powell	✓		I	Pembroke Boroughs
Hugh [illegible]	✓		I	
Richard [illegible]		✓	I	
William Salisbury		✓	I	Merioneth
Robert Bateman		✓	I	London
William Towerson		✓	I	London
Hugh Myddelton		✓	I	London
Sampson Eure		✓	I	Beaumaris
Total	7	8		

An Act for avoiding of vexatious delays caused by removing actions and suits out of inferior courts, 1621.[21]

HLRO, Main Papers, 20 April 1621.

Secondly read and committed on 20 April 1621.

Members	20 Apr.	Constituency
Edward Alford	✓	Colchester
Sir Thomas Hoby		Ripon
Drue Drury		Norfolk
Sir Jerome Horsey		East Looe
Richard Taylor		Bedford
Sir Edward Montagu		Northamptonshire
Sir Henry Poole		Malmesbury
Sir Francis Darcy		Middlesex
Sir John Crompton		Eye
Sir Francis Seymour		Wiltshire
Sir George More		Surrey
Robert Snelling	✓	Ipswich
Richard Amherst		Lewes
Sir Richard Worsley		Newport, I. of W.
Mr Coke, Clement or John		Dunwich or Warwick
Thomas Morgan		Wilton
Charles Howard		New Windsor
Burg. London		
Burg. Bristol		
Sir Nathaniel Rich		East Retford
Sir Francis Barrington		Essex
John Drake		Devon

[21] The measure did not emerge from committee in 1621 but it was enacted three years later as 21 James I cap. 23. The genesis of the act can be found in the tracts of Lord Chancellor Ellesmere. In 'Memorialles for Iudicature. Pro Bono Publico', he criticised the misuse of prerogative writs such as *certiorari, habeas corpus* and *procedendo*. He noted that the Clerks of Courts had often issued these writs either without the knowledge of judges or without adequate supervision from the judiciary. This had led to an increase of expensive actions in the central courts, delays in judgement and confusion when writs were issued from more than one court. The act therefore limited the ways in which actions could be removed from county courts to Westminster. On Ellesmere see Louis A. Knafla, ed., *Law and Politics in Jacobean England: The Tracts of Lord Chancellor Ellesmere* (Cambridge, 1977), pp. 274–81.

Sir Warwick Hele		Plympton Erle
Walter Earle		Poole
Nicholas Cage	✓	Ipswich
All to have voice		
Unnamed Members		
William Denny	✓	Norwich
Mr Glanville, Francis or John	✓	Tavistock or Plymouth
Richard Rosse	✓	Norwich
William Neale	✓	Dartmouth
Sir Francis Worsley	✓	Newport, I. of W.
Total	**8**	

Committee to Draft a Bill for Regulating the Court of Chancery, 1621.[22]

BL, Harl. MS 6806, fol. 276, 25 April 1621.

Appointed on 25 April 1621.

Members	n.d.	Constituency
Sir Edward Coke	✓	Liskeard
Edward Alford	✓	Colchester
Thomas Wentworth		Oxford
Sir Robert Phelips	✓	Bath
Sir Thomas Hoby		Ripon
Sir Edward Giles	✓	Totnes
Sir Miles Fleetwood		Westbury
Sir Edward Sackville	✓	Sussex
Sir Nathaniel Rich		East Retford
Serjeant Francis Ashley		Dorchester
Sir Thomas Roe		Cirencester
Christopher Neville	✓	Sussex
Sir Edwin Sandys		Sandwich
Sir George More		Surrey
Sir Humphrey May		Lancaster
Sir Henry Widderington	✓	Northumberland
William Mallory		Ripon
Thomas Ravenscroft	✓	Monmouth Boroughs
Sir Edward Wardour	✓	Malmesbury
Christopher Brooke		York
Sir Guy Palmes		Rutland
John Carvile		Aldborough
William Lord Cavendish		Derbyshire
John Pym		Calne
Sir Francis Barrington	✓	Essex
Sir Samuel Sandys		Worcestershire
Sir Henry Poole	✓	Malmesbury
Total	**11**	

[22] See Zaller, *Parliament of 1621*, pp. 93 and 207 n. 35.

An Act concerning the Purveyance and Taking of Horses, Carts and Carriages by Land or by Water, for His Majesty's Service, 1624.[23]

HLRO, Main Papers, 3 April 1624.

Secondly read and committed on 8 March 1624.

Members	10 Mar.	Constituency
Sir Gilbert Gerrard	✓	Middlesex
Sir William Fleetwood	✓	Buckinghamshire
Sir John Suckling	✓	Middlesex
Edward Alford		Colchester
Sir George More		Guildford
Sir Francis Seymour		Marlborough
Sir Francis Barrington		Essex
All to have voice		
Total	**3**	

---

[23] On the problem of early modern purveyance see Allegra Woodworth, 'Purveyance for the Royal Household in the Reign of Queen Elizabeth', *Transactions of the American Philosophical Society*, new ser. xxxv pt. 1 (1945); Pauline Croft, 'Parliament, Purveyance and the City of London 1589–1608, *PH* iv (1985), pp. 9–43; Eric N. Lindquist, 'The King, the People and the House of Commons: The Problem of Early Jacobean Purveyance', *HJ* xxxi (1988), pp. 549–70; G. E. Aylmer, 'The Last Years of Purveyance 1610–1660', *Economic History Review*, 2nd ser. viii (1957), pp. 81–93. The bill passed the Commons in 1624 but failed to emerge from committee in the Lords.

An Act for the securing of the Lordship or Manor of Goteland alias Gothland [Goathland] and the tenants of the same under the most excellent Prince Charles his Highness from the incumbrances of Sir Richard Etherington, Knight, 1624.[24]

HLRO, Main Papers Supplementary, 13 March 1624.

Secondly read and committed on 15 March 1624.

Members	18 Mar.	n.d.	15 Apr.	19 Apr.	n.d.	n.d.	n.d.	n.d.	Total	Constituency
Sir John Savile		✓	✓			✓	✓	✓	5	Yorkshire
Sir Thomas Hoby	✓	✓	✓						3	Ripon
Mr Wandesford	✓	✓	✓	✓		✓	✓		6	Aldborough or Richmond
Sir Thomas Savile	✓	✓	✓	✓		✓	✓	✓	7	Yorkshire
Sir John Walter		✓			✓	✓	✓	✓	5	East Looe
Sir Francis Cottington					✓				1	Camelford
Thomas Sherwill						✓		✓	2	Plymouth
K&B Yorkshire										
Sir Thomas Estcourt				✓	✓			✓	3	Gloucestershire
Sir George Dalston										Cumberland
Sir Henry Poole	✓	✓	✓	✓	✓		✓		6	Oxfordshire
Sir Thomas Trevor					✓	✓		✓	3	Saltash
Sir Gervase Clifton										Nottinghamshire

[24] The measure assured the tenants of their rights to hold the Duchy of Cornwall manor against the intrigues of Etherington. It was committed at the 2nd reading but proceeded no further. *CJ*, i. 686, 736.

Unnamed Members										
William Mallory	✓								1	Ripon
Christopher Brooke	✓								1	York
Sir Arthur Ingram	✓								1	York
Mr Wandesford	✓	✓							2	Aldborough or Richmond
Sir Ferdinando Fairfax							✓	✓		Boroughbridge
William Noy		✓							1	Fowey
William Sheffield		✓							1	Thirsk
Sir Thomas Belasyse		✓							1	Thirsk
Sir Thomas Denton			✓						1	Buckinghamshire
Sir John D[illegible]			✓						1	
Illegible			✓						1	
Added 20 Apr										
Edward Alford				✓	✓		✓		3	Colchester
Sir William Herbert					✓	✓			2	Montgomeryshire
Sir Clement Throckmorton				✓	✓		✓		3	Warwickshire
Sir Dudley Digges				✓					1	Tewkesbury
Mr Brereton, William or Thomas				✓	✓		✓		3	Cheshire or Taunton
William Booth				✓	✓		✓		3	Cheshire

Sir Edward Peyton						✓		✓	2	Cambridge-shire
Sir Thomas Walmesley				✓	✓	✓		✓	4	Lancashire
Sir William Cope					✓	✓		✓	3	Oxfordshire
Total	7	6	9	9	12	14	5	15		

An Act to make sale of the lands of Sir Anthony Aucher, Sir Robert James and John Wroth, 1624.[25]

BL, Harl. MS 6806, fol. 274.

Secondly read and committed on 7 April 1624.

Knights and Burgesses of Buckinghamshire and London added 12 April on the motion of Mr Saunders on behalf of the petitioners.

Members	n.d.	Constituency
Sir George Calvert		Oxford University
Sir Edward Coke		Coventry
Sir Robert Hitcham		Orford
Sir Henry Poole	✓	Oxfordshire
Sir Robert Hatton		Sandwich
Sir Guy Palmes	✓	Rutland
Sir Peter Heyman		Hythe
Sir Thomas Savile	✓	Yorkshire
George Mynne		West Looe
John Pym	✓	Tavistock
Sir Nathaniel Rich	✓	Harwich
Heneage Finch		London
K&B Kent		
Sir George Chudleigh		Tiverton
Sir George More	✓	Guildford
Sir Henry Slingsby		Knaresborough
Sir Edward Peyton		Cambridgeshire
Sir Edward Giles	✓	Totnes
Sir Roger North		Suffolk
Added 12 April		
K&B Buckinghamshire		
Burg. London		
Robert Bateman	✓	London
Martin Bond	✓	London
Sir William Fleetwood	✓	Buckinghamshire
Sir Thomas Denton	✓	Buckinghamshire
Sir Edmund Verney	✓	Buckingham
Total	**12**	

[25] The bill sought to sell the estates of Aucher *et al.* in order to repay their creditors. It proceeded no further than the committee stage. I am grateful to Andrew Thrush for information on Aucher and this measure.

Act for the Quiet Establishment of the Customs of Beaminster Second, Dorset, 1624.[26]

HLRO, Main Papers, 13 April 1624.

Secondly read and commented on 13 April 1624.
14 April 1624 Sir Edward Coke and Mr Drake (Francis/John) added to committee.

Members	15 Apr.	29 Apr.	30 Apr.	3 May	5 May	19 May	21 May	24 May	Total	Constituency
Sir Thomas Cheeke						✓			1	Essex
Lawrence Whitaker			✓		?				?2	Peterborough
William Whitaker	✓	✓		✓	✓	?			?5	Shaftesbury
Lawrence Hyde	✓	✓							2	Hindon
Sir Francis Barnham										Maidstone
Sir Robert Hitcham										Orford
Richard Taylor										Bedford
Martin Bond			✓						1	London
James Lord Wriothesley										Winchester
Sir John Stradling				✓					1	St Germans
Sir William Pitt	✓			✓			✓		3	Wareham
Sir Robert Hatton										Sandwich
Thomas Wentworth							✓		1	Oxford
John Selden	✓								1	Lancaster
Sir Edward Leech						✓			1	Derby
K&B Dorset										

[26] The measure remained in a Commons' committee when the Parliament was prorogued. *CJ*, i. 758, 764.

Added Members 14 April										
Sir Edward Coke										Coventry
Mr Drake, Francis or John										Sandwich or Devon
Unnamed Members										
Sir Walter Earle	✓		✓		✓	✓	✓	✓	6	Poole
Richard Bushrod	✓	✓		✓	✓	✓	✓	✓	7	Dorchester
Thomas Giear		✓		✓	✓	✓			4	Weymouth
Robert Browne		✓		✓	✓			✓	4	Bridport
William Whiteway		✓		✓	✓	✓	✓	✓	6	Dorchester
Sir John Strangways			✓					✓	2	Dorset
John Mostyn			✓	✓			✓	✓	4	Anglesey
Mr Pitt, Matthew or Edward				✓					1	Weymouth or Poole
John Trenchard							✓		1	Wareham
Robert Hassard							✓		1	Lyme Regis
Total	6	6	4	10	6	6	7	8		

An Act for the Relief of the Master, Wardens and Commonality of the Art or Mystery of Feltmakers of London against a Decree made in the High Court of Chancery at the Suit of Christopher Warwick, 1624.[27]

HLRO, Main Papers, 20 May 1624.

Secondly read and committed and 30 April 1624.

Members	3 May	4 May (1)	4 May (2)	7 May	10 May	Total	Constituency
Sir Edward Coke							Coventry
Sir Thoms Myddelton	✓	✓		✓		3	London
Robert Bateman	✓			✓		2	London
Sir John Savile							Yorkshire
William Coryton	✓					1	Cornwall
Sir Robert Heath				✓		1	East Grinstead
William Lord Cavendish			✓			1	Derbyshire
William Whiteway	✓	✓	✓			3	Dorchester
Richard Bushrod	✓	✓	✓	✓		4	Dorchester
Sir George Chudleigh		✓	✓	✓		3	Tiverton
Christopher Sherland							Northampton
Thomas Sherwill	✓	✓	✓	✓		4	Plymouth
Sir Anthony Forest							Wallingford

[27] The dispute dated back to 1611 when Warwick joined the Feltmakers in borrowing money to buy wool. Parcel of the sum raised was £500 borrowed from Lord Harington. Warwick alleged that he had made an agreement with the Company that he would discharge the debt to Harington and pay an equivalent amount to the Feltmakers on loan for one year. In exchange, he would be given the position of Clerk of the Company and at the end of the year he would be repaid his investment in addition to 10 per cent interest. When the Feltmakers failed to repay the money Warwick exhibited a bill in Chancery and this bill to Parliament. The measure passed the Commons but was 'allowed to sleep' in the Lords. Kyle, 'Parliament of 1624', pp. 454–7.

John Pym	✓					1	Tavistock
Sir William Cope	✓		✓			2	Oxfordshire
George Gerrard			✓	✓	✓	3	Newtown, I. of W.
Robert Brom-field							Southwark
Sir Peter Mutton	✓					1	Caernarvon Boroughs
Thomas Jermyn							Bere Alston
Added Members 4 May							
Sir Walter Earle		✓	✓	✓	✓	4	Poole
Samuel More			✓	✓		2	Hastings
Sir Erasmus Dreyden		✓	✓	✓		3	Banbury
Sir Francis Bar-rington				✓		1	Essex
Mr Whitaker, William or Law-rence			✓	✓		2	Shaftesbury or Peterborough
Total	4	7	12	11	7		

An Act to reverse a Decree, made in the Court of Whitehall, commonly called the Court of Requests, between Edwards the Elder and Edwards the Younger, 1624.[28]

HLRO, Main Papers, 20 May 1624.

Secondly read and committed on 16 April 1624.

Members	n.d.	n.d.	n.d.	n.d.	Total	Constituency
Sir Clement Throck-morton						Warwickshire
Sir Peter Mutton		✓			1	Caernarvon Boroughs
Sir Eubule Thelwall			✓		1	Denbighshire
Sir Walter Pye						Brecon
Sir Thomas Myd-delton			✓	✓	2	London
John Drake						Devon
Sir Thomas Wal-mesley	✓				1	Lancashire
Sir Thomas Fairfax	✓				1	Hedon
Sir Peter Heyman						Hythe
Sir Francis Bar-rington						Essex
Sir Henry Mildmay						Westbury
Sir Gilbert Gerard						Middlesex
Drue Drury						Thetford
Sir William Fleet-wood						Buckinghamshire
Sir Robert Pye						Bath
Thomas Charnock						Newtown
Robert Bateman	✓		✓	✓	3	London
All Lawyers						
K&B Wales						
Unnamed Members						
John Glanville	✓				1	Plymouth
Francis Berkeley	✓	✓			2	Shrewsbury

[28] The measure concerned the division of the senior Edwards' estate between his son and Richard Sherborne, the brother of the senior Edwards' first wife. It passed the Commons but stalled in the Lords where the Bishop of Bangor noted, 'Right is in the Son, Equity in the Father.' *LJ*, iii. 414.

Name					Count	Place
William Whitaker	✓				1	Shaftesbury
William Savage	✓				1	Winchester
Charles Jones	✓	✓			2	Beaumaris
Richard Digges	✓				1	Marlborough
John Wightwick	✓				1	Tamworth
John Saunders	✓		✓	✓	3	Reading
Timothy Levinge	✓				1	Derby
John Bankes	✓	✓			2	Wootton Bassett
Mr Wandesford, Christopher or John	✓	✓			2	Aldborough or Richmond
Edward Bysshe	✓				1	Bletchingley
George Herbert		✓			1	Montgomery Boroughs
James Price		✓			1	Radnorshire
Charles Price		✓			1	New Radnor Boroughs
Sir Hugh Myddelton		✓			1	Denbigh Boroughs
Sir John Hanmer		✓			1	Flintshire
William Ravenscroft		✓			1	Flint Boroughs
Sir Robert Mansell		✓			1	Glamorgan
William Price		✓			1	Cardiff Boroughs
Henry Wynn		✓			1	Merioneth
Sir James Perrot		✓	✓	✓	3	Pembrokeshire
Sir Walter Devereux		✓			1	Pembroke Boroughs
Sir William Herbert		✓			1	Montgomeryshire
John Mostyn		✓			1	Anglesey
Sir Henry Williams		✓			1	Breconshire
James Lewis		✓			1	Cardiganshire
Roland Pugh		✓		✓	2	Cardigan Boroughs
Richard Vaughan		✓			1	Carmarthenshire
Henry Vaughan		✓			1	Carmarthan
Thomas Glynne		✓			1	Caernarvonshire
John Carvile			✓		1	Aldborough
Christopher Herrys				✓	1	Harwich
Total	15	23	6	7		

An Act for the Restitution of the possession and the establishing and settling, of the manor of Prees, and other lands in the County of Lancaster, unto Robert Wolferstone, Edmond Wolferstone, and Charles Wolferstone, and the heirs of the said Sir Robert, according to the conveyances made to them thereof by John Skillicorne, 1624.[29]

HLRO, Main Papers, 8 April 1624.

Secondly read and committed on 14 April 1624.

Members	21 Apr.	n.d.	Total	Constituency
Sir Henry Poole				Oxfordshire
Sir Francis Barrington				Essex
Sir John Savile				Yorkshire
Sir Thomas Denton	✓	✓	2	Buckinghamshire
Edward Alford				Colchester
Sir Walter Pye				Brecon
Sir William Spring		✓	1	Suffolk
Francis Fetherstonhaugh				New Romney
Sir Walter Earle				Poole
Sir Robert Phelips				Somerset
Sir Charles Morrison				Hertfordshire
Sir Edwin Sandys				Kent
Sir Gilbert Gerard				Middlesex
Richard Knightley	✓		1	Northamptonshire
Sir Oliver Cromwell	✓		1	Huntingdonshire
Mr Brereton, Thomas or William				Taunton or Cheshire
Sir Francis Popham	✓	✓	2	Chippenham
William Wingfield	✓	✓	2	Lichfield
William Towse				Colchester
Sir Robert Hatton				Sandwich
Sir Edward Giles				Totnes
Sir George Hastings	✓	✓	2	Christchurch
Mr Drake, Francis or John				Sandwich or Devon
James Lord Wriothesley	✓		1	Winchester
Sir George Horsey				Dorset
Sir James Perrot		✓	1	Pembrokeshire

[29] The bill was ordered to be engrossed in the Commons but did not receive a third reading before the Parliament ended.

Unnamed Members[30]				
Sir John Radcliffe	?	?	1 or 2	Lancashire
Sir Robert Heath	?	?	1 or 2	East Grinstead
James Lewis	?	?	1 or 2	Cardiganshire
Robert Lewis	?	?	1 or 2	Reigate
James Price	?	?	1 or 2	Radnorshire
Charles Price	?	?	1 or 2	New Radnor Boroughs
Thomas Wolryche	?	?	1 or 2	Much Wenlock
William Price	?	?	1 or 2	Cardiff Boroughs
Total	7 (15)	6 (14)		

[30] It is not possible to determine whether the unnamed MPs attended one meeting or both.

An Act that Sheriffs, the heirs, executors and administrators, having *Quietus Est*, shall be absolutely discharged of their accounts, 1624.[31]

HLRO, Main Papers Supplementary, 27 May 1624.

Secondly read and committed on 23 April 1624.

Members	n.d.	n.d.	Total	Constituency
Sir Guy Palmes				Rutland
Sir Christopher Hilliard	✓		1	Hedon
Sir Robert More				Surrey
Sir Eubule Thelwall				Denbighshire
Sir William Cope				Oxfordshire
All to have voice				
Unnamed Members				
Sir Thomas Belasyse	✓	✓	2	Thirsk
Sir George Dalston	✓	✓	2	Cumberland
Robert Strickland	✓		1	Westmorland
Sir Thomas Fairfax	✓		1	Hedon
Sir William Sheffield	✓		1	Thirsk
Arthur Pyne	✓		1	Weymouth
Mr Lewis, James or Robert	✓		1	Cardiganshire or Reigate
Edmund Sawyer	✓		1	New Windsor
Mr Vaughan, Henry or Richard	✓		1	Carmarthen Boroughs or Carmarthenshire
John Sawle	✓		1	Mitchell
Sir John Fenwick	✓		1	Northumberland
Sir Peter Riddell	✓		1	Newcastle
William Mallory		✓	1	Ripon
John Carvile		✓	1	Aldborough
Arthur Mainwaring		✓	1	Huntingdon
Sir Robert Oxenbridge		✓	1	Hampshire
Nicholas Eversfield		✓	1	Hastings
Total	**12**	**7**		

[31] The bill was introduced by Sir Christopher Hilliard and enacted as 21 James I cap. 5. The process of *quietus est*, more commonly known as *abinde recessit quietus*, was used by Clerks of the Pipe and Auditors of the Exchequer as a final discharge of the account(s).

An Act against such, as shall levy any Fine, suffer any Recovery, or acknowledge any Statute, in other Men's Names, 1624.[32]

HLRO, Main Papers, 7 April 1624.

Secondly read and committed on 3 April 1624.

Members	5 Apr.	Constituency
Sir Edward Coke		Coventry
Sir Henry Poole	✓	Oxfordshire
Sir John Stradling	✓	St Germans
John Bankes		Wootton Bassett
Sir William Fleetwood		Buckinghamshire
Heneage Finch		London
Sir John Walter		East Looe
John Glanville		Plymouth
Sir Baptist Hicks		Tewkesbury
Sir Robert Hitcham		Orford
Sir Thomas Cheeke		Essex
Sir Nathaniel Rich		Harwich
Sir Thomas Lucy		Warwickshire
All to have voice		
Unnamed Members		
Sir Henry Slingsby	✓	Knaresborough
Sir Edward Peyton	✓	Cambridgeshire
Sir Thomas Myddelton	✓	London
Sir Erasmus Dreyden	✓	Banbury
Maurice Abbot	✓	Kingston
Mr Vaughan?, Henry or Richard	✓	
Total	**8**	

[32] Sir Henry Poole introduced the bill in 1621. The preamble noted 'that many lewde persons of base Condicion for very little reward or recompence have of late yeres used and still doe use to levy fynes and suffer recoveries of landes, and other heredytamentes, to knowledge statutes, recognizances, bayles and Judgementes in the name or names of any other person or persons not pryvie or Consenting to the same'. It then harshly enacted that anyone found guilty of this offense was to be deemed a felon. The measure passed both Houses with little trouble in 1624 and it was enacted as 21 James I cap. 26.

An Act that the County Palatine of Durham may send Knights, Citizens and Burgesses to serve in Parliament, 1624.[33]

HLRO, Main Papers, 8 May 1624.

Secondly read and committed on 25 March 1624.

Members	n.d.	n.d.	Total	Constituency
Sir John Savile				Yorkshire
Sir Henry Vane	✓		1	Carlisle
Sir Robert Heath				East Grinstead
Sir Francis Seymour				Marlborough
William Ravenscroft				Flint Boroughs
Christopher Pepper				Richmond
Mr Wandesford, Christopher or John	✓		1	Aldborough or Richmond
William Boswell				Boston
Francis Lucy				Warwick
Edward Kirton		✓	1	Ludgershall
Sir Clement Throckmorton				Warwickshire
John Lowther	✓		1	Westmorland
Sir John Danvers				Newport, I. of W.
Sir Thomas Wentworth				Pontefract
Sir Thomas Belasyse				Thirsk
Edward Lively	✓	✓	2	Berwick
Sir Anthony Forest		✓	1	Wallingford
Francis Fetherstonhaugh				New Romney
Sir Robert Hitcham				Orford
Sir Henry Mildmay				Westbury
K&B Yorkshire				
K&B Northumberland				
K&B Devon				
K&B Cornwall				
Unnamed Members				
Sir Robert Jackson	✓		1	Berwick

[33] See Andrew W. Foster, 'The Struggle for Parliamentary Representation for Durham, c.1600–1641' in David Marcombe, ed., *The Last Principality: Politics, Religion and Society in the Bishopric of Durham, 1494–1660* (Nottingham, 1987), pp. 176–201. The bill passed both Houses but was vetoed by James.

Sir Peter Riddell	✓		1	Newcastle
Sir John Jackson	✓		1	Pontefract
Sir Henry Anderson	✓	✓	2	Newcastle
Henry Rolle	✓		1	Callington
John Delbridge	✓		1	Barnstaple
William Nyell	✓		1	Dartmouth
Thomas Sherwill	✓		1	Plymouth
Edward Aglionby	✓		1	Carlisle
William Plumleigh	✓		1	Dartmouth
Sir William Carnaby	✓		1	Morpeth
John Carvile		✓	1	Aldborough
Sir Francis Brandling		✓	1	Northumberland
Total	**14**	**7**		

An Act to settle Jesse Glover, Presentee of Dame Grace Darcy, widow, and George Wilmore, esquire, Committees of the Body and Lands of Edward Darcy ... in the Church of Sutton, 1624.[34]

HLRO, Main Papers Supplementary, 15 May 1624.

Secondly read and committed on 7 May 1624.

Members	8 May	11 May	Total	Constituency
Sir Thomas Edmondes				Chichester
Sir Richard Weston				Bossiney
Sir Edward Coke	✓	✓	2	Coventry
Sir Humphrey May				Leicester
Sir Thoms Wentworth				Pontefract
Sir Francis Barrington	✓		1	Essex
Thomas Wentworth	✓		1	Oxford
Richard Taylor				Bedford
Sir John Stradling	✓	✓	2	St Germans
Sir John Walter				East Looe
Sir John Savile				Yorkshire
Mr Howard?				
Sir Guy Palmes				Rutland
Edward Alford				Colchester
Sir Robert Coke	✓	✓	2	Fowey
William Noy	✓		1	Fowey
Sir William Masham		✓	1	Maldon
John Drake	✓	✓	2	Lyme Regis
Sir Edward Giles	✓		1	Totnes
Sir Thomas Hoby	✓		1	Ripon
Sir Walter Earle	✓	✓	2	Poole
George Smyth				Bridgnorth
Thomas Gewen	✓	✓	2	Bossiney
Sir Henry Poole	✓	✓	2	Oxfordshire
Mr Wandesford, Christopher or John		✓	1	Aldborough or Richmond

[34] The bill was introduced after Lady Darcy had been foiled in her presentation to the Sutton parsonage by Lord Keeper John Williams who had introduced his own minister. It passed the Commons but was still under scrutiny by a Lords committee when the Parliament was prorogued.

Sir Thomas Cheke				Essex
Mr Brereton, Thomas or William	✓		1	Taunton or Cheshire
Sir Thomas Barrington				Newtown, I. of W.
Sir Robert Heath				East Grinstead
Sir Miles Fleetwood				Launceston
Sir James Perrot	✓	✓	2	Pembrokeshire
Total	**14**	**10**		

An Act concerning the Tithes or tenth of and for lead ore and lead mine …
within the Manor and Hundred of the High Peak and precincts thereof in the
County of Derby, 1624.[35]

HLRO, Main Papers, 9 April 1624.

Secondly read and committed on 17 April 1624.

Members	n.d.	Constituency
William Lord Cavendish		Derbyshire
John Guy		Bristol
William Coryton		Cornwall
Sir John Stradling		St Germans
John Pym		Tavistock
Sir Guy Palmes		Rutland
Edward Moseley		Preston
K&B Somerset		
K&B Devon		
K&B Cornwall		
All to have voice		
Unnamed Members		
William Denny	✓	Norwich
Samuel Owlfield	✓	Gatton
Sir Lewis Watson	✓	Lincoln
Mr Wandesford, Christopher or John	✓	Aldborough or Richmond
Mr Savage, John or William	✓	Chester or Winchester
Thomas Giear	✓	Weymouth
Edward Whitby	✓	Chester
Robert Bateman	✓	London
Total	**8**	

---

[35] The measure was introduced by Lord Cavendish and Derbyshire miners who sought
the removal of the tithe from lead ore which was payable to the Dean and parish of
Lichfield. The House on the report of the committee rejected it. See Kyle, 'Parliament
of 1624', pp. 466–8.

An Act for the Relief of the Artizan Clothworkers of the City of London, 1624.[36]

HLRO, Main Papers, 9 April 1624.

Secondly read and committed on 15 April 1624.

Members	19 Apr.	22 Apr.	28 Apr.	4 May	Total	Constituency
Sir Thomas Myddelton	✓		✓	✓	3	London
Sir Henry Poole			✓	✓	2	Oxfordshire
Sir John Danvers		✓			1	Newport, I. of W.
Sir George More	✓				1	Guildford
Sir Nathaniel Rich						Harwich
Sir Alexander St John						Bedford
Christopher Brooke						York
Sir Thomas Estcourt						Gloucestershire
John Guy		✓	✓	✓	3	Bristol
Robert Snelling		✓	✓		2	Ipswich
William Cage				✓	1	Ipswich
Francis Fetherstonhaugh						New Romney
John Barker						Bristol
Richard Tomlins	✓				1	Ludlow
Sir John Jackson						Pontefract
Sir Francis Barrington	✓				1	Essex
Robert Bromfield			✓		1	Southwark
John Pym						Tavistock
William Whitaker		✓	✓	✓	3	Shaftesbury
Edward Bysshe						Bletchingley
Edward Alford						Colchester
John Hawarde						Bletchingley

[36] The bill stated that any person who worked cloth in London must undergo an apprenticeship with the Artizan Clothworkers' Company. Unsurprisingly, the measure found little favour with the Corporation of London and it blocked the bill in committee. For a fuller analysis of the tactics used by the Corporation see Kyle, 'Attendance, Apathy and Order' (forthcoming).

William Mallory		✓			I	Ripon
Thomas Wentworth						Oxford
Robert Bateman	✓	✓	✓	✓	4	London
Burg. London						
Unnamed Members						
Martin Bond	✓	✓	✓	✓	4	London
Total	**6**	7	**8**	7		

An Act against the Extortions and Exaction of Customers, Comptrollers, Searchers, Waiters, Clerks, or Other Officers or Persons employed in or about the Custom of ... the King, 1624.[37]

HLRO, Main Papers, 20 May 1624.

Secondly read and committed on 24 March 1624.

Members	10 Apr.	14 Apr.	17 Apr.	19 Apr.	21 Apr.	24 Apr.	Total	Constituency
Sir John Suckling								Middlesex
Sir Edward Coke								Coventry
Sir Arthur Ingram								York
Sir John Strangways								Dorset
Sir John Savile		✓					1	Yorkshire
Sir John Stradling								St Germans
William Cage								Ipswich
Robert Snelling	✓		✓				2	Ipswich
Sir Thomas Myddelton								London
John Mostyn								Bridport
John Glanville	✓		✓			✓	3	Plymouth
John Jacob								Plympton Erle
John Bankes								Wootton Bassett
Sir Philip Carey	✓					✓	2	New Woodstock
Sir Edward Giles			✓				1	Totnes
Sir Thomas Estcourt								Gloucestershire

[37] The bill attempted to regulate the fees taken by those officers involved in the collection of customs duties. It was preferred in 1614, 1621 and 1624 but failed to gain the assent of both the Commons and the Lords in any Parliament. The measure was based upon the 1433 statute 11 Henry VI cap. 15 which forbade customers or controllers from taking any fee for entering or drafting warrants. It did not, however, apply to other officials in the Customs House. Thus the Jacobean bill enacted that merchants did not have to pay a fee for the warrant which stated that customs had been paid and it imposed heavy financial penalties upon any official who charged for a document.

Edward Hungerford									Wiltshire
John Whistler									Oxford
K&B Port Towns									
Added Members 2 Apr.									
Sir Edward Coke									Coventry
Sir Edwin Sandys									Kent
Unnamed Members									
Anthony Robinson		✓				✓		2	Gloucester
Sir Robert Killigrew	✓							1	Penryn
John Prowse	✓		✓					2	Exeter
William Price	✓							1	Cardiff Boroughs
Benjamin Cooper	✓		✓	✓				3	Great Yarmouth
John Delbridge	✓	✓	✓	✓		✓		5	Barnstaple
Thomas Sherwill	✓	✓	✓	✓		✓		5	Plymouth
George Hardware	✓		✓	✓		✓		4	Great Yarmouth
William Plumleigh	✓		✓	✓		✓		4	Dartmouth
John Lister	✓		✓	✓		✓		4	Kingston upon Hull
James Bagge	✓		✓					2	West Looe
William Nyell	✓		✓	✓				3	Dartmouth
Thomas Burges	✓					✓		2	Truro
Robert Bateman	✓					✓		2	London
Sir Peter Riddell	✓		✓			✓		3	Newcastle
Sir Henry Anderson		✓	✓					2	Newcastle
John Barker			✓					1	Bristol
Sir Robert Jackson			✓					1	Berwick
~~Sir Robert Knollys~~									

Sir John Drake			✓				1	Lyme Regis
Thomas Giear	✓	✓	✓			✓	4	Weymouth
Nicholas Rivett			✓				1	Aldeburgh
John More		✓	✓	✓			3	Lymington
Sir Robert Coke		✓					1	Fowey
Total	18	7	21	8	**Un-known**	12		

An Act for freer liberty of fishing and fishing voyages to be made and performed in the seacoasts and places of Newfoundland, Virginia, New England and other Seacoasts and parts of America, 1624.[38]

HLRO, Main Papers Supplementary, 4 May 1624.

Secondly read and committed on 15 March 1624.

Members	22 Mar.	24 Mar.	n.d.	n.d.	n.d.	n.d.	n.d.	Total	Constituency
Sir Edward Coke					✓			1	Coventry
Mr Wandesford, Christopher or John		✓						1	Alborough or Richmond
Christopher Brooke									York
Sir Thomas Myddelton									London
Henry Sherfield									Salisbury
Robert Bateman									London
Sir George Chudleigh	✓	✓		✓				3	Tiverton
Nicholas Duck		✓		✓				2	Exeter
Sir Walter Pye									Herefordshire
William Lenthall									New Woodstock
Henry Coke									Chipping Wycombe
Nicholas Ferrar			✓	✓			✓	3	Lymington
William Whiteway			✓	✓		✓		3	Dorchester
George Mynne	✓			✓				2	West Looe
Thomas Sherwill	✓	✓	✓			✓	✓	5	Plymouth
William Nyell	✓	✓	✓			✓	✓	5	Dartmouth
Sir Arthur Ingram									York
Burg. Seaports									

[38] The measure was introduced by West Country fishing interests in every Parliament of the decade but failed to reach the statute book. It was an attack on the patent of Sir Ferdinando Gorges for plantation of New England. See Conrad Russell, *Parliaments and English Politics, 1621–1629* (Oxford, 1979), p. 94; R. A. Preston, *Gorges of Plymouth Fort: a life of Sir Ferdinando Gorges, Captain of Plymouth Fort, Governor of New England, and Lord of the Province of Maine* (Toronto, 1953); *idem*, 'Fishing and Plantation: New England in the Parliament of 1621', *American Historical Review* xlv (1940), pp. 29–43.

Edward Pitt		✓						**1**	Poole
Sir Baptist Hicks									Tewkesbury
Sir Peter Mutton									Caernarvon Boroughs
Sir John Strangways									Dorset
Sir Edward Giles		✓	✓					**2**	Totnes
Sir Thomas Hoby									Ripon
Sir George Horsey		✓						**1**	Dorset
Unnamed Members									
John Glanville	✓	✓	✓	✓	✓	✓	✓	**7**	Plymouth
Matthew Pitt			✓	✓		✓		**3**	Weymouth
Thomas Giear	✓		✓	✓	✓	✓	✓	**6**	Weymouth
John Delbridge		✓	✓	✓		✓	✓	**5**	Barnstaple
Pentecost Doddridge		✓	✓	✓	✓			**4**	Barnstaple
Sir John Drake			✓					**1**	Lyme Regis
William Plumleigh			✓	✓	✓		✓	**4**	Dartmouth
Sir John Mill			✓	✓				**2**	Southampton
Arthur Champernowne			✓			✓		**2**	Totnes
Thomas Burges			✓	✓	✓	✓	✓	**5**	Truro
Sir Robert Killigrew			✓					**1**	Penryn
Sir John Danvers			✓					**1**	Newport, I. of W.
Mr F[illegible]			✓	✓				**2**	
Sir Walter Earle			✓	✓		✓		**3**	Poole
William Whiteway			✓				✓	**2**	Dorchester
John Guy	✓							**1**	Bristol
Edward Nicholas	✓							**1**	Winchelsea
Total	**4**	**7**	**25**	**16**	**8**	**11/9**	**10**		

An Act for Restraint of Assignment of Debts to the King, and for Reformation of Abuses in Levying of Debts for Common Persons in the Name and Under the Prerogative of the King, 1624.[39]

HLRO, Main Papers, 15 May 1624.

Secondly read and committed on 24 March 1624.

Members	n.d.	Constituency
Sir Edward Coke	✓	Coventry
Sir Robert Hitcham		Orford
John Glanville	✓	Plymouth
John Pym		Tavistock
Sir John Walter		East Looe
Christopher Brooke		York
Sir Edward Peyton		Cambridgeshire
John Lowther		Westmorland
King's Counsel		
Sir Arthur Ingram		York
Sir Edward Giles		Totnes
Sir Francis Seymour		Marlborough
Thomas Wentworth		Oxford
Richard Taylor		Bedford
John Bankes		Wootton Bassett
Mr Wandesford, Christopher or John		Aldborough or Richmond
William Noy		Fowey
Robert Bateman		London
All Lawyers		
Unnamed Members		
Sir Gilbert Gerard	✓	Middlesex
John Finch	✓	Winchelsea
Sir Francis Godolphin	✓	St Ives
William Ravenscroft	✓	Flint Boroughs
Nicholas [sic] Lawrence Hyde	✓	Hindon
Philip Fleming	✓	Newport, I. of W.

[39] The bill voided any debt which was not due to the King himself and forbade any officer of the King to claim a debt in the King's name. It was originally introduced as a grace bill in 1614.

Edward Ayscough	✓	Stamford
John Guy	✓	Bristol
Sir Erasmus Dreyden	✓	Banbury
Sir John Jackson	✓	Pontefract
Sir Richard Yonge	✓	Dover
John Hawarde	✓	Bletchingley
Mr Chomley, Hugh or William	✓	Scarborough or Great Bedwyn
Total	**15**	

An Act to Prohibit the Exportation of Wool, Woolfells and Fuller's Earth, 1624.[40]

HLRO, Main Papers, 27 April 1624.

Secondly read and committed on 6 March 1624.

Members	n.d.	Constituency
Sir John Suckling		Middlesex
Sir Edward Coke		Coventry
Sir George More		Guildford
Edward Alford		Colchester
Sir Henry Anderson	✓	Newcastle
Sir Robert Hitcham		Orford
Sir John Savile	✓	Yorkshire
Sir Thomas Savile		Yorkshire
Sir Robert Crane		Sudbury
Sir Thomas Estcourt		Gloucestershire
John Carvile		Aldborough
Sir Robert Jackson	✓	Berwick
Sir Henry Poole		Oxfordshire
Sir Peter Riddell	✓	Newcastle
All to have voice		
Unnamed Members		
Sir Robert Crane	✓	Sudbury
Total	5	

[40] Upon pain of felony, the bill enacted that no raw wool could be exported from England. Introduced in 1621 and 1624, it passed the Commons in the latter Parliament but stalled in committee in the Lords. Kyle, 'Parliament of 1624', pp. 80–6.

An Act for the Restitution in Blood of Carew Raleigh, son of Sir Walter Raleigh, Knight, late attainted of High Treason, 1624.[41]

HLRO, Main Papers, 1 May 1624.

Secondly read and committed on 8 April 1624.
16 April 1624 Knight and Burgesses of Devon and Cornwall added.

Members	16 Apr.	Constituency
Sir Heneage Finch		London
Sir Edward Coke		Coventry
William Noy		Fowey
John Selden	✓	Lancaster
Sir George More		Guildford
Sir Robert Hitcham		Orford
Sir Nathaniel Rich		Harwich
Sir Robert More		Guildford
Sir Thomas Wentworth		Pontefract
Sir John Walter		East Looe
Sir Edward Seymour		Callington
Sir Edward Peyton		Cambridgeshire
Sir Francis Seymour		Marlborough
John Pym	✓	Tavistock
Sir Benjamin Rudyard	✓	Portsmouth
Sir Henry Poole		Oxfordshire
Sir Thomas Cheke		Essex
Sir Thomas Estcourt		Gloucestershire
Sir Alexander St John		Bedford
Sir Peter Heyman		Hythe

[41] Restitution bills were designed to 'restore people to normal rights lost through the attainder, by act or at law, of ancestors whose blood ... had been corrupted through condemnation for treason and very occasionally for felony.' Elton, *Parliament 1559–1581*, p. 303. The bill's history spanned 1621–8 and involved not only Raleigh's restoration but his attempt to regain his father's property, Sherborne Castle, Dorset, which James had sold to John Digby, Earl of Bristol. The bill ran into serious difficulties as Bristol introduced a series of bills designed to give statutory confirmation of his right to Sherborne. Raleigh finally gained his restoration in blood in 1628 – the same Parliament in which Bristol's title to Sherborne was ratified by an act of Parliament. But Raleigh's quest for Sherborne continued. He was elected an MP for Haslemere in 1648 and petitioned the Commons for his property. Raleigh was again a Member during the Rump Parliament and similarly introduced a petition. He was unsuccessful in both attempts. Kyle, 'Parliament of 1624', pp. 442–7a; 3 Charles I caps 26, 37; *CJ*, vi. 595; viii. 131.

Henry Rolle		Callington
Thomas Morgan		Wilton
Sir William Pitt	✓	Wareham
Added Members 16 April		
K&B Devon		
K&B Cornwall		
Unnamed Members		
Sir George Chudleigh	✓	Tiverton
John Drake	✓	Devon
Bevil Grenville	✓	Cornwall
John Chichester	✓	Lostwithiel
Total	**8**	

An Act for Confirming an Agreement between the King and his tenants of Macclesfield in the County Palatine, Chester, 1625.[42]

HLRO, Main Papers, 23 June 1625.

Secondly read and committed on 26 June 1625.

Members	n.d.	n.d.	Total	Constituency
Sir James Fullerton				St Mawes
Sir Henry Vane				Carlisle
Sir Walter Earle				Dorset
Sir Edward Giles				Totnes
Sir Thomas Hoby				Ripon
Francis Downes	✓	✓	2	Wigan
Nicholas Hyde				Bristol
Henry Clerke				Rochester
Sir Arthur Ingram				York
Sir Robert Heath				East Grinstead
Sir Miles Fleetwood	✓		1	Newton
John Lowther				Westmorland
Sir Oliver Cromwell				Huntingdonshire
K&B Cheshire				
K&B Lancashire				
K&B Derbyshire				
Unnamed Members				
Sir Robert Cholmondeley	✓	✓	2	Cheshire
Sir Anthony St John	✓		1	Cheshire
Edward Whitby	✓		1	Chester
John Savage	✓		1	Chester
William Lord Cavendish	✓		1	Derbyshire
Sir John Stanhope	✓		1	Derbyshire
Sir Edward Leech	✓		1	Derby
Timothy Levinge	✓	✓	2	Derby
Sir Richard Molyneux	✓		1	Lancashire
Sir John Radcliffe	✓		1	Lancashire
Sir William Hervey	✓	✓	2	Preston

[42] The bill was enacted as 1 Charles I OA 8. Maija Jansson and William Bidwell, eds, *Proceedings in Parliament 1625* (New Haven, 1987), pp. 88, 90, 91, 95, 204, 226, 252, 257.

Henry Banister	✓	✓	2	Preston
Sir Humphrey May	✓		1	Lancaster
Sir Thomas Fanshawe	✓		1	Lancaster
James Stanley, Lord Strange	✓	✓	2	Liverpool
Edward More	✓	✓	2	Liverpool
Henry Edmondes	✓		1	Newton
Edward Bridgeman	✓	✓	2	Wigan
William Fanshawe	✓	✓	2	Clitheroe
Ralph Asheton	✓	✓	2	Clitheroe
Total	**22**	**10**		

An Act for the Naturalizing of Samuel Bave of the City of Gloucester, Bachelor in Physic, and An Act for the Naturalizing of Thomas Sotherne, born in Turkey, the son of Elizeus Sotherne, an English Merchant, 1626.[43]

HLRO, Main Papers, 27 April 1626.

On 27 March 1626 both bills were secondly read and referred to the same committee.

Members	n.d.	Constituency
Sir Thomas Myddelton	✓	London
Sir Maurice Abbot	✓	London
Sir Henry Poole	✓	Wiltshire
Sir Henry Whithed		Winchester
Sir Richard Buller	✓	Saltash
Sir John Stradling	✓	Glamorgan
John Lowther		Westmorland
Sir Thomas Cheke		Maldon
Sir Alexander Temple		Sussex
Christopher Brooke		York
John Carvile		Aldborough
William Coryton	✓	Cornwall
Unnamed Members		
Edward Bysshe	✓	Bletchingley
Sir Francis Barrington	✓	Essex
Sir George More	✓	Surrey
Sir Nicholas Saunders	✓	Winchelsea
Christopher Earle	✓	Poole
Sir Edward Peyton	✓	Cambridgeshire
Sir John Gill	✓	Minehead
Sir George Rivers	✓	Lewes
Robert Goodwyn	✓	East Grinstead
Walter Barttelot	✓	Bramber
Sir Thomas Canon	✓	Haverfordwest
Thomas Hele	✓	Plympton Erle
Edward Lyndsey	✓	Camelford
Total	**19**	

[43] Bave was born in Germany of Dutch parents. The text of his bill is reprinted in William B. Bidwell and Maija Jansson, eds, *Proceedings in Parliament 1626* (4 vols, New Haven, 1991–6), iv. 117–18. Neither bill was enacted in an addled Parliament. See *ibid.* iv. 86, 105.

An Act for the annexing of Freeford Prebend unto the Vicarage of St Mary's in Lichfield and for making St Mary's a Parish Church, 1626.[44]

Lichfield RO, MS D30/5/30.

Secondly read and committed on 18 February 1626.

Members	? 2 March	Constituency
Sir Thomas Edmondes	✓	Oxford University
Sir Robert Naunton	✓	Suffolk
Sir Humphrey May		Leicester
Sir George More	✓	Surrey
Sir John Suckling		Norwich
Richard Dyott		Lichfield
K&B Staffordshire		
Sir Robert Harley	✓	Herefordshire
John Pym	✓	Tavistock
John Selden		Great Bedwyn
Mr Wingfield, John or William		Grantham or Lichfield
John Drake	✓	Devonshire
Sir Henry Poole	✓	Wiltshire
Sir Arthur Ingram	✓	York
Mr Rolle, Henry or John		Truro or Callington
Sir Francis Barrington	✓	Essex
Sir William Constable	✓	Yorkshire
Sir Eubule Thelwall		Denbighshire
Sir William Bowyer		Staffordshire
Sir John Stradling		Glamorgan
Sir Henry Marten		St Germans
Sir John Danvers	✓	Oxford University
Unnamed Members[45]		
Sir John Skeffington	?	Newcastle-under-Lyme

[44] It is probable that the bill was introduced by Richard Dyott whose family held the manor of Freeford. Although Dyott was not recorded as present on this register, he attended a committee meeting on 28 February. The proceedings of this meeting were noted by Bulstrode Whitelocke, but as he recorded only a small number of speakers, not the attendees, it has not been included above. See Bidwell and Jansson, *Proceedings 1626*, ii. 32, 69, 70, 214, 217. I am grateful to Andrew Thrush for providing me with his transcription of the Lichfield manuscript.

[45] On the document the names below are noted alongside the annotation, 'Knights and Burgesses of Staffordshire.' It is not possible to ascertain whether they attended or not, but see n. 46.

John Keeling[46]	?	Newcastle-under-Lyme
Sir John Offley	?	Stafford
Bulstrode Whitelocke	?	Stafford
Sir Walter Devereux	?	Tamworth
Sir Thomas Puckering	?	Tamworth
Total	**11 (?17)**	

[46] Keeling reported the bill from committee on 7 March and it is probable that he attended the meeting. Bidwell and Jansson, *Proceedings 1626*, ii. 214.

Committee to consider of an Indifferent Course for the Naming of Committees, 1626.[47]

Hampshire RO, Jervoise MSS, Sherfield Papers 44M69/L22/2.

Appointed on 3 March 1626.

Members	n.d.	n.d.	n.d.	Total
Sir Dudley Digges	✓	✓	✓	3
Sir Humphrey May				
Sir Thomas Hoby				
Sir John Savile	✓	✓	✓	3
Sir Richard Tichborne			✓	1
Sir Walter Pye				
Sir Edwin Sandys				
Mr Herbert, Edward or William	✓	✓	✓	3
Henry Sherfield	✓	✓	✓	3
Sir Miles Fleetwood	✓		✓	2
Sir Francis Barrington	✓	✓	✓	3
Sir George More	✓		✓	2
Total	7	5	8	

[47] Notes on the deliberations of the committee are printed in Bidwell and Jansson, *Proceedings 1626*, iv. 196–200.

Committee to examine the heads of conference with the Lords, 1626.[48]

Port Eliot MS, vol. xi, fol. 105.

Appointed on 17 March 1626.

Members	n.d.	n.d.	Total
Sir John Eliot	✓	✓	2
Sir William Beecher	✓		1
Sir Thomas Hoby	✓	✓	2
Edward Kirton			
Sir Robert Pye	✓		1
Sir Richard Weston			
Sir John Coke			
Sir Henry Marten	✓		1
Sir Simon Weston	✓		1
Sir Dudley Digges	✓		1
Sir John Savile			
Sir Humphrey Newbury			
Sir William Armyne	✓	✓	2
John Pym	✓	✓	2
Sir Thomas Barrington	✓	✓	2
Sir Francis Goodwin	✓		1
William Coryton	✓		1
Sir William Spencer			
Sir Thomas Lake	✓		1
John Selden			
Sir Peter Heyman	✓		1
Sir Humphrey May			
Christopher Sherland	✓		1
Total	**15**	**5**	

[48] Bidwell and Jansson, *Proceedings 1626*, ii. 306; iv. 206.

Committee to examine the petition of Mark Willes, merchant, 1626.[49]

Port Eliot MS, vol. ix, fol. 103.

Petition committed on 8 March 1626.

Members	n.d.	n.d.	n.d.	n.d.	n.d.	Total
Sir Thomas Hoby	✓	✓	✓	✓		4
Sir John Eliot	✓	✓	✓		✓	4
Sir Dudley Digges	✓	✓	✓	✓	✓	5
Thomas Fotherley	✓	✓	✓	✓		4
Edward Kirton	✓					1
Christopher Wandesford	✓					1
John Drake						
Sir Francis Stewart	✓	✓				2
John Glanville						
Sir Henry Anderson	✓	✓	✓			3
Sir Henry Whitehead						
Oliver Lord St John						
John Pringle	✓	✓	✓			3
Mr Browne, George or John						
Sir Thomas Grantham			✓		✓	2
Sir John Strangways		✓	✓		✓	3
Sir Robert Mansell						
Walter Long		✓	✓		✓	3
Giles Greene			✓		✓	2
William Trumbull						
Roger Matthew		✓	✓			2
Sir Arthur Ingram					✓	1
Total	9	10	11	3	7	

[49] The petition and attendance list are printed in Bidwell and Jansson, *Proceedings 1626*, ii. 234; iv. 205–6. I have added further annotations on attendance which were not recorded by Bidwell and Jansson.

Committee to examine the words used by the Earl of Suffolk, 1628.[50]

Port Eliot MS, vol. ix, fol. 173.

Appointed on 14 April 1628.

Members	n.d.	n.d.	n.d.	Total
Sir Thomas Wentworth				
Sir Nathaniel Rich		✓	✓	2
Edward Kirton	✓	✓	✓	3
Sir John Eliot	✓	✓	✓	3
Sir Robert Phelips	✓			1
Edward Littleton			✓	1
William Coryton	✓	✓	✓	3
Sir Walter Earle	✓	✓		2
Sir Dudley Digges	✓		✓	2
John Pym	✓		✓	2
Sir Francis Seymour			✓	1
Mr Rolle, Henry or John				
Sir William Fleetwood		✓		1
Mr Alford, Edward or John				
Total	7	6	8	

[50] For the details of the case see Mary Freer Keeler, Maija Jansson Cole, and William B. Bidwell, *Proceedings in Parliament 1628* (6 vols, New Haven, 1977–83), iv. 563, index entry Selden/Suffolk business.

TACTICAL ORGANISATION IN A CONTESTED ELECTION: SIR EDWARD DERING AND THE SPRING ELECTION AT KENT, 1640

Jason Peacey

The document printed below, from a notebook compiled by the prominent Kentish gentleman Sir Edward Dering of Pluckley in Surrenden, was occasioned by the prospect of an electoral contest, and probable poll, in the Kent county election for what became known as the Short Parliament in the Spring of 1640. The contest in question was between Dering and his (second) cousin Sir Roger Twysden. The circumstances surrounding the Kent election are well known, and have been explored thoroughly by scholars such as Mark Kishlansky, Derek Hirst, and Alan Everitt.[1] Indeed, the election has been cited as evidence by historians with very different views on the nature of early seventeenth century elections. Everitt considered the election to indicate the importance of local and personal factors, while Hirst believed that it offered evidence of a new attitude towards MPs, as well as the degree to which elections could be dominated by 'political' issues, in this case Dering's record as a courtier, a supporter of Ship Money, and an opponent of religious dissent.[2] Hirst claimed that the Kent election is 'suggestive of the impact of political issues at elections', and that it indicates that 'the rumours branding Dering as pro-court and perhaps doubtful in religion had had a pronounced impact on the educated'.[3] Kishlansky, on the other hand, regarded the spring election in Kent as symbolising the transition in elections, and the growing element of ideology, although he considered that this was far from total or complete. He suggested

---

[1] M. A. Kishlansky, *Parliamentary Selection. Social and Political Choice in Early Modern England* (Cambridge, 1986); D. Hirst, *The Representative of the People? Voters and Voting in England under the Early Stuarts* (Cambridge, 1975); A. Everitt, *The Community of Kent and the Great Rebellion, 1640–1660* (Leicester, 1966); F. W. Jessup, 'The Kentish election of March 1640', *Archaeologia Cantiana* lxxxvi (1971), pp. 1–10; D. Hirst, 'The defection of Sir Edward Dering 1640–1', *HJ* xv (1972), pp. 193–208. See also F. W. Jessup, *Sir Roger Twysden 1597–1672* (London, 1965), pp. 137–42.

[2] See also J. H. Plumb, 'The growth of the electorate in England from 1600–1715', *P& P* xlv (1969), pp. 90–116.

[3] Hirst, *Representative*, p. 123.

that the 'accidental' contest in the spring led to a deliberate one later in the year, and that this represents evidence of 'new politicisation', and of the growth of contested elections: 'they no longer originated in muddles of misunderstanding and mistaken intention that could be sorted out by mediating authorities. Nor were they mainly affairs of honour that developed from feuds and slights. Men did not oppose each other, they sought a seat in the House'.[4]

I want to argue that this use of Dering's notes – as a prism through which to examine the nature of elections in the seventeenth century – has involved a subtle misunderstanding of the nature of the document itself, and of its value. The importance of the document lies in the insight which it offers into the degree of planning and preparation which went in to some contested parliamentary elections. While other early seventeenth century elections reveal evidence of concerted organisation, and even of the creation of poll books, documentary evidence about such activities is extremely rare. What this document provides, however, is new evidence regarding the mechanics of an election campaign. Dering, evidently aware of the popularity of his rival, Sir Roger Twysden, and of the organisation with which the latter sought to secure support prior to the poll, recognised the need to organise his own campaign. The result was a list of over 600 of the freeholders in the county, and Dering's notes thereon. In the weeks before the election, Dering identified those who planned to vote for himself and Twysden, in a way which indicates a concerted effort to undertake an 'opinion poll' across the entire county, and one which must have required the assistance of a number of friends. Furthermore, on the day of the election and in the weeks which followed, Dering endeavoured to record the way in which the freeholders voted, perhaps recognising – on the basis of past experience at Kent county elections – the possibility of electoral malpractice by the sheriff, and of a challenge to the election before Parliament. By keeping a record of events at the election, therefore, Dering may have felt prepared for any dispute, and any parliamentary investigation, as well as for any future election. Examination of Dering's list also offers important evidence about the areas within the county where he was most influential, as well as the patterns of voting, by parish and county region.

I

The spring election in Kent in 1640 was arguably more open than many recent elections, which had witnessed a great deal of influence

[4] Kishlansky, *Parliamentary Selection*; pp. 130–5.

and electioneering on the part of aristocrats, both local and national.[5] Initially, when news emerged of the forthcoming election, in December 1639, neither Dering nor Twysden planned to take part, supporting instead the claims of Norton Knatchbull of Mersham le Hatch, Sir George Sondes of Lees Court, and his friend Sir Thomas Walsingham of Scadbury. For the first seat Knatchbull was firmly supported by many influential cousins and neighbours, in particular the Scotts of Scots' Hall, and the Boys's of Fredvile. The second seat, however, was challenged not only by Sondes and Walsingham but also by Sir Henry Vane senior, Lord Treasurer of the Household, and, from February 1640, Secretary of State. Vane sought support from the Earl of Dorset and his kinsman, Sir John Sackville,[6] the latter of whom clearly worked zealously on behalf of Vane, together with 'my Lord of Dorset's bailiff and other agents'.[7] Dering heard about the election in the second week of December, and was initially encouraged to stand for Dover. He claimed that the charge for the knightship of the shire 'made me decline thought of that for myself', and he initially supported Knatchbull as knight of the shire, although it appears to have been clear that he would have offered himself to the freeholders if the latter had opted not to stand.[8] At this stage, Dering was evidently willing to support Sir Roger Twysden as well, even though he was confident that the latter was assured of a seat at either Rye or Winchelsea. On 20 December, he wrote to Twysden to say: 'If you be not fettered beyond all freedom, appear for yourself', adding that 'I did, with some eastern friends ... name you for a knight's service to the house, which was received with a cheerful desire'. Noting the strength of Knatchbull, Dering added: 'I hope to appear in that court in a lower sphere'.[9]

Although there was pressure applied to avoid 'clashing' in the election, the seeds of the future contest were clearly gestating, and these were nurtured by Vane's status as a prominent courtier.[10] Dering advised Twysden that, 'If you love Mr Treasurer, persuade his desistance. Sir Thomas Walsingham and Sir George Sondes have left many more voices free than they have taken. If Mr Treasurer should desist, join with Mr Knatchbull'.[11] On 24 December, however, Twysden informed

[5] J. K. Gruenfelder, *Influence in Early Stuart Elections 1604–1640* (Columbus, 1981), pp. 143–5.

[6] Everitt, *Community of Kent*, pp. 70–1; L. B. Larking, ed., *Proceedings Principally in the County of Kent* (Camden Society, old ser. 1862), pp. 3–6; BL, Stowe MS 743, fols 136, 140; BL, Stowe MS 184, fol. 10.

[7] *CSPD 1639–40*, pp. 526–7.

[8] Bodl. MS Top.Kent.e.6, pp. 81–2.

[9] Larking, ed., *Proceedings*, pp. 1–3.

[10] George Sondes clearly expected a contest: BL, Stowe MS 743, fol. 136. The pressure to avoid a contest came most noticeably from the Lord Chancellor: *ibid*.

[11] Larking ed., *Proceedings*, pp. 1–3.

Dering that he was engaged to help Vane, adding that 'I should be sorry (if he or any of his stand) they should not carry it, but without all opposition, and therefore am resolved never at all to appear, where there may be any contestation with such a friend'. He informed Dering that he was not assured of another seat, although he later wrote that Vane had promised to help secure a place in one of the boroughs. Whatever his own prospects, he was clearly resolved not to stand against Vane, unless the latter stood down: 'If the Treasurer give out I am free'. At this stage, Twysden, who seemed confident that Knatchbull was assured of one of the county seats, evidently felt able to convince Dering to support Vane: 'I doubt not but to give you such reasons for the Treasurer's election as shall with willingness persuade you to interest all your friends'.[12] Nevertheless, Twysden may have realised the problem which Vane faced. He later reflected that, 'truly the common people had been so bitten with Ship Money they were very averse from a courtier'. This realisation prompted Twysden to redouble his efforts on behalf of Vane. He said: 'I dealt with all my neighbours effectually, and had promise of many', although he admitted: 'yet could I not be confident of his being elected'. His response was important: 'I did therefore think the best way of facilitating it was to get all else but himself and one more sit down'. Twysden sought to ensure that the county would return Knatchbull and Vane by selection rather than election, in order to avoid a contest, and in order to maintain consensus. He apparently succeeded in persuading Sondes and Walsingham to withdraw, hoping thereby to secure for Vane their supporters in the northeast and northwest of Kent. He continued to feel confident that Dering supported his plan: 'I did then conceive him as firm for him as any man'.[13] However, Dering himself noted that, while he was prepared to solicit support for Knatchbull, he was determined to ignore Twysden's pleas on behalf of Vane: 'I was absolutely resolved that in times so desperate I would contribute no help to any privy counsellor or deputy lieutenant there standing'.[14]

It was at this point that Dering appears to have decided to stand for the election. He later noted that, when Walsingham and Sondes stood down, he was urged to offer himself as a candidate by Isaac Bargrave, Dean of Canterbury Cathedral, and George Strode of Westerham.[15] His version of events accords with that of Twysden, who timed it to the Spring assizes, held on 26 February 1640.[16] There, Dering spoke

[12] *Ibid.* pp. 3–5, 6.

[13] *Ibid.* pp. 6–7. The manoeuvring to get Sondes and Walsingham to withdraw was intended to be kept secret: BL, Stowe MS 743, fol. 138.

[14] Bodl. MS Top.Kent.e.6, pp. 81–2.

[15] *Ibid.*

[16] For the assizes, see: J. S. Cockburn, *Calendar of Assize Records. Kent Indictments, Charles I* (London, 1995), pp. 378–85.

'more coolly' of Vane, and 'after supper there was certainly some private consultation between him, Mr George Strode of Westerham and Isaac Bargrave, Dean of Canterbury, and the next day a resolution published that he would stand'.[17] Twysden's reaction to Dering's decision was clear from a letter sent on 9 March:

> I am and always have been so desirous to do you service that I cannot but be sorry you show yourself at a time in which I can not further your success. The truth is I took it very unkindly to see Sir Edward Dering from whom I hoped (and had good reason to do so) assistance, in the cause of a kinsman almost as near to him as to me, should be erected only to make a stop in the business, and was as sorry to see him for such a toy contract so potent enemies (which I was assured would follow) as for any other cause in it.

At this stage, it became clear that Dering's religious views were likely to become a factor in the election. Twysden affirmed as much, while seeking to distance himself from allegations regarding his cousin's Puritanism: 'but for that other imputation – will you be for Sir Edward Dering? He is none of our church – I will not go about to excuse it, much less defend it, if you have any opinion not of my wit, but that I have common sense'. Twysden said that he could see no difference between the two men on religion, 'unless on the affirming ... that you never would go up to the rails to receive the communion (which I do and justify the doing of). I did once say that there was some other cause in you for refusing to do so, for all the world know you were no Puritan, which I am confident you will not take ill'.[18]

Aside from the possibility that Dering's candidacy would threaten an election on religious issues, the result of his decision to stand was, as Dering himself noted, that 'Sir Henry Vane in great indignation did immediately sit down'.[19] Vane then asked Twysden to oppose Dering, and campaigned actively for him, not least by drawing attention to Dering's role in the collection of knighthood fines in the early 1630s.[20] Furthermore, 'in great fury' Vane set forward Sondes again, who was back in the frame by 4 March. However, Vane's withdrawal had freed up significant support for Dering, and when it became clear that, while Sondes could muster the support of the deputy lieutenants, the local militia captains supported Dering, Vane, 'in revenge', decided to support the candidacy of Twysden. The latter, according to Dering,

[17] Larking, *Proceedings*, p. 7.
[18] BL, Stowe MS 184, fols 10–11v.
[19] Bodl. MS Top.Kent.e.6, pp. 81–2.
[20] Larking, *Proceedings*, pp. 7–8; BL, Stowe MS 743, fol. 140.

decided that, 'since he could not make one kinsman (Vane) he would hinder another (Dering)', although Twysden himself noted that Vane's request presented him with a 'troublesome task'.[21]

II

It is in this context that Dering's list needs to be analysed. Derek Hirst felt able to conclude that 'the Kent poll list for the Spring of 1640 is of limited value. It was compiled by Dering partly for self-vindication after his defeat, partly for a check on his strength beforehand'. Hirst also points out that 'in many parishes he can only give the names of the gentlemen and ministers, although for the parishes around his own residence and that of his opponent Sir Roger Twysden, he is much fuller'.[22] Mark Kishlansky, on the other hand, considered that the context in which it ought to be studied is the election for the Long Parliament later in the year. Kishlansky considered that in the Autumn, Dering 'composed a list of the imputations made against him and sketched a self-justifying narrative of events. He even went so far as to attempt a rough calculation of the support he had received, compiling a parochial calendar of the county for this purpose'.[23] While not entirely wide of the mark, such comments, I believe, offer a somewhat misleading interpretation of the nature of Dering's list. Although it was possible that the forces of consensus would ensure that a contest was avoided before the date set for the election, preparations clearly needed to be made in case of a poll. It seems clear that Dering's list formed part of such preparations, and that its nature has been misinterpreted and misunderstood by scholars in the past. Dering's comments on the list, and his description of the election indicate that the list was almost certainly intended to be exploited in either a challenge to the election result in March, or employed in a subsequent election campaign, or both. However, a close examination of the portion of the document which contains the list of names indicates that it was compiled before the Spring election, and in preparation for a contest. Once this is recognised, the document can be regarded as providing valuable evidence relating to the organisation of an election campaign, rather than as a tool for the examination of the nature of the election, and a means of interpreting its result.

It is clearly true that Dering's list offers a far from complete picture

---

[21] Bodl. MS Top.Kent.e.6, pp. 81–2; BL, Stowe MS 743, fols 138, 140; Larking, *Proceedings*, p. 8.

[22] Hirst, *Representative*, pp. 122–3.

[23] Kishlansky, *Parliamentary Selection*, p. 132. See also Jessup, 'Kentish election', p. 1.

of the support received by both himself and Twysden. Dering claimed that 2,325 people were polled at the election on 16 March, out of a potential electorate of some 10,000. His list, however, contained only 642 names, of which the preferences of only 194 are recorded.[24] However, this represents a limitation on the importance and value of the document only if it is regarded as a means of interpreting the outcome of the election. If examined with a view to understanding how Dering prepared for the election, this limited list is of far greater interest. In order to understand the value of Dering's list it is important to explore the nature of such lists in general, and this list in particular. Only when it is understood why Dering sought to compile the list, and how he might have used it before the election, will it be possible to reach conclusions about its value, and the light that it sheds on the Kent election.

Lists of electors and freeholders were prepared for a number of reasons. In many cases they represented official records of votes cast, while on other occasions they were compiled after an election in pursuance of a complaint or election dispute in Parliament. On yet other occasions, however, as in Yorkshire in 1621 and Huntingdonshire in 1625, they were clearly prepared as lists of prospective supporters.[25] Although the kind of *canvassing* that took place in Kent in 1601 was forbidden by the Privy Council in 1604, and although there was widespread hostility to the idea of votes being actively sought prior to the election, the practice of compiling lists of voters, and lists of likely supporters, remained in use.[26] While it is possible, and indeed probable, that such documents could be used for the purposes of canvassing, they were not in themselves indicative of canvassing having taken place.

Dering's list, it seems clear, was prepared before the election, rather than afterwards, and as a check on his likely support. Dering proceeded by producing, in a small notebook, a list of the 355 parishes in the county, leaving space for the inclusion of names of parishioners who were freeholders, and their predicted or avowed voting intentions. Dering then inserted the names of parishioners, and indicated their predicted allegiance in the forthcoming election by means of marks

[24] Hirst, *Representative*, p. 117. Dering may have over-estimated the size of the potential electorate, which was probably nearer 6,000: B. D. Henning, ed., *The House of Commons 1660–1690* (3 vols., London, 1983), i. 274; Magdalene College, Cambridge, Ferrar Papers, Sir Edwin Sandys to John Ferrar, 12 Jan. 1624. I am grateful to Andrew Thrush for this last reference.

[25] Hirst, *Representative*, pp. 33, 36–7, 258. See: S. Baskerville, P. Adman and K. F. Beedham, 'Manuscript poll books and English county elections in the first age of party: a reconsideration of their provenance and purpose', *Archives* xix (1991), pp. 384–403.

[26] Hirst, *Representative*, pp. 15–16; BL, Add. MS 34828, fol. 15: list of names of those to whom letters were sent before the election in 1601. I am grateful to Andrew Thrush for this last reference.

alongside their names. For this task Dering used red ink for his own supporters, and black for those of Twysden. Furthermore, he placed a horizontal dash next to the names of men whose views could be predicted before the election, and then, at or shortly after the poll, he added a vertical crossing mark for those whose actual allegiance he was able to determine. That Dering prepared his list of parishes before acquiring the names of the freeholders, and thus that the document was compiled before, rather than after the election, is clear from the fact that some pages are empty of names, while in other cases he found himself with insufficient room to include all of the names, necessitating the production of appendices at the end of the book. Furthermore, his having devised a system of marks by which to indicate predicted and actual votes also reveals that the names were inserted before the poll, and that the book was taken to the to the election, and amended during the proceedings as Dering observed the events.

This means that Dering expected a poll to take place, at the point when it became clear that he and Twysden were in the running for the second place, behind Knatchbull.[27] The method by which it was prepared and compiled indicates that it was not produced as part of a campaign of complaint and self-vindication after his defeat in March. Although it might have formed part of his subsequent grievance, the nature of the document would arguably have done little to support his substantive complaints. Rather, Dering probably endeavoured to secure information on likely voting patterns before a poll. This may have been done by writing to actual or potential supporters, and by asking them to work on his behalf, or alternatively by physically travelling to different areas in order to measure opinion. It is of interest that in the entry for the parish of Egerton, Dering noted the names of those who 'were not there as I suppose', a probable reference to those absent during canvassing. Indeed, Twysden's comments on the election support this interpretation, since he recorded that after the assizes, when Dering's candidacy became clear, he 'did never lie still, but rode up and down soliciting everybody, yea such as were for Sir Henry Vane he strove to get a promise of, that, he giving out, they would be for him'.[28] Added impetus to Dering's campaign of information gathering was probably provided by the activity of Twysden and his friends, who expended a great deal of energy in order to ensure his success.[29] Furthermore, it is possible that opinion in the county 'gradually slid towards the mild Sir

---

[27] For the parish of Chilham, Dering included among his probable supporters three men who supported him 'post Sondes', which I take to mean after Sondes withdrew from the election.

[28] Larking, ed., *Proceedings*, p. 8.

[29] Everitt, *Community of Kent*, p. 73; BL, Add. MS 34173, fol. 18.

Roger, and Dering's followers became alarmed', not least by the efforts on the part of Vane in favour of Twysden.[30]

Between the assizes and the election, Dering had a little over two weeks to organise and muster support. He may only have had time to concentrate on areas where he had good contacts, and where he felt likely to be able to gather support, and his list may also have been biased towards those areas where he had ready support. Prior to the election, Dering was able to gather information on the likely voting pattern of at least some of the freeholders in 112 parishes (32%), and found support for himself in 101 of these places. His core support, in terms of those places where he could rely on a significant number of men, lay in 29 parishes. He was able to identify some 485 supporters, as opposed to 62 for Twysden. In terms of the geographical distribution, the pattern of parishes for which Dering was able to acquire some information suggests, somewhat predictably, that he knew most about the area nearest to his own seat, in a broad band of central Kent, as well as about the major towns and ports in the county, such as Canterbury, Sandwich, Dover, Folkestone, and Thanet. Aside from these areas, Dering was able to acquire information from a number of scattered parishes, mainly in west Kent, and around the Medway towns (Rochester, Strood, and Gillingham). Unsurprisingly, his core support, at least as he predicted, lay in a ring of parishes around Pluckley, in which his own seat lay, as well as in Canterbury, Sandwich, Dover, Folkestone, Maidstone, and Ashford.[31]

It seems likely that Dering's intention was partly to prepare a list of voters on whom he felt he could rely, and partly to produce a document to assist in canvassing support. It is probable that, prior to the election, Dering concentrated his attentions on those areas where he felt most able to rely on support, rather than on areas where he felt sure that he stood little chance of finding favour. Dering recorded relatively few names of Twysden supporters, and there is little indication on his list of the existence of parishes where Twysden dominated.[32] It is likely that Dering made little attempt to monitor levels of support in places where he knew that he stood little chance of success. Most obviously, Dering recorded little information for the parish of East Peckham, where Twysden resided, or indeed the majority of those parishes which surrounded it.[33] There were exceptions to this pattern, in that Dering

[30] Everitt, *Community of Kent*, pp. 73–4; BL, Stowe MS 743, fol. 140.

[31] For comments on the geography of Dering's support, see Jessup, 'Kentish election', p. 6.

[32] One exception to this pattern is Hartlip, near Rainham.

[33] Parishes such as Hadlow, West Peckham, Brenchley, Horsmonden, Marden, Hunton, Linton, Boughton Monchelsea, East and West Farleigh, Mereworth, Teston, East Barming, East Malling, Leybourne, Offham, Addington, Ryarsh, Snodland, and Birling.

attempted to gauge support in Nettlested, to the north of East Peckham, where he found only Twysden supporters, and in another of Twysden's neighbouring parishes, Yalding, although he would quickly have realised that this too was solid Twysden territory. Dering's realisation of the fruitlessness of surveying certain areas may explain why he recorded information for few parishes in the north-west of the county or in the north-eastern area, along the north Kent coast. He may have realised that this was an area where Twysden was likely to secure support, if only through the efforts of Sir George Sondes and Sir Thomas Walsingham.[34]

Dering made efforts to record the names of supporters in parishes which offered the core of his support, and which were close to his own seat. Here, Dering may have needed to do little in the way of campaigning. These parishes included his native Pluckley (17 supporters), as well as see Ashford (43), Bethersden (34), Charing (43), Egerton (28), Godmersham (13), Hothfield (15), Smarden (17), and Westwell (18). Dering also recorded important levels of support in towns such as Dover, to which he had an established connection during his time as Lieutenant of Dover Castle in the 1630s. Moreover, Dering's brother-in-law, Anthony Percivall, was captain of the forts and customer of the port of Dover, while another prominent local gentleman was Dering's friend, Humphrey Mantle.[35] In these places, Dering recorded supporters and no opponents. Among other parishes to which Dering devoted some attention in recording likely voting patterns, it is likely that he had good reason to hope to be able to employ the influence of powerful friends and kinsmen in order to gain new supporters from dependant or client freeholders. He would certainly claim later that Sir Thomas Culpeper was able to control the votes of 'his dependsness',[36] and John Sedley mentioned that Dering's supporters would bring 'all they can make'.[37] Dering may have paid attention to some parishes on the grounds that he hoped to secure support through the efforts of kinsmen to muster support.[38] Alternatively, he may have targeted leading gentry figures, in the hope that they would bring votes with

[34] Everitt, *Community of Kent*, p. 71; Larking, ed., *Proceedings*, pp. 6–7; BL, Stowe MS 743, fol. 136.

[35] Everitt, *Community of Kent*, pp. 71–2; Larking, ed., *Proceedings*, pp. 2, 7.

[36] Bodl. MS Top.Kent.e.6, p. 84.

[37] BL, Stowe MS 743, fol. 140. Later in the year it was reported that George Sondes would help Dering 'at least in his friends and tenants', and that one Mr Thomas, lieutenant to Sondes, 'hath promised to engage his company': *ibid*. fol. 155.

[38] Barfreston (Anthony Dering), Boughton Malherbe (Edward Dering), Charing (Brent Dering, Nicholas Dering), Eastwell (James Dering), Lodesdowne (Anthony Dering), Newington (Sittingborne), (Henry Dering, clerk), Pluckley (Henry Dering), Ringwold (Francis Dering clerk).

them.[39] This may mean that the parish of Eastchurch was important, electorally, for Dering, despite the fact that he only recorded one supporter. That supporter was Sir Michael Livesey, who was clearly the dominant gentry figure in the area, and Dering may have been relying upon him to muster more votes. In Elmstede, Dering recorded only the support of Sir John Honywood, and in Langley only Edward Partherich, both of whom were leading members of the county gentry. In a parish such as Boughton Aluph, furthermore, Dering recorded the names of only two men, both supporters, Walter and Thomas Moyle, while for Burham he identified Henry Hawle, and in Chartham he recorded only James Kent. Perhaps Dering hoped, and expected that all of these men would be able to control substantial numbers of freeholders. In other places, meanwhile, Dering may have targeted clerics for the same reason. It is interesting that he identified twenty-four such clerics as supporters before the election.

Beyond those areas where Dering felt assured of support, or felt that he had powerful friends upon whom he could rely, he may have concentrated on areas which were more 'marginal'. There are a number of parishes for which he gathered information which were clearly divided, such as Dover, where ten names were recorded as supporters of Dering, five as supporters of Twysden, and eight more were recorded whose intentions were unknown. In Eastwell, furthermore, Dering found that he had two supporters to Twysden's three; while in Hollingborne he found support from Sir John Culpeper and opposition from Sir Thomas Culpeper. In part such marginal areas were urban centres, where the greater independence of the electorate meant that it was important to try and canvass support.[40] Maidstone, for example, the county town, was equally split between supporters of Dering and Twysden, including some of Dering's key supporters (such as Sir Humphrey Tufton) and leading opponents (such as Sir Francis Barnham).

At, or shortly after, the poll, Dering was able to record that 133 of the 485 whom he had identified as supporters had actually voted for him in the poll, while eighteen of Twysden's sixty-two recorded supporters had been identified as having cast their vote as predicted. Dering's list also provides some evidence regarding those areas where his support was most solid, in the sense that his potential supporters turned up at the election and voted for him. Pluckley was, unsurprisingly, one of the parishes on which Dering proved able to rely, and thirteen of the seventeen supporters were marked as having voted in the poll,[41] while all five supporters at Brokeland, all six at Chart Parva (Little

[39] Hirst, *Representative*, p. 116.
[40] *Ibid.* p. 123.
[41] Hirst concluded that men local to Dering were the most loyal: *ibid.*, p. 123.

Chart), and six of the ten at Dover did likewise. Hirst noted that Dering 'was forced to record many defaulters, or failures to turn up, even among the voters from his own parishes'.[42] However, while it is true that only 27% of Dering's supporters are recorded as having actually voted for him, the likelihood that they were 'defaulters' is lessened if we regard the document as having been prepared before the election, and annotated at, or after, the poll, rather than having been compiled *ex post facto*. This is because questions must be raised regarding the method by which Dering recorded such votes, and the accuracy with which he was able to do so. In the circumstances of a poll, it is unlikely that he would have been able to gather accurate information regarding the identity of individual voters, as opposed to gaining some impression of numbers. For some parishes, Dering was evidently able to confirm the votes of those leading figures with whom he was probably personally familiar, and whom he was able to recognise more easily than their dependants and the lesser freeholders.[43] For the parish of Smarden Dering recorded a list of those who had 'defaulted', which may refer to those freeholders who did not attend the election, or to those potential supporters who had failed to register their vote for Dering, although none of their names were recorded on the original list of supporters. Dering was also able to list (under Ashford) the names of four men who had indicated support when canvassed but who turned out not to be freeholders, and who were thus ineligible to vote. Dering may have been able to look at the official poll papers, and to gather information in the weeks which followed, but neither may have been particularly reliable or efficient methods of collecting names.

III

Having outlined the context of the election, and provided an analysis of Dering's list of freeholders, it is necessary to consider the significance of this document, and the extent to which it offers evidence of growing politicisation. The list certainly provides evidence for analysing the ways in which some of the most important gentry figures in the county voted in the election. Dering, therefore, can be demonstrated to have received support from John, Edward and Robert Darell, Sir Michael Livesey, Mark Dixwell, Thomas Broadnix, Sir John Culpeper, Sir William Meredith, Sir Thomas Peyton, Sir Humphrey Tufton, Norton Knatchbull, Thomas Westrow, Sir William Brockman, Edward Scott

[42] *Ibid.*, p. 116.
[43] See the parishes of Charing, Eastchurch, Folkestone, Meresham, Newington (Hythe), and Westwell.

of Smeeth, Anthony St Leger, Sir Thomas Palmer, Sir James Oxenden, Henry Oxenden of Wingham, Anthony Aucher, and Sir John Rayney. His rival, Sir Roger Twysden, on the other hand, secured support from men such as Sir Thomas Culpeper, Sir Francis Barnham, and Sir Edward Boys. Interesting though such evidence is, it seems clear that there is no obvious split between future royalists supporting Twysden and future parliamentarians supporting Dering.[44] Nevertheless, it is possible, however, that the list offers some scope for suggesting the politicisation of elections in the mid-seventeenth century. As Hirst correctly indicated, the list also provides evidence that Dering's predicted and actual supporters included a number of clerics who would be removed from office by Parliament during the 1640s, while of Twysden's clerical supporters the majority suffered after 1660.[45] Furthermore, it seems clear that, if we regard Dering's list as having been prepared before the Spring election, then the first election, and the first contested election, of 1640 was perhaps less accidental than Kishlansky asserts. There were clearly forces at work which sought to ensure that it would be uncontested or unpolitical, but as early as December 1639 there were signs of disagreement, and by early March 1640 it was clear that a number of the leading protagonists were willing to see a contest, and one which would be fairly fiercely fought. However, the degree to which the election was 'political' remains somewhat ambiguous, since the issues – Dering's religion and his service as a crown official in the 1630s – are not entirely clear.

This is evident from events at the election, on 16 March 1640. Dering probably arrived feeling confident as to the strength of his support, but his campaigning was to prove to no avail. As was so often the case, there were moves to avoid a poll. It was noted by one contemporary, for example, that Sir George Sondes, 'perceiving he had fewest voices on his side gave it over'; while it was clear that Norton Knatchbull had secured the first place.[46] However, there remained two candidates, Twysden and Dering, for the second place. Even at this point, attempts were made to avoid a poll. Dering claimed that he 'was offered to cast dice for the choice [and] when three of us stood the sheriff offered to draw lots between me and Twisden and the clerks offered in the afternoon to cast dice again'. Dering claimed, however, that he 'wished the field in each side to be set in rank and file, but the sheriff was made to warp strongly to Twysden'. Dering claimed that 'the strength with me in eye and ear was a thousand more than on the other side',

---

[44] Jessup, 'Kentish election', pp. 6–7. Jessup concluded that the document 'must be used with utmost caution as evidence of political affairs in the Spring of 1640' (p. 9).

[45] Hirst, *Representative*, p. 123.

[46] Bodl. MS Rawlinson D.141, p. 4.

adding that 'all the gentry of Kent and most of the clergy were with me, and a mighty advantage of freeholders, yet the poll must be taken'. Dering also alleged that one of Twysden's supporters, Sir Francis Barnham, claimed that a poll would be useless, at which point many left to return home. As a result, Dering alleged, out of 10,000 in the field ('which in all sense could not be less than six thousand for me') only 2,325 were polled. Dering claimed that the result of this poll was that Twysden received 1,231 votes to Dering's 1,094, although he alleged that the clerks were 'industrious' for Twysden, and that one sheet of names of Dering's supporters were 'embezilled'. He concluded that, 'plain it is that ye Puritan faction made Twysden', by 'foul play, false clerks and [a] warping sheriff'.[47]

Neither the information from the poll list, nor the evidence from the election itself, provides grounds for a firm conclusion regarding the degree to which the Kent election was dominated by political issues. If Hirst underestimated the extent to which the forces of consensus remained present in 1640, then Kishlansky underestimated the degree to which issues of national as well as local concern were impinging on the county election. That the way in which such issues affected the outcome is not straightforward does not nullify their importance, and it is perhaps inevitable that the politics of the Kent election should be somewhat inscrutable, given the complex nature of Dering's own views. The weakness in Kishlansky's argument, however, is one which stems from a mistaken belief that the Dering list was prepared in the aftermath of the election, or in preparation for the election to the Long Parliament, rather than in preparation for the Spring election. It is possible that the narrative account of the election, which Dering composed at the back of the notebook containing his list, was composed later in the year.[48] This gave Dering a chance to vent his frustration at the 'obscure and peevish sort' – the religious radicals – who had made allegations about his religion and his support for Ship Money and wine patents, as well as to catalogue what he described as the 'black artifices' of his opponents.[49] Furthermore, his experience in the Spring may have contributed to the contested nature of the Kent county election later in the year,[50] when support was quickly marshalled, by friends and

---

[47] Bodl. MS Top.Kent.e.6, pp. 83–7; MS Rawl. D.141, p. 4; Larking, ed., *Proceedings*, p. 5.

[48] Bodl. MS Top.Kent.e.6, pp. 81–7; 'A briefe passages concerning knights of the shire 1639 et 1640', reprinted in Jessup, 'Kentish election', pp. 2–4.

[49] Bodl. MS Top.Kent.e.6, p. 83.

[50] On 2 September 1640, one of his supporters, George Strode, wrote to Dering saying that 'I conceive you do yourself a great deal of right in resuming your pretension, which in my apprehension was most unequally carried in the last election': Larking, ed., *Proceedings*, pp. 8–9.

agents, letter campaigns, and personal persuasion.[51] However, close reading of Dering's list itself makes clear that it must have been compiled in preparation for the Spring election, rather than merely in response to it: he sought to gain an understanding of the nature of his support in advance of the election. Whatever his reasons for finding out how people had voted on the day of the poll, and however the election centred on political issues, it is clear that Dering knew, in late February or early March 1640, that there was going to be an election contest for one of the county seats.

Beyond providing evidence to suggest that a contest was considered likely, if not inevitable, in the weeks before the election, the value of this list of the freeholders of Kent lies in the evidence it provides of the energy which figures such as Dering were prepared to expend in securing election, the effort which they were prepared to put into an election 'campaign', and the methods by which support could be garnered. Dering was prepared to undertake an opinion poll of the freeholders, and to supplement this with a degree of canvassing, both in terms of personal persuasion and letter-writing, and the influence of powerful supporters. Furthermore, Dering appears to have recognised the boundaries of the area in which he was able to exert influence, and the parishes from which his core support came. He probably understood that some parts of the county would produce a negligible return from vigorous canvassing, and that it was more advisable to muster support in areas of proven influence, and to target urban areas, not least because, in what was a very short campaign, they provided a concentrated source of freeholders whose opinions could be polled. Furthermore, Dering also appears to have been prepared to exploit, and rely upon, the influence of significant gentry figures, whose names he could include on his list in a kind of shorthand for a larger number of probable supporters, and who effectively held a 'block' vote. For Dering the Spring election was not going to be 'fixed' in advance by a consensual decision by the county elite. Rather it was going to be contested by rivals, and this meant that voters had to be both polled and canvassed. As such, his list of the freeholders is an important element in the catalogue of neglected documents relating to the way in which Parliament operated in the wider world, and a means of exploring the procedure of seventeenth century elections.

---

[51] Larking, ed., *Proceedings*, pp. 9–11; BL, Stowe MS 184, fols 15–16; Kishlansky, *Parliamentary Selection*, p. 132. For Twysden's attitude see: Stowe MS 184, fol. 17: Sir Roger Twysden to Sir Edward Dering, 24 Oct. 1640. In the event, the election on 26 October saw another poll, in which Browne was 'put by', and Culpeper and Dering were returned, although only 'at length [and] with much ado': Bodl. MS Rawl. D.141, p. 6.

Note on the text

Dering's list is contained in a small paper notebook (18 × 15cm) containing 92pp, to which a board cover has been attached at some point. It is owned by the Bodleian Library (Bodl. MS Top. Kent.e.6). In this transcription of the list, Dering's red ink (for his supporters) is represented in **bold** type, while black ink (for Twysden's supporters) is represented in *italics*. Dering used these different coloured inks only on the marks at the side of the names on the list, but for the purpose of making such identifications clear I have chosen to use **bold** type and *italics* for the whole name. A mark '−' alongside a name indicates the way in which Dering expected a particular freeholder to vote, and a '+' indicates confirmation of their vote at, or after, the poll, and represents a later emendation of the list. Where Dering recorded no names for a parish, I have compressed his spacing, and I have also underlined the names of parishes, for the sake of greater clarity. I have retained Dering's use of two columns per page of his notebook.

p.1   A Booke of Freeholders made since ye 16 of march. 1639 wherein
are entred all the names that I can learne throughout ye shire
memd. they that are marked redd were for my elecion to be
knight of ye shire att Penenden Heath, and if crossed did stay
and give in theire names. They who are marked blacke were
there for Sr Roger Twisden.

p.2   Acrise   Aylesford
       – Hamon Lewkenor ar[mig]

       Addington   Aldington

       Adesham   Aldington

p.3   All Hallowes   Apledore

       Allington   Ash iuxta Sandwich

       Alkeham   Ash iuxta Mepham

p.4   Asherst   Badelsmere

       Ashford   Badsell
       + Jo[hn] Maccubie cl[er]icus
       + Baptist Pigot cl[er]icus
       – Ric[hard] Martin gen[t]
       + Steph[en] Betenham gen[t]
       – Rich[ard] Knatchbull gen[t]
       – Edw[ard] Woodward gen[t]
       – ... Stourton gen[t]
       – Jo[hn] Dine gen[t]   Bapchild
       – Elyas Sanderson
       – Rich[ard] Topliffe
       – Daniel Nower
       – Jo[hn] Nower
       – Nic[holas] Sudale
       – Jo[hn] Hawtrey gen[t]
       – Peter Paris
       – Tho[mas] Pope
       – Willia[m] Worseley
       – Jo[hn] Dufty
       – Rich[ard] Line
       – Jo[hn] Morris sen[ior]
       v.pag.60

p.5   Barfreston   Bedgebury
       – Anthony Dering gent
       – Edward Meryweather gen[t]

Barming

Beckenham

p.6 Bekesborne
Jacob Wilsford ar[mig]
Tho[mas] Hartfleete ar[mig]

Bedenden

Berham
Hen[ry] Oxenden ar[mig]

West Beere

Begham

Berghstead
+ Raphe Freake ar[mig]
 ...Cage gen[t]

Bethersden
+ Thomas Withersden
+ Isaac Hunt
− Gregory Odierne
− Raph Abbot clark
− Jo[hn] Dine
− Tho[mas] Waterman
− Hen[ry] Stonestreete
− Rich[ard] Hunt
− Rich[ard] Waterman
− Tho[mas] Parker
− Vavasor Barnham
− Jo[hn] Armestrong
− Tho[mas] Whitaker
− Jo[hn] Spicer
− Michael Peirce
− Rob[ert] Bull
− Hen[ry] Bowyer
− Tho[mas] Milsted
− Nico[las] Milstead
− Will[ia]m Hooke
− Jo[hn] Davy
− Rob[er]t Rich
− James Bateman
 vide phires pag. 59

p.7 Betshanger
 − Boys

Bexley

Bidborough

p.8 Birchington

Birling

Blackmanston

~~Bobbing~~

Bidenden
Rich[ar]d Taylor

Bikenore

Bilsington

Bobbing

Bokeland

Bonnington

Borden

Blen

p.9 Bishopsborne

Little Borne

Patrickes Borne
- **Rich[ard]d Spaine**
- **Tho[mas] Yong**

Boughton Aluph
- **Walter Moyle gen[t]**
- **Tho[mas] Moyle gen[t]**

p.10 Bourdfield

Boxley

Brabourne

p.11 Brenchesley

Brenset
+ **Laurence Burre**

Broke

Brokeland
+ **Robert May**
+ **Tho[mas] Marsh**
+ **Wil[ia]m Den**
+ **Tho[mas] Mombrey**
+ **John Owen**

p.12 Capell

Chalke

Boughton Blen

Boughton Malherbe
- **Edw[ard] Dering**
  ar[mig]
  Tho[mas] Dering F eius

- **... Wilkinson gen[t]**
- **Anthony Diue**

Boughton Montchensy

Brasted
Geo[rge] Hussey esq

Bredgare

Bredge

Bromefield

Bromeley

Burham
+ **Hen[ry] Hawle gent**

Canterbury
+ **Sir Edw[ard] Master**
+ **Jo[hn] Nutt ar[mig]**
- **Allan Eppes gen[t]**
-      **Eppes gen[t]**
- **Cliue Carter**
- **Paul Countrey**
- **Jo[hn] Crux**
+ **Rich[ard] Birkenhead**
-      **Jenkin**
- **Leonard Browne**

Challock
- **Gibbon Hawker gent**
- **Richard Giles**

Charing
+ **Brent Dering gent**

+ **Nicolas Dering gen[t]**
+ **Thomas Hutchin**
+ **Geo[rge] Wightwicke**
− **Humphrey Whitlocke**
− **Jo[hn] Morse**
− **Jo[hn] Hart**
− **Hen[ry] Tayler**
− **Simon Beeching**
− **Rich[ard] Beeching**
− **Tho[mas] Henneker**
− **Will[ia]m Barett**
− **Tho[mas] Knolden**
− **Tho[mas] Cooke**
− **Jo[hn] Payne**
− **Geo[rge] Cuckow**
− **Jo[hn] Cuckow**
  v.pag. 59 et 60.

p.13 Charleton

Chart Magna
− **Nicolas Toke ar**
+ **Geo[rge] Chute ar**

Chart Parva
+ **Jo[hn] Darell ar[mig]**
+ **Ed[wa]r[du]s Darell gen[t]**
+ **Rob[er]t Darell gen[t]**
+ **Henricus Swift**
+ **Isaac Loriman**
+ **Gilbert Edwardes**

p.14 Cheriton
− **... Strout cl[er]icus**
− **Rob[er]t Hobday**
− **Rich[ard] Jacob**
− **Will[ia]m Writtle**
− **Rich[ar]d Alden**
− **Steph[en] Pilcher**
− **Thomas Froude**

Chart iuxta Sutton

Chartham
+ **Jacobus Kent gen[t]**

Chelesfeild

Chilham
− **Belke**
  cl[er]icus   ⎫
− **Mr Vaughan** ⎬ p me
− **Hamon**   ⎪ post
  Watson   ⎭ Sondes[52]
− **Jo[hn] Goodlad**
      p me principally
− **Hen[ry] Tayler**

[52] I take Dering to mean that these voters indicated that they would support Dering only if Sondes withdrew, while John Goodland and subsequent freeholders, supported Dering ahead of Sondes.

	− Caleb Kennett
	− Hen[ry] Austen
Chetham	**− Tho[mas] Austen**
	− Tho[mas] Henneker
Chidingston	**− W[illia]m Fishenden**
Thomas Backet	**− Hen[ry] Samon**
	− Rob[er]t Dixon

Chillenden
− Anthony Hamon esq

Chiselherst

Chistlet

p.15 West Cliffe   Colrede
+ *Tho[mas] Gibbon*

Coudham

Swale Cliffe

Cowling

Cliffe att Hoo
+ Georg[e] Parrett   Fotes Cray

Cobham

p.16 North Cray   Crayford

Paules Cray   Cranebroke
S[i]r Tho[mas] Henley
Peter Courtop ar[mig]

St Mary Cray

Crondall
− Geo[rge] Carter
− Steph[en] Thomas
− Will[ia]m Chapman
− Steph[en] Launcesfeild
− Peter Marsh

p.17 Cuckestan   Denton
~~Hen[ry] Oxenden gen[t]~~
Ja[mes] Marsh
Darent   *− Jo[hn] Swan cl[er]icus*

Dartford

Deptford

Deale

Detling

p.18 Devington   [Dover cont.]
+ Tristram Stephens

Dunchurch

Ditton

Dover
+ **Ed[ward] Kempe**
+ **Anth[ony] Percivall ar[mig]**
+ **Daniell Skinner**
+ **Luke Pepper**
  Tho[mas] Collen
− **Thomas Kitchill**
− **Will[ia]m Stratfold**
+ **Humphrey Mantle**

− **Peter Nepen**
− **John Jacob**
  Arnold Braemes
  Tho[mas] Garret
  Jo[hn] Harrison
  Tho[mas] Wimbleton
  Will[iam] Eaton
  Jo[hn] Golder
− *Randoll Patridge*
− *William Richardes*
− *Tho[mas] Fidge*
− *Edw[ard] Chambers*
− *Tho[mas] Oldfield*
  Abraham Skinner

St Dunstan

Eastbridge
+ **Will[ia]m Bateman**

Eastchurch
+ **S[i]r Michael Livesey
  bart**

p.19 Eastrey

Eastwell

+ **Ja[mes] Dering gen[t]**

+ *W[illia]m Sanford cl[er]icus*
+ *Jo[hn] Lamben*
− **W[illia]m Sprat**
− *Tho[mas] Farley*

Ebeney

Egerton

− **Tho[mas] Prude gen[t]**
− **Jo[hn] Tucker gen[t]**
− **Jo[hn] Turner**
+ **Hen[ry] Hudson**
− **Tho[mas] Steed**
− **Edw[ard] Lambe gen[t]**

[Egerton cont.]
− **Geo[rge] Powell**
− **Edw[ard] Fenner**
− **Rich[ard] Maplesden
  gen[t]**
− **Steph[en] Lambe
  iun[ior] gen[t]**
− **Jo[hn] Barling sen[ior]**
− **Rich[ard] Barling**
− **Tho[mas] Barling**
− **John Barling iun[ior]**
− **Hen[ry] Bridge**
− **Abel Pemble**
− **Geo[rge] Powell**
− **Rich[ard] Iden
  sen[ior]**
− **Hen[ry] Austen**
  vive pag. 59

Eighthorne

Elham

– Rich[ard] Woller gen[t]
– Jo[hn] Beane
– Anth[ony] Gender
– Jo[hn] Hogben
– Jo[hn] Boughton

p.20 Elmstede
+ Sir Jo[hn] Honywood knt

Eltham

Eryth

Eseling

Euering
... Salmon

Ewell

Fayrefeild

Falkeham

E[ast] Farley

p.21 W[est] Farley

Farmingham

Fauersham
+ Rob[er]t Greenstreete
Nathanael Besbeeche
      Besbeeche

N[orth] Fleete

Flimwell

Folkestan
+ Marke Dixwell esq
+ Will[ia]m Reade gen[t]
–   Harrison
– Tho[mas] Marchall
– Tho[mas] Beane
– Jo[hn] Godwin
– Michael March
– Tho[mas] Den
– William Yong

Fordwich
+ Tho[mas] Hodleston
+ ... Lukin
  ... Bigge
  Valentine Parker gen[t]

p.22 Frendsbury
+ Henr[y] Yong

+ Edm[un]d Ellis gener

Frensted

Frithenden

St Giles Thanet

Gillingham
+ Jo[hn] Orwell sen[ior] gen[t]
+ Jo[hn] Orwell iun[ior] gen[t]
– Jacobus Cripse

Goceston
– Jo[hn] Gardener

Godmersham
+ Tho[mas] Broadnix

iun[ior] gen[t]
- **Jo[hn] Broadnix gen[t]**
- **Rob[ert] Broadnix gen[t]**
- **Tho[mas] Hull cl[er]icus**
- **Tho[mas] Smith**
- **Norton Downe**
- **Jo[hn] Fearne**
- **Simon Chapman**
- **W[i]ll[ia]m Court**
- **Henr[y] Mathewes**
- **Jo[hn] Mathewes**
- **Rich[ard] Somes**
- **Rich[ard] Barling**

p.23   Godneston

Goudherst
- **James Bunce**

Graveney

p.24   Halsto

Ham

Harbledowne

upp Hardres

p.25   Hastingleigh
- **Tayler cl[er]icus**

Hawkerst

Hawkinge

Hedcorne
- **... Britt cl[er]icus**
- **Rich[ard] Fowle**
- *Jo[hn] Wollet*
- *Jo[hn] Ramesden*

Greenwiche

Hadlow

Halden

Nether Hardres
- **... Pulford cl[er]icus**

Harrisham
+ **... Leech cl[er]icus**
- **Adman**
  ... Lyden

Hartley

Hartlip
- *Jo[hn] Besbeeche*
- *Jo[hn] Brunger*
- *Will[ia]m Bridge*
- *Rich[ard] Brunger*
- *Will[iam] Fullager*

Henxhill
- **Kennet Backe**
- **Tho[mas] Andrew**
- *... Wood cl[er]icus*

Herne

Hith
- **George Reeve**
  ... Reynoldes
- **Jo[hn] Browning**
- **... Downe**

p.26 W[est] Hith

Hollingborne
+ *S[i]r Tho[mas] Colpeper*
+ **S[i]r Jo[hn] Colpeper**
- **... Thatcher**

Hoath

Hothfeild
- **Jo[hn] Viney cl[er]icus**
+ **Abraham Godfrey**
- **Jo[hn] Broadnix**
- **Henry Thompson**
- **William Henden**
- **Robert Bull**
- **Rich[ar]d Paris**
- **James Sharpe**
- **John Taylor**
- **Rich[ar]d Hall**
- **Thomas Willmot**
- **Rich[ar]d Knolden**
- **William Missing**
- **Geo[rge] Atkin**
- **Tho[mas] Godfrey**

Hoo

Hope

Horsmonden

p.27 Horton Kirkby

Horton Monachorum
- **Geo[rge] Rooke gen[t]**

Hougham
+ **Tho[mas] Fineaux gen[t]**
Tho[mas] March iun[ior]

Hackinge

Hunton

St James att Hoo

Ifield

p.28 Ightham
- **S[i]r Jo[hn] Sedley
  mil[itus] bart**
- **Isaac Sedley ar[mig]**
- *Will[iam] James ar[mig]*

Iwade

Kemsing

Kenardington

Ilkeham
- **Dr Kingsley archdeacon**

St John Thanet

Kenington
- *... Player cl[er]icus*
- **Ed[ua]r[du]s Hawker**

Ivichurch

– Sampson Farbrace

p.29 Kevington

Kingsdowne
– xpofer Bacheler cl[er]icus
Tho[mas] Finch

Kingsnoth
+ John Bing

Kingeston

Knolton
**+ S[ir] Tho[mas] Peyton
bart**

Lamberhurst
+ ... *Porter*

E. Langdon
**– Rich[ard] Master
ar[mig]**
– Tho[mas] Marsh
– *Fran[cis] Marsh*

W. Langdon
– *Jac[obus] Dunkin*

Langley
**– Edw[ard] Partherich
ar[mig]**
... Kenard gen[t]

p.30 St Laurence Thanet
+ Adam Sprackling gen[t]

+ Rob[ert] Sprackling gen[t]

Leedes

**+ S[i]r W[illia]m Meredith
bart**
Leyborne

Lenham
**+ Mr Rob[ert] Mariot
clark**
+ ... Hulkes
+ Mr James Perry
**+ Tho[mas] Henman
iun[ior]**
+ Rich[ard] Elmeston
+ Geo[rge] Codde
+ Tho[mas] Codde
– Rob[ert] Dane
– Rich[ard] Rooke
– Tho[mas] Clarke
– Tho[mas] Forde

Leueland

Lewseham

p.31 Lyd
– ...... Baillif
– John Bate

Limne

Linsted
**+ Jacobus Hugheson
ar[mig]**

Lidden

Liminge
+ **Nich[olas] Salkins gen[t]**
+ **Will[iam] Salkins gen[t]**
− **Jo[hn] Hogben**
− **Jo[hn] Hogben**
  Penfold

p.32 Lodesdowne
+ **Jo[hn] Johnson cl[er]icus**
+ **Anthonius Dering gen[t]**

Lollingston

Longfield

Loose

+   **Wilkinson gen[t]**

Linton

Ludenham

Maydeston
   Bigge maior
+ *S[i]r Francis Barnham knt*
+ **S[i]r Humphrey Tufton knt**
+ *Rob[ert] Barnham ar*
+ *... Barnham gen[t]*
+ **... Lambe gen[t]**
+ **Abraham Clarke**
− **J. Davy**
− **... Couert Dr**
+ *Tho[mas] Swinocke sen[ior]*
+ **Rob[er]tus Swinocke iurat**
+ **Tho[mas] Swinocke gen[t]**
+ *... Swinocke*
+ **Caleb Bankes iurat**
   Jacobus Franklin gen[t]
   ... Cowper gen[t]
   Peter Manwood gen[t]
− **Geruais Maplesden gen[t]**
+   **Maplesden gen[t]**
+   *Maplesden*
   Rich[ard] Marsh

p.33 East Malling

Towne Malling

Maplesdown

p.34 Marden   St Martin

St Margaret att Cliffe
- Rob[er]t Fineaux
- Will[iam] Allan

St Margaret pp Rochester
+ Alexander Witherley

St Margaret att Hoo

p.35 Mepham

Mereworth

Midley

Milton pp Grauesend

p.36 Mongeham p[ar]ua

Mongeham magna
+ *S. Sampson*

Monketon

p.37 Newington iuxta Hith

+ S[i]r W[illia]m Brockman
knt
- ... Sandford cl[er]icus
- Edw[ard] Rucke
- Rich[ard] Beane
- John Webbe
- Mathew Goddard
- Rich[ar]d Markes
- John Rolfe
- Jo[hn] Cheeseman
- Jo[hn] Marshall
- Jo[hn] Pilcher

Newington iuxta Sitingborne
+ Henr[y] Dering cl[er]icus

Merseham
+ Norton Knatchbull
+ Tho[mas] Westrow
ar[mig]
+ ... Lott
+ ... *Lott*
- Searle Prude ar[mig]
- Hen[ry] Spicer
- Jo[hn] Netter
- Rob[er]t Johnson
... Swinocke cl[er]icus

Milton pp Sitingborne

Moldash
- Henr[y] Chapman

Moreston

Nackington

Nettlested
- *Edward Salmon*
- *Jo[hn] Henbury*

Newchurch

St Nicolas att Wood in
Thanet

Nockholt

Nonington
+ *S[i]r Edw[ard] Boys knt*
+ Gabriel Richards

St Nicolas Thanet

p.38   Norborne
    + Edw[ard] Nicolls
      cl[er]icus

Ofham

Ore

Orgareswike

p.39   Otham
    ... Wilson cl[er]icus
    ~~Ellis Ellis~~ gen[t]

Oxney
Jo[hn] Benden
Ric[hard] George

Padlesworth ship

Padlesworth tilesf

p.40   Pensherst
    − Rob[ert] Baker gen[t]

Pepenbury

p.41   Pluckley
    − Hen[ry] Dering gen[t]
    − Jo[hn] Betnam ar[mig]
    + Franc[is] Betnam gen[t]
    + Jo[hn] Betnam gen[t]
    + Roger May
    + Daniel Nower
    + Rich[ard] Posse
    − W[illia]m Posse
    + Tho[mas] Forman
    + Tho[mas] Benchkin
      sen[ior]
    − Hen[ry] Pollard
    + Jo[hn] Nepecker
    + Edw[ard] Nepecker
    + Jo[hn] Copley cl[er]icus

Orpington

    + Rich[ard] Spencer ar[mig]

Osprenge

Oteringden

Otford

E[ast] Peckham

W[est] Peckham

St Peter Thanet

Petham
    − Timothy White

Peuington
    − Edw[ard] Spice
    − Jo[hn] Spice

Postling

Preston

Queenborough

Raynham
    − ... Kenard gen[t]

+ **James Posse**
+ **Joshua Lambin**
+ **James Oxley**

Plumsted

p.42 Reculuer   Ringewold
                                   + **Francis Dering**
                                     cl[er]icus
      Ridley   + **Tho[mas] Yong**
                                   – **Jo[hn] Yong**
      Riersh   – **Hen[ry] Elgar**
                                   – *Ric[hard] Boll*

                                   Ripple
                                   d. ... Francis cl[er]icus
                                   d. ... Gokin[53]
                                      ... Den

                                   River

                                   Rochester
                                   – **Rich[ard] Lea ar[mig]**

p.43 Rodmersham   Roluenden

      Rokinge   Romney uetus
      – **Jo[hn] Barman**

                                   Romney noua
                                   – **... Weyuele maior**
                                   – **Sam[uel] Smith**
                                     Jo[hn] Wilcocke
                                     Smith Tookey
                                     Peter Knight clarke

p.44 Rookesley   Sandhurst

      All Saints Thanet   Sandwiche
                                   + **Henry Forstall iurate**
      Saltwood   + **Solomon Hougham**
                                     iurate
      – **Jo[hn] Turney gen[t]**   – **Andrew Gosfreight**
      – **Tho[mas] Turney gen[t]** –   **Gosfreight**
                                   –   **Gosfreight**
                                   – **Rob[ert] Berham**

[53] I presume that this signifies that these freeholders died before the election, or before
Dering ascertained their voting intention.

- **Tho[mas] Elwood**
-          **Elwood**
-          **Wildes**

p.45 Seale   Seuenoke
                              - **... Bloome**
     Seasalter   - **... Bloome**

     Selling iuxta Fauersham Seuington
     - **Rob[ert] Thomas**

                              Shadockesherst
     Selling iuxta Hith   - **Rob[er]t Springet**
     - **Pet[e]rus Hayman miles**
     - **Henricus Hayman ar[mig]**
     - **Tho[mas] Godfrey ar[mig]**
     - **Tho[mas] Godfrey gen[t]**
     - **Searle March**

p.46 Sharestede   Sholden

     Sheldwicke   Shoreham

     Shiborne   Siberteswold

p.47 Sitingborne   Smeeth
                              + **Ed[ua]r[d]us Scott
                                ar[mig]**

     Smarden   Snaue
     + **Jacob Turner**
     + **Thom[as] Cheeseman** Snargate
     + **Francis Whitfield**
     + **Rich[ard] Barow**
     - **Jo[hn] Goldwell**
     + **William Byham**
     - **James Tong**
     - **George Haffenden**
     - **Sander Haffenden**
     - **John Hopper**
     - **Geo[rge] Downe**
     + **Tho[mas] Moter**
     + **Will[ia]m Bixe**
     + **Rob[ert] Greene**
     + **Tho[mas] Swift**
       v. pag. 59.

p.48 Snodland   Stanford

     Speldherst   Stanstede

Stacefeild

Staple

p.49 Stapleherst

Stodmersh

Stelling

Stone
    Rich[ard] Reynoldes
    widow Blackamore ⎱
    Daniel Tilden   ⎰ d.[54]

Stockbury

Stowting

p.50 Stroode
    + Ric[ard]us Backensall

Sutton att Hone

East Sutton

Sturrey

Sutton Valance

Sundredge

p.51 Sutton iuxta Douer
    − *Foche*

Tenham

Tenterden
    − Jo[hn] Austen ar[mig]
    − John Witherden gen[t]
    **+ Rob[ert] Curteys·
       gen[t]**

Swinkefeild

Tanington

p.52 Teston

Tilmanston
    − ... Capell clark
    − Rich[ard] Fogge gen[t]

Thornham

Throughley

Tong

Totesham

p.53 Trotescliue

Ulcombe
    **+ Antho[ny] St Leger
       ar[mig]**
    + ... Horsmonden Dr

Tudeley

Tunbridge
    + *Ed[ua]r[du]s Ashbornham cl[er]icus*

Waldwarschare
    + *Ed[ua]r[du]s Monins ar[mig]*

p.54 Walmer
    Will[iam] Hugheson gen[t]
    − *Tho[mas] Gillo*
    − *Jo[hn] Gillo*

E[ast] Well u Eastwell

Westwell
    + James Taylor gen[t]

---

[54] I presume that this signifies that these freeholders died before the election, or before
Dering ascertained their voting intention.

Waltham

− Tho[mas] Beakon
Watringbury

+ **Anth[ony] Aucher
gen[t]**
+ **James Sharpe gen[t]
sen[ior]**
+ **... Wollball**
− **Rich[ard] Aucher
gen[t]**
− **Thomas Taylor**
− **John Taylor**
− **James Sharpe iun[ior]**
+ **Jo[hn] Sharpe of Nash
gen[t]**
− **William Sharpe**
− **Thomas Sharpe**
− **Daniel Bourne**
− **John Millen**
− **James Philpot**
− **John Knolldan**
+ **Gervais Gervais**
− **Paul Lofty**
+ **Ralfe Wolgate**

St Werbergh att Ho

p.55 Werehorne

Westerham
− Geo[rge] Strode ar[mig]

− ... Strood gen[t]

Whitstaple

Wy
− **Ric[hard] Godfrey
ar[mig]**
− **Rob[ert] Weyvile
ar[mig]**
− **... Wyvile gen[t]**
− **... Steel gen[t]**
+ *Jo[hn] Tilden gen[t]*

p.56 Wicheling

E[ast] Wickham

W[est] Wickham

Willesborough
− **Edwin Aucher ar[mig]**
+ **Tho[mas] Cobbes**
− **... Andrewes**
− **Nicolas Bargrave**
− **Ed[ua]r[d]us Master
gen[t]**
− **Geo[rge] May
cl[er]icus**
− **Rob[ert] Sprakling
gen[t]**

- ~~Tho[mas] Cobbes~~
- **Will[ia]m Wellins**
- **Sim[on] Philpot**
- **Hen[ry] Hall**
- **Edw[ard] Master**
- **Jo[hn] Geffrey**
- **Jo[hn] Pilcher**
- **Tho[mas] Elham**
  qu de Boys[55]

Wilmington

Wimingswold

p.57 Wingham
+ **S[i]r Tho[mas] Palmer
  bart**
+ **S[i]r James Oxenden knt**

+ **Henry Oxenden ar[mig]**
–   **Boys gen[t]**

Witerisham
Mr Jo[hn] Odierne
Nic[holas] Tufton ⎤
Giles Dauy   ⎬ d.[57]
Ric[hard] George ⎦

Woodchurch

p.58 Wormeshill

Wotton
        Carington cl[er]icus

Wrotham
+ **S[i]r Jo[hn] Rayney bart**
  Henry Keble
  Rich[ar]d Browne

Wodnesborough

d ... Greene cl[er]icus[56]
Tho[mas] Blechenden
ar[mig]

Woldham

Wolwich

Yalding
– *J[ohn] Kenard sen[ior]*
– *Geo[rge] Penhurst*
– *Geo[rge] Salmon sen[ior]*
– *Geo[rge] Salmon iun[ior]*
– *Jo[hn] Kenard iu[ior]*
– *Jo[hn] Fleete*
– *Jo[hn] Furner*]
– *Rich[ar]d Hatch*
– *Rob[ert] Kenard*
– *Walter Broke sen[ior]*

[55] Possibly a note by Dering to himself to make further enquiries after Mr Boys.

[56] I presume that this signifies that this freeholders died before the election, or before Dering ascertained his voting intention.

[57] I presume that this signifies that these freeholders died before the election, or before Dering ascertained their voting intention.

– Reginald Figge
– Henry Morice
– W[illia]m Dan
– Rob[er]t Allen
– John Coueney
– Tho[mas] Mannering
– Walter Ford
– Hugh Hatch

p.59   Egerton
   – Rob[er]t Knocke
   – William More
   – Edward Lucas
   + Geo[rge] Rayner
   – Rich[ar]d Cary
   – Rich[ar]d Mond
   – ... Bishop gen[t]
   + Edw[ard] Fenner
   – Giles Andrewes

These of Egerton were not
there as I suppose
Steph[en] Lambe sen[ior] gen[t]
... Skeere
Clement Rickard
Rob[er]t Tilbey
Reynold Filmer
Daniel Brattell
John West
Rob[er]t Bocher
Tho[mas] Winter
John Tilden

Bethersden

   – Henry Honey
   – Geo[rge] Gadfly
   – Tho[mas] Lawe
   – Rich[ar]d Carde
   – Francis Austen
   – Steph[en] Chapman
   – Geo[rge] Witherden
   – Edw[ard] Verser

Smarden
   – Hen[ry] Sharpe
   – Simon Hernden

These of Smarden defaulted
Tho[mas] Bishopenden
Tho[mas] Grinoll
Moyses Hopper
Tho[mas] Piper
Tho[mas] Monke
Joseph Meade
Jo[hn] Jewherst
Jo[hn] Thorpe
Tho[mas] Welles
Jo[hn] Coke
Jo[hn] Poute
Richard ~~Pete~~ Peter
Sam[uel] Chitenden
Tho[mas] Bridge
Tho[mas] Iggleden
Rob[ert] Tilden

Charing
   **– Thomas Simons
   sen[ior]**
   **– Tho[mas] Simons
   iun[ior]**
   – Nic[holas] Spillet
   – Tho[mas] Hickes
   – Jo[hn] Hickes
   – Tho[mas] Willes
   – Gregory Scot
   – Tho[mas] Thunder
   – Will[ia]m Bird

- **Joseph Bull**
- **Tho[mas] Browne**
- **Jo[hn] Perkins**

p.60 Charing

- **Steph[en] Scot**
- **Godfrey Hill**

- **Tho[mas] Rade**

- **Rob[ert] Elvy**

- **Tho[mas] Michell**
- **Rob[er]t Willard**

- **Francis Hodges**
- **Tho[mas] Yong**
- **Will[ia]m Ashby**
- **Jo[hn] Weekes**
- **Rich[ard] Baldocke**
- **Jo[hn] Jones**
- **Elyas Tong**
- **James Clement**
- **W[i]ll[ia]m Nepecker**
- **Tho[mas] Stephans**
- **Tho[mas] Gervais**

Ashford

- **Rob[ert] Goldhacke**
+ **Tho[mas] Robins sen[ior]**

+ **Tho[mas] Robins iun[ior]**
- **Tho[mas] Hall sen[ior]**

- **Rob[ert] Cowper**
- **Jo[hn] Austen ye bocher**

- **Rob[er]t Badnor**
- **Ralph Tritton**
- **Tho[mas] Master**
- **Jo[hn] Pope qu.**
- **Jo[hn] Coueney**
- **Rich[ard] Vewtrell**
- **Hen[ry] Gibbes p etcon**
- **Rob[er]t Dunne**
- **Leonard Armestrong**
+ **Tho[mas] Carpenter**
- **Jo[hn] Buckhurst**
+ **Tho[mas] Cuckow**
- **Jo[hn] Cuckow**
- **Ric[hard] Morecocke**
- **Jo[hn] Fenner**
- **Rob[ert] Horton**
- **Dan[iel] Morecocke**

these no freehold
- **Will[ia]m Wise**
- **Jo[hn] Den**
- **Nathaniel Bridge**
- **Jo[hn] Morris jun[ior]**

'PARTICULAR BUSINESSES' IN THE LONG PARLIAMENT: THE HULL LETTERS 1644–1648

David Scott

One of the least studied aspects of the Long Parliament is its role in addressing the legislative needs of private or sectional interests such as trading companies and borough corporations. In the field of parliamentary studies, the dissolution of the 1628–9 Parliament represents a major watershed. The pioneering work of Geoffrey Elton, Conrad Russell and others has allowed us to appreciate a long-overlooked facet of Parliaments before 1629 – their function as a 'market-place of legislative business'.[1] But the Parliaments called after the collapse of the Personal Rule tend to be scrutinised in a very different light. Understandably, perhaps, the focus is almost exclusively upon the debates and factionalism that attended the nation's slide into civil war and subsequent endeavours to restore peace. The general assumption among historians of the civil war period is that the two Houses were so preoccupied with the great issues of the moment that they had little time to devote to any business of a more private nature. There is certainly no denying that the Long Parliament was often consumed with 'greate & weightie affaires',[2] nor that many of the MPs who remained at Westminster after the outbreak of war were under little pressure to promote the interests of their constituents or indeed of any private individuals. Even so, where the relationship between a serving Parliament-man and those who had elected him remained strong, it is unlikely that he could have ignored entirely his obligation to act as their spokesman and lobbyist. One of the best and yet most neglected sources for examining the role of MPs as promoters of 'particular businesses'[3] in the Long Parliament is the Hull letters.

[1] Conrad Russell, *English Parliaments and Politics, 1621–1629* (Oxford, 1979), ch. 1; G. R. Elton, *The Parliament of England, 1559–1581* (Cambridge, 1986); Conrad Russell, 'Parliamentary History in Perspective, 1604–29', *History* lxi (1976); M. A. R. Graves, 'The Management of the Elizabethan House of Commons: The Council's 'Men-of-Business', *PH* ii (1983), p. 11; idem, *Elizabethan Parliaments 1559–1601* (2nd edn, London, 1996); David M. Dean, *Law-making and Society in Late Elizabethan England* (Cambridge, 1996).

[2] HCA, L330; L418; L420; L421; L426; L449: hereafter letter nos only are given in the notes.

[3] L420.

The Hull letters are the largest surviving cache of pre-Reform municipal correspondence anywhere in England. The collection, housed at the Hull City Archives, comprises over 1,300 letters, the bulk of which cover the Tudor and Stuart period.[4] Most of the correspondence consists of letters to the mayor and aldermen from the town's MPs, its friends and agents in London, or from local and central government. The town's correspondents include some distinguished names, most notably Andrew Marvell, who served as an MP for Hull from the late 1650s. His letters to the corporation during the 1660s are an important source for the debates and proceedings of the Cavalier Parliament. Twenty years earlier, the letters of another of Hull's MPs, Peregrine Pelham, and of the town's recorder, Francis Thorpe, open a similar window on the workings of the Long Parliament.

Over a four-year period beginning in the autumn of 1644, Pelham and Thorpe wrote 130 letters to the corporation, most of them from London. Even by the voluminous standards of the Hull letters, this is rich vein of correspondence. Before the autumn of 1644 the town's official contacts with its friends and representatives in the metropolis seem to have been patchy at best. For the first two years of the fighting the town's links with the outside world were blocked to landward by the Royalists. Its only reliable line of communication with the capital was by ship, and foreign privateers made the journey by sea a perilous one. With the parliamentarian victories in the north of 1644, however, the royalist grip on Yorkshire and the East Midlands was finally broken, and the town was able to receive a regular stream of letters from Pelham and Thorpe overland. This stream seems to have dried up between November 1646 and December 1647, when the two men may have been deterred from regular attendance at Westminster by the ascendancy of the Presbyterians. Thorpe resumed a fairly regular correspondence with the corporation in December 1647, which continued until August 1648; but Pelham wrote just one more letter to the corporation – in November 1648. Thereafter, the two men either ceased corresponding with the town or their letters have not survived. It is possible that the support that both men showed for bringing the king to trial, which in Pelham's case extended to signing the death warrant, strained to breaking-point their relations with the town's Presbyterian-dominated bench. The historian has to wait until Marvell's correspondence during the 1660s before the Hull letters reveal another seam of Westminster news of comparable richness.

The Hull aldermen's thirst for information from Westminster was probably unusual among town fathers of the period; but then Hull was itself an unusual borough. Its commercial vantage-point on the Humber estuary had made it the most prosperous northern town after Newcastle. In volume of trade it ranked fourth among the outports, serving as an entrepôt to the vast commercial hinterland drained by the Rivers Trent, Aire, Wharfe, and Ouse. Almost all of the West Riding's vast output of textiles passed through Hull, which exported more cloth than any other outport. On the import side, Hull merchants brought in a wide variety of commodities, although the bulk of this trade was in raw materials from the Baltic.[5] The town's commercial prosperity had pushed its population up to around the seven or eight thousand mark by the 1630s, making it one of the ten largest urban centres in England.[6] The Civil War led to a sharp curtailment in the town's trading activities, with cloth production in the West Riding virtually grinding to a halt and Hull itself enduring several royalist sieges during 1642 and 1643. In 1644 the corporation informed the Commons that the town had 'of late years bene very much impoverished by meanes of these unnaturall warres, most of the inhabitants depending upon traid, being merchants & seamen, who for dyvers yeares together have beene deprived of theire traid & callings by reason of the ... enemies stopping all passages ...'.[7] This slump in trade, coupled with a severe outbreak of the plague in 1637, had an adverse effect upon the town's population, which had dropped to around the six thousand mark by mid-century.[8] Nevertheless, the town retained a vigorous municipal life and a large degree of independence in the conduct of its affairs. By its charter of incorporation, Hull enjoyed its own county status and jurisdiction independent of the East Riding, and was governed principally by a mayor and twelve aldermen, who held office for life and served as JPs for the borough.[9] Unusually for a town of Hull's size, there was no common council or second chamber – the mayor and aldermen conferring directly with the leading freemen on important matters. In practice, this seems to have allowed the aldermen and the 'best' inhabitants considerable leeway in governing the town and determining its interests at Westminster. Moreover, as the aldermen and leading townsmen were merchants almost to a man, the town's dealings with Parliament tended to revolve around commercial issues.

[5] *VCH, East Riding* (6 vols, London, 1969–84), i. 134–9.
[6] *VCH, East Riding*, i. 161; *Hull's Managing of the Kingdoms Cause* (London, 1644), p. 2 (BL, E51/11).
[7] HCA, Hull bench book 5, pp. 652–3, 669–71; L369; BL, Lansdowne MS 890, fols 132v, 141–2; *VCH, East Riding*, i. 138.
[8] *VCH, East Riding*, i. 161.
[9] *Ibid.* i. 29, 35, 38, 126; David Scott, draft constituency article, Hull 1640–60, History of Parliament Trust.

Hull was also unusual, at least among northern boroughs, in that it remained in Parliament's hands during the entire course of the war. In addition, and again unusually, both of its MPs – Sir Henry Vane junior and Peregrine Pelham – retained their seats throughout the 1640s, which in the turbulent times ensured considerable continuity in the relationship between the town and its Parliament-men. That relationship was strengthened in the autumn of 1645, when Francis Thorpe, the town's recorder, was returned as a 'recruiter' for the Yorkshire borough of Richmond. Hull now had, in effect, three representatives at Westminster. One of these, however, Sir Henry Vane, was a politician of national stature and apparently devoted little time to Hull's parliamentary affairs.[10] The bulk of town's business at Westminster was handled by Pelham and Thorpe; two men of very different character and background.

Pelham was descended from a cadet branch of the distinguished Sussex family, the Pelhams of Laughton.[11] He was born in Sussex in 1602, but grew up mainly in Lincolnshire, where his family settled during James's reign.[12] His father was apparently a man of modest wealth, which would explain his willingness to have Pelham, his eldest son, apprenticed to a Hull merchant. Granted his freedom of Hull in 1626, Pelham quickly established himself as one of the town's most successful overseas traders, exporting lead and importing large quantities of French wine.[13] His commercial success was reflected in his progress along the town's *cursus honorum*. He served as chamberlain in 1630–1, sheriff in 1636–7, and was elected an alderman in September 1641.[14] His return as the town's MP on 18 January 1641, in place of the deceased Sir John Lister, was almost certainly upon the corporation's interest. By the summer of 1645, he was firmly aligned with the nascent Independent faction at Westminster, claiming that the war would never be won while Parliament countenanced the Earl of Essex and other 'disobliged' figures.[15] He was even more distrustful of the king, par-

---

[10] See Violet A. Rowe, *Sir Henry Vane the Younger: A Study in Political and Administrative History* (London, 1970).

[11] For Pelham's life and career see David Scott, draft biography of Peregrine Pelham, History of Parliament Trust.

[12] Kenneth H. Macdermott, 'Extracts from the Parish Registers of Bosham, Sussex', *Sussex Archaeological Collections* liv (1911), p. 57; HCA, PE185/1 (St Mary Lowgate parish register), unfol.; PE158/1 (Holy Trinity parish register), unfol.; A. R. Maddison, *Lincolnshire Pedigrees* (Harleian Society lii), p. 765.

[13] Cambridge University Library, Mm.1.46, p. 84; PRO, C 7/275/91, 94; *CSPD Addenda 1625–49*, p. 249; *CSPD 1628–9*, p. 313; *VCH, East Riding*, i. 142.

[14] HCA, BRG1 (Freeman register 1396–1645), fol. 179; Hull bench bk. 5, pp. 234, 422, 542, 821.

[15] BL, Harl. MS 166, fol. 218; Michael Mahony, 'The Savile Affair and the Politics of the Long Parliament', *PH* vii (1988), p. 218.

ticularly after hearing extracts from Charles's correspondence seized at Naseby. Indeed, the Hull letters suggest that such disclosures had a deeply corrosive effect upon the loyalty of many of Charles's subjects.[16] Thorpe believed that 'the designes discov[er]ed in his [the king's] since intercepted lres have taught the House that wisedome which otherwise they could nott have learned'.[17] In Pelham's case, the Naseby letters convinced him that the king was fighting to establish Catholicism, and that there were 'noe hopes of peace but by the sword'.[18] Despite his alignment with the Independent interest, Pelham had little sympathy for the sects, and in a letter to the aldermen expressed the hope that the 'multiplicitie of opinions w[hi]ch swarme generally (of w[hi]ch your towne is much infected as I heare) will ere long be reduced to government'.[19] He seems to have favoured 'orthodox' divines such as Hull's minister, William Styles (removed from his living in 1650 for refusing the Engagement) and the strongly erastian Thomas Coleman, who was opposed both to the gathering of churches and the 'rigid' Presbyterianism of the Scots.[20]

In contrast to Pelham, Thorpe was of true county gentry stock. He was born in 1594, the heir to a cadet branch of a long-established East Riding family, the Thorpes of Thorpe.[21] His father was a JP and sewers' commissioner for the East Riding, and served as one of James I's gentleman ushers and quarter waiters.[22] Thorpe received a gentleman's education at St John's College, Cambridge (graduating BA in 1614), and Gray's Inn.[23] He was called to the bar in 1621, and in 1624 was elected recorder of Beverley.[24] In the mid-1630s he was retained as a counsellor-at-law by the future Independent grandee, Algernon 10th Earl of Northumberland, and it was possibly on the earl's recommendation as lord high admiral that Thorpe was appointed recorder of Hull in 1639.[25] Thorpe was operating as one of Hull corporation's

[16] L375; L376; L379; L383; L424; L426; L430; L463; L464; L465.

[17] L424; L426.

[18] L375; L383; L463; L465; L477.

[19] L428.

[20] L401; L428; L444; L476; L481; T. Tindall Wildridge, ed., *The Hull Letters* (Hull, 1887), p. 103.

[21] Joseph Foster, ed., *The Visitation of Yorkshire Made in the Years 1584/5* (London, 1875), pp. 52–3.

[22] PRO, C181/3 fols 96, 187v; C193/13/1, fol. 30v; REQ2/413, fol. 216v; SP14/33, fol. 20.

[23] *Alumni Cantabrigiensis*; Joseph Foster, ed., *The Register of Admissions to Gray's Inn, 1521–1889* (2 vols, London, 1889), i. 125.

[24] Reginald J. Fletcher, ed., *The Pension Book of Gray's Inn, 1569–1800* (2 vols., London, 1901–10), i. 242, 300, 310, 343; *VCH, East Riding*, vi. 205.

[25] Alnwick Castle, Duke of Northumberland MSS, U.I.5., unfol. ('The Generall Accompte 1636') [BL, Mic. 390]; J. Tickell, *The History of the Town and County of Kingston upon Hull* (Hull, 1798), p. 685.

men-of-business in London by December 1644 at the latest,[26] and continued to serve the town's interests even after his election for Richmond on 20 October 1645 (probably on the interest of Philip Lord Wharton).[27] Indeed, in several of his letters to the aldermen he implied that he himself was more diligent on their behalf than either of the town's MPs.[28] His correspondence reveals that he shared the Independents' distrust of the king and their desire to impose a stringent settlement upon him.[29] He also emerges as a supporter of Hull's Presbyterian preacher, John Shawe, whose attempts to impose godly discipline upon the townspeople may have incited charges of sectarianism in some quarters.[30] Although Thorpe played no part in the king's trial and execution, he subsequently defended the revolution and enjoyed a high profile legal career under the Rump.[31]

The differences in background of Pelham and Thorpe probably contributed to the contrast in their style as Parliament-men. Thorpe's approach was very much that of the lawyer – cautious, judicious, and mindful of precedent. Pelham, on the other hand, shared his fellow aldermen's impatience with legal niceties and red tape. He emerges from his letters as a man of forthright views and abrasive personality. He also seems to have been a rather arrogant and boastful character – which is as well for us, for his letters are exceptionally frank about how a less than scrupulous MP liked to operate at Westminster. Pelham concentrated a good deal of his attention upon the chairmen of standing committees – the men who were charged with actually executing parliamentary orders, and whose position often gave them quasi-judicial authority. Pelham targeted a number of these individuals, and in particular Miles Corbett and Laurence Whitaker (joint chairmen of the Committee for Examinations); John Blakiston (the Committee for Petitions); John Wylde (the Committee for Sequestrations); Gilbert Millington (the Committee for Plundered Ministers); and Sir Thomas Widdrington (the Northern Committee and Northern Association Committee). Only rarely, it seems, did he attempt to influence proceedings on the floor of the House, and then it was to have his 'friends' secure orders for transferring legislation to standing committees where the members or chairmen were open to friendly persuasion. One of his favourite methods of exerting leverage in these committees was

[26] L325.
[27] PRO, C 219/43/3/119; David Scott, draft constituency article, Richmond 1640–60, History of Parliament Trust.
[28] L370; L426; L427.
[29] L424; L426; L429; L434.
[30] L417; L418; L421; L426; L448; L468; L471; L491.
[31] For Thorpe's life and career see David Scott, draft biography of Francis Thorpe, History of Parliament Trust.

through simple bribery. In a letter to the mayor and aldermen of 8 April 1645 he made an extraordinary claim: 'My desposition is such yt I care for noe chairman noe further then I finde him for ye publique ... I am confident you neede not feare any committee to doe you any p[re]iudice. I doe not spend £500 p[er] ann[um] here for nothing'.[32] Five hundred pounds is roughly the equivalent of half a million pounds today. Some of this money may have gone on legal advice (although with Thorpe available for consultation this seems unlikely) and in above board expenditure such as the fees due to the clerks and other parliamentary officials. However, it is hard to avoid the conclusion that this was a slush fund that Pelham used to treat or bribe other MPs in return for services rendered. The source of this money is not clear. The town's accounts do not survive for most of the 1640s, but since £500 represented about a third of Hull's pre-war income it is unlikely to have come entirely from municipal coffers.[33] In all likelihood it was a 'Parliament fund', to which the aldermen and other leading Hull freemen contributed, of the kind that some London trading companies set up to prosecute their various businesses at Westminster.[34]

One less controversial form of political currency that both Thorpe and Pelham splashed around at Westminster was Hull ale – a heady brew, and much in demand among Parliament-men. In November 1645, for example, Thorpe informed the corporation that he had received the two barrels of ale they had sent him 'and shall bestow them with some reference to yo[u]r advantage'.[35] Similarly, in 1646 the corporation sent two barrels of ale to Samuel Browne, a prominent MP and Lincoln's Inn barrister, 'as a present from ye towne ... Mr Pelham having gyven intimac[i]on soe to do'.[36] Pelham was confident that Browne would be 'a true freind to your towne. He is a very solid lawyer & a man in very great esteeme ... he strikes a greate stroke [in the Commons], as in other affaires'.[37] Another recipient of Hull ale was the Speaker of the Commons, William Lenthall. Lenthall's reputation as one of the most venal members of the Commons is confirmed by the Hull lettters. Not only did he solicit Pelham for Hull ale, but also a douceur of £5 a year.[38] But he was just one of a queue of Parliament-men keen to sample the town's largesse, as Pelham informed the corporation:

[32] L348.
[33] I am grateful to Simon Healy for information concerning Hull's municipal revenues before the Civil War.
[34] David M. Dean, 'Public or Private? London Leather and Legislation in Elizabethan England', *HJ* xxxi (1988), p. 535.
[35] L417.
[36] HCA, Hull bench bk. 5, p. 709.
[37] L444.
[38] L347; L350; L404.

I am much importuned for Hull ale dayly, both by Lords and Commons, who are willing to further me in any thing that concerns your towne, and I shall have occasion to use my friends ... If it please you to send to me a tonne of Hull ale, and leave it to my desposeing, it will not be lost, but will be wellcome, although it be late. In steade of jug-heads I will make bottled many of our friends...[39]

The term 'friends' was frequently employed by both Pelham and Thorpe, and had served for decades, possibly centuries, as the standard euphemism for bribed Parliament-men.[40] It is possible to identify a number of men who were certainly very well disposed towards Hull, of which the most important (if one excludes Lenthall) were Robert Goodwin (MP for East Grinstead, Sussex);[41] Sir William Strickland (MP for Hedon, Yorkshire);[42] and Sir Thomas Widdrington (MP for Berwick-upon-Tweed).[43] Widdrington became friendly with the aldermen through his role as man-of-business to Hull's governor, Ferdinando Lord Fairfax.[44] Strickland had an eye towards establishing an electoral power base for himself in the town.[45] Goodwin, on the other hand, like his brother and fellow MP John, has been identified as a bag-carrier and fixer for leading Parliament-men, and was precisely the kind of figure who would respond well to the inducements the corporation had to offer.[46] But while the corporation's ale barrel politicking proved effective with the more biddable element at Westminster, it helped to alienate many of Hull's neighbours, confirming them in their mistaken belief that the town had profited from the war while the region as a whole had been ruined. 'The Yorkshire men say they are all undone & you are growne rich', Pelham told the corporation.[47] Both Thorpe and Pelham regularly remarked that Hull had 'very ill neighbours', and complained that their MPs were endeavouring to frustrate the town's parliamentary affairs.[48] 'I expect no assistance

[39] L293.

[40] Dean, 'Public or Private?', pp. 545, 546; Ian Archer, 'The London Lobbies in the Later Sixteenth Century', *HJ* xxxi (1988), pp. 344, 349.

[41] L362; L371; L419; L473.

[42] L353; L360; L371; L425.

[43] L360; L362; L378; L396; L399; L404; L425; L428; L463; L480.

[44] For Widdrington's life and career, see David Scott, draft biography of Sir Thomas Widdrington, History of Parliament Trust.

[45] BL, Add. MS 21427, fol. 262; HCA, Hull bench bk. 6, p. 277.

[46] J. S. A. Adamson, 'Parliamentary Management, Men-of-Business and the House of Lords, 1640–49', *A Pillar of the Constitution: The House of Lords in British Poitics, 1640–1784*, ed. Clyve Jones (London, 1989), pp. 32 n. 58, 33 n. 62; Adamson, 'The English Nobility and the Projected Settlement of 1647', *HJ* xxx (1987), p. 598.

[47] L369.

[48] L368; L369; L373; L424; L426; L468; L480.

by your neighbours', Pelham informed the aldermen, 'those that serve for remote p[ar]ts are my best friends'.[49] Thorpe also acknowledged the role that MPs from other parts of the country – 'strangers' – played in securing the town's ends.[50]

Most of Hull's particular businesses in Parliament were routine in nature – securing timber to shore up the banks of the Humber; money from dean and chapter lands to augment the stipend of the town's minister; abatement of the town's fee farm rent arrears etc. But the aldermen's zeal to do right by the town, as well as their own pockets, occasionally got them into trouble at Westminster; as in early 1645, when they became embroiled in a dispute with the Committee for Examinations over their penal taxation of non-free traders, and in particular one James Nelthorpe, who would be returned as a recruiter for Beverley later in the year. The revelation that the corporation had imposed a 50-shilling-a-week fine on Nelthorpe was not well received by the committee.[51] Even the town's own governor, Ferdinando Lord Fairfax, was moved to write to the committee on Nelthorpe's behalf.[52] The corporation argued, through Pelham, that it was simply enforcing its right under the town's charter to proceed against interlopers. However, there was a strong suspicion at Westminster that it was pursuing a vendetta against Nelthorpe because he was an exciseman.[53] Thorpe advised the corporation that its penal taxation of unenfranchised traders was illegal, but Pelham brushed his arguments aside.[54] From early April, however, Pelham and his ale barrel fraternity began to lose ground in the committee as a group of London merchants added their voice to the complaints against the corporation. The activities of Dunkirkers and royalist privateers in the English Channel had forced some London merchants to sell their cargoes at Hull, but not being freemen the corporation had mulcted them as it had done Nelthorpe.[55] Outraged, they petitioned the committee, complaining about 'the great assessments of cittizins [i.e. Londoners] & others ... when the best men in towne pay but 1s.'.[56] The committee expressed surprise that 'such violent courses ... should be taken against persons of knowne integrity and fidelity to ye Parliament ...'. It ordered the corporation to regulate its assessments proportional to the petitioners' estates, and that if they

[49] L293.
[50] L371.
[51] L332; L335; L342; L347; L351; L360; Wildridge, *Hull Letters*, p. 52.
[52] L342.
[53] L342.
[54] L331.
[55] L345.
[56] L347.

had committed any misdemeanours 'to take remedy by Law'.[57] Needless to say, Pelham and the corporation ignored these orders. 'You have allways an appeale to the House of Commons', Pelham told the aldermen, 'and there you shall have right'.[58] He even admitted to one of the committee's joint chairmen that 'whatsoever they doe at the Committee of Examinations ... the towne of Hull will finde freinds in the House of Commons'.[59]

The corporation's determination to pursue its own advantage regardless of the public interest, or indeed of Parliament's 'great businesses', was even more starkly revealed over the summer of 1645. At the start of the year the Long Parliament's principal executive body, the Committee of Both Kingdoms, had set about re-organising the northern parliamentarian forces in anticipation of another summer's bloody campaigning.[60] The committee drew up a draft ordinance for associating Yorkshire and six other northern counties, and in mid-April this was referred for fine tuning to the Northern Committee.[61] As soon as the mayor and aldermen got wind of this new legislation they wrote to Pelham urging him to get Hull exempted. Jealous as ever of their corporate privileges and Hull's county status, they feared that inclusion in the association would undermine municipal authority and result in the town's incorporation with the East Riding. In fact, as many MPs believed, the corporation's fears were entirely groundless. Martial law would apply only to the garrison; the town's new governor, Lieutenant-Colonel John Mauleverer, had been a man of the corporation's own choosing; and there was no question of Hull's civil government being merged with that of the East Riding.[62] When Pelham began canvassing the possibility of having the town left out of the association he seems to have got short shrift from most of his fellow MPs: 'They say you escape better then any of your neighbours'.[63] Similarly, when Thorpe and Widdrington tried to put the town's case in the Northern Committee they were rebuffed; but then the committee was dominated by those self-same neighbours, who were determined that Hull should bear the same military burdens as the rest of the region. Pelham did not even bother to turn up at the committee, for as Thorpe informed the corporation: 'he thincks to get it stoppt in the House when the ordinance coms to be voted their'.[64] In other words, Pelham was hoping to use

[57] L345; L358
[58] L360; L361; L365.
[59] L360; L368.
[60] CJ, iv. 9.
[61] Ibid. 110.
[62] L362; L369.
[63] L360; L361.
[64] L362.

his ale barrel fraternity in the Commons to overrule Hull's resentful neighbours in the Northern Committee. Against the day when the ordinance was reported to the Commons, Thorpe advised the corporation to write to the Speaker and to Sir Henry Vane junior, who could use their influence to have the letters read, and so provide the cue for Pelham and his friends to press the case for Hull's exemption.[65] This tactic looked like working when the ordinance was read in the Commons on 30 May, for Hull's concerns were the main topic of debate. But in the end the ordinance was referred back to the Northern Committee, where Hull's enemies were waiting. When the Committee convened again early in June there was a 'a verye full companye', and after a long and apparently divisive debate the vote went against Hull for the second and final time.[66] On 7 June Widdrington reported the ordinance to the Commons again, and it was sent to the Lords for their assent.[67]

That the Northern Association took so long to become law, in fact not until well into the 1645 campaign season, was due in no small part to Hull and its friends at Westminster. This at any rate was Thorpe's assessment, as he confided to the corporation in June: 'your business to that purpose haveing bene the onely subiect of debate' the ordinance had, '& much opposic[i]on about yo[u]r exempcon yo[u]r freinds, w[hi]ch were very many, made in it'.[68] What made the town's private interest politicking particularly reprehensible was its timing. While Hull's concerns were being pored over in the Northern Committee and on the floor of the Commons, the king's main field army was poised to strike into Yorkshire. In juggling the various forces at its disposal, the Committee for Both Kingdoms had left a massive gap in its northern defences, and it was very fortunate for the Yorkshire Parliamentarians that the Royalists could not make up their minds how to exploit this power vacuum, and spent a fortnight dithering in the Midlands before being defeated at Naseby on 13 June. By delaying the introduction of the Northern Association – legislation that was vital for the region's military security – at precisely the moment when Parliament's defences in the north were at their most vulnerable, Hull corporation was potentially jeopardising the entire parliamentarian cause.

Although Thorpe accepted the decision of the Commons with a good grace and got on with advising the corporation about implementing the new legislation, Pelham resorted to the last desperate gamble of the

[65] L362.
[66] L368; L369; L370.
[67] *CJ*, iv. 166–7.
[68] L371.

frustrated Parliament-man – a petition.[69] By the mid-1640s, petitions represented an admission of parliamentary impotence; a failure or inability to 'cog in'[70] with the grandees and their men-of-business in the executive committees. Pelham's petition came to nothing, and Hull was duly incorporated in the Northern Association. But the corporation continued its private interest-building at Westminster, and in November 1645 even tried to engage the services of one of the grandest of the Independent grandees, Oliver St John, the solicitor-general. Thorpe, who knew that St John was too busy with 'public engagements' to do or care much for Hull's little businesses, had to remind the corporation that '[it is] not an easy thing to get a man of M[r] Sollic[i]tor's imploym[en]ts leasur'.[71] In May 1646, the corporation sought another exemption, this time from an ordinance concerning the pay and government of Hull's garrison, and once again its exaggerated fears for the town's privileges gummed up the legislative works. Thorpe informed the corporation that its friends would endeavour to have a suitable proviso inserted in the ordinance during its passage through the Lords (Hull evidently possessed a bicameral interest at Westminster),[72] 'but this will occasio[n] a delay by retorning it back to o[u]r House w[i]th the amendm[en]t, & their debating it anew'.[73] By this stage, Thorpe himself was becoming exasperated by the aldermen's paranoia about military enroachment:

> And as touching yo[u]r fears of martiall law & desyre to be exempted from it, I thought you had bene longe since satisfyed yt the martiall law extends onely to martiall men, & is to be exercised only ov[er] them, & cannot nor ought not to be exercised but in case of martiall discipline, & their can be no exempc[i]on by ordinance from that w[hi]ch is not. And I thinck you need no more feare the exercise of martiall law to the p[re]judice of yo[u]r civill authoritye then you need fear the exercise of the forrest law w[i]th you.[74]

As Thorpe feared, the amended ordinance ran into difficulties in the Lords, 'and what they will send back to us or when we know not. So the mayne is delayed'.[75] But on this occasion the corporation eventually

[69] L373.

[70] [David Buchanan], *An Explanation of Some Truths* (London, 1646), pp. 53, 55–6 (BL, E314/15).

[71] L416.

[72] Thorpe engaged Philip Lord Wharton to speed the ordinance through the Upper House: L464; L468.

[73] L456.

[74] L454.

[75] L458

got its way, for after much debate the ordinance was passed 'w[i]th more exempc[i]ons' than any garrison town had yet obtained.[76] Yet even then the corporation was not entirely satisfied, causing Thorpe to exclaim that 'it is the best p[ro]vision we cold [*sic*] gett & the best service I cold [*sic*] do you to p[ro]mote it soe far. And if yo[u]r selves had bene here to have sene the troubles of attending it, besides the labour of freinds for it, I hope you might have bene bett[er] satisfyed there was no omissio[n]'.[77]

On the face of it, much of the corporation's politicking at Westminster, particularly its efforts to secure exemption from the Northern Association, smacks strongly of localism. But Pelham's 'Parliament fund' and use of sweeteners in one form or other are reminiscent of the lobbying methods favoured by the London trading companies in the Elizabethan era. Moreover, the vast majority of the locality and its MPs resented the town and did their best to hinder its business at every turn. Similarly, there is the strong suspicion that most of the matters Pelham and his 'friends' prosecuted at Westminster benefited the aldermen and their fellow merchants more than they did the townspeople as a whole.[78] The corporation operated at Westminster as a vested interest, and like most vested interests it relied not upon community spirit but upon money and treating to get its way. In order to disguise the often self-interested nature of the corporation's particular businesses, Pelham used Hull's reputation of loyalty to the Parliamentarian cause to develop the notion that anything that was beneficial for the town must also, by definition, be beneficial for the kingdom generally. This mindset is evident in his indignation that the Committee for Examinations could have the effrontery to summon Hull men to London to answer Nelthorpe's charges against them: 'This day I spoke w[i]th the chairman of examinations, Mr Whitterkers. I tould him I wondred he would send for the maior upon such informations, himselfe and the towne having done such good service for the publique'.[79] Having created this convenient fiction that Hull's good was synonymous with that of the public, Pelham was particularly anxious to preserve the town's loyal reputation at Westminster. If once that reputation was tarnished then the *pro bono publico* disguise in which he sought to dress the town's dealings in Parliament would be stripped away. He was understandably upset, therefore, when he was told by

---

[76] L468.

[77] L475.

[78] Robert Tittler has argued that municipal legislative initiatives often favoured the interests of the governing élite at the expense of 'frequently voiceless majority': Robert Tittler, 'Elizabethan Towns and the 'Points of Contact': Parliament', *PH* viii (1989), p. 279.

[79] L391.

two prominent MPs in October 1646 that Hull's merchants had sent an address to the king asking him to intercede with the Dutch for the return of some captured shipping. Pelham quickly riposted that it was the York merchants – Hull's old rivals – who had sent the address. But in private he berated the aldermen for their foolishness: 'I know it would give a great occasion of offence to the House if they should heare of it. It might p[ro]ve very p[re]iudiciall to the affaires that I have in hand for the towne. I hope better of you'.[80]

Overall, despite its grumbling, the corporation did pretty well out of the Long Parliament. Fortified by Pelham's £500 a year and plenty of Hull ale, the town's caucus of friends at Westminster may well have rivalled that of London, which by 1645 was a deeply divided city. Thereafter, however, as the hostility between Presbyterians and Independents in the capital spilled over into the kingdom at large, the aldermen began to draw fire from more powerful groups than the town's jealous neighbours. By 1648, the Presbyterian leanings of the aldermanic bench and its highly publicised arguments with the town's sectarian deputy-governor, Colonel Robert Overton, had excited the suspicion of the more radical element at Westminster.[81] In July, at the height of the Second Civil War and with royalist ships ranging up and down the East Coast, the corporation sent a delegation to Westminster, headed by Alderman John Ramsden, demanding Overton's removal.[82] Once again, the leading office-holders feared enchroachment by the military upon their privileges, but their action in sending a delegation could not have been more ill-timed. For several months the London newsbooks, both royalist and parliamentarian, had been spreading rumours that Hull was arming for the king.[83] Thorpe was amazed at the corporation's wilfulness:

> Touching yo[u]r business for w[hi]ch M[r] Ramsden & the rest are come up; all I shall say at p[re]sent is yt if you wold have vouchsafed to have consulted yo[u] freinds here before yo[u]r ingagem[en]t to that und[er]taking, I p[re]sume you wold, as rationall men, have receycd a satisfaccon to yo[u]r contentm[en]t, & wold have bene p[er]swaded not to indanger the disturbance of a publick peace for any pryvate intrest.[84]

What Thorpe saw as the workings of a private interest, the par-

[80] L482.
[81] L500; L506; L507; *CSPD 1648–9*, pp. 138, 226; Bulstrode Whitelocke, *Memorials of the English Affairs* (4 vols, Oxford, 1853), ii. 279–80.
[82] L501; *VCH, East Riding*, i. 106.
[83] For example, see *Mercurius Melancholicus*, no. 38 (London, 8–15 May 1648), p. 228 (BL, E442/14); L500.
[84] L501.

liamentary radicals regarded as crypto-Royalism. Although Thorpe, Pelham, and Sir Henry Vane junior all retained their seats at Pride's Purge, the triumph of the army and its supporters left the corporation in a vulnerable position. Yet just when it needed its friends most they began to fall away. Thorpe was obliged to resign as Hull's recorder by reason of his 'weighty employments' as a baron of the Exchequer;[85] and in December 1650 Pelham died, leaving the corporation with only Vane to rely on, and he was heavily engaged in national politics. The corporation's weakness during the early 1650s was cruelly exposed when the garrison built a brick wall right down the middle of the town church to make room for a sectarian congregation.[86]

A selection of the Hull letters, including many from the civil war period, was published by Thomas Tindall Wildridge in 1887. His transcriptions are generally accurate, but the edition lacks both a scholarly introduction and annotations to help the reader make sense of the letters and elucidate their context. His selection begins with the commencement of Charles's reign in 1625 and ends in mid June 1646 with the king's 'imprisonment' (although Charles was effectively a prisoner of the Scots from mid-May). However, in terms of political developments at Westminster, or indeed the content of the letters themselves, June 1646 is a date of little significance. Moreover, Wildridge never adequately explains the basis of his selection between 1625 and 1646. He omits many important and revealing letters before June 1646 for no discernable reason. This present selection of the Hull letters features many of the letters that Wildridge transcribed, and most of those for the period 1644–8 that he did not. It is at once both more and less comprehensive than Wildridge's edition. More, in the sense that it extends beyond June 1646 and fills in some of the more glaring gaps in Wildridge's selection; less, in that very few of the letters are transcribed in their entirety. The main value of the letters for the mid-1640s is the light they shed on the workings of Hull's parliamentary interest.[87] The town's affairs in other fora, for example the law courts, are generally unremarkable (as a glance at Wildridge's edition will confirm) and have been omitted here. Similarly, the inclusion of general news matters – reports of battles, the progress of the war etc. – has been limited to material not likely to be found in other sources or where it is revealing of the opinions and prejudices of the writer and his audience.

---

[85] HCA, Hull bench bk. 5, p. 820.
[86] *VCH*, East Riding, i. 108.
[87] A point that T. Tindall Wildridge himself conceded: Wildridge, ed., *Hull Letters*, p. xiii.

Note on the Text

The letters have been arranged in date order, rather than by manuscript number. Unless otherwise stated, the letters are addressed to the mayor and aldermen of Hull. The letters with manuscript numbers in bold type have been published by T. Tindall Wildridge. Punctuation and capitalisation have been modernised.

The Hull Letters, 1644–1648

L326: Pelham, Westminster 24 Dec. 1644
 ... I shall acquainte Mr Coleman[88] w[i]th your desires. I have often spoken to him. I doubt not but wee shall p[re]vaile w[i]th him to come to you when the Assembly will dispence w[i]th him (although I heare his parishioners are very unwilling to part w[i]th him). Multiplicitie of businesse in the House of Commons doth yet hinder the report of your businesse.[89] I doe often put the chaireman[90] in mind of it. I shall take care to have your p[ar]ishes devided according to your desires...
 The ordinance yt noe member of either House shall inioy any office millitary or civill during this war is past in the House of Commons. It now remaines in the House of Lords ... I desire to know from you who you would have to command at Hull...

L330: Pelham, Westminster 14 Jan. 1645
 ... I cannot as yet accomplish your desires by reason of such great immergent affaires in the House of Commons. The House hath resolved to receive noe privat businesse until they have setled a constant p[ro]vision for the payment of there armies, agreed upon the treaty for a well grounded peace, setled church government, & alsoe made

---

[88] Thomas Coleman was appointed minister of St. Peter's, Cornhill, after he had been driven from his living at Blyton, Lincolnshire, by the Royalists during the Civil War. In a letter to the mayor of Hull, dated 18 Sept. 1645, Coleman declared that while he looked upon the Independents as 'honest men', he disliked the gathering of churches, and 'on the other side I am no rigid presbyterian, nor can I comply w[i]th the Scots': L401; Wildridge, *Hull Letters*, pp. 103–4; Clive Holmes, *Seventeenth-Century Lincolnshire* (Lincoln, 1980), p. 195.

[89] This is a reference to a petition that the corporation had had drawn up in London and presented to the Commons 'for p[ro]cureing from the Parliam[en]t a settled mainteynance for o[u]r ministers, & to have the election of o[u]r owne ministers, and for cutting off the dependence of the parishes from Hessle and Ferreby, and for monies to repaire the ruines about the town as have beene occasioned by the warres ...': HCA, Hull bench bk. 5, pp. 652–3.

[90] This is probably a reference to John Blakiston, MP for Newcastle-upon-Tyne, the chairman of the Committee for Petitions.

p[ro]vision for the navy. Then, I doubt not but they will take care for a guard for our northerne coast. I have acquainted divers of my freinds what great losses our p[or]te sustaine for want of it...

The treaty is appointed to be at Uxbridge ... If they at Oxford be as desirus of peace as wee, I hope God will give a blessing to it ... You may p[er]ceive how active they are when they are about a treaty, but it pleaseth God to blast there designes...

L331: Pelham, Westminster 11 Feb. 1645
... As for treaty at Uxbridge, I expect noe good issue; more then halfe of the tyme being expended & nothing concluded ... You may p[er]ceive what counsells are p[re]domina[n]t; wee conceive the queen's (though absent). Our great businesse now is to have a good army in the feild & a navy by sea, w[hi]ch I hope ere long wee shall inioy. S[i]r Tho: Fairfax is expected dayly, w[hi]ch I hope may settle our army...

I did advize you formerly to make use of your charters to p[re]vent unfree men for [*sic*] trading in your towne ... if any thing happen to your disadvantage let me suffer (although your recorder's advice be to the contrary).

Old S[i]r Henry Vane hath beene w[i]th me divers tymes about yo[u]r fee farme[91]...

L333: Pelham, Westminster 18 Feb. 1645
... Wee expect noe good by the treaty ... Wee hope wee shall have an army in the feild very shortly, to be commanded by S[i]r Tho: Fairfax, and a navy at sea now yt the House hath made choyse of new commissioners to mannage the customes...

Coronell Overton[92] hath written to me to desire yt he may be in Hull w[i]th his regiment when there is an alteration of government. You may doe as you please. I conceive they have beene allwayes faythfull to you...

This New Moddell causeth a great alteration; there are greate distractions in our army (I pray God unite them)...

L334: Pelham, Westminster 25 Feb. 1645
... This day I have not seene Mr Coleman. I make noe question but he is yours, as he hath tould me. But in regard the treaty is ended, I hope w[i]thin few dayes wee shall have the report made for the maintenance of your preachers. I conceive it better to forbeare to desire his possitive answere until yt be done.

[91] Sir Henry Vane senior, MP for Wilton, Wiltshire, was chairman of the Committee for Revenue.
[92] Colonel Robert Overton.

Our commissioners came yesterday from Uxbridge. They have taken a great deale of paines. As they tould me they sate up often until 4 a clocke in the morning ... The witte of Oxford could not outwit them. Our intentions were really for peace, the others did nothing but equivocate ... Our businesse in the House is now to have a good navy at sea and a good army under the commaund of S[i]r Tho: Fairfax, w[hi]ch I hope will speedily be accomplished. The Londoners, having incurragement from the House, will raise a great army, as divers of them have informed me...

The States' ambassadors, who came lately from Oxford, were rec[eived] into the House upon there desires. There herangue in French gave noe great content...

In man's iudgment this is like to be a bloody summer, except God in his mercy doe reconcile these grand distractions...

L335: Pelham, Westminster 4 Mar. 1645
... This day I spoke w[i]th Mr Corbut[93] and acquainted him w[i]th what he had written to you.[94] He tould me he was inioyned by the committee to write to you. When I was at the committee they were of another mind. I tould them he[95] was soe assest for his greate trade, being not a free man. I am of sev[er]all other committees yt I seldome attend that committee. His letter is very faire to doe that w[hi]ch is agreeable to law & justice. I tould him this day that by yt rule they might assesse him £5 p[er] weeke in regard of his greate trading. He will gaine nothing by contending w[i]th the towne of Hull. I am confident the House doe nothing to your p[re]iudice. Thefore I desire you that you would p[ro]ceede against unfree men...

L340: Pelham, Westminster 11 Mar. 1645
...I spoke w[i]th Mr Corbut this day and did acquaint him of the inconvenience to have witnesses examined at Yorke concerning the sub-commissioners for excise. He tould me he was willing it should be examined at Hull. This afternoone they had soe much businesse that I could not git a motion made. Against the next post I hope to p[ro]cure an order to have the businesse examined at Hull...

[93] Miles Corbett, MP for Great Yarmouth, Norfolk, and joint chairman with Laurence Whitaker of the Committee of Examinations.

[94] For the Committee of Examinations' letter to the mayor, signed by Corbett, see Wildridge, *Hull Letters*, p. 52. Corbett informed the mayor that the committee had upheld the complaint of James Melthorpe (a mercer and alderman of Beverley, and a sub-commissioner for the excise at Hull) that he had been over-assessed by the town authorities. The committee order the mayor to make appropriate redress to Nelthorpe. The town's dispute with Nelthorpe can be followed in the Hull letters and in the corporation minute books: HCA, Hull bench, bk. 5, pp. 620, 651, 652, 664, 712.

[95] i.e. Nelthorpe.

L342: Pelham, Westminster 18 Mar. 1645

... W[i]th some difficultie, at the Committee for Examinations, I p[ro]cured an order to have the businesse betwixt our neighbours & the sub-commissioners examined at Hull by the maior, the governer,[96] and S[i]r Mathew Boynton.[97] I assure you I was strongly opposed by the commissioners for excise. They had divers that spoke for them to have the businesse examined at Yorke by that committee. Nelthorpe writs yt he doth not keepe open his shop, as yt you have assest him at 50s p[er] weeke merely because he was a sub-commissioner. I tould them it was in respect of his great trade. They thought 50s p[er] weeke was very much. He p[ro]cured a letter from my Lord Fairfax one [*sic*] his behalfe of his good service & how he had suffered.[98] Mr Corbut was p[re]sent, but Mr Whitterkers[99] had the chaire that day. They were vext they had not there wills to have the witnesses examined at Yorke.

This day I did not meete w[i]th the chaire man for sequestrations,[100] therefore I can write nothing at p[re]sent concerning S[i]r Michael Wharton[101] ...

L347: Pelham, Westminster 8 Apr. 1645

... Upon the receipt of yours to the Committee for Sequestrations, I acquainted the chairman, Sergeant Wilde, who ordered yt you should have a copy of S[i]r Michael Warton's petition ... The chairman tould me there is sufficient to make him a delinquent.

There was a petition p[re]ferred against the towne of Hull at the Committee for Examinations for the great assessments of cittizins[102] & others; some say £3 a weeke, when the best men in towne pay but 1s. I was not p[re]sent at the deliv[er]y of the petition, but some friends in my absence spoke for our towne, & since, I have spoken w[i]th Mr Corbut ...

The Speaker tould me you were in his debt £5 p[er] ann[um]. I askt him how many years. He replyed 6 or 7, but would not advise me to write to you ...

---

[96] Ferdinando 2nd Lord Fairfax, MP for Yorkshire; appointed governor of Hull in July 1643.

[97] Sir Matthew Boynton resided at Barmston, which lay about 20 miles north of Hull. He was elected a recruiter MP for Scarborough, Yorkshire, in October 1645. The Committee of Examinations order was dated 18 Apr. 1645, and was signed by Laurence Whitaker: HCA, M217.

[98] In a letter dated from York, 6 Mar. 1645 (L337), Fairfax informed the mayor that he had written on Nelthorpe's behalf to the Committee of Examinations.

[99] Laurence Whitaker, MP for Shaftesbury, Dorset, and joint chairman, with Miles Corbett, of the Committee of Examinations.

[100] John Wylde, serjeant-at-law and MP for Worcestershire.

[101] Sir Michael Wharton of Beverley, Yorkshire.

[102] i.e. Londoners.

L348: Pelham, Westminster 8 Apr. 1645

. . . I am glad you hold Nelthrope at stave's end. I imagine our townsmen will make good profe against him. I wonder he should say I p[ro]mist any mittigation of his assessment or delivery of his goods, or yt I should show your letters to his freind. I have showed somthing to Corbut as the reason why he was soe assest. My desposition is such yt I care for noe chairman noe further then I finde him for ye publique. I tould Mr Corbut that I wondered he would send for Hull men soe far, when there intentions were for the publique. I expected better respects from him. He tould me he did not know they were Hull men. I am confident you neede not feare any committee to doe you any p[re]iudice. I doe not spend £500 p[er] ann[um] here for nothing. I have noe end of my owne. My ambition is to doe you & your towne service . . .

L350: Pelham, Westminster 15 Apr. 1645

. . . Yours of the 12th instant I rec[eived], whereby I p[er]ceive how you are oprest by the Londoners. I shall doe what I can to p[re]vent complaints to the House, but if they doe complaine I suppose they will have small incurragement to offer any iniery to the towne of Hull.

I askt the Speaker this day for what he should have rec[eive]d a fee from the towne of Hull, & yt if you had knowne of any such fee due to him you would not have beene in arrears. He was unwilling to tell me what it was for, but sayd you did usually pay him such a fee, but now he tould me he was not in counsell for you. I askt him if it were concerning the blockhouses etc. He tould me yes, but would not have had me written to you. This I leave to your consideration.

I spoke this day w[i]th Mr Coleman. I hope he will be w[i]th you ere long . . .

The Lords & Commons being now displaced out of all offices civill & millitary, there are sev[er]all committees of Lords and Commons named, and to be named, for the admiraltie, the revennue, and for placeing of new governers in castles & townes yt were commanded by members of either House. That committee should have sate yesterday, where I did attend, & have acquainted divers of them of your desires. I p[er]ceive there is a designe to put in a stranger upon you, and noe northerne man, w[hi]ch I hope, by the meanes of my friends, I shall p[re]vent. But I know noe other way then by nominating S[i]r Tho: Fairfax, w[hi]ch I intend to morrow. This afternoone I waited upon him, & tould him my intentions & your desires, w[hi]ch he tooke very kindly, & hath p[ro]mist me yt if it be conferd upon him, he will substitute Mr Malleveror[103] according to your desire. I p[er]ceive by

---

[103] Colonel John Mauleverer. Mauleverer had served as deputy-governor of Hull under Lord Fairfax, and commanded the regiment that garrisoned the town: Charles Firth and Godfrey Davies, eds, *The Regimental History of Cromwell's Army* (Oxford, 1940), p. 529.

your northerne Burgesses yt they have noe desire yt Mr Malleveror should command at Hull. They say he is strange to them & soe he is to most of the House. He would not have beene nominated in the House w[i]thout much difficulty. I hope the other way will take...

L351: Pelham, Westminster 22 April 1645

... As I writ you, there was much labouring to have put a new governor uppon you, w[hi]ch was one of the Earle of Laister's sonns.[104] I did acquaint divers of my friends of your desyres for Collonell Mauliverer. It seemes he lives far remote from our Yorkshire Burgesses; they tould me they did not know him. P[er]ceiving that he was not knowne to the House, it being a towne of that consequence, I saw small hopes to accomplish your desires by nominating him, although the nomination was referd to a committee of Lords & Commons to p[re]sent names to the houses. In the interim, I tooke the boldnesse in the House of Commons to desire that S[i]r Tho: Fairfax might be the governor of Hull, w[hi]ch past both houses that day w[i]th little opposition. I did acquaint S[i]r Tho: Fairfax the day before w[i]th my intentions and your desires for Collonell Mauliveror. He tooke it as a great favour, and p[ro]mist before S[i]r Tho: Widdrington[105] and my selfe that if he were made governor, you should have him you desired ... S[i]r Tho: Widdrington hath p[ro]mist by this post to write to my Lord Fairfax[106] to desire his Lordship to write to S[i]r Tho: Fairfax to substitute Collonell Mauliverer, soe that I make no question but you will have asmuch as you desyred, and one of the most eminent p[er]sons in the kingdome in the eye of the Parliament, who, I am confident, will be ready to doe you any curtesie.

... There was a letter read at the committee[107] this afternoone from Mr Nelthorpe, that his great assessment is continued, notwithstanding there were sev[er]all letters written to the maior from this committee, & some other obiections, w[hi]ch I answered, & tould them the committee should heare from you by the next post ... I did acquaint the committee of your greivances; I desire you to write at large of your sufferings by

---

[104] Robert Sidney, 2nd Earl of Leicester, had two sons: Philip Sidney, Viscount Lisle, and Algernon Sidney. It is likely that Algernon Sidney was the son referred to here. In 1645, Algernon Sidney was appointed governor of Chichester, which lay close to the Sussex estate of his uncle, the Earl of Northumberland, who had been the younger Vane's patron at Hull in the elections to the Long Parliament: Jonathan Scott, *Algernon Sidney and the English Republic, 1623–1677* (Cambridge, 1988), p. 43.

[105] Sir Thomas Widdrington, MP for Berwick-upon-Tweed. Widdrington was Lord Fairfax's son-in-law and man-of-business. He was also chairman of the Northern Committee.

[106] Governor of Hull until forced to resign his commission under the self-denying ordinance.

[107] i.e. The Committee of Examinations.

interlop[er]s to the Speaker and to the Committee of Examinations the next post, that if there come any complaints to the House we may be ready for an answere ... They did nominate some others to this committee w[hi]ch I would not accept against.[108] I tould them our desire was that the truth might be discov[er]ed ...

L353: Pelham, Westminster 1 May 1645
... Upon the post day I was long at the Committee of Examintions & had your letter read. To morrow is appointed for that businesse, where I intend to be w[i]th divers of my friends ...

It hath pleased the House of Commons to hono[u]r me w[i]th another imployment. They have appointed one lord & two of the House of Commons to command their summer fleete[109] ... so that I feare I shall not be able to doe you any service here in p[er]son this 6 mounthes,[110] but my freinds have p[ro]missed me to doe what they can for the towne of Hull. Mr Whitterkers coming amongst the rest to salute me, I desired him to take noe informations against the towne of Hull. He p[ro]mist faire. I am confident the House of Commons hath a very good opinion of your towne. When you have any occasion to write, I desire you to addresse your letters to S[i]r Will[ia]m Strickland,[111] who doth much respect your towne & hath p[ro]mist me to doe what lyeth in his power for you. I have divers other friends w[hi]ch I could have made bould w[i]th, but I thincke him the fittest man in regard he is your neighbour & a man that you may confide in. I assure you, in my absence you will not be destitute of freinds in the House of Commons ...

L360: Pelham, Westminster 13 May 1645
... I have spoken w[i]th the chairemen at the Committee of Examinations.[112] Mr Corbut tould me the assessments were to high. I answered 'let them desist from trading & there assessments should be remitted'.

---

[108] On 22 Apr. 1645, the Committee of Examinations ordered that John Anlaby, Thomas St. Nicholas, and Richard Darley (all leading Yorkshire committeemen) be added to the committee set up on 18 March, consisting of the mayor, Lord Fairfax, and Sir Matthew Boynton, to examine the dispute between the sub-commissioners of the excise and the Londoners trading at Hull, and the town authorities (see L342): HCA, M220.

[109] On 28 Apr. 1645, the Commons appointed Pelham and Alexander Bence to serve alongside the Earl of Warwick as commissioners to command the fleet over the summer. Pelham and Bence were chosen as experienced seamen: *CJ*, iv. 125, 128; BL, Add. MS 31116, pp. 413–14.

[110] In the event, the appointment of Commons' commissioners to assist the Earl of Warwick was blocked in the Lords, and thus Pelham remained at Westminster: see L361.

[111] Sir William Strickland, MP for Hedon, Yorkshire.

[112] Miles Corbett and Laurence Whitaker.

Whatsoever they doe at the Committee of Examinations, I tould him the towne of Hull will finde freinds in the House of Commons.

I have spoken to divers to leave out Hill out of the Northerne Association, but I feare it will not be graunted. They say you escape better then any of your neighbours. If you cannot be exempted I have taken care for a committee for Hull. I thincke the charge will not be much...

The reason why there is nothing done for your ministers is because as yet I could never git Mr Blakestone[113] to make his report. To morrow is appointed for hearing of petitions. He hath p[ro]mised me, if he can be heard, to make yt report to morrow. Yours was the first petition yt was reade at the committee...

I have spoken w[i]th the Parliment's gunnfounder, w[i]th whom I am well acquainted, about the touch hole of your basilisce[114] ... You may consider uppon it, & if I be called suddenly to Sea, S[i]r Will[ia]m Strickland, S[i]r Tho: Widdrington, my cousin Henry Pelham,[115] who is well acquainted w[i]th this gunnfounder, have p[ro]missed to doe what lyeth in there power for the towne of Hull, & soe have divers others. Soe that I hope in my absence you will not want freinds. S[i]r Will[ia]m Strickland's lady being in the cuntry causeth his absence sometymes from the House...

I heare now yt the chairman of examinations[116] hath written to you about the assessments. You have allways an appeale to the House of Commons, and there you shall have right...

L361: Pelham, Westminster 20 May 1645

... Yours of the 17th instant I rec[eived]. Mr Whitterkers I have not seene since. I spoke w[i]th Mr Corbut this day. He tells me he knoweth nothing of the businesse. If it come to the House of Commons I doubt not but you will find favour. I have indeavoured to oppose your associatio[n] w[i]th the northerne p[ar]ts at the committee. There was noe hope to p[re]vaile. When it comes to the House I shall use the best meanes I can to p[re]vent it.

As yet I cannot git the report made for the maintenance of your ministers, although I have importuned him[117] divers tymes. I hope to remaine here to doe you service; the Lords not concurring w[i]th the

---

[113] John Blakiston, the chairman of the Committee for Petitions.
[114] A large brass canon throwing a shot of about 200 pounds weight.
[115] Henry Pelham, MP for Grantham, Lincolnshire.
[116] This is a reference to letters from the Committee of Examinations (L345, L358), dated in April and May, and signed by Laurence Whitaker, ordering the mayor to reduce the 'heavy and unheard of' assessments that the town had laid upon Nelthorpe and citizens of London trading in Hull.
[117] John Blakiston.

House of Commons about our command at sea. Our House hath inioyned the Committee for the Admiraltie to give a commission and instructions to Cap: Battin[118] to command in cheife, w[hi]ch I heare hath displeased the Earle of Warwicke. His Lordship p[ro]ffered me many curtesies. It is sayd he dislike my p[ar]tner[119] ...

L362: Thorpe, London 20 May [1645]

... yest[er]day afternoone, being a comittee day for o[u]r northern ordinance, I acquainted them as before w[i]th yo[u]r desyres of being left out of the Associac[i]on. Then S[i]r Tho: Widdrington p[ro]duced yo[u]r lre writt to M[r] Pelham, & by him deliv[er]d ov[er] to S[i]r Thom[as], w[hi]ch was redd, but the reasons theirin, or what I cold [*sic*] say, p[re]vayld not to leave you out, and yo[u]r allegacon that yo[u]r civill gov[er]nm[en]t wilbe trampled upon & you made p[ar]cell of the East Riding was conceyvd a mistake. Afterward, M[r] Pelham came in & I acquanted him what had past, & I p[er]ceyv he thincks to get it stoppt in the House when the ordinance coms to be voted their. Ag[ain]st w[hi]ch tyme, and I beleyve it wilbe next week at furthest, I thinck it is not amiss you write to S[i]r H. Vayne jun[ior] & to the Speak[er] ... That though you desyre not, nor thinck yo[u]r selvs able, to stand alone, yet you haveing a gov[er]nor whom you know, & of whom so great & good testimonyes have bene given, you fear, if yo[u]r town shalbe subiected to other comands & comand[er]s, yo[u]r townsmen may be disgusted by it, & p[er]haps distracted by cross & co[n]trary comands ... This letter now sent to the Speak[er] is rec[eive]d well, yet if you transcribe it agayn, and leave out that last part (as to interruption to yo[u]r civill gov[er]nm[en]t), and add some of these now aminded to you, I think it wilbe bett[er], and may come tyme inough next week, but if the occasion require it sooner, I shall deliv[er] this and speak to S[i]r Henry Vayn and do what I can. But things of the House must be done in the House, and M[r] Pelham and yo[u]r frends their must labor it for you...

I have deliv[er]d yo[u]r letter to M[r] Goodwin,[120] whose goodwill and good affecons to you is not to be doubted...

L365: Pelham, Westminster 27 May 1645

... I doe p[er]ceive how the businesse is p[ro]secuted for Nelthorpe at the Committeee of Examinations. I spoke w[i]th Mr Corbut about yt businesse. He tould me he knoweth nothing of it. This day in the House I spoke w[i]th Mr Whitterkers. I tould him I thought your

---

[118] Captain William Batten.
[119] Alexander Bence.
[120] Robert Goodwin, MP for East Grimstead, Sussex.

reasons might have given good satisfaction, & further that I would move the House of Commons how the towne of Hull sufferd by unfree men trading there etc. He desired me to forbeare and that they would take some course in it. I know Gosse,[121] the sollicitor for the commissioners of excise, is p[re]valent at yt committee,[122] yet I have beene an occausion of his quitting the room, & have still a higher apeale. I have spoken often about your feefarme rent ... I intend to speake w[i]th some of yt committee[123] at the first opp[or]tunitie ... As for your ministers, Association etc., you shall finde my best assistance. S[i]r Henry Vane hath p[ro]mist to ioyne w[i]th me ...

L366: Thorpe, London 27 May [1645]
... I have rec[eive]d yo[u]rs w[i]th the inclosed, but I have deliv[er]d none yet till the season approch nerer. The ordinance is not fully finisht w[i]th the comittee,[124] But aganst [sic] that tyme & the reporting th[er] of to the House I shall take my opportunityes.

I intend also to wayte upon both the committees of Reven[n]ue & Exa[m]i[n]ac[i]ons when they sitt to know the result of yo[u]r lres to them, and shall do what service I may theirin ...

L368: Thorpe, 3 June [1645]
... Fryday last was the northern ordinance reported to the House, & much debated concerning you, and th[er]upon recom[m]itted to the comittee back agayn, who met yest[er]day theirupon, & where was a verye full companye & where the matt[er] was fully agitated. But after long debate, as I p[er]ceyve (for all who were no memb[er]s were putt out), The matt[er] is voted agayn against you, & yt you shalbe ioyned to the Associac[i]on ...

Touching yo[u]r feefarm arrers: I was w[i]th M[r] Pelham the oth[er] day befor the Comittee of Reven[n]ue, & had much debate & disco[u]rse about the business. But for conclusion, no remedy but mony ... Affirmacons are here, w[i]th much vehemencye, urged of yo[u]r great wealth & advantage you, and onely you, have made of these tymes, w[hi]ch though opposed by those who are sensible inough of the co[n]trary, yet is not heard nor beleyvd. Howbeit, I must do yo[u]r p[ar]ticul[er] frends right, to whom you have made yo[u]r addresses. They have donn their p[ar]ts.

Touching the Comittee of Exa[m]i[n]acon business: M[r] Pelham

---

[121] Possibly Samuel Gosse, a citizen of London and receiver of moneys at Guildhall: *Calendar of the Committee for Advance of Money*, pp. 128–30.
[122] The Committee of Examinations.
[123] The Committee for Revenue.
[124] The Northern Association ordinance in the Northern Committee.

tells me he doubts not but to rectify it in the House howev[er] they dispose it their.

... I deliv[er]d yo[u]r lres upon Fryday morning last to M[r] Pelham yt he might deliv[er] them to the Speaker & S[i]r Hen: Vayn in the House when the ordinance was reading, having my self first acquainted them w[i]th the business & ingaged them to the care of it.

L369: Pelham, Westminster 3 June 1645
... I deliv[er]d the letters you sent to the Speaker & to S[i]r Henry Vane. They were both willing to doe you any curtesie. Your letter was read at the committee.[125] There was a long debate about your associating w[i]th the northerne counties. Very much was sayd for it & against it. In the conclusion it was voted yt you should associat ... Divers of our House would p[er]swade me that it is better for yout to associat, but I am not of that beleefe. One obiection was that you could not defend the towne of your selves. I tould them you had done it...

It was demanded how you should take notice of such an ordinance. Wee ought not to give notice untill the businesse be done. You writ me of names inclosed, but there was none but those names yt you sent to the Speaker, [which] the chairman[126] hath. When it comes to the House wee will see what can be done. The Yorkeshire men say they are all undone & you are growne rich. I tould them yt I was informed yt £10,000 would not make all good about the towne yt you had suffered dureing these warrs...

I was sent to by the Committee for the Revennue. I sent to Mr Thorpe to be there, who came thither. They were very forward to have sent for Mr Raikes.[127] I cannot conceive any any meanes how to p[re]vent the nonpayment of the fefarme...

L370: Thorpe to the mayor [c.3 June 1645]
... The Northern Associac[i]on is now to be establisht, wherein you must consider both the military & civill pow[er] to be exercised their by the comittee of the Associac[i]on.
... Touching yo[u]r town: The whole afternoon upon Thursday last was spent in debate, but yo[u]r burgess not attending by reason, I p[re]sume, of his great[er] imploym[en]ts,[128] all I cold [*sic*] say according to yo[u]r short instruccons I did say, and all I cold [*sic*] obtayn is this: that this ordinance of Association shall not hinder or alt[er] any monyes form[er]ly ordred or dyrected for pay of yo[u]r garrison, nor hinder or

[125] The Northern Committee, chaired by Sir Thomas Widdrington.
[126] Sir Thomas Widdrington.
[127] The mayor of Hull.
[128] This is probably a sarcastic reference to Pelham rather than Vane.

alter any pow[er] form[er]ly given to S[i]r Tho: Farfax as gov[er]nor...

S[i]r, you see of what consequence these things may be to you. Bethinck yo[u]r selvs of it, & write yo[u]r lres to be seasonably deliv[er]d when their is cause, for to write to p[er]sons who can do you no good, or to write lres at unseasonable tymes (though to fitt p[er]sons) p[ro]duces the same effect − of nothinge.

... Touching yo[u]r business about yo[u]r tradesmen & M[r] Nelthorp, I can give you noe account because no p[ro]ceeding th[er]bouts hath bene communicated to me here since I came up, nor wheth[er] the certificate I drew for you to be deliv[er]ed, nor what effect it hath p[ro]duced. But yo[u]r lre to the Speak[er] in this cold [*sic*] be of litle· use because the businesse passes not that way...

And touching yo[u]r minist[er]: that is a House business, & must be p[ro]moted & attended their, but I shall do what I can abroad...[129]

I doubt the men you are put upon in the House will not do much in yo[u]r affayres; the one seldom attending, & the other being at p[re]sent not well, & when well extreme full of business.[130] But I shall observ if they do any thing, & give you notice to thanke them.

L371: Thorpe, 10 June [1645]
... This week brings you the news that our ordinance for the Northern Associac[i]on is past & you are ioyned in it, your business to that purpose haveing bene the onely subiect of debate it had, & much opposic[i]on about yo[u]r exempcon yo[u]r freinds, w[hi]ch were very many, made in it. But at last it is resolved as before, yet w[i]th such qualificac[i]ons touching you as do much prevent any of those dang[er]s you feare. And for the gent[leman] you name,[131] he hath nothing to do alone, nor can any thing be donne in the millitary p[ar]te concerning you w[i]thout consent of yo[u]r gov[er]nor ... I dare assure you, you are much beholdeing to M[r] Rob[er]t Goodwin, & to S[i]r Will[ia]m Strickland. Other men who serve for you or who are strang[er]s to you I name them not, though theire is a dett of thankfulness due to them all...

L373: Pelham, Westminster 10 June 1645
... As I writ you formerly, there was very much sayd against your associating w[i]th the rest of the northerne counties, but by our

[129] Thorpe was not an MP at this stage.

[130] Thorpe appears to be referring here to Pelham and Vane respectively. Pelham was named to just eight committees in 1645, which may suggest that he did not attend the Commons on a regular basis.

[131] The gentlemen the corporation named was evidently Sir Matthew Boynton: see L378. The corporation feared that Boynton was eager to promote religious Independency in the town: Wildridge, *Hull Letters*, p. 38.

neighbours one [sic] both sides the river, w[i]th divers others, it was carried against us ... I p[er]ceive wee have very ill neighbours. I conceive the best way for you will be to petition the House of Commons, & to let them know what you have done & suffered ... Git as many hands to it as you can, and when Mr Henry Barnard,[132] or some other of our neighbours, come up, you send it. A few may serve to deliver it at the barr. I hope it will stop the mouthes of those that conceive you to be soe rich etc.

L375: Pelham, Westminster 24 June 1645

... This day in the House of Commons I spoke w[i]th Mr Corbut & Mr Whitterkers, the chaire men at the Committee for Examinations. I acquainted them how you suffered by unfree men trading there ... I tould them likewise how there order was disobeyed. I suppose you will heare noe more of them. I shall be putting them in mind of your sufferings, and shall still presse our chaireman[133] to make a report about our ministers ...

The king's cabinet was taken [at Naseby], wherein were great store of letters.[134] The reading of p[ar]t of them tooke up yesterday, the House sitting untill 9 a Clocke at night. Divers were not reade. They are all referred to a committee. There are many caracters or figures in them. I hope a key will be found to open there locks. Enough is discov[er]ed to demonstrate what religion the king fights for ...

L376: Thorpe, London 24 June [1645]

... Yo[u]rs I r[eceive]d & shall not fayle to serve you in yo[u]r desyres touching yo[u]r businesse here.

I send here inclosed what both you & I have long desyred, viz. the ordinance for the Northern Associacion. You will p[er]ceyve by it how all things are settled & how the form[er] co[u]rse is alterd. I wish I were w[i]th you at yo[u]r first entring upon the execuc[i]on of it, for many things are considerable, especially to men that desyre to p[ur]sue their rule. And I do assure you I see the danger in other men's business here of treading awrye.

I can write you litle news this week save what the prints bring ... Yesterday was wholly spent in the House of Comons in p[er]using the lres & pap[er]s taken in some cabbinetts in the last fight, [and] sayd to be the king's & many secretts are now layd open, & I belevye [sic] layd more open th[er]by. But nothing yet is published of them.

---

[132] Henry Barnard was an alderman of Hull.

[133] John Blakiston.

[134] These letters revealed Charles's plans for using Irish and foreign troops in England. The bulk of this correspondence was published by Parliament.

L378: Sir Thomas Widdrington to the mayor, 30 June 1645
... The letter written by yourselfe & the aldermen of Hull to Sir
Thomas Fairfax ... was sent by him to a friend of his in towne, w[i]th
his earnest care to have yo[u]r desires therein effected as much as
might be. And my selfe being acquainted therew[i]th I thought fitt in
his absence (he being now gone into the west w[i]th his army) to give
yow this accomptt for the exemption of Hull from ye Northerne
Association. Though it were much desired & insisted upon by some,
yet it could not be effected ... In this ordynance[135] there be, besides
the Members of the House, sev[er]all gent[lemen] named in ye sev[er]all
rydings and other counties for man[n]ageing the military p[ar]te ...
And for yt purpose Sir Mathew Boynton is named for ye East Ryding &
Hull, but by yt p[ar]ticular designac[i]on hath noe more powre ov[er]
Hull then the rest of the com[m]ittee have...

L379: Pelham, the Fish Yard, 1 July 1645
... If it please God to give our army a victory in the west to beate
the king's army, it will be very difficult for his ma[jes]tie to raise another
army. When his letters are published I doubt not but it will much
obstruct his p[ro]ceedings.
    I will speake with the chairemen[136] about there last order ... I have
divers tymes spoken about the imployment of Henry Appleton's ship &
for ordnance for her; I spoke to my Lord of Warwicke when he had
command, to S[i]r Henry Vane, & divers of the Committee for the
Navy. I spoke likewise w[i]th yt was lieutenant of the ordnance.[137] He
tould me there was noe iron ordnance in the store ... I have spoken
w[i]th the Committee for the Revennue. I tould them yt by this last
ordnance,[138] all the arrears for the king & queen's revennue are to be
imployed in the north for maintenance of that army[139] ...
    Those names that you sent for the committee I gave to the chairemen,
but I p[er]ceive there hath beene some omission – divers left out. I
spoke to S[i]r Tho: Widdrington about it.
    I am not unmindful of maintenance for your ministers. The chai-
reman[140] hath had sufficient tyme to have made his report...

[135] The ordinance for the Northern Association.
[136] Miles Corbett and Laurence Whitaker, chairmen of the Committee of Examinations.
[137] Sir Walter Earle, MP for Weymouth and Melcombe Regis, Dorset. He was forced
to resign his place as lieutenant of the ordnance by the self-denying ordinance.
[138] The ordinance for the Northern Association.
[139] The Northern Association army.
[140] John Blakiston.

L383: Pelham, Westminster 15 July 1645

... I have had of late extraordinary businesse w[hi]ch did p[re]vent my writing to you. Your letters I delivered. As for the maintenance for your ministers, I have spoken divers tymes about it. It is conceived that will be a generall businesse throughout the kingdome. There is noe hopes at p[re]sent to alter the ordinance for Association. Our generall & your governor hath gained soe much hono[u]r yt you shall not need to fear yt any thing will be p[re]iudiciall to you or his government...

I have sent you by the post the king's letters etc.,[141] whereby you may p[er]ceive that there is noe hopes of peace but by the sword...

L384: Pelham to the mayor, Westminster 16 July 1645

... I did appeare at the committee for the navy w[i]th the East Cuntry m[er]chants, and will assist the best I can when it comes to the House...

L389: Pelham, Westminster 29 July 1645

... I have spoken to divers of my friends about the imployment of Mr Appleton & his ship. I have some hopes from freinds to accomplish your desires ... W[i]th the first opp[or]tunitie I will speake w[i]th the chairman for sequestrations[142] (who is my freind)...

L391: Pelham, Westminster 11 Aug. 1645

... I did confer with S[i]r Tho: Widdrington about the ordinance for maintenance for your ministers. He had heard of some defecte in it. When that ordinance comes in question in the House I doubt not but to have yours incirted. There hath beene a fault in the chairma[n][143] that did not make the report, yours being the first petition of yt nature yt was read at the committee. As an opp[or]tunitie doth p[re]sent I shall use the best meanes for obtaining those two you writ for.

This day I spoke w[i]th the chairman of examinations, Mr Whitterkers. I tould him I wondred he would send for the maior upon such informations, himselfe and the towne having done such good service for the publique etc. I will take such a course that I hope there shall be noe contempt for non aparance.

This day it was ordred yt your garrison should be payd out of the customes & excize. It is thought by diverse of the House yt the customes & excize are to much to maintaine yt garrison. There was much obiected in regard the customs are usually imployed for the navy...

[141] The king's letters captured at Naseby.
[142] John Wylde.
[143] John Blakiston.

L394: Henry Barnard to the mayor, London 19 Aug. 1645

... This is to accquaint you that at my coming to London on Fryday last I repared to Mr Pellam his lodging, where I desired to be informed whither any thing had bene moved either in P[ar]lament or elsewhere to the p[re]iudice of o[u]r towne by any sinister meanes. His answer was that he was no way privy to any such thinge, but wished me to be confident that nothing should be effected for oure disadvantage without timely intelligence both of the authors & ther intents. My request unto him was that he would be myndfull of the contents of yo[u]r last letter ... I told him we must rely wholy now upon his vigillanc[e], especially now in the absenc[e] of his fellow burgesse S[i]r Henry Vane.[144] I doubt not but if his late coniugall imployment[145] be not som hinderanc[e] he will take all care that may be for o[u]r towne's wellfare...

I suppose the motions of the king's army ar better knowne to you then here at London, for reports are very various. Som reporte he is surrounded by the Parlament's forces at Webecke howse;[146] other [sic] that he is gone northwardes toward Scotland; others at Newarke. So that fame maketh him at present ubiquitary...

L396: Barnard to the mayor, Hull[147] 26 Aug. 1645

... I have now brought my owne busines to a period, & shall now, dureing my short time of stay, endeavour to agitate any thing within reach of my capacity for the advantage of the towne. I have bene this afternoone with S[i]r Thomas Witherinton, & have had some conferenc[e] with him how we may revive the deade coales of o[u]r dying peticon for the maintenance of our ministers. We could not resolve upon a way at present, but I have promissed to attend him at Westminster on Thursday next in the afternoone, & there to conferre with him self & Mr Pellham upon the speediest course to be taken for the effecting o[u]r desires. I doe verily believe we shall find him an espetiall frend to the towne of Hull, if we doe not undervalew desertes.

Mr Pellham, as I writt you before,[148] did wish me taike no care about mr maior his appearanc[e] at London. Nevertheless, at my earnest intreaty we both repaired this afternoone to the Committy of Exam-inations ... but after 3 houres attendance of him within & my self without, we could not have p[er]mission to p[re]ferre o[u]r motion. The reason was a bussines of great importanc[e] did take up ther time the whole afternoone ... I must confesse, I fynd Mr Pellam a cordiall

[144] By September 1645, certainly, Vane was preoccupied with fortifying Raby Castle, in County Durham: Rowe, *Vane*, p. 82.
[145] Pelham had just married Dame Jacoba van Lore, widow of Sir Peter van Lore.
[146] Welbeck House, Nottinghamshire, where the king arrived on 15 Aug. 1645.
[147] Although dated from Hull, Barnard is evidently writing from London.
[148] In L394.

man for the towne of Hull, if his owne new undertaken busines[149] doe
not impede ours...

L397: Pelham, Westminster 9 Sept. 1645
... I rec[eived] sev[er]all letters from you, w[hi]ch I did not answer,
having little newes to acquaint you w[i]th, & hearing of the inrodes of
those of Newarke in the post's way, wee conceived all our letters would
be intercepted.

I doe now hope to accomplish your desires for maintenance for your
ministers, having now another chairman,[150] who will not lose [*sic*] his
reporte as the last[151] did, else, no question, the businesse had beene
dispatched long since. This chairman hath p[ro]mist me to doe what
he can the next Fryday in that behalfe. The vote being past at the
committee, I shall git [*sic*] it speedily reported to the House.

This day I spoke w[i]th my Lord Fairfax about 2 or 300 trees for
repairing the defects in your blockhouse etc. I tould him I conceived
the best way was for S[i]r Tho: Fairfax to write to the House about it,
he being governor of the towne. His lordship tould me he thought it
would be fit to move it at the Committee for the North[152] & they to
report it to the House. If our way faile I hope the other will not.

For newes this day wee rec[eived] intelligence from S[i]r Tho: Fairfax
that this weeke they intend to storme Bristoll. At the same tyme our
ships are to send a number of seamen. Prince Rupert is obstinat. S[i]r
Tho: Fairfax sent a trumpet to him to render the towne, w[hi]ch they
heare he hath hanged. This messenger sayeth yt S[i]r Tho: Fairfax will
hang S[i]r Barnard Ashley, one of his prisoners. Those yt come out of
the towne report yt 9 p[ar]ts of 10 are for the Parliament. They beginne
to be straightened for p[ro]visions: a pound of butter being sould for
5s; a loaf of bread at the same rate. 5,000 clubmen are come to S[i]r
Tho: Fairfax & say that they will live & die w[i]th him. Wee heare the
Scots have raised the seiege of Heriford...

L399: Pelham, Westminster 13 Sept. 1645
... I writ to you by the last post that I was in good hope to have
the businesse dispatched at the committee[153] for maintenance of your
ministers, w[hi]ch accordingly was p[er]formed yesterday. The chairman[154] is ordered to make the report of it to the House. I will much

---

[149] i.e. His recent marriage.
[150] The new chairman of the Committee for Petitions was John Goodwin, MP for
Haslemere, Surrey: L419; *CJ*, iv. 317.
[151] John Blakiston.
[152] The Northern Committee, chaired by Fairfax's son-in-law, Sir Thomas Widdrington.
[153] The Committee for Petitions.
[154] John Goodwin.

importune him for the efecting of it. I moved for £300; some thought
£200 to much. S[i]r Tho: Widdrington was our freind...

L404: Pelham, Westminster 23 Sept. 1645
... Your letter to our noble generall was sent by a freind of mine
this morning, who hath p[ro]mised to take care of the businesse; it is
in his power to doe it, being secretary to S[i]r Tho: Fairfax.[155] I deliverd
your letter to S[i]r Tho: Widdrington, who desires to be kindly
remembred to you. Upon the first opp[or]tunitie I will indeavour that
the report be made to the House for maintenance for your ministers...

I have had intimations from the Speaker for some Hull ale. I desire
you to remember him. He takes it for a great favour when you
remember him...[156]

L411: Pelham, Westminster 21 Oct. 1645
... I hoped to have given you a good accompt concerning maintenance for your ministers, but as yet the chairman[157] cannot git [*sic*] it
reported to the House. As for the timber you desire, there is no answere
comed as yet from our noble generall. For your garrison, it will be
reduced to a smaller number. I suppose there will be an establishment
setled for 500 souldiers.

I was sorry to heare of your great losse. Before I heard from you I
had conference w[i]th divers of the Committee for the Admirallitie &
of the Navy about that businesse. If it weere a Hollander, the best way
will be to p[ro]cure a letter from the Admirallitie to our Agent in
Holland. It will be requisit to know whither the shipps & goods were
carried. I hope there will be restoration or satisfaction made. Some are
the more unwilling to graunt a convoy in regard the navy hath noe
benefit from our port, w[hi]ch is not your fault, it being ordered by
the state.

The House is now p[re]paring p[ro]positions to be sente to his
ma[jes]tie. Our generall intended to storme Tiverton Castle in Dev-
onshire upon Saturday last. The malignant gentry come in a pace, &
divers of Goring's officers & souldiers. It is hoped that w[i]th God's
assistance there will be a speedy conclusion of those unhappy warrs...

L413: Thorpe [c. Oct. 1645]
... Touching monyes to be p[ro]cured for yo[u]r rep[ar]ac[i]ons: it
wilbe a hard task (all things put together), yet I shall p[ro]miss you yt

---

[155] John Rushworth, the secretary of the army.
[156] This last sentence was omitted in Wildridge's transcription.
[157] John Goodwin.

w[i]th the first opportunity I will do my indeavo[u]r in it, but you must be content to expect a seasonable tyminge of it.

Touching yo[u]r minister's stipends: if you please to send me up the orders for those stipends w[i]th dyreccons what you desyre & what the mistakes are w[hi]ch you wold have alterd, I shall effect for you what may be obtayned...

Touching o[u]r affayrs here: all at p[re]sent remarkeable are yt we are preparing new proposicons to send to the king. But what the answer & success th[er]upon will be, no man can c[er]tanly know but may p[ro]bably ghess. Mean tyme, let all good men be earnestly zealous in their prayers to God for his mercyes, & yt he will not deale w[i]th us after o[u]r sinnes, nor reward as according to o[u]r iniquityes...

L414: Widdrington to the mayor, 30 Nov. 1645
... Touching those shipps & goods mentioned in y[ou]r letter taken at sea & now at Amsterdam: I have very lately recyved a letter from Mr Strickland[158] w[hi]ch shewes what he [has] done about them, a coppy whereof I herew[i]th send inclosed. I shall joyne w[i]th y[ou]r other frinds here [to? – MS damaged] doe further herein what I am able. Touching y[ou]r other busines for p[ro]curing of a warrant from the Parliam[en]t for tymbers: the generall[159] hath writt about it as you desyred, but nothing is yet further done. But I will give my best assistance I can when opportunity is offered, as also touching that other of setling means for a minister. But the report of that is not yet made to the House...

L416: Thorpe, London 12 Nov. [1645]
... Thursday next is appointed for the business of yo[u]r garriso[n], where [? – MS damaged] I hope to effect what you desyre ... Touching yo[u]r business of £200 p[er] ann[um] for [your? – MS damaged] minist[er], I shall not fayle in [? – MS damaged] tyme & place to [? – MS damaged] it for you, but where [? – MS damaged] or why it sticks I know not [? – MS damaged]. But when I am informed [of the? – MS damaged] obstackle I shall labor to [remove? – MS damaged] it.

I [have? – MS damaged] not yet mett w[i]th S[i]r Thomas [Widdrington's? – MS damaged] counsell, nor have [? – MS damaged] bene w[i]th me to appoint a tyme, & [it is? – MS damaged] not an easy thing to get a man of M[r] Sollic[i]tor's[160] imploym[en]ts leasur. Therefor I thinck you [? – MS damaged] best go on w[i]th yo[u]r

---

[158] Walter Strickland, the Parliamentary agent in Holland.
[159] i.e. Sir Thomas Fairfax.
[160] Oliver St John, MP for Totnes, Devon, and solicitor-general.

sesm[en]t till [they? – MS damaged] stirr & let those who are cold [blow? – MS damaged] the cole...

L417: Thorpe, London 25 Nov. [1645]

... I have r[eceive]d yo[u]r 2 barrells of ale & shall bestow them with some referenc to yo[u]r advantage...

M[r] mayor, I praie you excuse me to M[r] John Shawe[161] yt I wrote not to him.

L418: Thorpe [c.2 Dec. 1645][162]

... Touching yo[u]r garrison: the first day the establishm[en]t was voted I attended & got it effected. But since, a comittee for the north cold [*sic*] nev[er] be gott togeth[er] by reason of other great affayres...

L420: Thorpe, London [7 Dec. 1645]

... Yo[u]r establishm[en]t is fully past the Northern Comittee & is now to be transmitted to the Comittee for the Army, where, if other more publick ingagem[en]ts (whereof I have many in my hand) do not impede me, I shall attend to forward yo[u]r work.

I have now discov[er]d the obstruccon yo[u]r ordinance hath had for yo[u]r minist[er]s their, w[hi]ch was by making it a p[ar]ticul[er] petitio[n] & a p[ar]ticul[er] business, before w[hi]ch other things of publick nature are always p[re]ferrd. Oth[er]wise it might have bene putt in to the ordinance w[i]th York, w[hi]ch yesterday was redd twice & hath past the House & is now w[i]th the Lords for their concurrenc.[163] But yet I have gott good men's p[ro]misses & ingagem[en]ts yt upo[n] the next petition day the report shalbe brought in touching the town, & if I once gett it past the House we shall soune make ready the ordinance for it, & give it what dispatch can be gott therin. And if the speed be not so swift as you expect you must not attribute it to a slackness in yo[u]r friends but to the naturall slowness of all p[ar]ticul[er] businesses in their mocon in the House.

For news you may please to recyv this inclosed w[hi]ch I writt from the originall. The answer to w[hi]ch is this day retornd by the same trumpet who brought it, is that the houses will send an answer by messeng[er]s of their own w[i]th all convenient speed. W[hi]ch answer wilbe o[u]r owne p[ro]posicons, w[hi]ch will suddenly now be finisht,

---

[161] John Shawe was lecturer at Trinity Church, Hull: HCA, Hull bench bk. 5, p. 675. For his life and career see Charles Jackson, ed., 'The Life of Master John Shaw', *Yorkshire Diaries and Autobiographies in the Seventeenth and Eighteenth Centuries*, ed. *idem* (Surtees Society, lxv, 1875); A. G. Matthews, *Calamy Revised* (Oxford, 1934), pp. 434–5.

[162] Received 5 Dec. 1645.

[163] An additional ordinance for the maintenance of ministers in the northern parts passed the Commons on 6 Dec. 1645: *CJ* iv. 367; *LJ*, viii. 50.

for the House hath agreed to sitt fro[m] day to day upon that business onely till they be donne...

L419: Pelham to the mayor, Westminster 9 Dec. 1645

... this day I was p[ro]mist by Mr John Goodwin, the chairman for petitions, to make the report for the maintenance for your ministers, but he hath further p[ro]tracted the tyme untill the next day he can make a report. I have ingaged him & his brother[164] & S[i]r Henry Vane yt he will p[er]forme. Alsoe, upon the first opp[or]tunitie, I have a p[ro]misse that the letter concerning your timber shall be reported to the House...

L421: Thorpe, London 16 Dec. 1645[165]

... Since my last I have soe farre proceeded in the busines for your ministers as to gett itt drawne through those straites in which itt does stickle & would have stucke for ever. And I have got itt putt into such a cleare passage as I hope wilbe more open for itt (viz) by removing itt fro[m] the Com[m]ittee of Petic[i]ons to the Com[m]ittee of Plundered Ministers by whom I am assured itt will receive such expedic[i]on as other greater businesses of the House can p[er]mitte.[166] Howbeitt, if that expedic[i]on be nott such as may answeare the suddennes of your desires you must be content to rest in the assureance that nothing shalbe wanting in me to promote itt for you in due time & place and att the last to give you good accommpt of itt.

The ordinance for Yorke which was talked on above a yeare and was soe long since imp[er]fectly past is butt nowe in mending & lies with the Lords for their Concurrence.

Upon a resoluc[i]on this last weeks that Wressell garrison should be slighted, I moved & itt is ordered accordingely that all the ordinance & am[m]unic[i]on there shalbe deliv[er]ed ov[er] to you. I shall send you the order soe soone as itt can be gotten drawne. In the meane time you may take notice of that busines.

The settlem[en]t of your garrison is, according to our votes att the Northren Com[m]ittee, represented to the Com[m]ittee for the Warre,[167] soe it rests theire debate, resoluc[i]on, & reporte thereupon.

The king's offer of p[ro]posic[i]ons & the House's resoluc[i]on to send theire owne (newe framed & in framing) proposic[i]ons & the Scotts' pap[er]s latelie putt in to the House (and without whose

---

[164] Robert Goodwin.

[165] This letter was not written in Thorpe's hand, but in that of his clerk.

[166] In fact, the town's petition for maintenance of its ministers seems to have remained with the Committee for Petitions: see L420.

[167] The Army Committee.

concurrence nothing canbe done in this treatie) intimateing theire
desires with theire reasons thatt we should onely stand upon the old
proposic[i]ons sent to Uxbridge, filles the House with soe much buisines
in the debates and disputes upon these subiectes as that, during these
agitac[i]ons, all other matters wilbe laid aside...

L422: Pelham, Westminster 16 Dec. 1645
... I cannot as yet give you yt acco[unt] w[hi]ch I desire concerning
the maintenance for your ministers, & timber for your occausions [*sic*].
Mr Goodwin, the chairman for petitions, did p[ro]misse me yesterday
to make that report for the ministers, being solicited by S[i]r Henry
Vane & his brother Robert Goodwin, who doth p[ro]fesse much his
best respects for the towne of Hull. At p[re]sent I cannot much blame
the chairman, being soe much importuned by widowes & others very
much necessitated, although at the committee it was ordered yt it
should be the first petition to be reported...

L423: Widdrington to the mayor, 16 Dec. 1645
... You were pleased to send unto me 2 barrells of Hull ale in Mr
Popple's shipp, for w[hi]ch I desyre hereby to returne you thanks...

L424: Thorpe, Gray's Inn 23 Dec. 1645[168]
... Since my last I have had meeting with Mr Browne,[169] one of the
commission[er]s for the great seale, touching S[i]r John Barrington's[170]
buisines. I find matter of p[ro]ffitt is the thing they aime at. They
affirme that they are told by some of your neighbours that you make
£700 p[er] ann[um] of that water ... I wish some of your neighbours
have nott hands in this business, & that yo[u]r waterpipes have nott
carried a streame of newes of theire benifitt into Essex.
... Our proposic[i]ons to be sent to the king are in prepareing with
what speed may be, with resoluc[i]on nott to treate butt to desire
positive answeares upon them. For the great advantages gained by the
king upon the last treatie, & the designes discov[er]ed in his since
intercepted lres have taught the House that wisedome which otherwise
they could nott have learned...
This day the establishem[en]t of your garrison hath beene debated
att the Com[m]ittee for the Army. But the busines for fire & candle
would nott be listned unto. Your establishem[en]t wilbe pursuant to
that of Bristoll and other the Parl[iamen]t garrisons of the like nature,
and we must be content to accept it...

[168] This letter was written in the same hand as L415.
[169] Samuel Browne, MP for Dartmouth, Devon: see L444, L449, L453, L462, L465.
[170] Sir John Barrington of Hatfield Broad Oak, Essex.

L425: Pelham, Westminster 23 Dec. 1645

... Your letters came soe late that I had little tyme to speake to my freinds concerning your further charge for fire & candle. I conceive you are to deepe already in payments, haveing soe well defraied as the towne of Hull hath done. Yesternight S[i]r Tho: Widdrington & my selfe stayed late in the House of Commons expecting, according to the chairman's[171] p[ro]misse, to have the report made for the maintenance of our ministers, but still refered w[i]th a p[ro]misse to the next day, w[hi]ch is ev[er]y Munday in the afternoone. I am much impatient w[i]th delayes.

This day I spoke w[i]th S[i]r Will[ia]m Strickland about your cloth shipps. He tould me he rec[eived] letters lately from his brother[172] that there is great hopes of restoration. I assure you those whom it doth concern are much obliged to Mr Strickland for his great paines. When he hath finisht the businesse he deserves a good reward.

All the other good newes that I have to acquaint you w[i]th is that Heriford, a place of great consequence, is taken w[i]th little effusion of blood. I hope the rest of the townes that stand out will come in ere long, that wee may have a happy conclusion of these unhappy warres ...

L426: Thorpe, London 30 Dec. 1645[173]

... Since my [last? – MS damaged] what progresse your busines about your minister hath had, [the? – MS damaged] inclosed order will informe you. The difficulty was in the midst of these greate & weightie affaires now in hand to gett your petic[i]on redd ag[ains]t soe much opposic[i]on. The some granted you is equall to them of Yorke Minster.[174] It was publiquely said by some that itt was a shame you should have any thing, considering what wealth you have gott and what advantage you have made by these distracted times. Yet nottwithstanding this & much more, thus farre I have brought itt for you without helpe of your owne Burgesses. I hope now, therefore, if need be for any further agitac[i]on to gett this order into an ordinance, that you will engage them to itt, for I have soe much other more publicke busines upon my hand that I cannot possibly further attend itt as I have done. Perhaps this order may serve your turne. Mr John Penrose of Yorke is receiver of that revenue, and he will informe you what probabillitie of wealth theire wilbe comeing into pay you. I desire that in the deposic[i]on of this pay, when it comes, Mr Shawe may be

---

[171] John Goodwin.

[172] Walter Strickland.

[173] This letter was written in the same hand as L415.

[174] On 29 Dec. 1645 the Commons passed an order for the payment of £150 per annum out of the York dean and chapter lands for the maintenance of a preaching minister at Hull: CJ iv. 389–90.

p[ar]ticulerlie lookte upon with your approbac[i]on...

The newes of the kinge's comeing to towne to treate of peace doth nowe fill all men's mouthes & eares ... itt is gen[er]allie conceived this overture of trreaty att best is butt to gaine time till some forraigne forces, whereof we have notice to be in preparac[i]on, can be gott readie, and in the meane time to sowe seedes of discenc[i]on and disobligac[i]on betwixt the two nac[i]ons, as the three proposic[i]ons treated on att Uxbridge and expounded by one of the king's lres taken att Naseby doe plainely showe, and which proposic[i]ons his ma[jes]tie drives att againe to be first considered upon ... Butt five yeares experience hath taught English men another lesson then to be catcht twice with one stale.[175]

Itt is true that to vulgar apprehensions itt may seeme strann that the king should p[ro]pound to treate first by com[m]issioners and after in p[er]son, and yett nott be embraced. Butt those men must knowe who soe presume to censure, that as they are nott acquainted with the p[ar]ticulers & secretts of the affaire, soe they must be contented to intrust themselves in the handes of [that? – MS damaged] assemblie who nev[er] yett failed ye kingdome. God will in [due? – MS damaged] time settle such a peace and by such meanes as may be a saftie and not a snare to his people...

L293: Pelham [n.d. but c. 1645–6][176]

... I am much importuned for Hull ale dayly, both by Lords and Commons, who are willing to further me in any thing that concerns your towne, and I shall have occasion to use my friends. I expect noe assistance by your neighbours. Those yt serve for remote p[ar]ts are my best friends. If it please you to send to me a tonne of Hull ale, and leave it to my desposeing, it will not be lost, but will be wellcome, although it be late. In steade of jug-heads I will make bottled many of our friends w[hi]ch are best knowne to me...

L427: Thorpe, 13 Jan. [1646]

... Touching yo[u]r order for yo[u]r minist[er]: I got it past our House & then expected that yo[u]r own Burgess[177] wold have gotten it drawn up into an ordinance as it ought to be, & th[er]by to have ascertaynd the tyme of paym[en]t, when to begin, by whom, & to whom to be payd. All w[hi]ch the ordinance shold have supplyed. But

---

[175] A stale was a decoy bird used to entice other birds into a snare or net (*OED*).

[176] L293 somehow ended up in private hands. Hull City Archives only possess a 19th century typescript of it, in which the spelling has been modernised. Wildridge evidently saw the original, and transcribed the section included here, before it was sold. Its whereabouts are now unknown: Wildridge, ed., *Hull Letters*, p. 134.

[177] Thorpe is probably referring to Pelham here rather than Vane.

now I finde the order was by too much zeal to do somth[in]g suddenly taken away before it was drawn into an ordinance, and sent up to the Lords & so the order is onely past their,[178] w[hi]ch mends the matter nothing, for you are still as defective as before, if you be not somthinge worse. But I p[re]sume care wilbe taken to amend all ...

Touching our ordinance of Associacon: it is now und[er] dispute whether we shall co[n]tinue it or not, as also whether their shalbe any more comittees or not, eyther w[i]th us or any where else becaus of the many & great complants [sic] w[hi]ch are dayly made agt them eyther for und[er]doinge or ov[er]doing their duty. Some here have tasted depely of the punishm[en]t due to those who p[re]sume to execute arbitrary justice at their pleasure, w[i]thout rule or reasons. And I do beleyve some others wilbe made more publick examples for it ...

Our much disputed lre is now gone to the king this day in answer to his about a p[er]sonall treaty & co[n]tayning the reasons why denyed. The prince being now in head of an armye in the west & having sent out a p[ro]clamacon in his own name sum[m]oning those cou[n]tryes to come in to his assistance, though it hath p[ro]duced litle effect their, yet it hath begot a com[man]d to him from hence to desist such attempts & to lay down his armes ...

God hath blest us this week w[i]th very good news both out of Ireland, where before Sleegoe the rebells have had a great defeat, as also out of the west, where our army hath taken 400 horse & kild & taken div[er]se p[ri]son[er]s indeavoring to releyve Exet[er] ...

L428: Pelham, Westminster 13 Jan. 1646

... Upon the post day for the north I had an occausion [sic] to be out of towne w[i]th Mr Speaker. The next day your letter came to hand. As for the report for the maintenance of two ministers for Hull, I did attend about a yeare & a halfe, but yt day when the report was made I had occasion to be absent, & I did acquaint S[i]r Henry Vane & others of my freinds that I could not then be in the House. S[i]r Tho: Widdrington tould me he did attend after candles were lighted & noe report was made. If our freinds had beene there I p[re]sume the order might have beene more amply drawne ... Some of the House doe report there are factions in the towne, & did desire me to move the House to send you downe a minister. I hope all these differences will be composed. In my opinion, you cannot pitch uppon an abler, orthodox devine then Mr Stiles[179] ...

---

[178] *LJ*, viii. 80, 81.

[179] William Styles, vicar of Hull. A 'moderate Puritan', he was displaced as vicar in 1650 for refusing to take the Engagement: *VCH, East Riding*, i. 108; *CSPD 1650*, p. 385; *CSPD 1651*, p. 22.

As concerning the monneyes deposited from Ipswich in Mr Denman's hands, I spoke w[i]th Mr Gurden[180] I alsoe spoke w[i]th Mr Corbet...

S[i]r Henry Vaine hath p[ro]mist me to make the report about your timber w[i]th the first opp[or]tunitie.

... I desire God's assistance for the setling of church government. I hope the multiplicitie of opinions w[hi]ch swarme generally (of w[hi]ch your towne is much infected as I heare) will ere long be reduced to government...

L429: Thorpe, London 20 Jan. 1646[181]

... I bes[eech? – MS damaged] you take care thatt the negative oath ... be strictlie executed with you upon all such [as have? – MS damaged] beene in the king's quarters or garrisons and are [now? – MS damaged] come to live within you, for the neglect thereof is looked upon as a very great disservice, and therein, therefore, I am very desirous to present you blamelesse upon all occasions.

Touching the Ipswich money: The answeare is itt was a p[ar]ticuler gifte by some p[ar]ticuler men to S[i]r John Meldrum[182] in relac[i]on to some p[ar]ticuler services and favours he hadd done to them, and therefore he being dead before the money was paid to him the sev[er]all owners doe stand upon their [former? – MS damaged] ownership of the money and require it backe againe. [I? – MS damaged] have laboured whatt I can & ingaged those Burgesses [as? – MS damaged] Mr Bacon[183] and Mr Gowrden[184] who have for [? – MS damaged] used theire uttermost in the buisines...

The king hath writt 2 more lres within these 3 or 4 daies still pressing his p[er]sonall treatie and comeing to London. But [upon? – MS damaged] most iust grounds, as will hereafter appere ([though not? – MS damaged] yett fitt to be published), the counsells stand [for refusall? – MS damaged] of a treatie and to adhere to the sending of proposic[i]ons. In the meane time I knowe thatt to country apprehensions itt will seeme strange that soe faire & plausible an overture should be withstood. But I believe, withall, thatt wise men will consider thatt as they cannot at first sight [? – MS damaged] doe not knowe the dimensions of those obiectes whereof [they?] see butt the outward figure and sup[er]ficies, you [will have? – MS damaged] a declarac[i]on shortelie sett out, which will tell [you the? – MS damaged] whole trueth and describe the solidd bodie att [length? – MS damaged]. And

---

[180] John Gurdon, MP for Ipswich, Suffolk.
[181] This letter was written in the same hand as L415.
[182] Sir John Meldrum, a Scot serving in Parliament's northern armies, was killed at the siege of Scarborough in May 1645.
[183] Francis Bacon, MP for Ipswich, Suffolk.
[184] John Gurdon.

till thatt com[m]e you must rest yo[u]r assureance upon [this? – MS damaged] principle, thatt the Parliam[en]t of England nev[er] did, nor can, betray the kingdome. And till that come I send you the inclosed to shewe you whatt trucking theire is in Ireland[185] while treaties are p[ro]pounded in England…

L430: Pelham, Westminster 20 Jan. 1646
… I send you here inclosed an ordinance of the Lords & Commons for the maintenance of a minister. I payd the clarke of the Lords [MS damaged] 14s 6d. I send you [MS damaged] Irish Cabinet[186] as [MS damaged] to the view of the world [MS damaged] you may p[er]ceive what good intentions his ma[jes]tie hath for peace, notwithstanding all the spetious p[re]tentions…

L433: Thorpe, 27 Jan. [1646]
… The ord[er] past in the Lords' House for yo[u]r £150 p[er] an[num][187] is no more but the sume w[hi]ch was before & w[hi]ch will not serv you, for it was nev[er] intended to be past in that man[n]er, but to have an ordinance drawn up upon it to be past both Houses compleat, as an act of P[ar]lam[en]t is past…

L434: Thorpe, London 5 [Feb. 1646]
… We have sitten all this day till now w[i]thin night in answer of anoth[er] lre fro[m] the king, sent upon Satturday last, pressing still for a p[er]sonall treatye at Westminst[er] & holding forth some plausible things to the people who wold have peace upon any terms. But there is so much art in the co[n]tryvances in the lre [it would? – MS damaged] not admitt a condiscenc[i]on, as will appere by the lre & answer [w[hi]ch? – MS damaged] will both shortly be published…

L435: Pelham, Westminster 24 Feb. 1646
… For the timber, I have prest it very much to S[i]r Henry Vane, who rec[eived] the letter from our noble generall long since…

---

[185] This is a reference to the Glamorgan Treaty – Charles's attempt to make peace with the Confederate Irish and secure Irish troops for use in England. The treaty was brokered for the king by the Earl of Glamorgan. Copies of documents relating to the treaty reached Westminster on 16 Jan. 1646 and were subsequently published (see below): Samuel Rawson Gardiner, *History of the Great Civil War 1642–1649* (1987 edn, 4 vols, London), iii. 30–42.

[186] *The Irish Cabinet: or, His Majesties Secret Papers, for Establishing the Papall Clergy in Ireland* (London, 1646), BL, E316/29.

[187] For the town's ministers.

L436: Thorpe [received 27 Feb. 1646]

... yo[u]r own business about settling the pay of yo[u]r garrisonn, though very earnestly labourd by yo[u]r frends & sollicited by M[r] Watson,[188] we cannot gett on, for we still follow the cras[h]e[189] where the game lyes, and thincks of other places at leasure, but tyme and patienc will worke it ...

L438: Pelham, Westminster 10 Mar. 1646

... As for the timber, S[i]r Henry Vane was then in the cuntry, & hath not as yet made your request knowne to the House. This day I spoke w[i]th him. He tould me, as formerly, that he had our generall's letter in his pocket, & that w[i]th the first opp[or]tunitie he would acquaint the House w[i]th it ...

I have acquainted divers of my freinds that you conceive 600 men to be sufficient for yt garrison ...

L440: Pelham, Westminster 17 Mar. 1646

I shall take the best care I can about marshall law ... As for your timber, I prest S[i]r Henry Vane about it. I tould him the great necessitie of it. This day he tould me he waited only for the first opp[or]tunitie to p[re]sent it to the House ...

L441: Pelham, Westminster 24 Mar. 1646

... This day was appointed for setling the Northerne Association, but the speeding of the p[ro]positions to reconcile the differance betweene the Parliament and the Scotch commissioners did intervene. S[i]r Henry Vane tould me he had rec[eived] letters from you. When the businesse was in agitation he did acquaint the House of our generall's desire for timber for your towne. I have often importuned him about it, & shall still be vigilant, when the northerne affaires are in question, to have a care for your timber & martiall law. I have acquainted divers of my freinds w[i]th it, who have p[ro]mist there best assistance ...

L444: Pelham, Westminster 31 Mar. 1646

... This day was appointed for the Northerne Association, but it is still deferd by reason of other great affaires ... When that businesse is in agitation, I shall desire S[i]r Henry Vane & other of my freinds to be p[re]sent. About the number of the garrison, timber, etc., I am confident Mr Samuell Browne will be a true freind to your towne. He is a very solid lawyer & a man in very great esteeme ... Mr Browne is

---

[188] Possibly John Watson, a Hull freeman: HCA, BRG/1, fol. 195.
[189] The outcry made by hounds when they find the game (*OED*).

one of the keep[er]s of the greate seale. There are 4 of the House of Commons, & 2 Lords yt keepe it, but he strikes a greate stroke there, as in other affaires. If you write to him, the sup[er]scription may be for your ho[nou]rable freind, Samuell Browne Esq[ir]e.

As for your classes, you will heare more. The Assembly are not well pleased that the appeale is to commissioners. It hath pleased God of late to take to himselfe one of the Assembly, a freind of ours, Mr Coleman.[190]

We rec[eived] letters lately from Mr Strickland, our agent in Holland, that there is great hopes our m[er]chants will rec[eive] satisfaction for there cloth that was taken...

L447: Pelham, Westminster 14 Apr. 1646
... Our northerne businesse hath had very ill successe. As I remember, there hath beene 15 dayes appointed about yt businesse, & as yet nothing setled...

L448: Thorpe to the mayor, Gray's Inn 21 Apr. [1646]
... I p[er]ceyv yo[u]r business for yo[u]r garrison hath had slow mocons in o[u]r House of late; 19 dayes appointed but none held. I know not what I shalbe able to do, but shall do what I am able for forward it. I praie you tell Mr Shaw I did dispatch his business at Lincoln according to dyrecco[n] & shall do what I may here as he desyres for his mony...

The west is totally clere. S[i]r Tho: Farfax coms to morrow to before Oxford. Many of the army being their already. It is thought the king will come to him...

My service to yo[u]r gov[er]nor...

L449: Pelham, Westminster 21 April 1646
... As yet I can give noe further acco[unt] of our northerne businesse; other pressing affairs doe p[re]vent the p[ro]gresse of it.

The p[ro]positions for peace are not as yet agreed upon by the Scottish commissioners. Oxford is beseeged. Our noble generall is uppon his march out of the west. I suppose w[i]thin few dayes he will be neare Oxford. I doubt not but those few garrisons w[hi]ch the king hath in those p[ar]ts will be speedily reduced to the obedience of the Parliamente. Wee heare Pendennis is upon treaty and the Mount[191] yelded. I have some confidence that S[i]r Tho: Fairfax will be a happy instrument to make a good peace in this kingdome.

---

[190] Coleman evidently died in March 1646, not early in 1647 as some authorities state: *DNB*, under 'Thomas Coleman'.
[191] St Michael's Mount in Cornwall.

I was desired by Mr Browne[192] to give you thancks for your ale, &
he tould me farther that he would not thancke you in words but in
deeds, w[hi]ch was that he would make a conclusion w[i]th S[i]r John
Barrington about your spring water.

I send you inclosed a declaration of the House of Commons.[193] You
will have a greater number sent you by messengers expresly. Soe soone
as they come to your hands I desire they may be published in all your
churches both in towne & county according to the order of the House
of Commons...

I send you alsoe inclosed a letter from the Committee of the Navy.
You may returne what answere you please...

L450: Thorpe, London 28 Apr. 1646
... But as touching the Northern Associac[i]on, I cannot say any
thing is settled, nor is the ordinance yet renewed or continued ...
Many dayes have bene appointed for debating o[u]r northern affayres,
but they come on cold as our clymate...

... It is now thought yt the king will put him self upo[n] S[i]r Th:
Farfax, & cast himself wholly upon the P[ar]lam[en]t, so as by God's
blessing we may lyve to see a happy issue of all o[u]r miseryes, if we
do not fall out among o[u]r selvs...

L451: Pelham, Westminster 28 Apr. 1646
... I hope our brethren[194] may shortly returne home, the work being
neare a period in the app[re]hension of many...

L452: Thorpe to ?, 31 Apr. [1646][195]
This day Coll[onel] Rainsbourow came to the House and gave us
informac[i]on that upon Tuesday last the Duke of Lynox, S[i]r Will[ia]m
Fleetewood, Earle of Linesay, Mr Sidnam, and some other eminent

[192] Samuel Browne. On 26 Mar. 1646, Hull corporation ordered that 'two barrells of
aile shall be sent as a present from ye towne unto Mr. Browne ... Mr. Pelham having
gyven intimac[i]on soe to do': HCA, Hull bench bk. 5, p. 709.
[193] *The Answer of the Lords and Commons Assembled in the Parliament of England at Westminster
to the Several Papers of the Commissioners of Scotland* (London, 1646), BL, E333/14. This
declaration was drawn up in response to papers presented to Parliament by the Scots
commissioners the previous Autumn. So blunt was it in reproving the Scots for the 'free
quarterings disorderly plunderings' of their army in the northern counties, that the Lords
apparently refused to join with the Commons in ordering it to be printed. On 14 Apr.
1646, therefore, the Commons ordered it to be printed and published on their own
authority: *CJ* iv. 317, 327, 338, 342, 347, 353, 371, 508; *LJ*, viii. 34–6; Keith Lindley and
David Scott, eds, *The Journal of Thomas Juxon, 1644–1647* (Camden Soc., 5th ser., xiii,
1999), pp. 114–15.
[194] i.e. The Scots.
[195] This letter was written neither in Thorpe's hand nor that of L415.

courtiers came to him to him to Woodstocke and rendred themselves prisoners. And the duke told him that upon Mounday morneing by two a clocke the kinge with Mr John Ashbournam and a minister, conceived to be Docto[u]r Steward,[196] weere gonne away privately out of Oxford, but whither or upon what designe he could not tell, though, as he said, he prest him earnestly, being in his chamber the same night to know it. But the king denied to tell him, saieing it was a secrett and therefore charged him noe further to move him in itt. That the next morneing S[i]r John Mounson came to render himselfe a prisoner and brought the same relac[i]on of the kinge's departure, and that he had on a white perriwig and a reed mountearay,[197] and rid upon a bay horse, & went out at the East Gate, and that soe soone as they weere oute they ridd away soe fast as they could. And that for certaine his designe was to ride to London.

The Coll[onel] said further that the same day the two princes Rupert & Morris and other lordes had sente for passes to have leave to come in, but weere denied till the pleasure of the House weere knowne. He said alsoe that this businesse of the kinge's departure (as he did p[er]ceive by some of those offic[er]s that came from Exeter upon sourrender thereof) had breed [sic] soe greate confusion & distraccon in Oxford as they weere all ready to cutt the throates one of another, and that he beleeved as soone as the gen[er]all came upp with the whole body of foote before it the sold[ier]s would yeild it.

[?May the – MS damaged] first. The intelligence continues certaine of the kinge's being gonne from Oxford, but to what place is yett variously reported. Some say into Scotland, some into Ireland, and others to London.

Monday.[198] A vote passed the House that whosoever shall harbour and conceale the kinge and not forthwith discov[er] him to the speakers of both Houses shall die without m[er]cy and forfeit as in case of high treason.

Newes was brought to the House that upon Friday last the gen[er]all, comeing before Wallingford, the gov[er]nour of the castle sent to desyre him to forbeare any attempt upon the towne least by the assault the towne's people might receive hurt and the towne be endangered, and therew[i]thall p[ro]mist that if he heard nothing from the king w[i]thin eight daies he would surrender the castle & towne to the P[ar]liam[en]t. Upon this promise the gen[er]all forebore to attempt the towne and

---

[196] The doctor who accompanied Charles on his flight to the Scots was in fact Dr Michael Hudson.
[197] i.e. A Montero, a Spanish hunter's cap, having a spherical crown and a flap capable of being drawn over the ears (OED).
[198] 4 May 1646.

wente away. And that night & next day after the gov[er]nour of the castle, one Blake, burnt all the towne to the ground.

No c[er]tayn news is yet come where the king is.[199]

L453: Thorpe [early May 1646]
... This post brings you ... this touching yo[u]r businesses ... That upon Thursday last[200] the ordinance for settling yo[u]r garrison was redd twice & then comitted to the Comittee of the Army w[i]th an addicon of more gent[lemen] to be added to it (quoad this business), w[hi]ch I co[n]fess I und[er]stand not, yet do beleyve & shall hope it is for the best.[201] I was not in the House when the business came on & th[er]fore shall give it my good wishes & what more I can.

And this for the p[re]sent is all I have, save to tell you yt the next week S[i]r Jo: Barrington, M[r] Brown, & my self are to treat about yo[u]r waterworks ... I beleyve you will have an assizes at York this som[er], and if you have any need w[i]th you, the judg may be easily brought to you. Write yo[u]r minde.

L454: Thorpe to the mayor and aldermen [n.d. but from internal evidence, 12 May 1646]
... Yo[u]r ordinance for the garisonn is not yet carryed up to the Lords, but w[i]th the first opportunity I shall gett it donne. And as touching yo[u]r fears of martiall law & desyre to be exempted from it, I thought you had bene long since satisfyed yt the martiall law extends onely to martiall men, & is to be exercised onely ov[er] them, & cannot nor ought not to be exercised but in case of martiall discipline, & their can be no exempc[i]on by ordinance from that w[hi]ch is not. And I thinck you need no more feare the exercise of martiall law to the p[re]iudice of yo[u]r civill authoritye then you need fear the exercise of the forrest law w[i]th you...

Touching yo[u]r ordinance for yo[u]r minister: I wold willingly c[on]tribut my paynes & service in it if I did not see an impossibility to get it sodanly donne, & as the state of affayrs now stand. But this expedienc I wold offer you: if you can inquyer of any p[ar]sonages improp[er]iate nere you w[hi]ch form[er]ly did belong to the dean & chapter of York of the vallew in yo[u]r ordinance, I will do my indeavor to get them by name assigned to you or your vallew out of them, w[hi]ch is now lately found out to be the easyest & surest way to ascertay[ne] yo[u]r paye.

[199] This sentence is in Thorpe's hand.
[200] i.e. 30 Apr. 1646.
[201] The MPs added to the Army Committee to consider the ordinance for the pay of Hull garrison included Sir Matthew Boynton: *CJ*, iv. 527.

The news from henc is various: that Newark & Banberry & Dudley are rendred I know you have heard, & yt Oxford is beseiged; that the kinge in the Scotts army is gon back northward, but whether or where they will staye ammazes us here. But we in Yorkshir shall feel it ...

The Lords the last week denyed to ioyn w[i]th the Com[m]ons' Hous in any their votes about disposall of the king's p[er]son & th[er]for to morrow a co[n]ference is appointed to satisfy them w[i]th reasons.

Yesterday it was voted yt the Scotts comission[er]s and Scott's gen[er]all[202] shold be sent to & desyred yt it shold be demanded of the king yt all the forts, towns & holds [*sic*] held by the king or his p[ar]ty in England, Scotland, Ireland, Wales, or the Iles shold be forthw[i]th rendred into the P[ar]lam[en]t.[203] But by the effect of to morrow's co[n]ferenc touching the king's p[er]son we shall und[er]stand what the Lords aym at & how they will stand inclyned to their concurrenc in this.

Here is great iealosye & doubt of differenc w[i]th o[u]r brethren. But I hope things wilbe so wisely attempted as to p[re]vent more blood ...

The debate about this vote & about disposall of S[i]r Tho: Farfax spare horse fro[m] Oxford & the [? – MS damaged] Newark, held till late yesternight, together w[i]th the [miseries? – MS damaged] of those countryes where the [armyes? – MS damaged] lye, & about some differences & [? – MS damaged] w[hi]ch had bene in Cumb[er]land between the Scotts & countrymen their, for taking care to p[re]vent the like in our country ...

L456: Thorpe, 14 May [1646]

... Yo[u]r frends here are so tend[er] to satisfy yo[u]r desyres about martiall law yt we resolv to get this proviso, whereof the coppy is inclosed, inserted into yo[u]r ordinance in the Lords' House, but this will occasio[n] a delay by retorning it back to o[u]r House w[i]th the amendm[en]t, & their debating it anew. Howev[er], I shall not fayle you in my p[ar]t ...

L458: Thorpe, 19 May [1646]

... What I feard is come to pass. I sent you by M[r] Lilly[204] the coppy of an addic[i]on drawn for your satisfaccon to the ordinance of yo[u]r garriso[n]. But the Lords stick at it, & what they will send back to us or when we know not. So the mayne is delayed.

This day was spent till two of clock upo[n] debate about the

[202] Alexander Leslie, first Earl of Leven.
[203] *CJ*, iv. 542.
[204] Richard Lilly, the clerk of the corporation.

co[n]tents of a lre sent fro[m] the comittee at Yorke touching the state of the country, & the Scotts forces lying at North Allerto[n], & o[u]r forces lying about thier, & of their clashing about qu[ar]ter; the one requyring the other remov furth[er] northward, & they agayn requyring a removal further southward.[205] The result was these votes:

1. That the House declares that the kingdome of England hath noe more neede of the Scottes army w[i]thin this kingdome...[206]

Touching the blockhouse decayes: it is the first menc[i]on yt I rememb[er] yt you have made, & it coms now suddenly & mony is scarce here. Therfore you must first thinck of an expedient wher & how to rayse the mony nere you, & the some you desyre, & then a petic[i]on must be p[re]pared w[i]th a recomendac[i]on fro[m] the gen[er]all yo[u]r gov[er]nor. This, if you will speed, must be the way, oth[er]wise whatsoev[er] is told you [is? – MS damaged] butt words...

L459: Pelham, Westminster 19 May 1646

... I have lately taken a house in Axe Yard in Westminster, where I have had soe many visits that I had noe tyme to write to you; notwithstanding, I was not unmindfull of your desires, & yt day that the ordnance past in the House of Commons I did put S[i]r Henry Vane in mind of the timber. Wee were then soe desirous to have it past, it was not thought fitting then to make any further request. This day he hath againe p[ro]mist me to take the first opp[or]tunitie to move for timber. The ordnance yet lyeth w[i]th the Lords...

I did acquaint S[i]r Henry Vane of the ruine of the north block-house...

L460: Thorpe, Gray's Inn 26 May [1646]

... This post will bring you from all hands the tydings of the king's lres to the Houses of P[ar]lam[en]t of England, of Scotland, & to the comittees of both kingdoms, & to the citty of London, & his warrant to surrend[er] Oxford upon ho[noura]ble terms – all holding forth a smilinge face of peace. But what is inlye ment, God onely knows, & good men doubt & wise men fear, becaus they forsee: yet I hope well. You will hear also of a remonstrance brought in to o[u]r House this day by the Comon Counsell of London in terms high enough. The whole day hath bene spent upon an entrance into the debate of these,

---

[205] Bodleian Library, Oxford, Tanner MS 59, fol. 195: the county committee of York to Lenthall, 15 May 1646. The committee complained that the Scots, having imposed 'intollerable leavies' on the North Riding, were intent on moving southwards. They ask the Commons to order the removal of the Scots army from the county.

[206] This sentence and the four additional Commons' resolutions passed that day and related by Thorpe are in the same hand as L452. For the Commons' resolutions concerning the Scots army, see *CJ*, vii. 551.

together w[i]th an interveening accidentall speach w[hi]ch fell from a
Memb[er] in the House touching another Memb[er] ...[207]

Touching yo[u]r business in the Lords' House about yo[u]r ordinance & martiall law: M[r] Watsonn may, if he will, tell you what paynes
it hath cost me, & labor amongst my best frends their, yet the business
remaynes und[er] comitm[en]t their. But what feet may be added to
hasten the p[ro]gress shall not be wanting ...

L461: Pelham, Westminster 26 May 1646
... I did acquaint S[i]r Henry Vane w[i]th your desires about the
blockhouse. He is very willing to doe any service for the towne of
Hull ...

The indeavours of the House of Commons are for a well grounded &
a safe peace, but they diverted by some that intend to sow sedition ...

I deliv[er]ed your letter to the chaireman for the Committee of the
Navy w[i]th your respects ...

L462: Thorpe [2 June 1646]
... This tells you I have had conferenc w[i]th Mr Brown & S[i]r Jo:
Barringto[n] touching yo[u]r wat[er] ...

This day a new peticon cou[n]t[er] to that of the Cittye's the last
week was brought in.[208] We are working hard upon the p[ro]posicons
(God give good success) as being the most p[ro]bable way to peace ...

L463: Pelham, Westminster 2 June 1646
... Wee have very lamentable complaints out of the north. It is
ordered that the report shall be made to the House of Commons the
next day.

The king's letters doe not so much amaze us. Wee have known his
stile long, both to us & to our enemies. My desire to you is that you
would have a great care of your towne.

Newes was expected this day from Oxford. The Speaker tould me
yt our generall sent in articles upon Saturday last, and yt they within
Oxford desired two dayes respite & then they would returne an answere.
But Newcastle is much p[re]fered before Oxford, w[hi]ch is not yet

---

[207] This is possibly a reference to a Commons' speech by George Thomson, MP for
Southwark, on 26 May. Thomson was highly critical of lord mayor of London, Thomas
Adams, but it is not known whether he also attacked a member of the House: Lindley
and Scott, eds, *Juxon Journal*, p. 124; BL, Browne papers (uncat.): William Garway to
Richard Browne, 28 May 1646.

[208] *The Humble Acknowledgement and Petition of Divers Inhabitants in and about the City of London*
(London, 1646), BL, E339/12; *CJ*, iv. 561.

surrendred.[209] I have a p[ro]clamation from his ma[jes]tie to disband all his forces in Scotland, w[hi]ch was reported to be done w[i]th acclamations. I have not much good newes to acquaint w[i]thall, but yt our forces have taken Ludlow Castle; a strong place in Wales. Sir Henry Vane desired me to p[re]sent his service to you w[i]th this inclosed letter from Mr Strickland.[210] S[i]r Tho: Widdrington did alsoe desire me to p[re]sent his service to you and have both promised to use there best indavours for you, w[hi]ch I am confident of...

L464: Thorpe, 9 June [1646]

... I can give you no result this post of yo[u]r business w[i]th S[i]r Jo. Barrington; his ma[n], upon whom he relyes, not being in town.

I receyv inclosed in yo[u]r lre a case to be p[re]sented to ye Comittee of Lords & Comons for Sequestracons, supposing it to be of difficulty, w[hi]ch I co[n]fess I finde not in it ... In gen[er]all it is yo[u]r best way to leave p[ar]tyes to p[ro]secute there owne business before the comittees here, & not, und[er] cullor of favor or desyres to help freinds, indanger to do wrong to the comonwealth...

The treaty at Oxford p[ro]ceeds and we look dayly for a good accou[n]t of it. That ye Duke of York shall come hither and the 2 princes Morris & Rup[er]t goes beyond sea is already agreed. The great stick is ye great lords and p[er]sons excepted in the p[ro]posicons...

The king's lre to the E[arl] of Ormond in Ireland, and their discov[er]d, and from thenc sent hither by the lords iustices & comittee their, & whereby his design of going into ye Scotts army is clearly discov[er]ed, and answering other intelligences, all concurring yt it was to devide & imbroyle the 2 nations & to rayse a new warr. Great stirr we now have here upon it.

Yo[u]r ordinance for yo[u]r establishm[ent] is not yet finished w[i]th the Lords, though I have got my Lo: Wharton[211] p[ar]ticul[ar]ly to speed it their.

I write things breifly. I p[re]sume you have others who send you diurnalls & printed pap[er]s...

This day is a comittee appointed to collect together the causes we have of iealosy ag[ains]t ye Scotts,[212] & these are to be sent into Scotland

---

[209] Newcastle was held by the Scots. Parliament had been pressing the Scots to remove their garrisons from Newcastle and other places in northern England since the summer of 1645.

[210] This is probably the letter from Walter Strickland to Sir Henry Vane (L442) that is printed in Wildridge, *Hull Letters*, pp. 145–6. It concerns his efforts to secure redress at Amsterdam for several Hull merchants whose ships had been seized by the Dutch.

[211] Philip Lord Wharton.

[212] Those MPs nominated to this committee included Sir Henry Vane junior, and Thorpe: *CJ* iv. 570.

to the States[213] their in a fayr way & w[i]th desyres yt ther army may be recalld; the House having declared we have noe furth[er] use of them...

L465: Pelham, Westminster 10 June 1646

... I spoke w[i]th S[i]r John Barrington about yo[u]r spring water, but I expected noe satisfactory answere from him, he being governed by my freind Mr Samuell Browne, who hath p[ro]mist me to finish the businesse, & I doubt not but it will be to your content. The letter from our generall concerning your timber etc. is not come to the Speaker. When it doth come you will want noe freinds to further his requests...

The businesse in the north troubles many more then in the south. I pray God send a good agreement...

This day wee had another letter in print signed by Ormonde & the king's commissioners in Ireland, a true coppy thereof (w[hi]ch I tooke in the House of Commons) I send you inclosed; the printed pap[er]s not having all the truth. Upon w[hi]ch letter the House of Commons past this vote: that upon the letter from the king to the Marquisse of Ormond of the 3[d] of Aprill 1646, that the king went into the Scotts army upon a designe to set devision betweene the two kingdomes of England & Scotland, and to continnue the warr against the Parliament of England...

L466: Thorpe, 16 June [1646]

S[i]r John Barringto[n] & I are at two stands: he stands upon it not to exceed 21 yeres & 40 m[ar]k rent; I stand at 20s & in fee farm. Where we shall meet I know not. But at the most I p[re]sume the town of Hull is able to kepe their wat[er] in its due co[ur]se, & I hope the House of Com[m]ons will take care their garrison shalbe supplyed at least not depryved of soe necessary a p[ro]vision as aqua omnia. Mean tyme, & when I hear, you shall heare more.

Their is like to be an assizes at York, but how it may com[m]ode you I know not. Yet if you please & yt you thinck it necessary I shall gett comissions for it.

We had yest[er]day lres fro[m] the king signifying his desyre to hasten the p[ro]posicons for peace & for his com[m]ing to London, & w[i]th many more good words for disbanding forces & sparing shedding blood & the like. Div[er]se other pap[er]s were also com[m]unicated by the Lords to o[u]r House at a conference, all tending to the same subiects & touching the prince his retorning back into England.

Oxford treaty is finished & Thursday next, if it hold, is appointed for rendring the towne. We hear very bad news out of Ireland of a

[213] i.e. The Committee of Estates.

great defeat given to o[u]r forces their, but I am co[n]fident it is not so bad as it is made by some who heighten it for other purposes.[214]

The proposicons for peace are ready to be sent to the Scotts com[missioner]s for their concurrence & so wilbe speedily sent to the kinge. And I hope God will p[ro]duce good for us by them.

We are in expectacon of an imbassado[u]r out of France. The last week the Russia imbassador came into both Houses of P[ar]lam[en]t to take his leave & to receyve his lres of gratulac[i]on to the emp[er]or . . .

L467: Pelham, Westminster 23 June 1646

. . . The letter from our generall concerning timber is not yet written; notwithstanding the ordinance passing yesterday for the garrison of Hull. S[i]r Henry Vane did move for 300 trees out of the Lord of Dunbar's parke.[215] The felling of timber was opposed. I beleeve the House of Commons will be more inclineable to furnish you w[i]th a some of monney to buy timber from foraigne parts then to cut downe our English Oakes, there having beene such a great consumption made of Oakes by papists formerly. The House was then full of businesse. At some other tyme I hope they will graunt you either trees or monney. As for your suffering by Cap. Dewet's[216] taking of your goods, the way that you p[ro]pound at p[re]sent is not seasonable. It is admired yt you would have such a thing moved in the House of Commons.[217]

The king and that House doe not stand upon such good tearmes as yet. Yesterday the Lords & Commons agreed upon the p[ro]positions & they are now w[i]th the Scots commissioners. There is a committee appointed to p[ro]pound a way how they should be sent to the king. If they be assented unto by his ma[jes]tie then I doubt not but there will be a good union. Untill then they will not admit of any such addresse to the king. In the interim, patience is the best remedie that I know.

I have sent all the ordinances that I find for the setling of church government. What other ordinances that concerns you I shall send you. In the ordinance that past for martiall law for Hull the civill government is exempted.

For newes: Oxford & Farrington are to morrow to be deliv[er]ed to

---

[214] This is a reference to the defeat of the Scots' Ulster army by the Irish Confederates at Benburb, County Tyrone, on 5 June 1646. The 'some who heighten it for other purposes' is probably a reference to the Scots' more vociferous enemies among the political Independents.

[215] The Catholic peer and 'delinquent', Henry Constable, first Viscount Dunbar [S], was lord of seigniory of Holderness and owned extensive property in the Hull area.

[216] i.e. The Hollander, de Witt, who Thorpe mentions in L468.

[217] i.e. For permission to petition the king for his help in securing the release of several Hull merchantmen captured by the Dutch: see L468.

S[i]r Tho: Fairfax. The articles were but this day read in the House. The printed coppy is false. A true coppy was this day ordered to be printed, w[hi]ch I shall send you. Anglice²¹⁸ in Wales is reduced to the obedience of the Parliament. I doe not know above 4 garrisons in England & two in Wales yt the king hath left…

L468: Thorpe, London 23 June [1646]
This post brings you tidings of the surrend[er] of Oxford & deliv[er]y th[er]of upon articles. Yesterday was the ordinance past for yo[u]r garriso[n]. The matt[er] about martiall law having had much debate & yo[u]rselves being saved fro[m] it, as you may p[er]ceyve, w[i]th more exempc[i]ons then any garriso[n] ev[er] yet had; howbeit the articles for London & Westminst[er] are made to extend to you.

This day I got the establishm[en]t for the pay of yo[u]r garriso[n] carryd up to the Lords, & shall follow it w[i]th what dilligenc may be to get it finisht.

Yo[u]r 300 trees were moved for yest[er]day by S[i]r Hen: Vayne, & debated a litle but was layd aside agayn for want of tyme to conclude it. I finde it wilbe much opposed in regard of the scarceness of timber in those p[ar]ts & the great use Humb[er] banckes hath of timb[er] for saving the country, & yt some of yo[u]r good freinds & neighbors say you have had 500 trees already, for w[hi]ch no account is given to the state.

I receyved a lre by M[r] Taylor of York, as oth[er]s did from you, touching a desyre of leave to move the king for a lre into Holland about their goods taken by De Witt. But we all to whom the lres are dyrected agred in a great wond[er]m[en]t you shold make such a p[ro]posic[i]on, & we all I thinck shall. Howev[er], I shall tell you it is not be desyred w[i]thout p[re]iudice to the desyrers, & I am sure will not be granted.

The p[ro]posicons are all agreed upo[n] & remayn now w[i]th the Scotts com[missioner]s, where we can[n]ot expect they shold finde any rubb, & then they are to be speeded away to the king … My service to M[r] Gov[er]nor & M[r] Shaw.

L470: Pelham, Westminster 6 July 1646
The last weeke I heard little worth your notice. I have spoken with one that hath beene the chairman at Gouldsmiths' Hall.²¹⁹ He tould me unless they [delinquents] have £10 p[er] ann[um] or £200 in monneys you are not to meddle w[i]th them. He tould me you were guided by Mr Thorpe. When the p[ro]positions are printed I will send

---

²¹⁸ i.e. Anglesey.
²¹⁹ Pelham is probably referring here to John Ashe, MP for Westbury, Wiltshire.

them to you. Yesterday they were appointed to be sent to the king. Two Members of the House of Lords and foure of the House of Commons are to carry them. They are appointed not to stay above 10 dayes to desire his ma[jes]tie's possitive answere to all the p[ro]positions.

As for your timber, it is referd to the Northerne Committee to consider of it. The House is unwilling that any timber should be sold, especially neare rivers. Yet as I writ your formerly I hope you will have either monney or timber.

The House of Commons hath past this resolution that twenty thousand p[er] ann[um] of delinquents' lands that are excepted out of pardon shall be sould for the carrying on of the warr against the Irish rebells. There is a letter written to the king to desire his ma[jes]tie that Dublin, Trogida[220] & all the rest of his garrisons may be delivered into such hands as the Parliament shall appoint & that his ma[jes]tie would write to the Marquisse of Ormond to that effect. Wee heare by letters out of France that the prince was the last weeke at S[t] Germans...

L471: Thorpe, 7 July [1646]

... I have comunicated the lre you sent up touching Richard Brown to the Comittee of Goldsmiths' Hall, & M[r] Stevens,[221] the charman [*sic*] their, much wond[er]s at it. He hath showed it to Hoyle[222] who subscribed it (the rest disclayming). And I do not finde but upon the whole matt[er] but you are left to the ordinance of P[ar]lam[en]t to see for power to take of a sequestracon, w[hi]ch I cannot learn of any such power. I have not yet receyvd the lre back but when I get it I shall send it back to you. Howev[er], I beleyve the business of sequestrac[i]on wilbe put into another way, & comittees wilbe eased of it, & yo[u]r own pow[er] at p[re]sent being in suspenc till the ordinance be renewd, w[hi]ch I beleyv will not be in hast.

The proposicons for peace are now, w[i]th in a very litle, concluded upon & the lords & others appointed to carry them are agreed upon: E[arl of] Pembrok, E[arl] of Suffolk, S[i]r Walt[er] Earle, S[i]r John Epsly, M[r] Goodwin & Mr Robinson.[223]

These 2 last dayes have bene spent in debates touching the disposall of the Scotts army. We have desyred the Lo[rds'] concurrenc in the vote yt we have no furth[er] use of them, and yt the comons of England can no longer pay them. And upon these debates we still are. God put an end to o[u]r troubles & send us peace.

---

[220] i.e. Drogheda.
[221] John Stephens, MP for Tewkesbury, Gloucestershire.
[222] The identity of this man has been impossible to establish.
[223] The commissioners to present the Newcastle Propositions to the king were the Earl of Pembroke, the Earl of Suffolk, Sir Walter Earle, Sir John Hippisley, Robert Goodwyn, Luke Robinson.

The prince is got into France.

My service to yo[u]r gov[er]nor & Mr Shaw

L472: Thorpe, 14 July [1646]

... The business for yo[u]r timb[er] does not rest w[i]th the Northern Comittee as it seems you are informed, but in my report of the whole northern affayrs last week, being aminded [*sic*] fro[m] some of yo[u]r selves touching Drypoole banks, & remembering also Humb[er] ba[n]ks both upon Holderness & Howdenshir coasts, & yt the estates w[hi]ch shold mayntayn them were for the most p[ar]t und[er] sequestra[c]on, & how yo[u]r ba[n]ks were cutt for saving the town by ov[er]flowing the grounds, & looking out also for the declarac[i]on whereby the Hous declared long since yt they wold repayre p[ar]ticul[er] losses occasioned th[er]by, did take occasion to speake of these losses & of these rep[ar]acons, & did desyre yt some p[ro]porcconall allowances might be made out of those sequestracons both in Howdenshir & Hold[er]ness who were lyable to repayre these bancks. And upon [debate][224] of this it is referrd to the Northern Comittee to state the case, & to inform themselvs of the costs & charges in repayringe & what estates in all placs [*sic*] are lyable to make them good & what timb[er] wilbe necessary, & to p[re]sent their opinions. And thus the business stands before the comittee, as I thinck.

The French imbassador is come in & hath audienc to morrow, being come to the P[ar]lam[en]t, as his credentialls p[re]tend. Great is the expectacon of the message...

L473: Pelham, Westminster 14 July 1646

... I am beholding to you for your care of me. I shall use my best indeavours to requite you when the report comes to the House concerning timber & the breaches in the bancks neare Hull. I hope you will rec[eive] some satisfaction. I could wish you had Mr Hillyard's mannor house given to the towne, although the state rebated him the vallew [of – MS damaged] his composition ... For my p[ar]t I doe not hold it convenient that any man that hath declared himselfe in the least measure against the Parliment should have any shew of power in a towne of such consequence that hath stood firme to the Parliament.

As for newes, wee have little at p[re]sent. This day the p[ro]positions for a well-grounded & a safe peace weere deliv[er]ed by the Speaker to our freind Mr Rob[er]t Goodwin to be p[re]sented [to – MS damaged] his ma[jes]tie, who beganne there [*sic*] iourney this day. What the successe will [be only? – MS damaged] time will p[ro]duce.

[224] Thorpe has missed out a word, presumably 'debate', in turning over to write on a new sheet.

Some of the garrisons yt yet stand out are in [? – MS damaged] ... I
sent you yest[er]day by Mr Deering a booke intitled *Manifest truth*,[225]
w[hi]ch may be worth your reading.

L474: Pelham, Westminster 21 July 1646
    ... The House of Commons having adiurned 4 dayes past I could
doe nothing about your towne's affaires. You may expect I [will -MS
damaged] use my best indeavours to fulfill your desires when the
opp[or]tunitie shall p[re]sente. This day was a day of thanksgiving for
the reducing of Oxford, & since this day was appointed it hath pleased
God to deliver Leachfeild to the Parliament. And this day wee heare
that Worster is surrendred to the Parliament upon honorable conditions.
Our generall sent articles for the surrendring of Wallingford, but the
House of Commons would not agree to them. I send you inclosed the
p[ro]positions sent to his Ma[jes]tie; as alsoe the articles for Lichfeild.
    An ambassader from France came [to – MS damaged] both Houses
upon Fryday last. He desired to goe to the king & to the Estates of
Scotland. I am somthing dubious that his embassie is not for the good
of this nation. If it please God to send us a good peace at home, wee
shall not much fear foraigne forces...

L475: Thorpe, 21 July [1646]
    ... I am sorry you thinck you are not so well p[ro]vided for in yo[u]r
establishm[en]t as you desyred. Beleyve me, it is the best p[ro]vision
we cold [*sic*] gett & the best service I cold [*sic*] do you to p[ro]mote it
soe far. And if yo[u]r selves had bene here to have sene the troubles
of attending it, besides the labour of freinds for it, I hope you might
have bene bett[er] satisfyed there was no omissio[n].
    The French imbassador came to the Houses upo[n] ~~Fryday~~ Thursday
last. He made his speaches in French & deliv[er]d in his credentialls.
His errand, as he p[re]tends, is to negotiat the peace betwixt the king &
the P[ar]lam[en]ts of the two kingdomes, so his first address to the
Houses was but to tell them soe, & yt he did w[i]th one breath salute
them & bidd them farewell. The Lords have given him a passe to go
to the king & so into Scotland. But it is not assented as yet in o[u]r
Hous. I beleyve he is come away this day. What the issue wilbe God

---

[225] *Manifest Truths, or an inversion of Truths Manifest* (London, 1646), BL, E343/1. This
tract was written by the Yorkshire Presbyterian minister, Edward Bowles, in answer to
that of the Scottish apologist, David Buchanan, *Truth its Manifest* (London, 1645), BL,
E1174/4. Bowles was particularly concerned to challenge Buchanan's criticism of the
Parliamentary commissioners in the north (who were mostly political Independents), to
whom Bowles had served as chaplain: Bodl., Nalson MS III, fol. 315; David Scott, 'The
"Northern Gentlemen", the Parliamentary Independents, and Anglo-Scottish Relations
in the Long Parliament', *HJ* xlii (1999), p. 364 and n. 94.

knows. But we heare for c[er]tayn yt if the king do grant to the p[ro]posicons yet their is a declarac[i]on drawen in France & to be sett out in the name of the prince now their whereby he p[ro]tests ag[ains]t them & appeales to all Christia[n] princes theirupon how the king, being as it were und[er] a custody, is thus inforced by his subiects to yeild to things derogatory to this crown & his posterity, & to monarchy it self. A few weeks will let us see furth[er] into these things. God almighty prepare us for his mercyes & kepe us all honest men...

L476: Pelham, Westminster 28 July 1646
... your letter this day I deliv[er]ed to the Speaker from our noble generall. When the business for the north comes in question I will put the Speaker in minde of it, or before. As for the maintenance for ministers, I hope there will [be a course? -MS damaged] taken throughout the kingdome that the Gospell may [be? – MS damaged] preached in all the dark corners of England & Wales, & a competent [? – MS damaged] for orthodox devines...

L477: Pelham, Westminster 4 Aug. 1646
This weeke p[ro]duceth little newes, onely of a castle or two in Wales yt are reduced to the Parliament. Wee have noe newes from our commissioners concerning the p[ro]positions. There is noe good expected. I am informed that the king will not graunt them, and that he hath written to the Marquisse of Ormond to p[ro]secute the queen's designes & to follow hir directions. I doubt not but God will blast them all.

I have acquainted S[i]r Henry Vane & divers of my freinds about Mr Hillyard's house, that the House would give it to the towne as a marke of there favour for your good services. They thincke it very reasonable. I doe intend to speake w[i]th Mr Hillyard. I heare he will be willing to part w[i]th it & to have it allowed in his second payment for his composition. I desire to have an estimate from you of the vallue of it.

I am not unmindful of your ministers, nor timber...

L478: Pelham, Westminster 25 Aug. 1646
... I have [MS damaged] the chaireman[226] for plundered [ministers – MS damaged] about your £150 p[er] ann[um] for your ministers. I did acquaint him w[i]th the imp[ro]priations you write of. If the cure be p[ro]vided for in those parrishes there will be great hopes you may have a supply from thence. I doe not forgit [sic] the magazin nor

---

[226] Gilbert Millington, MP for Nottingham.

timber. Mr Hillyard is very well contented yt you should have it.[227] I p[er]ceive by him there hath beene some undermineing to have purchased it of him for some other man. He hath ingaged himselfe to me.

I have not much newes at p[re]sent, but that Pendennis Castle, Ragland in Wales & I thincke all the rest of the king's garrisons in England and Wales are reduced to the obedience of the Parliament. The House of Commons have beene in consideration how to give our brethren satisfaction yt they may quit this kingdome & returne for Scotland...

L479: Pelham, Westminster 8 Sept. 1646

... I writ to you formerly that the chairman for plundred ministers desires to be satisfied whither [?the – MS damaged] cures of those imp[ro]priations be p[ro]vided for. That being done I hope to obtaine our desires.

The House of Commons of late have spent most of there tyme about an agreement w[i]th our brethren of Scotland. They are very desirous to have them out of the kingdome, that the northerne p[ar]ts may be eased of that intollerble burthen under w[hi]ch they have soe long groaned. Many doe verily beleeve yt upon an exact accompt they are in our debt. Yet the House of Commons, out of there brotherly affection, have voted to give them £400,000, whereof £100,000 to be paid p[re]sently upon there removeall. They doe accept the some in grosse, but alledg yt they canot take lesse then £200,000 p[re]sent for the disbanding of there army, wherein I conceive they doe not requite our kindness – £100,000 in former tymes had been a considerable some in Scotland. Wee have appointed a committee to try if they can borrow £200,000 in London for the use of the states[228] & to know of the commissioners for Scotland if they have any instructions to make any other demands. Untill this great businese be dispatched I have small hope to effect any businese for you...

L480: Pelham, Westminster 15 Sept. 1646

... As for timber, I writ you it was referd to the Northerne Committee, w[hi]ch I thincke hath not sate this 3 mounthes. Now, I suppose wee shall meete w[i]thin few dayes. This day S[i]r Tho: Widdrington came to the House. He tells me he is much obliged to you for your great respect shewed to him, for w[hi]ch I give you thancks. I have allwaies found him a faythfull freind to the towne of Hull. Wee have many of our neighbours yt p[re]tend asmuch, but are not soe. My intention is

---

[227] i.e. The manor house.
[228] i.e. The Committee of Estates.

to write noe more of those p[ar]ticulars untill something be really p[er]formed, unlesse you have some new subiect [you? – MS damaged] may spare your penne.

I have little newes to acquainte you w[i]thall. The Earle of Essex dyed yesterday. £200,000 will be raised. Our brethren & wee are not yet fully agreed. I conceive they will not refuse our monney. This day wee had great complaints against them from the northerne committees...

L481: Pelham, Westminster 29 Sept. 1646

... I have gotten £200 p[er] ann[um] for your ministers. I cannot send you the order by this post. I doubt not but to have the ord[er] framed as you please out of those delinquents' imp[ro]priations you write of. You write of one that belonged to S[i]r Phillip Constable. Although he be my kinsman, yet I question whether his honor will reduce our triall. If he did not rec[eive] knighthood before the greate seale was carried away from the Parliament it may p[re]iudice your businesse if you pitch upon yt. My motion was in generall to have yt some of £200 p[er] ann[um] out of those imp[ro]priations you sent me. My desire is yt Mr Stiles may have £100 p[er] ann[um] out of this. I conceive him to be an able and an orthodox devine. I desire to heare from you. I suppose I can have the order drawne as I please.

I hope to p[re]vaile for the magazin; yt you shall have the inheritance of it if it is rated but at £2,400. I can p[ro]misse nothing, but I hope the House will not denie mee such a poore request. And for your timber, I will look for [money? – MS damaged] for you w[i]thall expedition...

As for the classes, there is an ordernance of Parliament for the regulateing of it w[hi]ch I conceive you have.

And as for Ch: Ligard,[229] I wonder he durst write any write any such thing. I p[re]sume he dare not attempt it. My condition was w[i]th S[i]r Tho: Fairfax, before I had the hono[u]r to make him gover[er] of Hull, yt Mr Mallevery, who you desired, should be his deputy. I am confident you neede not feare any such thing. He is well he comes of as he doth concerning his kinsman, S[i]r John Hotham...

L482: Pelham, Westminster 13 Oct. 1646

... I have deliv[er]ed your letters to the chairmen of Gouldsmiths' Hall & plundered ministers.[230] I have likewise spoken to the clarke[231] to

---

[229] Colonel Christopher Legard of Anlaby, a near kinsman of Sir John Hotham: J. Digby Legard, *The Legards of Anlaby and Ganton* (London, 1926), pp. 27, 84–5.

[230] John Stephens and Gilbert Millington.

[231] Probably the under-clerk of the Parliaments (clerk of the Commons), Henry Elsynge.

rectifie the mistake. The House sate soe late that the committee did not sit. The clarke hath p[ro]mist to draw the order against the next day.

The House hath beene lately imployed in turning some of the p[ro]positions into lawes, & about ye great seale. To morrow wee are to have a conference w[i]th the Lords about it. Here are commissioners come from the Lord Ormon [*sic*] & the rest of yt bourd w[i]th some instructions concerning Ireland. There is a committee appointed to heare what they have to say.

Two of the Committee of Both Kingdomes tould me that they had rec[eived] letters that the towne of Hull had made there adresses to the king. I tould them I heard it was some of Yorke. I should be very sorry you should commit such a grosse error. I gave you my advice concerning that p[ar]ticuler. I desire to be informed of the truth; yt if there hath beene any such thing I may excuse it aswell as I can. I know it would give a great occasion of offence to the House if they should heare of it. It might p[ro]ve very p[re]iudiciall to the affaires yt I have in hand for the towne. I hope better of you . . .

L325: Thorpe, London 21 Dec. [1647][232]

By this post you will und[er]stand that yest[er]day our com-[missioner]s went away w[i]th the 4 bills to the kinge, & by me you will und[er]stand yt I have litle caus of hope that the king will assent to them.

The Schotts com[missioner]s have sett out a sharpe declarac[i]on ag[ains]t the P[ar]lam[en]t p[ro]ceedings th[er]abouts, & wold have a p[er]sonall treaty in London before ought else be asked, & wold also have a sight of o[u]r bills, w[hi]ch yet (not relatinge to them or their nation) is conceyvd to be ag[ains]t the English intrest.

Our comission[er]s from the armye the last week brought us good satisfaccon touching their complyance & concurrenc w[i]th the P[ar]l-am[en]t. And accordingly we are now p[ro]ceeding upon their p[ro]-posalls for their arrers & futur mayntenance, & disbanding super-numeraryes, & taking of free quart[er] . . .

L484: Thorpe, London 28 Dec. [1647]

. . . Our comission[er]s who went w[i]th o[u]r 4 bills are not yet retornd, but this day we heard from them & did receyve a coppy of the pap[er] deliv[er]d by the Schotts com[missioner]s to the king, wherein they signify their dissent from us, & upon the matt[er] do p[ro]test aganst both the bills & the new p[ro]posicons theirw[i]thall sent to be treated upon, so as we ghess what temp[er] the bills will

---

[232] This letter has been misdated in the calendar as 21 Dec. 1644.

finde the kinge in. And how the Schotts & we shall hit it upon these opposit points, God knows & a little tyme will manifest it to ev[er]y man.

This post brings down the ordinances both old & new for the sesm[en]ts w[i]th the lres & instruccons for present raysing the 6 months paym[en]t for paying of the sup[er]numerayes & taking away free quart[er]. I p[re]sume yo[u]r Burgess[233] gives you an account of it, the matt[er] being by o[u]r House comended to the Burgesses in each county to take care to send down, & Memb[er]s being sent down into ev[er]y county to agitate the business. M[r] Scowen[234] did assure me the ordinance was mended in that point concerning yo[u]r county, but he being now w[i]th the army I cannot at p[re]sent learn wher the order rests...

L489: Thorpe, London 25 Apr. [1648]

... After a wett & dirty iorney, being now got to London, I have not yet any thing of yo[u]r peculiar concernm[en]t save yt this day & lre from the gen[er]all, Lo: Farfax, was redd about fortefying yo[u]r town & for re-edifying your walls & blockhouses. £6,000 is voted for you, but where or whence to be had is referrd to the Northern Comittee here, & I beleyve wilbe found difficult to be raysed suddenly...

The prints will tell you the news: that the Lo: Inchiquin hath betrayed his trust in Ireland; that the Duke of Yorke made an escape upon Fryday night last from St James House, but how got away or whether gon is not yet known; that you need not trouble yo[u]r selvs about a foolish report, much fomented here, of the armye's coming to demand a million of the Citty, & of their resolucon to disarm & plund[er] all those who refused to ioyn in their assistance; that the forces in Wales increase but not much; that we do look for the Schotts coming in.

L490: Thorpe, London 9 May [1648]

... The ordinance for yo[u]r £6,000 is past as M[r] Pelham tells me (for he hath taken the sole care of it)...

I wish unity may be found in yo[u]r town in relac[i]on to com[m]on security...

L491: Thorpe, London 16 May [1648]

... This week hath not here brought forth any thing of business concerning yo[u]r town & I am not in a condic[i]on to write news, having so much oth[er] business upon my hand.

---

[233] He probably means Pelham rather than Vane.

[234] Robert Scawen, MP for Berwick-upon-Tweed and chairman of the Army Committee.

It ioyes me when I heare from all other p[ar]ts of the kingdom about their rysings & distempers in their affayres at this coniuctur of tyme that yet we hear nothing of any disquyetnesses or disord[er]s among you. And I assure you it is a blessing next to that of peac to be at unity w[i]thin yo[u]r selvs. And for the matter of Sectaryes, whereof you make mecon in yo[u]r lre this post, you need not fear yt they can rule or trouble you much when peace & gov[er]nm[en]t is settled. And in the mean tyme their noyse is but like the hum[m]ing of a flye, onely we must beware that good men, who are truly so called & approved, but not reproved w[i]th the name of Sectarye.

I beleyve the gen[er]all comes down upon Fryday next & I p[re]sume you will acquaynt him w[i]th yo[u]r affayrs & receyv his dyreccons in ord[er] to publick safety & yo[u]r own p[re]servac[i]on in these tymes of danger...

P[er]haps you may heare of some great fighting here this afternoon, w[hi]ch in truth was nothing but that some Surrey men coming w[i]th a petition to the House, & a throng pressing to come in & being resisted by the guard & not warnd w[i]th reasonable warnings, a musket or two was shot of, & one is slayne & another hurt. And that is all as farr as I can learn.[235]

L492: Thorpe to the mayor, Gray's Inn 17 May 1648[236]
   Sir, I writt in my last of the tumult here upon Tuesday in afternoone, w[hi]ch so farr as I then understood, toucheing that upon the staires, was true. But since I understand that the greatest tumult & hurte was in the Pallasse Yard & in the Hall, where many weere wounded, and as I heard aboute five or six are since dead. And as is conceived it was a thing purposely plotted by div[er]s who have beene in armes against the Parliam[en]t under collo[u]r of comeing along w[i]th the peticon[er]s, and then exasperateing the sold[er]s, who weere upon theire guard, calleing them traiters & rebells & endeavoreing to take some of theire weapons from them, from whence grew all the disorder...[237]

L493: Thorpe, London 'Tewsday 9 of clock at night' [c. 23 May 1648]
   ... I send you inclosed a pap[er] of the passages here; diurnalls & occurr[en]ces I know you will have from oth[er]s. M[r] Pelham is designed for one to attend & go along w[i]th the navye. Our great

---

[235] CJ, v. 561–2.
[236] This letter was written in what seems to be the same hand as L452.
[237] For contemporary accounts of this fracas at Westminster, see *A True Relation of the Passages between the Surrey Petitioners and the Souldiers at Westminster, May the 16. 1648* (London 1648), BL, E443/5; *The Sad, and Bloody Fight at Westminster between the Souldiers of the Parliaments Guard and the Club-Men of Surrey* (London, 1648), BL, E443/17.

new ordinance for the Northern Associac[i]on is now und[er] the ham[m]er,[238] & you are brought in for a part. If you desyre any thing, or to have any other men of your committee, write up about it yet, it may be donne...

I desyre my service may be p[re]sented to yo[u]r gov[er]nor, w[i]th thanks for his care ov[er] us w[i]th his guard.

L494: Thorpe, 23 May [1648]
... Yest[er]day is an ordinance past for putting the form[er] Northern Associaccon into a posture of defence & for settling the militia their; & yo[u]r selves being p[ar]t of that Associac[i]on and concerned in it I shall send you an ordinance so soune as I can get some printed, and then it wilbe necessary for som of you to meet w[i]th the rest at York to advise w[i]th them in relacon to yo[u]r selves & yo[u]r own town & county If you shall so think it convenient for you. The towne being a garrison already, whereto I p[re]sume you will gov[er]n yo[u]r selves as may best suite w[i]th publicke safety & yo[u]r owne, according to the example of oth[er] towns in like condicon.

I am sorry to heare yt mony is so hard to rayse w[i]th you upon the security of an ordinance of P[ar]lam[en]t, w[hi]ch all men here take for good...

I doubt not but this post will bring you tydings of the prince landed at Sandw[i]ch in Kent, but the mean[n]ess of the p[er]son, his habit, his no [sic] attendance, makes the thing yet lookt upon as a fable & fictitious p[er]son sent ov[er] for some oth[er] end, w[hi]ch a day or two more will fully discov[er]. Tomorrow is appointed for the debate for a p[er]sonall treaty w[i]th the king...

L495: Thorpe to the mayor and aldermen [c. June 1648]
... The most important business to you ward [sic] is yt div[er]se shipps of the navy, or the greatest p[ar]t th[er]of, hath declared for the king & turnd of their vice admirrall, Coll[onel] Raynesborrow. What caution this may be to you to be beware of any of those shipps I leave to yo[u]r selvs, but do hope you wilbe carefull. It is true we have voted my Lo: Warweek admirall agayn, & he is forthw[i]th to go down among them upon some pryvate intymacons yt all wold be well agayn if the pow[er] be put into his hand, & yt it was but a p[ar]ticul[er] dislike taken by the seamen against Raynsborrow. But I shalbe glad to see what I heare of that nature, & do in the mean tyme p[er]ceyv much distraccon to be upon that occasion.

[238] An ordinance for 'settling the Militia in the Northern Counties' was passed in the Commons on Monday 22 May, and Thorpe was appinted to carry it to the Lords for their concurrence: *CJ*, v. 569.

The prints, I p[re]sume, will tell you of the armyes now in Kent & of the intended design here, from w[hi]ch good Lord deliv[er] us hereafter as he hath donn hitherto.

You will receyv inclosed the new ordinance for the militia, w[hi]ch you may make use of as occasion serve. I am sorry to hear yt some of yo[u]r company is like to come to question, & do hope the accusacon here is not fully such truth as p[re]sented.

I have sent you also another ordinance touching the last sesm[en]ts for the army. And the reason w[hi]ch I send it is because yo[u]r neglect wilbe a blame upon you, & I wold not have you looked upon as those are whose remisnes draws them into suspicons & questions ...

L496: Thorpe, London 6 June [1648]
... The news fro[m] henc is the great & good success & victory w[hi]ch God hath given us in Kent, where things are quyeted & quyet ... Some litle stirr their is still in Essex but not co[n]siderable.

The E. of Warweek is retornd fro[m] the shipps & denyed recepcon, yet it is thought yt they wold now thanke him to come agayne. Hower[er], I praie you be mindefull. I am extrem sorry to heare yt Pontefract is surprised, but I hope it will teach all oth[er]s more watchfulness ...

L498: Thorpe, 12 June [1648]
Yo[u]rs I receyvd & theirw[i]th good satisfaccon, as also by M[r] Barnard, of yo[u]r unanimity in the towne, and shall heartily wish & dayly praie to continue it among you. I also showd yo[u]r lre to yo[u]r Burgess, S[i]r Hen: Vayne, especially touching that passage of some offic[er]s in yo[u]r town in whom you canot confide. And he hath promissed to examin the matt[er] p[ar]ticul[er]ly & w[i]thin two or three dates to give me an account of it.

The greatest matt[er] heer in relacon to you is the shipps w[hi]ch have bene at Yarmouth & tendred the Kentish peticon & demanded victualls & men, but were stoutly answerd by the town yt they would send up to the P[ar]lam[en]t to know their pleasur & then, as they receyvd dyreccon so they wold bear themselvs. Wherupon shortly after the shipps dep[ar]ted & came into the Downes, but rath[er], som say, are gonn into Holland. Howev[er], I do not p[er]ceyv but that they stand doubtfull.

The scene of business is now in Essex, or upon the skirts of Suffolk & Cambridgshir to intercept Goring's forces from coming northward ...

L499: Thorpe, London 20 June [1648]
... I need not say much in relacon to yo[u]r selvs save that I am informed by a lre from York (w[hi]ch yet I do not beleyve, because not

having it from you) that one of the revolted shipps is in Humb[er]. Howev[er], I suppose you will kepe good scoutage that way, for I must co[n]fess I look more at the shipps then the Scotts.

You will receyv answer from yo[u]r P[ar]lam[en]t men touching you[r] desyred guards, for the Comitee of Darby House I p[er]ceyve takes care in it & have writt to the gen[er]all about it, & as I am informed some who have troubled you are to be removed from you ...

I praie God p[re]serv you from trechery, w[hi]ch I p[er]ceyve is much practisd in these dayes, & wherew[i]th I am informed Scarbrough had very like to have bene catcht the last week ...

L500: Thorpe, 28 June [1648]

... Having an opportunity to informe the House of the state of the north, & of the enimye's intencon to fortify at Ayre mouth, I acquanted them w[i]th yo[u]r readiness to send out men & p[ro]visions for p[re]vention of that designe. And it is very well taken from you. Also I have obtaynd an ord[er] th[er]upon for bringing in an ordinance to give you leave to disburse £500 of the sequestracon money arising w[i]thin yo[u]r iurisdiccon toward paying the people sent out & toward yo[u]r repayrs & to reimburs the same upon yo[u]r £6,000 ordinance, when it comes in. And furth[er], yo[u]r Burgess, M[r] Pelham, & my self are ordered to repayre to the comittee of excise, & to press them w[i]th what argum[en]ts of necessity we can to advance speedily some p[ar]t of that ordinanc mony for yo[u]r p[re]sent service ...

A letter was also redd from the gen[er]all to the Comittee at Darby House & by them reported this day to o[u]r House desyring their might be a troope of horse assignd for yo[u]r garrison, & it so referrd to the comittee here for northern affayrs to consider how they may be mayntayned.

And this at p[re]sent is all I have concerninge you, save that I am glad to see you give the printed pamphlets here the lye ...[239]

L501: Thorpe, 11 July [1648]

... Touching yo[u]r business for w[hi]ch M[r] Ramsden[240] & the rest are come up; all I shall say at p[re]sent is yt if you wold have vouchsafed to have consulted yo[u]r freinds here before yo[u]r ingagem[en]t to that und[er]taking, I p[re]sume you wold, as rationall men, have receycd a satisfaccon to yo[u]r contentm[en]t, & wold have bene

[239] From May 1648 some of the newsbooks were reporting that Hull was arming for the king: *Mercurius Melancholicus*, no. 38 (London, 8–15 May 1648), p. 228 (BL, E442/14).

[240] Alderman John Ramsden. The corporation instructed Ramsden to deliver letters to Pelham, Thorpe, Vane, and Widdrington, and to 'desire their sev[er]all assistance': HCA, M232: Instructions to John Ramsden, 20 Dec. 1647.

p[er]swaded not to indanger the disturbance of a publick peace for any pryvate intrest. Howev[er], now, I p[re]sume yo[u]r Burgesses, to whom it belongs, will take care for you, & yt you may receyve such satisfaccon as the business requires; their being, as I p[er]ceyve, mutuall complaynts & mutuall dislikes...

You tell me of two gent[lemen] taken in Lincolnshir & sent by the gov[er]nor[241] to you for popish recusants, w[hi]ch kinde of p[ro]ceeding, law ward, I do not und[er]stand, & th[er]for till I heare more p[ar]ticul[er]s & informacons of the fact I cannot advise my self or you as iustices of peace. Onely I doubt how the business of a massinge preist can be made the question, unless you have some kind of evidence for it...

L502: Thorpe, 25 July [1648]

... I am extreme sorry that our lett[er]s miscarryed the last post; the rath[er] because some informac[i]ons being sent up hither of an extraordinary numb[er] of pistolls closely conveyd to yo[u]r town in one of yo[u]r shipps. Many app[re]hend it as a designe attending yo[u]r petition here, & my desyre was, & is, to have the matt[er] cleered as much as may be by a strict exa[m]i[n]ac[i]on of it & of the p[er]sons ingaged in it. W[hi]ch by this post was expected wold have bene retornd. And it is much wond[er]d yt you do not so much as menc[i]on the business in any of yo[u]r lres (though as news). I praie you, retorn by the next how the business stands, for I hope the towns people are clere of it. And send up the names of those who freighted these things in the shipps & who payd or was to pay for the freight of them, & oth[er] circumstances relating, to ascertayn any p[er]sons who have to do in the business...

If I can gett leave to come down (w[hi]ch is hardly now granted), & the memb[er]s ord[er]d to be calld upo[n] Monday com senight, I intend to be w[i]th you, if God please, at next sessions...

Notice is come hither of 19 shipps before Yarmoth w[i]th the prince, & some indeavo[u]r to land their. Gent[lemen], now is the tyme of all men's tryalls. I shall praie for yo[u]r stedfastness to God & his cause...

L504: Thorpe, 1 Aug. [1648]

... as I did not doubt before, so yet I am glad of the satisffaccon you give me touching the pistolls.[242] It is true here are many iealosyes &

---

[241] Colonel Robert Overton. The New Model Army and its supporters had become suspicious of Hull's Presbyterian-dominated bench, and late in 1647 Oliver Cromwell had prevailed upon Sir Thomas Fairfax to replace Colonel Mauleverer with Overton, a sectarian, as his deputy-governor: BL, Sloane MS 1519, fol. 169; L486.

[242] For the matter of the pistols, see L502.

suspicous, w[hi]ch I am confident their is no cause for...

M[r] Harry Darley,²⁴³ M[r] James Challon[er]²⁴⁴ & my self are appointed to go down to the gen[er]all touching div[er]se businesses, whereof yo[u]rs is the cheif.²⁴⁵ And to morrow morning, by God's leave, we set forward, so by the next we shall be able to give you some bett[er] satisfaccon...

L506: Thorpe, 15 Aug. [1648]

... I doubt not but you have heard, or will heare by this post, how the prince sent lres lately from the revolted shipps to Yarmoth to invite that town to joyn w[i]th him, & yt howev[er] specious his p[re]tences by yt the lres p[re]vayled not w[i]th them. It is sayd here you will have the like sum[m]ons & it is hoped, or rather assured by yo[u]r friends (howev[er] oth[er]s not well affected to you upon this single occasion of yo[u]r difference w[i]th yo[u]r gov[er]nor suspect the contrary),²⁴⁶ that your resolucon is aswell sett as theirs at Yarmoth. The accons of publicke men are now writt in grand capitall lres & ev[er]y man gazes upon them, & God suffers them to be in this condicon for tryall of their faith & constancye. I shall wish & praie for unanimity among you, p[r]incipally in relac[i]on to the publicke, as also to you[u]r selves, in regard of yo[u]r pryvate differences, w[hi]ch I wish had nev[er] bene begunn. But being begunn I doubt not but yo[u]r own Burgesses, to whom it solely belongs to inform you & direct you, do accordingly adv[er]tise you of all the emergencyes; I my self, in the condic[i]on I stand, being uncapable to serv you in that kinde. Howev[er], I am otherwise ingaged to the towne & shall ev[er], as that duty & obligac[i]on bindes me, be ready to disch[ar]ge my self as yo[u]r assured friend & serv[an]t...

L507: Thorpe, 18 Aug. [1648]

... I have no more to write, but am sorry to see the devisions in yo[u]r towne to increase so much as they do, to the disturbance of yo[u]r owne peace & indangeringe the publick intrest. And th[er]for I do heartily wish quietness to you & among you...

²⁴³ Henry Darley, MP for Northallerton, Yorkshire.

²⁴⁴ James Chaloner, MP for Aldborough, Yorkshire.

²⁴⁵ Pelham and Vane appear to have been more active in this role than Thorpe, Chaloner and Darley: *CJ*, v. 615; *CSPD 1648–9*, pp. 88, 102, 104, 105, 110, 111, 112–13, 115, 118, 119, 124.

²⁴⁶ Relations between the town authorities and the garrison became strained in 1648 as a result of the billeting of troops in Hull and Overton's sectarian sympathies: L487, L488; HCA, M234; *VCH, East Riding*, i. 106.

L508: Thorpe to the mayor and aldermen [received 25 Aug. 1648]
... It is c[er]tayn, as I am informed by good intelligence, the prince is come northward for Scotland, & how he may call upon you by the way is yet lookt upon as doubtfull. But I beleyv the defeat given to that army, whereof we had notice yesterday here, will turn his course. And howev[er], I am confident of your resolucons & stedfastness, whereof you have so oft given assurance & testimony.

Here is little more news then what the prints tell you, to w[hi]ch I referr you; *The diurnall* being the p[er]fect relacon of the passages touching the treaty for peace, w[hi]ch I know you most desyre...

L509: Thorpe, 29 Aug. [1648]
... The inclosed will acquant you w[i]th the news here, & theirin the wond[er]s of God's mercyes to the kingdom...

The E. of Warweek is gone out of Thames w[i]th 18 tall shipps; the prince hath 14. It is thought their wilbe a very sudden ingagem[en]t...

L510: Pelham, Westminster 30 Nov. 1648
I have long forborne to write unto you because I could not give you a good accompt that Mr Hillyard had past assurance of the Manor house, w[hi]ch is now fully p[er]formed; an indenture sealed and a fine past w[i]th the advice of Sergeant Thorpe, Mr Hales[247] and others. I have put in all the aldermen by name as feffees in trust and by another indenture you are all to seale to declare yt it is for the benefit of the maior & burgesses for ever, w[hi]ch indenture & fine I have sent by Mr Lilly.

I have borrowed £100 uppon ye interest of your £6,000 w[hi]ch was, as I thincke, due this mounth, for w[hi]ch I shall be accomptable to you. In the interim, what monneys are, or shall be, due to me, you may detaine in your hands untill I give you an account. I know not yet the charge about yt mannor house, nor for some other businesse yt concernes your towne w[hi]ch I hope shortly to dispatch.

Here is little newes at p[re]sent. Our commissioners were ordered to come away from ye Isle of Wight upon Tuesday morning last. I doe not as yet heare yt they are come to towne. I never expected any good tydings from thence. When I can let you p[ar]ticipate [*sic*] of any good newes I will not faile to give you notice...

---

[247] Probably the distinguished lawyer, Matthew Hale.

INDEX